REGNUM DEI

THE BAMPTON LECTURES, 1901

REGNUM DEI

EIGHT LECTURES ON THE KINGDOM OF GOD IN THE HISTORY OF CHRISTIAN THOUGHT

BY

ARCHIBALD ROBERTSON, D.D.

LATE FELLOW OF TRINITY COLLEGE, OXFORD
HON. LL.D. GLASGOW, HON. D.D. DURHAM
PRINCIPAL OF KING'S COLLEGE, LONDON
EXAMINING CHAPLAIN TO THE LORD BISHOP OF BRISTOL

ΟΥ ΤΗϹ ΒΑϹΙΛΕΙΑϹ ΟΥΚ ΕϹΤΑΙ ΤΕΛΟϹ
SYMB. ECCLES. HIEROSOL.

REGNVM ERGO ET IVSTITIA DEI BONVM NOSTRVM EST
ET HOC APPETENDVM ET IBI FINIS CONSTITVENDVS
PROPTER QVOD OMNIA FACIAMVS QVAECUNQVE FACIMVS.
ST. AUGUSTINE

Wipf & Stock
PUBLISHERS
Eugene, Oregon

PIAE MEMORIAE

S

VENERANDI PRAESVLIS

BROOKE FOSS WESTCOTT S T P

QVI OBDORMIVIT IN CHRISTO

VI KAL AVG MCMI

Wipf and Stock Publishers
199 W 8th Ave, Suite 3
Eugene, OR 97401

Regnum Dei
Eight Lectures on the Kingdom of God in the History of Christian Thought
By Robertson, Archibald
ISBN: 1-59244-954-9
Publication date 10/18/2004
Previously published by Methuen & Co., 1901

EXTRACT

FROM THE LAST WILL AND TESTAMENT

OF THE LATE

REV. JOHN BAMPTON,

CANON OF SALISBURY.

——"I give and bequeath my Lands and Estates to the Chancellor, Masters, and Scholars of the University of Oxford for ever, to have and to hold all and singular the said Lands and Estates upon trust, and to the intents and purposes hereinafter mentioned; that is to say, I will and appoint that the Vice-Chancellor of the University of Oxford for the time being shall take and receive all the rents, issues, and profits thereof, and (after all taxes, reparations, and necessary deductions made) that he pay all the remainder to the endowment of eight Divinity Lecture Sermons, to be established for ever in the said University, and to be performed in the manner following:

"I direct and appoint that upon the first Tuesday in Easter Term, a Lecturer be yearly chosen by the Heads of Colleges only, and by no others, in the room adjoining to the Printing-House, between the hours of ten in the morning and two in the afternoon, to preach eight Divinity Lecture Sermons, the year following, at St. Mary's in Oxford, between the commencement of the last month in Lent Term, and the end of the third week in Act Term.

EXTRACT

"Also I direct and appoint, that the eight Divinity Lecture Sermons shall be preached upon either of the following Subjects—to confirm and establish the Christian Faith, and to confute all heretics and schismatics—upon the Divine authority of the Holy Scriptures—upon the authority of the writings of the primitive Fathers, as to the faith and practice of the primitive Church—upon the Divinity of our Lord and Saviour Jesus Christ—upon the Divinity of the Holy Ghost—upon the Articles of the Christian Faith, as comprehended in the Apostles' and Nicene Creeds.

"Also I direct that thirty copies of the eight Divinity Lecture Sermons shall be always printed within two months after they are preached; and one copy shall be given to the Chancellor of the University, and one copy to the head of every College, and one copy to the Mayor of the City of Oxford, and one copy to be put into the Bodleian Library; and the expense of printing them shall be paid out of the revenue of the Land or Estates given for establishing the Divinity Lecture Sermons; and the Preacher shall not be paid, nor entitled to the revenue, before they are printed.

"Also I direct and appoint, that no person shall be qualified to preach the Divinity Lecture Sermons, unless he hath taken the degree of Master of Arts at least, in one of the two Universities of Oxford or Cambridge; and that the same person shall never preach the Divinity Lecture Sermons twice."

PREFACE

Certains auteurs parlant de leurs ouvrages disent : Mon livre, mon commentaire, mon histoire, etc. Ils sentent leurs bourgeois qui on pignon sur rue, et toujours un *chez moi* à la bouche. Ils feraient mieux de dire : Notre livre, notre commentaire, notre histoire, etc., vu que d'ordinaire il y a plus en cela du bien d'autrui que du leur.—PASCAL.

THE following pages, the result of the writer's reflexion with a view to his own guidance in life, must be regarded as an enquiry rather than as leading up to a predetermined conclusion. They are published in the hope that a theme, which has been fruitful of instruction to himself, may be not unfruitful, at any rate by way of suggestion, to some others.

So far as the enquiry has led to definite results, which I would be understood to hold with diffidence and with full consciousness that much is still to be learned, those results are briefly as follows.

The Kingdom of GOD is the Christian answer to the most vital question that man has to solve, the question of the purpose of his being. Our Saviour's teaching on the subject is closely connected with hopes and convictions in full currency at the time of his Advent on earth; but he so used these convictions and hopes as to give a new meaning to life, and to open a new direction to human aspiration and effort. The Kingdom of GOD in his hands is a many-sided conception ;

to do justice to it has been the problem set to his followers in the long and varied course of the Church's existence.

Between the Church itself and the Kingdom of GOD there exists the closest correlation, although neither our Lord himself nor his immediate Disciples treat the two as strictly identical. In early Christian times the Church on earth, as present, was contrasted with the Kingdom of GOD as future; either specially (as by Tertullian, Irenaeus, etc.), with the Millennial reign of Christ on earth, or simply (as by Cyprian and others), with the Kingdom of GOD in which the saints are to reign in heaven. St. Augustine, without in any degree abandoning the latter contrast, added to it a deeper conception of the Church, based upon the contrast between the phenomenal and the real. He conceived the present Church as the Kingdom of Christ in so far as it consists of those who are in truth reigning with Him, in whose hearts and wills Christ is reigning now. These constitute the *civitas Dei*, which to Augustine consists of GOD'S elect, in contrast to the *civitas terrena*, which consists of the reprobate. But Augustine also, in applying his fundamental view of life to the interpretation of history, incidentally hinted at a more external interpretation of the thought of the Kingdom of GOD, namely as embodied in the exercise of divine power delegated to human hands in directing the affairs of the Church and of mankind. This interpretation, remarkably absent from earlier Christian thought, occupies in Augustine's own writings a quite subordinate position; none the less it struck the keynote for the most imposing attempt in Christian experience to give practical embodiment to the idea of a Kingdom of GOD on earth, namely the theocratic system of the Middle Ages. That attempt, so far as it succeeded, succeeded at the cost of the more fundamental and spiritual side of Augustine's mind, and of the unity of the Christian ideal. For the confusion and conflict which have resulted, the remedy must be found in renewed recourse to the record of our Lord's own teaching, and in the attempt to apply it in relation to the complex needs of modern life. In attempting this, the lessons of Christian experience must be our principal aids; and among these lessons, it will probably be found that the Church of to-day has more to learn from St. Augustine than from any other ancient interpreter of the mind of Christ and of the Apostolic Church.

That in some respects, as has been apparent from the time of Dante, Augustine's vision was limited, may be due to the fact that a low estimate of civil government and of social life was inevitable in the age to which he belonged. But his fundamental contention that the source of social decay is the love of self, and that the love of self can only be effectually overcome by the Love of GOD, is as fully borne out by the signs of our times as by those of the decline of Ancient Rome.

It has been no part of my purpose to deal with controversies relating to Christian doctrine. They have been referred to in some cases, but only in so far as they have affected the development which is the subject of this volume. I have neither concealed, nor I hope unduly obtruded, my personal convictions; in speaking of individual characters, it has been my principle to give them all possible credit for the best motives. Even the gravest moral blunders of great men are as a rule due to their enthusiasm for some cause greater than themselves; zeal for GOD is the leaven of life, but none the less it has at times blinded men to the complexion of their own acts.

In a book which is in no sense a compilation, it is difficult to do justice to obligations to other writers. Those recorded in the notes are far from exhausting the very many which are really due; if the genesis of the volume has been in the reflexion of some few years, its actual composition has been in the somewhat scanty intervals of present duties which leave but little time for systematic study. It is inevitable that many authorities which have gone to design the structure have not been consulted in the course of its actual execution. For example, in the first three lectures the reader will miss references to many important and obvious authorities. The reason partly is that in writing them I have worked mainly with the biblical text itself, with the object of gaining my final impression so far as possible at first hand. But in doing so, I am fully aware how illusive in such a case is the appearance of a *tabula rasa*. Lectures VI. and VII. have been furnished with somewhat longer notes, in order to enable readers who are less at home in the subject there dealt with to follow the allusions in the text. I hope that historians, if any should read the Lectures, will pardon the large amount of obvious matter, which is not meant for their instruction. I would also apologise for occasionally, especially in the

PREFACE

Fifth Lecture, referring to what I have written elsewhere. My object in doing so is merely to avoid self-repetition.

Inequality of reference in the notes does not, I fear, stand alone among the signs of discontinuous production which I have been unable wholly to remove from the book. But were I to begin an apology for its shortcomings, the Preface would threaten to be a long one.

My fervent hope and prayer is that, whatever its faults, this volume of Lectures may do nothing to hinder, but by GOD'S mercy may rather in some degree, however slight, set forward the Kingdom of Christ and of GOD. I would make my own the prayer of one of my predecessors: "Domine Deus, quaecunque dixi de tuo, agnoscant et tui; si qua de meo, et Tu ignosce et tui."

KING'S COLLEGE, LONDON
Michaelmas Day, 1901

TABLE OF CONTENTS

LECTURE I

INTRODUCTORY. THE KINGDOM OF GOD IN THE OLD TESTAMENT

                                                                                                  PAGE

I. The idea of Purpose at the root of the Problem of Life . 3
The verification of religious conviction reached not so much by speculative theism as by the appeal to the religious experience of mankind. The Christian Religion the central channel of this experience. The Christian conception of purpose summed up in the idea of the Kingdom of GOD. Aim of these Lectures: to interrogate Christian experience as to the meaning of the Kingdom of GOD. General plan of the Lectures . 4

II. Foremost place of the Kingdom of GOD in our Saviour's teaching as the summary of his message. Its relation to the expectations of the Jewish People 8

III. (a) Roots of the hope of the Kingdom of GOD in the Old Testament: the "Golden Age" of Israel was a future age. But this presupposed the thought of Israel itself as a Divine Kingdom. This idea primitive: earliest unity of Israel as a nation founded on Religion 11
But this does not explain the conception of the Kingdom of GOD *as future*. Result of the Monarchy. Religious aspect of the Hebrew monarchy (1) as a concession to a lower religious ideal; (2) as the foundation of a new religious and national ideal. Prophetic contrast of ideal and actual. Dawn of eschatological hope in this connexion. Widening of prophetic outlook in eighth century B.C.—Amos, Hosea, Isaiah 14

(b) Prophecy at the close of the Judean monarchy—Universalism and the Righteousness of Faith. Spiritual culmination in Jeremiah. The Exile. Rise of "eschatology of the individual." Doctrine of a future life 21

(c) Later eschatology: Daniel; Apocalypse as a form of Jewish literature. Daniel's legacy of hope. The Maccabean movement and dynasty 27

CONTENTS

PAGE

IV. Summary of the pre-Christian history of belief in a Kingdom of GOD: Old Testament idea of GOD,—its history that of real revelation 32

LECTURE II

THE KINGDOM OF GOD (I.) IN THE GENERATION BEFORE CHRIST; (II.) IN THE EPISTLES OF ST. PAUL; (III.) IN THE SYNOPTIC GOSPELS

I. The Lucan canticles and the Psalms of Solomon. Date and provenance of the latter. Daniel and the Psalms of Solomon. Their evidence as to Jewish expectation of the Kingdom of GOD. 39

II. Sharp contrast between St. Paul and the Psalms of Solomon. The early apostolic Church and the Kingdom of GOD; preparation for distinctive work of St. Paul. St. Paul places the Kingdom of GOD (*a*) in the future, (*b*) in the present. Distinguishes between the Kingdom of GOD and the mediatorial kingdom of Christ. The Kingdom of GOD and the Church of Christ. "Kingdom" or "Reign"? St. Paul's complete spiritualisation of Jewish hopes. Was it wholly St. Paul's work? 46

III. The Kingdom of GOD in the Preaching of Christ. Synoptic tradition. The "Gospel" of the Kingdom. "Kingdom of Heaven" in St. Matthew. Our Lord supersedes national claims by moral conditions. The Kingdom present, and "taken by force." "Receiving" the Kingdom: character the test of Membership. Difficulty of entrance. "Becoming as little children" 61

The Kingdom of GOD and Eternal Life. The Kingdom of the Son of Man and the Kingdom of the Father. The Return of Christ "in his Kingdom." The mediatorial Reign of the Messiah. The Kingdom of GOD, present and future, in relation to the twofold Advent of Christ. Kingdom and Church 68

LECTURE III

THE KINGDOM OF GOD IN (*a*) THE SYNOPTIC GOSPELS (*concluded*), IN (*b*) THE FOURTH GOSPEL, AND (*c*) IN THE REMAINDER OF THE NEW TESTAMENT

I. Synoptic tradition (*concluded*). The transition from old to new; the "discipled scribe." Did the Kingdom of GOD come as an Idea, as an Institution, or as a Life? Ideas implicit in Nature and in Life 81

CONTENTS

The Kingdom of GOD as a process; the Parables unfold the "mysteries" of its growth. Parables "of the Kingdom". 87
The Beatitudes link on the Synoptic to the Johannine aspect of the Kingdom of GOD 89
II. The Fourth Gospel. The Kingdom of GOD as Life; Timeless, and therefore both Future and Present . . . 90
Unity of Pauline and evangelical tradition in this respect. Relation of Christian to Jewish conception of the Kingdom of GOD 94
Summary of results. Christ's Kingdom in relation to the Society of his followers. Function of the Spirit as *vicarius Christi.* Problems left to the experience of later Christendom. Did our Lord provide a complete system of government? . 96
III. Epistles of St. James and St. Peter; Epistle to the Hebrews: the City of GOD 103
IV. The Apocalypse of St. John; the first Christian philosophy of history. Contrast with St. Paul in respect to secular society and government 105
Contents and structure as bearing on its interpretation . 108
The Kingdom of Christ on earth. The Thousand Years and the question of realistic interpretation . . . 113

LECTURE IV

THE KINGDOM OF GOD IN THE FIRST FOUR CHRISTIAN CENTURIES

I. Alternative interpretations; a Millennium not unnaturally associated with imminence of the Parousia. But the latter a more universal belief than the other. Realistic eschatology of primitive Church, and the authority of the Apocalypse . 119
II. Predominance of Realistic Eschatology in the pre-Nicene age, and in the West till the time of St. Augustine. Examples of this. Favouring conditions: immaturity of theological thought; the Church and civilisation; intensity of primitive faith. Reasons for evanescence of Millenniarism; its latent antagonism to the organised Church. Montanism. Was it conservative or revolutionary? Its eschatology conservative. Its rigorism narrowly so. Its downfall discredited eschatological Realism 124
III. Rise of philosophical theology. Contrast with earlier Christian thought. The Gnostics. The Alexandrine School. Christianity and Philosophy. The Alexandrian Theology made eschatological Realism (*i.e.* Millenniarism) impossible. Permanence of Origen's influence 147
IV. Other causes of the decay of Millenniarism. The Christian

Empire. Divergence of East and West. Tendency in the West to an ecclesiastical conception of the Kingdom of GOD. Monasticism. Its original aim, and its influence . 158

LECTURE V

THE KINGDOM OF GOD IN ST. AUGUSTINE

I. Position of Augustine in the history of Christian thought with reference to the Kingdom of GOD. His early Millenniarism. His change of mind: The "first Resurrection" spiritual only; the "thousand years" the life of the Church on earth. The Kingdom of GOD twofold: The perfect Kingdom belongs to the next world; but Christ already reigns in his true members. Augustine's opinion misrepresented in modern times. Augustine and his predecessors. What was Augustine's own opinion? His explanation of the Apocalypse. The conception of the present Church as Kingdom of GOD subordinate to that of the Eternal Kingdom 169

II. Relation of this question to his fundamental principles. Peculiar difficulty of formulating these in case of Augustine. (*a*) Augustine's Theism, at once experimental and metaphysical. Idealism and Universalism. His religious debt to Plato. (*b*) His devotion to the Catholic Church. Debt of Western Christendom to him in this respect. The note of "catholicity" and the "Orbis Terrarum." (*c*) His Doctrine of Grace; not first formulated in antagonism to Pelagians. His change of mind in the year 396. "*Domine da quod iubes.*" Predestinarianism, *vocatio non congrua.* Influence of "Augustinianism" in the Church . . 181

III. Augustine's doctrine of the Church, how affected by his doctrine of Grace. The *communio externa* and the *communio sanctorum*; which of the two is primary? Influence of his transcendentalism. Practically, the *communio externa* has the attributes of the *communio sanctorum*; but no true synthesis of the two; the latter not wholly included in the former. Practical result in the Church of the age following. Legacy of difficulty for later times. Impossibility of an intellectual solution 194

IV. The new religious philosophy of history. The *de Civitate Dei.* Problems involved in the fall of Rome. Augustine urged to deal with them; growth of his plan of reply. The two *civitates.* Origin of earthly kingdoms: *grande latrocinium.* Church and State, how far to be identified with the two *civitates*? mutual dependence; but the civil society ideally

CONTENTS

dependent on the Church. Keynote of medieval system. Persecution: Augustine's change of mind . . . 206
V. Twofold character of Augustine's conception of the Kingdom of GOD. The ideal and the empirical, reason and authority, unreconciled. Three great questions left for the Church of later ages. Summary of results 217

LECTURE VI

THE KINGDOM OF GOD IN THE MEDIEVAL THEOCRACY

I. Augustine's legacy to the medieval Church: an ideal, but not a system. The early Middle Age favourable to practical development of system rather than to analysis of ideas. Gregory the Great, his work as a builder-up of papal power 225

II. The dark ages. (*a*) Before Charles the Great. Birth of a new Order. The house of Pipin. Temporal power of popes. Donation of Constantine. Charles: temporary revival of the Christian Imperial ideal. Feudalism in the Church . 231

(*b*) Post-Carolingian period. Break up of Caroline system. The Pseudo-Isidorian decretals; their effect upon medieval idea of the Church. Nicolas I. Temporary arrest of the development of the papal system. Moral decay of the papacy. Rome under Alberic and John XII. The Saxon emperors. The Holy Roman Empire. Second phase of the medieval embodiment of the Kingdom of GOD on earth. The German popes; regeneration of the papacy. Gerbert, Henry III., Leo IX., Nicolas II. The College of Cardinals . . 235

III. (*a*) Hildebrand and his successors. Alexander II. Hildebrand virtually pope. The Cluniac order; its ideal of Church Reform: earlier life and election of Hildebrand. His ideal of the kingdom of Christ; no later pope could add to it in principle. Collision with the crown. Investiture. Feudal headship of emperor or pope? . . . 248

(*b*) Gregorian and Augustinian ideas. Limitation of Gregory's view. Necessity of statecraft to his ideal. Cheapening of the censures, etc., of the Church. The popes and the emperors. Canossa 254

IV. The Hohenstaufen. Rise of the Schools. Arnold of Brescia; the typical medieval reformer. His death. Frederick Barbarossa, Adrian IV., and Alexander III. Defeat of imperial idealism. Innocent III.: gradual deterioration of papal ideal. The Lateran Council. Frederick II. and the popes of the early thirteenth century: significance of the contest. Triumph of Papacy over Empire 259

V. Rise of the new nations. Thomas Aquinas on Church and

b

king. Decline of the medieval system. Beginning of concordats. Review of the theocracy of Gregory VII. Gregory X.; inherent weakness of imperial ideal; success of papacy as a religious power, how far complete? its failure as a political influence. Papal extortions, spiritual injury to local Churches. Failure to appreciate moral forces. Persecutions. Blame not to be fixed on individuals. Conclusion: Augustine and the medieval system; contrast of ideals . 270

LECTURE VII
THE KINGDOM OF GOD IN THE DIVERGENCE OF MODERN IDEALS

I. Intellectual and Moral break-up of medieval convictions. Dante and Augustine; (*a*) Dante and the *de Monarchia* . . 286
(*b*) Historical conditions. The Franciscan ideal and Arnold of Brescia. Abbot Joachim and the Spiritual Franciscans. Dante and the Spirituals. John XXII. and the Franciscan ideal. Cesena, Ockham, and Lewis of Bavaria . . 294
(*c*) Importance of reign of Lewis. Ockham; his criticism of the Papacy as an institution in the Church. Ockham a modern mind; not an imperialist; his love of truth; tendency to blind faith 305
(*d*) The *Defensor Pacis*. Marsilius primarily a constructive political thinker. Account of his main principles; sovereignty of People, function of Prince, coercive power, constitutional Government in modern sense. Accuracy in treating ecclesiastical terms. The priesthood and the Sovereign power. The Church and the Papacy. Councils; persecution, Church and State. Strong, and weaker, elements in the Marsilian idea. His practical tendency towards separation of Church and State 311
(*e*) Summary. Conflict of the Gregorian ideal with political philosophy and with spirit of constitutional self-government. Arnold of Brescia and the medieval ideal of life: movements in favour of Poverty converge, in Dante and Marsilius, with new idea of Society 322
II. Doctrinal reaction and the Eve of the Reformation. The above movements almost wholly orthodox in doctrine. Wycliffe and Hus compared to earlier reformers. The conciliar movement for reform; its defeat. Despair of practical Reform. Contrasts of the fifteenth century. The Reformation not due to individual will 326
III. Divergence of ideals in Reformation and Counter-Reformation.
(*a*) Work of the Counter-Reformation. The Council of Trent and its legacy of unsolved problems: (α) Augustinian doctrine of Grace. (β) Relation of Pope to Episcopate and to Tradi-

CONTENTS

	PAGE
tion. (γ) Direction of moral conduct and Probabilism; Victory of the latter against the better judgment of the Church	333
(b) Connexion of these three questions: the interpretation of the Kingdom of God as the Church-State. Authority and morality: Legalism in Ethics. The Church and modern civilisation	343
IV. Conclusion: diversity and Christian unity	347

LECTURE VIII

THE KINGDOM OF GOD IN MODERN THOUGHT, WORK, AND LIFE

I. The Reformation. Why not a period of construction? The Reformers and an "invisible church." What did Luther and Calvin hold? Position taken by the English Church. The question of the Kingdom of God on earth not definitively solved 353

II. New study of the question, why called for. Ritschl's conception of the Kingdom of God: how related to that of the Church; twofold character of the idea of the Church. His system criticised. Ritschl and St. Augustine. Moral aim of human Society. The Church in relation to this . . . 357

III. Summary of ideals. An earthly realisation of the Kingdom of God to be looked for. The Church, how thought of in this relation. Negative result of our enquiry in reference to millennial and to medieval interpretations. Positive ideal; its assertion by Butler; lacks necessary element of Brotherhood. Church legislation. In forming ideals, our view not to be limited by what appears practical. The true remedy for a false individualism 364

IV. Other ideals (a) the purely ethical ideal. The Church and moral earnestness. Good in non-Christians. Has the Church a moral interest in public matters? GOD the Source of all good 373

(b) Christian Socialism. State action, how far able to produce morality? But social life demands Christian principles, and conversely. Christian Socialism a summons to neglected duties. But social reform alone will not constitute the Kingdom of GOD on earth 377

V. The Christian ideal and the World to come. St. Paul and "otherworldliness." Real teaching of Scripture on this point. The Chief Good must be eternal. Limited duration of the world. Are the highest ideals perishable? Purpose and method in the Universe: purpose in Existence and Life. 381

INDEX 389

LECTURE I

THE KINGDOM OF GOD IN THE OLD TESTAMENT

For however great uncertainty may still hang over the details of Old Testament history, the history of the Jews is, in its broad and unquestionable outlines, the history of a people who believed, and who, with all their failures and relapses, lived as believing, in the intercourse of GOD and man : who believed in the kinsmanship of men as made by GOD for His glory : who believed in the righteous sovereignty of GOD, guiding the affairs of the world to an issue corresponding with the purpose of Creation.

WESTCOTT.

REGNUM DEI

LECTURE I

INTRODUCTORY. THE KINGDOM OF GOD IN THE OLD TESTAMENT

Thy kingdom is an everlasting kingdom, and thy dominion endureth throughout all generations.—Ps. cxlv. 13.

THE doubts and distractions of our age, and the questions at issue between the various systems which compete for the allegiance of the modern man, appear to turn ultimately upon the two kindred questions of the Government of the World and the purpose of Life. The two questions are not identical, for the former is speculative, and relates to the constitution of the world around us, while the other is strictly practical, and upon the answer to it depends the tone and colour of the individual life. But they are closely connected, for the practical question cannot receive even a practical answer without an implied assumption upon the wider issue. Common to both is the idea of purpose. Theoretically, if we can gain the conviction that purpose sways the forces of the universe and guides its history, it follows that man can only find the true end of his being in subordination to and in harmony with the Supreme Will which embraces nature and man in one. But practically, the process is reversed; the more intense our sense of purpose in our individual life— the more lasting and comprehensive and satisfying the purpose which guides and sustains us as individuals, the more energetic becomes our hold upon the supreme truth of the Divine Government of the World, the deeper our homage in deed and thought to the absolutely Holy Will. The conviction of purpose in the individual life and the conviction of purpose in the universe, in short, act and react. The vigour of the one strengthens, the weakness of the one enfeebles, the other. Individual lives furnish exceptions to this general truth, but I speak of the tendency which asserts itself in the average and mass of human life.

To say this is to appeal to experience, the experience not only of the individual but still more of the human race. Believers have differed as to the theoretical cogency of the speculative proofs offered in support of the fundamental truths of God and the soul. I do not join in the tendency to disparage the proofs in question, on the contrary I believe them to be, so far as they go, indispensable and of great importance. But the mere fact that these proofs carry conviction, to equally sincere and religious minds, in very unequal degrees, must make us cautious of expecting too much from them. Moreover it is not as a matter of fact by means of them that we reach belief in God, or in ourselves as responsible beings. These priceless convictions come to us in all cases through those who possess them, and who have put them to the test of life. The

RELIGION AND PURPOSE

religious experience of mankind is a fact unquestionable and unquestioned; the stream of religious conviction has flowed down to us from sources not all of which we can any longer trace, it has received tributaries, it has run in many channels and in varying degrees of depth and clearness and power. But wherever it has flowed it has kept alive that belief in the ultimate sovereignty of truth and right which is the central faith of all good men; it has upborne those who have faced with cheerfulness and courage the sharpest trials of life, and have raised and cheered the lives of their fellow-men. It is in the religious experience of mankind alone that the verification of religious conviction is to be found.[1]

That the Christian Religion, and its antecedent development, recorded in the Old Testament, constitute the centre and heart of the religious experience of mankind will not be disputed, even by those who regard all religious experience as founded upon illusion. Here, that which underlies all religion, though in many religions so mingled with heterogeneous matter as to be hard to discover, the simplest instinct of man's thirst for a living GOD,—finds its simplest expression, its simplest satisfaction. Here too we find prominence

---

[1] No two regions of thought could well be wider apart than that of the physicist reiterating his conviction, founded upon minute investigation of the building up of molecules and the behaviour of atoms, of "the rationality of all natural processes" (Dr. Larmor at the British Association, *Times* of Sept. 7, 1900), and that of Deborah (Judg. v. 11) rehearsing "the righteous acts of Jehovah toward his villages in Israel." The one is approaching God by intellectual steps, the other is drawing full-handed from religious experience. But both processes already meet in the prophecy of Amos as really, though not as analytically, as they do in the pages of St. Augustine himself.

given to the most elemental needs of our moral nature, both in its ideal loftiness and in its actual humiliation and weakness. Nowhere else are mythical and incongruous elements, fanaticisms and superstitions, so markedly absent, or, if present, so readily disengaged from the religion itself.

It is then worth while, or rather it is of the highest importance, to examine Christian experience with reference to the great twofold problem of life,—the purpose of God in guiding the affairs of man, and the supreme purpose—the *summum bonum*—which we are severally to set before us as the goal of our life.

Both aspects of the problem before us come, in the teaching of Christ, under the general conception of the Kingdom of GOD, the kingdom in which the consummation of the ages will find its final issue, and which we are each one of us first of all things to pray for and to seek, in the confidence that if that is gained, all subordinate good things will be added in GOD'S own time.

It is the purpose of these Lectures to contribute something, however small, toward the interpretation, and thus to the vindication, of the supreme goal set before us by our Lord under the name of the Kingdom of GOD.

To interpret it adequately or worthily, even in its imperfect earthly manifestation, is a task wholly beyond individual power; the task is imposed upon the Society of all who bear Christ's name, and even so the interpretation must be progressive and subject to correction, and must remain imperfect in the end.

OUR LORD'S TEACHING

To promise a decisive and rounded-off conclusion would therefore condemn our attempt in advance. But what we can do is to interrogate Christian experience as disclosed in the history of the Christian Society. So far as the life and thought of that Society has been moulded by different conceptions of the Kingdom of GOD, those conceptions have been put to the test of experience, and as they have emerged confirmed or discredited, the result should enable us to distinguish between the more transitory and the more lasting elements in the Master Idea; and so we may learn to correct and purify our own ideals, and bring our working aims and convictions into closer correspondence with ultimate reality.

We must begin with the attempt to understand, so far as is possible, the meaning which our Lord himself gave to the Idea. This will occupy three Lectures; the present Lecture will sketch the Old Testament antecedents, the second, after placing in comparison the conceptions of the Kingdom of GOD entertained respectively by those whom our Lord found "waiting for" it, and by St. Paul the great Pharisee of the generation which had learned from Christ, will show how the points of agreement and difference alike presuppose the teaching of Christ as recorded in the synoptic Gospels. The third Lecture will complete this subject, and will consider the evidence derivable from the Fourth Gospel, the remaining Epistles, and the Apocalypse. The fourth Lecture will deal with the realistic eschatology of the primitive Church, as influenced in part by the Apocalypse, in part by other causes. This marks a very important, though transitory, phase in the Christian conception of the Kingdom of GOD. The fifth Lecture will aim at doing justice to the influence of St. Augustine, as closing an epoch of Christian thought on this subject, and as opening a new epoch in which opposing conceptions, both rooted in Augustine's thought, are destined to contend for the mastery. In the sixth Lecture, the medieval papacy will be treated as the attempt to give effect to one of these alternative conceptions, viz. that of the Kingdom of GOD as an omnipotent Church, an attempt in which theory followed the lead of practice. The seventh Lecture will describe the intellectual and moral break-up of this system, and how, from being the ideal of Christendom as a whole, it became theoretically elaborated as that of a party in Christendom. Then, after dealing briefly with the reassertion, at the Reformation, of one distinctively Augustinian conception of the Church and with its consequences as affecting the subject of our study, it will be endeavoured to gather up the result of the whole enquiry, and to bring its results to bear upon some problems which confront the Christian in modern life. To do this will be the object of the eighth and last Lecture.

II

One point must impress us at the outset of our enquiry. Whatever difficulties may attend the attempt to do justice to the fact in modern theology, there can be no question that in our Lord's teaching the Kingdom of GOD is the representative and all-embracing summary of his distinctive mission. The Baptist came to an-

OUR LORD'S TEACHING

nounce that the Kingdom of GOD was at hand,[1] and when Jesus himself began to teach, what he taught is summed up in the same words,—"repent, for the kingdom of GOD has come near."[2] And it was not only the beginning of his teaching but the end as well. In the forty days before he was taken up, "he was seen of them, and was telling them the things concerning the kingdom of GOD."[3] Throughout, his message is "the good news of the kingdom,"[4]—the kingdom which comes with his coming,—to accept his gospel is to receive the Kingdom of GOD,[5] the first prayer he taught his disciples to address to their Father in heaven was "Thy kingdom come." Devout Israelites like Joseph of Arimathea and many others who pass before us in the gospel pages have this as the goal of their hopes, they are "looking for the kingdom of GOD."[6] It is to be the goal of Christian life and effort.[7] It sums up the preaching of the Apostles after the Lord's visible presence was withdrawn. Philip in Samaria, St. Paul at Ephesus and at Rome, preach and teach "concerning the kingdom of God."[8] "Descriptions" it has been truly said "of the characteristics of the kingdom, expositions of its laws, accounts of the way men were actually receiving it, forecasts of its future, make up the whole central portion of the synoptic narrative."[9]

But our Saviour did not begin by defining the

---

[1] Matt. iii. 2.   [2] Matt. iv. 17, parallel with Mark i. 15.
[3] Acts i. 3.   [4] Matt. iv. 23, xiii. 19.
[5] Matt. xii. 28; Mark x. 15; Luke xviii. 17.
[6] Mark xv. 43.   [7] Matt. vi. 33; Luke xii. 31.
[8] Acts viii. 12, xix. 8, xx. 25, xxviii. 23, 31.
[9] Stanton, *The Jewish and the Christian Messiah*, p. 206.

Kingdom of GOD. He simply announced it. And this implies that his hearers, even those who were not, in the signal and pre-eminent sense, "waiting for the Kingdom of GOD," were prepared to attach some meaning to the phrase. Even the hostile Pharisees ask "when the kingdom of GOD is to come."[1] Christ is not introducing an idea wholly new to his hearers, but is making use of one which already existed, and was exercising a spell over men's minds. What is told us of select individuals was true in a real, though a lower and less intimate sense of the nation as a whole. Christ found Israel as a nation looking for the Kingdom of GOD. This fact stands in the closest connexion with the national hope of a Messiah, an anointed king, who was to be raised up by GOD in the latter days to "restore again the kingdom to Israel,"[2] to bring back national independence, and to revive all the splendour and national well-being which tradition associated with the kingdom of David. This hope varied doubtless in its character according to the spiritual capacities of those who cherished it; some thought more of the external and political, others of the religious blessings of which the Messiah-King was to be the bearer,—but it was universal, and in the more spiritual minds the idea of political deliverance was subordinated entirely to that of religious reformation and enlarged moral opportunity. Their hopes are expressed in the verse of the *Benedictus*: "That we being delivered from the hand of our enemies might serve him without fear, in holiness and righteousness before him, all the days of our life."[3] In

---
[1] Luke xvii. 20.   [2] Acts i. 6.   [3] Luke i. 74.

EARLY HEBREW IDEAL

proclaiming that the Kingdom of GOD was at hand, Jesus Christ takes his stand upon the national hope of Israel. What then was the hope actually entertained by the nation? and how far did Christ really make it his own? This question can only be answered as we proceed; but meanwhile we may say thus much: Our Lord gradually untaught his Disciples the hope as they held it at the first, and taught it them again in a wholly transformed shape.

III

(*a*) Their hope had come down to them from the past. Like the Religion of Christ generally, this "exhaustive category" of Christ's teaching has its roots in the Old Testament. We shall indeed search the Old Testament in vain for the *phrase* "Kingdom of GOD" or "Kingdom of Heaven." It belongs to the vocabulary of the New Testament, not of the Old. But it has its antecedents and elements in the Old Testament; and for these we must now enquire. The most direct Old Testament source for the New Testament idea of the Kingdom of GOD is without doubt the book of Daniel, which in two passages—to be referred to more particularly later on—speaks of a kingdom to be set up by the Most High himself, a kingdom which his saints are to possess.[1] But the book of Daniel itself comes at the end of a long process of development or of divine schooling, in the

---

[1] Dan. ii. 44, vii. 14, 27. Dalman, *Worte Jesu*, p. 109, makes a distinction between the sense of βασιλεία in these two passages which I cannot wholly follow.

course of which Israel was led to frame its ideal of a Golden Age. Whereas other nations looked sadly back to their golden age over a long series of successive declensions, Israel alone "placed its golden age in the future." The religions of antiquity were pessimistic and despairing in their philosophy of history; the religion of Israel was a religion of hope. From early times the germ of this phenomenon may be detected in the consciousness of a relation of the people to its GOD unlike anything that could be found in any other people—a relation which carried with it a peculiar consecration and an exceptional destiny. Their tradition of the great deliverance from Egypt told how Moses had promised them in Jehovah's name that if they would obey his voice they would be "a peculiar treasure unto me above all people—for all the earth is mine:—and ye shall be unto me a kingdom of priests and an holy nation."[1] The passage is regarded by critics as Deuteronomic in style and date, *i.e.* as tinged with the influence of the later prophets; but in substance the idea expressed is as old as any prophecy of which we know. The prophecies of Balaam describe how "It is a people that dwell alone, and shall not be reckoned among the nations"[2]—Israel was thought of, at any rate by its religious leaders, as marked off from other nations,—governed by no human king—over whom "Jehovah shall reign for ever and ever"[3]— Gideon refuses the throne for this reason: "I will not rule over you, neither shall my son rule over you: Jehovah shall rule over you."[4] When the people

[1] Ex. xix. 5, 6.   [2] Num. xxiii. 9.
[3] Ex. xv. 18.   [4] Judg. viii. 23.

EARLY HEBREW IDEAL

demand a king, it is not Samuel, but Jehovah himself, whom they are deposing, "they have not rejected thee, but they have rejected me that I should not be king over them."[1] "When ye saw that Nahash king of the children of Ammon came against you, ye said unto me, Nay, but a king shall reign over us; when Jehovah your God was your king."[2] This protest means that Israel is, as a nation, a kingdom of GOD; the practical demand involved is for the surrender of the nation's self to the rule and guidance of their God, Jehovah, who had by his mighty works made himself known to them as their deliverer, "I am Jehovah thy God who brought thee up out of the land of Egypt,—thou shalt have none other god but me."[3] To assign a time for the origin of this ideal is I think not possible; in germ it appears coeval with the beginnings of the distinctive nationality and religion of Israel. But we may ask with more prospect of a definite result when and how this ideal became energetically formulated, and by what steps it led to the expectation of a future Kingdom of GOD.

Israel comes before us in its earliest scarcely dateable records as a group of tribes, very loosely organised, but able, when great occasions arose, to co-operate

---

[1] 1 Sam. viii. 7.   [2] 1 Sam. xii. 12.

[3] Ex. xx. 2, and often. What is contended is not that other peoples of antiquity, and Israel's nearest neighbours (Moab as in Mesha's Stone) were not theocratic, but that the moral character of Jehovah, and the moral link between him and his people, were conceived by the earliest religious teachers of the Israelites in a way to which the religion of other peoples does not furnish a parallel. That the reciprocal relation between Jehovah and Israel is *moral* is involved in germ in the idea of Covenant. (See W. Robertson Smith, *Prophets of Israel*, chap. ii. [1st ed.]; Ritschl, *Unterricht*, § 7, and Dr. Davidson's art. "Covenant" in Hastings' *Dict. of the Bible*.

more or less completely as a whole. And when they do so, the bond of union between the tribes is Jehovah. Defaulters are traitors to him. "Curse ye Meroz, said the angel of Jehovah, curse ye bitterly the inhabitants thereof; because they came not to the help of Jehovah —to the help of Jehovah against the mighty."[1] The wars of Israel are recorded as "the wars of Jehovah";[2] the cause of the nation is his cause; scandalous offences are sins against the collective national conscience— "folly in Israel."

But we do not trace in the earliest history any such profound sense of the unfitness of the people Israel to be the vehicle of a spiritual idea as to lead them to lean upon *the future* for the realisation of the golden age of a true kingdom of GOD.

This deepening of the national conscience was the work of the nation's experience under the Monarchy. The Monarchy is presented to us in tradition under two contrasted but really complementary aspects.

(1) On the one hand the religious conservatism of the people, and the religious idealism of their teachers, alike resented the centralisation of political power. The language of Samuel already quoted gives strong expression to this resentment. The warning of Deuteronomy[3] as to the evils which would attend the establishment of a kingdom are in harmony with those of Samuel,[4] and both find their verification in the reign of King Solomon.[5] There are many indications that

[1] Judg. v. 23.   [2] Num. xxi. 14.
[3] Deut. xvii. 14.   [4] 1 Sam. viii. 10-18.
[5] In Deut. the warnings are directed against (1) multiplication of horses, (2) intercourse with Egypt, (3) multiplication of wives, (4) multiplication of silver and gold, (5) overweening pride. Samuel assumes (1) (4) and (5)

EARLY HEBREW IDEAL

the monarchy was established before the nation was politically ripe for it—the reign of David over Judah was for some years confronted with the allegiance of Israel to Ishbosheth; the details of Absalom's revolt show that the ascendency which David succeeded in establishing over Israel was purely personal, and maintained itself in spite of a deep cleavage between the Northern and the Southern portions of the kingdom.[1] The census of the whole nation was an innovation amounting, in the eyes even of Joab, to sacrilege, and when it was carried out Judah and Israel were still treated as separate units. Solomon's reorganisation of the country for the purpose of taxation [2] looks [3] like an attempt to supersede the tribal organisation by one conceived on fiscal and political lines, centralised round Judah. The principal fiscal officer [4] appointed by Solomon was stoned as soon as the great king was dead—and even when he was at the height of his

---

and adds (6) forced labour, a standing army (practically identifiable with (1), and heavy taxation in kind (cf. (4)), coupled with (7) confiscations of real property (v. 14). All these apply to Solomon except (7) of which there is no direct evidence, and (6) which also seems doubtful (comp. 1 Kings ix. 22 with xii. 4, etc.).

[1] 2 Sam. xix. 41.   [2] 1 Kings iv. 7 sqq.

[3] Four tribes are ignored: Simeon, Dan, Zebulon, and Reuben—and of course Levi. Judah is not provided for, excepting that the Philistine border is administered as two departments. Four tribes are left as departments: Benjamin, Naphthali, Ephraim (i.e. its hill country), and Asher. The latter receives an added district. Probably Western Manasseh may be added, or at least that part which included the plain of Sharon (Naphath-Dor). Eastern Manasseh, Gad, and Issachar are curiously subdivided. The N. division of Issachar has the tribal name, but may have included part of Zebulon. The two Eastern tribes form three departments not easy to delimit. The outlying and especially the richer districts seem to receive careful reorganisation; the whole plan suggests that Judah is the only tribe whose allegiance can be taken for granted.

[4] Adoniram (or Adoram), 1 Kings iv. 6, xii. 18.

power, the voice of prophecy, in the memorable scene between Ahijah and Jeroboam, had doomed the precarious fabric of a united Israel to an early fall. Ahijah, it is true, bases his message upon the personal sin of Solomon, not upon any condemnation of monarchy as such. He may not, for all we know, have shared the feelings of Samuel on that subject. But Samuel's influence was too great to die with him, and of his view of the monarchy no doubt is permitted to us: he looked upon it as an apostasy from the nation's religious ideal.

(2) But the Monarchy has another and widely different aspect in religious tradition. On purely utilitarian grounds, indeed, the advantages of a central authority were obvious and tangible. Men looked back with relief from the times of monarchy, with all its faults, upon the anarchy which had preceded it. "In those days there was no king in Israel: every man did that which was right in his own eyes."[1] But this was only a small part of the truth. The reign, the achievements, and the personality of David formed the nucleus of an ideal which struck deep and lasting root in popular feeling. Amid their later vicissitudes, the Hebrews forgot the many failures of David's reign in comparison with its unquestionable splendours. Under David the Hebrew kingdom had been—for its opportunities—great and successful, its foreign wars untarnished by defeat, its king reigning in closest loyalty to Jehovah, the home life of the people protected from invasion, but not interfered with by the state. Oriental peoples are as a rule little appreciative

[1] Judg. xvii. 6, xviii. 1, xxi. 25.

EARLY HEBREW IDEAL

of civil organisation; they will *respect* only a strong ruler; but they will *love* a monarch who is in sympathy with their character. Like the Persians who remembered Cyrus as a Father,[1] Cambyses as a master, Darius as a tradesman, the Hebrews, apparently in Israel and Judah alike, cherished the memory of David as the symbol of a glorious past, and the highest embodiment of their hopes for a happier future. Even Amos, whose mission is in Northern Israel, and Hosea, a north-Israelite by birth and sentiment, equally with Micah the prophet of the Judean peasantry, contrasting later kings and later reigns with the traditional glories of David, associate the future resurrection of national life with a new David and a new national unity under a regenerated dynasty of David's line.[2]

Secondly, the monarchy did in a very real sense centralise the national conscience; this allowed the contrast between the ideal and the actual to come to a head, and thus the way was prepared for the growth of a more definite hope of an age to come. This contrast was heightened by the manifest and increasing decay of social life, and the divorce of religion from conduct, both of which evils are lashed by Amos and Isaiah, and by that assimilation of the religion of Jehovah to local worships which is denounced by

[1] Herod. III. lxxxix.: ὅτι ἤπιόσ τε καὶ ἀγαθά σφι πάντα ἐμηχανήσατο. The contrasted reference is to Darius' careful organisation of the finances of his empire.

[2] I take the passages in question as they stand, though fully aware that Professor Sayce (*Higher Criticism and Mon.*, chaps. ix. and x.) and others hold that Amos and Hosea bear marks of Judean editing; the identification of these marks appears somewhat subjective, and I cannot follow Professor Charles (*Eschatology*, p. 83) in extending the principle to most of the Messianic passages in the four earliest prophetical books.

2

Hosea. These corruptions were linked, in the prophetic survey of the times, with the overhanging peril of Assyria, which the prophets interpreted as the scourge which was to purify the life of Israel and bring about the establishment of a regenerated kingdom.

From the death of Solomon down to that of Uzziah—or the contemporary close of the reign of Jeroboam II.—the name " Israel " belongs specially to the northern kingdom.[1] The main volume of national life, the chief vicissitudes of religious history, the great prophetic personalities, and the very important though somewhat obscure institutions of prophetic fraternities, from which the great and individually inspired prophets stand out like peaks from a range of lower heights, all are found in the kingdom of Israel, and lend undying interest to its records. With the death of Uzziah and the call of Isaiah we find Israel already hastening to political effacement and Judah fully ripe to continue the development for a time. About this time we trace the earliest form of eschatological hope, the germ from which both the definite expectation of a personal Messiah-king and that of a kingdom of GOD derive their origin—viz. the hope of a restored and purified Israel. The great pre-canonical prophets, indeed, were concerned with the present rather than with the future. Elijah, no doubt, when he despairs of Israel as it is, is rebuked[2] by the reminder of the seven thousand who have not bowed the knee to Baal;—and this conception of a faithful minority,

---

[1] Reference may be permitted to an article by the present writer which aims at doing justice to the Biblical estimate of Northern Israel (*The Thinker*, Jan. 1895).

[2] 1 Kings xix. 14-18.

EARLY HEBREW IDEAL

who were to form the nucleus of a regenerated people, was destined to become fruitful in the hands of later prophets. But his main mission, and that of Elisha also, was different, namely to be "very jealous" for the Lord of Hosts—to vindicate the *exclusive sovereignty* of Jehovah over Israel. Both Elijah and Elisha exemplify the growing prophetic consciousness that Israel is far below the ideal of a " people of Jehovah." But Elisha's direct mission is simply to supersede a sinful dynasty ; and he lives long enough to see how little such a remedy can really effect.

With Amos and Hosea begins a new prophetic epoch; not merely the beginning of written prophecy, although this implies much, but the opening out of a wider outlook upon the forces which were moulding the future of the world, and a longer vista of time—an outlook upon a future of which we do yet see to the end. The contemporaries of Amos had the expectation of a " day of the Lord " — they hoped for some decisive intervention by Jehovah in favour of his people which would relieve the anxieties which were crowding round them, and proclaim Jehovah and his people Israel victorious over their foes. To these hopes Amos sternly gives the lie. The day of Jehovah would come indeed, but not such a day as they expected. " Woe unto you that desire the day of the LORD. Wherefore would ye have Jehovah's day : shall not Jehovah's day be darkness and not light—even very dark and no brightness in it ? " Jehovah has indeed a special care for Israel, but the first result of this will be sharp and speedy vengeance upon their sins. " You only have I known of all the families of the earth—therefore I will punish you for your iniquities."[1] And Hosea, though he dwells upon the unquenchable love of Jehovah for Israel, holds out no hope of escape from the terrible collapse of the nation which the immediate future is to bring. Both prophets however look for restoration, to follow, and to be effected by, the furnace of affliction, and both associate the regeneration of the people with a revival of the monarchy of David. Here then we have the contrast between the ideal and the actual formulated with all possible clearness, and while the actual present is painted with ruthless severity, the ideal is assured in the future. But it is in Isaiah that this new germ of prophecy is ripened to a head. His denunciation of the present is most marked and unsparing in the prophecies which immediately follow his call "in the year that King Uzziah died,"[2] *i.e.* in the early days of Ahaz. "How long?" is the keynote of these earlier utterances. Then under Ahaz comes the combination of denunciation and promise, when special prominence is given to the thought of a king under whom the divine guidance of Israel shall once more be the ruling reality of the nation's life. Immanuel will appear, and that very shortly, and the land of Israel is his destined kingdom. Meanwhile, Isaiah has collected round him a band of disciples, who will, so it would seem, form a nucleus for the remnant that shall escape the overflowing scourge and constitute the beginnings of a new and worthier people of Jehovah. Under Hezekiah the promise is more clearly formulated. The personality of the Messiah-king is now less pro-

---

[1] Amos v. 18-20, iii. 2. See Charles, *Eschatology*, pp. 82, 84 sqq.
[2] It is impossible to assign any considerable time for an independent reign of Jotham.

PROPHECY AND THE CAPTIVITY 21

minent, but the regenerate kingdom fills the prophet's imagination.[1] It is linked on with the actual Israel by the remnant that will be spared when the scourge of Jehovah's anger has passed over the land: but although the realisation of the blessed future will be in and for Israel, the whole world will share in it. The regenerate kingdom will be a channel of blessing to all mankind; even Assyria and Egypt, the two signal representatives of the hostile world-empire, will be numbered with Israel as God's people and the work of his hands.[2]

(*b*) The next period of prophecy, under Josiah and his sons, coincides with the discovery of Deuteronomy, in which book Moses is interpreted to the people by the prophets—the ancient law passing, through the medium of prophecy, into the national consciousness. As a result, the faithful minority become more sharply defined; and at the same time their world-wide mission is again emphasised. " Seek ye Jehovah, all ye meek of the earth—it may be ye shall be hid in the day of Jehovah's anger." " For I will turn to the peoples a pure language, that they may all call upon the name of Jehovah, to serve him with one consent." " But I will leave in the midst of them an afflicted and poor people, and they shall trust in the name of Jehovah."[3] Here we very nearly reach the universalism of the 87th

---

[1] Isa. xxxiii.

[2] Isa. xix. 16–25. The universalism of this passage is a splendid paradox in the mouth of a contemporary of Hezekiah. But to put the passage far later than the Assyrian period (Charles, p. 113) is surely a more startling historical paradox. Micah, the prophet of the Judean peasantry, has in common with Isaiah the hope of a renewed purity of national life, and of a Davidic prince. But unlike Isaiah, he demands the destruction of the sinful capital (iii. 12, iv. 10, i. 5). In this, he anticipates Jeremiah.

[3] Zeph. ii. 3, iii. 9, 12. For another side to Zephaniah, see Charles, p. 98.

Psalm, in which the thought of Isa. xix. is carried to its highest development—

> I will make mention of Rahab and Babylon as among them that know me.
> Behold Philistia, and Tyre, with Ethiopia;
> This one was born there.
> Yea of Zion shall it be said, This one and that one was born in her.
> The LORD shall count, when he writeth up the peoples,
> This one was born there.

To this period, again, belongs the first formulation of the underlying principle of universalism [1] in the famous verse of Habakkuk, which furnished St. Paul with the text for his Epistle to the Romans, " The just shall live by his faith." [2] And even more explicit is the superb passage of Jeremiah,[3] " Behold the days come, saith Jehovah, that I will make a new covenant with the house of Israel . . . but this is the covenant that I will make with the house of Israel after these days, saith Jehovah: I will put my law in their inward parts and in their hearts will I write it; and I will be their GOD and they shall be my people: and they shall teach no more every one his neighbour, and every one his brother saying know Jehovah: for they shall all know me from the least of them unto the greatest of them, saith Jehovah; for I will forgive their iniquity, and their sin will I remember no more." The great passage to be thoroughly appreciated must be read with its whole context.[4] The entire section is the

---

[1] By universalism, in this connexion, is meant the principle of a universal religion, in which there is no difference before GOD between "Jew and Greek" (Gal. iii. 28, etc.).

[2] Hab. ii. 4. By "faith" here is meant not merely "integrity" but "trust in God." See Riehm, *AT. Theol.* § 74. 4.

[3] Jer. xxxi. 31 sqq.   [4] Jer. xxx., xxxi.

PROPHECY AND THE CAPTIVITY 23

ripest fruit of the prophetic picture of a perfect kingdom in which GOD himself is King. In one verse [1] Jeremiah recalls Hosea's prophecy of a Davidic monarchy,[2] but throughout the passage as a whole it is the direct reign of GOD in the hearts and lives of his people that is really in contemplation. It may be questioned whether the Christian conception of a kingdom of GOD upon earth has ever, even at its highest, done more than touch the height here attained. Certainly it has often done less.

Ezekiel in one passage [3] partially reproduces the thought of Jeremiah. Generally speaking, however, universalism, though present, is not prominent, in Ezekiel. Certainly in the earlier part of his prophecy (i.–xxiv.) he shows that the existing kingdom and priesthood [4] are not to be identified with the promised kingdom. The growth of the tender shoot to a goodly cedar, in whose shadow shall dwell "fowl of every wing," [5] reminds us of the mustard seed of the Gospels; and the hope of restoration is expressly extended even to the most profligate of heathen cities.[6]

In the second and reconstructive part (xxxiii.–end) we have the wonderful anticipation [7] of the Parable of the Good Shepherd, the stony heart replaced by hearts of flesh,[8] and above all the great prophecy of the bones,[9] which—once again in the spirit of Hosea—promises resurrection to Israel and Judah equally under the

---

[1] Jer. xxx. 9.   [2] See Briggs, *Messianic Prophecy*, p. 255 sqq.
[3] Ezek. xi. 16–20.   [4] xxi. 26, 27.
[5] xvii. 22–24. I venture to dissent from Professor Charles' view (p. 106, note) that "all fowl of every wing" cannot refer to the Gentiles.
[6] xvii. 53.   [7] xxxiv. 11–31.
[8] xxxvi. 25–35, cf. xi. 16–20.   [9] xxxvii. 1–24.

monarchy of David. This prophecy certainly extends far beyond mere restoration from exile ; it is a *spiritual* restoration above all that is promised. And the great picture of a restored and reorganised Jewish Church-People culminates in the waters of life, which are to revive even the Dead Sea,[1] as those of Paradise watered the whole earth.

We see then the seed of universalism steadily unfolding and striking root at the beginning of the Exile. And if we are to yield to the evidence which brings down to the period of exile large portions of our present book of Isaiah, the continuity of development is illustrated by them in a remarkable way. National regeneration is to follow upon the overthrow of Babylon. The faithfulness of Jehovah will bring into being a renewed Israel who will inherit the nations. The servant of Jehovah is not only to embody the ideal character which is to emerge from the long discipline of the nation, but he is also to be a light to the Gentiles.[2] And all culminates in a new Palestine, a very heaven on earth,[3] and in a renewal of the Heavens and Earth themselves.[4] Here we have for the first time the germ of a purely eschatological conception of the kingdom, eschatological in the sense of transcending altogether the conditions of earthly existence, and reserved for a future world. The eschatology of the Prophets is, so far, almost wholly concerned with the life of the nation, and with what shall befall it in the last days. But the thought upon which we have just touched opens the

---

[1] Ezek. xlvii. 12, cf. xvii. 53.
[2] Isa. xlix. 14-23, li. 1-8, liv. 1 sqq., lvi. 6, 7, lx.   [3] Isa. xxxv.
[4] lxv. 17 sqq. See Charles, *Eschatology*, p. 122 sqq.

PROPHECY AND THE CAPTIVITY 25

way to a fusion of the eschatology of the nation—the distinctive theme of prophecy—with the eschatology of the individual, which had hitherto played no part in the accredited religious training of GOD'S people, though we can trace in popular belief and custom,[1] and occasionally in the language of prophets themselves, the existence of some belief at any rate in a personal existence continued after death. What we have specially to take note of at this period,—that of the Exile, from Jeremiah to Haggai,—is a conception of a resurrection from death as the privilege of the righteous individual—the direct germ of the distinctively Christian doctrine of a resurrection from the dead. The comparison is instructive between the resurrection-language of Hosea[2] and that of the 26th chapter of Isaiah[3] which in some ways recalls it. In Hosea the resurrection is clearly and definitely that of the nation. In the later passage the thought of individual resurrection begins to make its presence felt, though the predominant thought is still — as in the great prophecy of Ezekiel—that of corporate revival.

On the whole, we seem to detect a transition in its beginnings. We may say that the downfall of the Jewish State deepened and widened the hopes of the Nation by preparing the transition to the idea of a kingdom of GOD in a new life, and *therefore* based upon the resurrection of at any rate the righteous dead. This has as its necessary correlative an increased concentration of interest upon individual righteousness and holiness, individual religion; and this again centres

[1] See Charles, *Eschatology*, pp. 56, 62, 69–76, 125.
[2] Hos. vi. 2, xiii. 14.
[3] Isa. xxvi. 19 and context, see Charles, p. 126 sq.

attention upon the inward and spiritual state as the ground of righteousness in God's sight.

We have noticed the characteristic declaration of this everlasting truth by Habakkuk as well as Jeremiah, Ezekiel and the rest. The kingdom to which these later prophets look forward is, accordingly, Jewish in its origin, but for the benefit of all mankind; Zechariah (if the chapters in question belong approximately to this period) insists [1] upon the religious attraction which will draw all the world to Jerusalem,[2] Haggai[3] sees them pouring all their treasures into the house of Jehovah, and fierce as is the vengeance which Joel denounces upon those who have enslaved and sold the children of Jerusalem, there is no need to interpret more narrowly than did the Apostles his prophecy that the LORD in time to come would pour out his Spirit "upon *all* flesh," and that "whosoever shall call on the name of the LORD shall be saved."[4]

---

[1] Zech. viii. 23, xiv. 16. On the current view of the dates, see Charles, pp. 117, 121.

[2] The "Apocalypse" of Zechariah xii. 1–9, xiv. has features in common with Zephaniah (Charles, 98), Ezekiel xlvii. 1–12 (see Charles, 106), and with Joel iv. 18 (Charles, 118). See also Isa. xxxiv., xxxv. It represents a final capture of Jerusalem by the heathen, leading to a signal Theophanic Deliverance, followed by the gathering in of the Nations round a nucleus of believing Israelites. This final struggle has a long sequel in the history of Apocalyptic vision. See Charles, pp. 122 (Daniel), 177 (Sibyl), 191 (Enoch *Ethiop.*), 247 (Jubiles), 288 (4 Esdras), 348 sq., 381. "The doctrine of a final overthrow of living enemies—enemies of Israel according to Jewish belief, enemies of GOD and his true kingdom according to the more spiritual view of Christians—retained its place among the Last Things . . . even when the doctrine of a universal eternal judgment upon every human being, dead as well as living, was added" (see Stanton, *The Jewish and the Christian Messiah*, pp. 136 sq., 304–310).

[3] Hag. ii. 6–9.

[4] Joel ii. 32. Charles, p. 119, mainly on the ground of iii. 2 sqq., which I regard as inconclusive, insists upon a "particularist" sense of this verse.

The Exile then, or rather the experiences of the people which led to it, accompanied it, and followed it, prepared the faithful Israelites for the thought of (1) a kingdom of GOD within them, (2) a kingdom of GOD spiritual and world-wide, and (3) a kingdom of God in a life to come.

(*c*) The subsequent history gives increased definiteness and force to this hope, but at the same time forces it into a somewhat narrower channel. The ideal of the Exile seems at first sight to lose something of the sanguine sympathy and world-wide range of its early promise.

The hope of the Prophets is in fact attuned by Daniel to the faith of an oppressed people, struggling for independence, and conscious that the institutions distinctive of their religion are at stake in the struggle. Whether Daniel wrote under the present stress of the Maccabean struggle, or foresaw it in the minuteness of detail of which chap. xi. is the witness, that chapter is at any rate enough to show the situation to which the book is closely addressed. Faced with the alternative of apostasy or annihilation, the pious Israelite is to learn that stedfast loyalty to his GOD will come out triumphant however the odds to which it is opposed. This, the common creed of prophecy, Daniel enforces by a new method,—new, that is, in its literary vehicle, but with its roots in the prophetic past. Daniel stands first in the great series of Apocalypses. Viewed as they formerly were from a distance, the visions of Daniel and of St. John towered aloft into the light of heaven, two solitary mountain peaks connecting heaven and earth. We have now been brought by the study of comparative material to a nearer point of view; we see that the giant masses are connected and surrounded by a long series of lesser heights; Apocalypses of Moses, of Eldad and Medad, of Elijah and Isaiah, of Enoch and Abraham, of the XII Patriarchs, of Ezra and Baruch, and of Peter. Apocalypse is a type of literature as distinctive of Judaism as the drama is distinctive of the Greeks, and there are characteristics which are common to the whole Apocalyptic series. But it remains as true as formerly that in the whole range two peaks alone catch the sunlight of Inspiration.

Apocalypse furnished the Jew with a philosophy of history in relation to religion and life. This had in a measure been the work of prophecy and of certain other classes of Hagiographa. But Apocalypse addressed itself directly and comprehensively to the history of the world, with the history of the Chosen People as its centre, viewed in the light of the ultimate purpose of GOD, and the final consummation of his Kingdom.

In the book of Daniel three points claim our special attention. First the history of the world is reviewed twice over (chaps. ii., vii.); it culminates in a hostile power, apparently centred in an individual king (vii. 8, viii. 9, 21, xi., all apparently identical in reference), which is to be overthrown by a divine, a perfect and an eternal kingdom, reigned over by " one like unto a Son of Man," *i.e.* by the people of the saints of the Most High.[1] Secondly, this kingdom is inaugurated by judgment—a judgment with books[2] and penal fire for the enemies.[3]

---

[1] Dan. vii. 13. On the meaning of this see Driver, *Daniel*, p. 108.
[2] Dan. vii. 10, cf. xii. 2.
[3] Dan. vi. 11, cf. Isa. lxvi. fin.; Charles, pp. 132, 181.

JEWISH ESCHATOLOGY 29

The resurrection which ushers in the judgment is still not conceived as universal; but it is individual, and it includes bad as well as good. Thirdly, the intensity and definiteness of the whole is undoubtedly gained at the expense of the older prophetic universalism. The nationalism of Daniel is intense. But it is tempered by deep national contrition (ix. 3–19); and the seer has learned, before St. Paul was there to teach him, that "not all are Israel" who are of Israel's seed.[1] Those only who are written in the book are delivered, and not all endure to the end. Still, we certainly miss here the hope held out by the prophets for all mankind. True, there is nothing to forbid proselytism, but even that has no special mention, still less anything beyond it. But though this is so, the reign of the Son of Man is to include all mankind: "that all people and nations and language should serve him." The possession of the kingdom is, indeed, reserved to the saints,—*i.e.* to those against whom the tyrant has waged war,[2]—but it will—under conditions not defined—include all the world. There are two factors in the idea of the Messianic kingdom in the maturity of Jewish prophecy,—the idea of universal dominion, and the idea of a universal conversion of mankind to the worship of Jehovah—the political and the purely religious conception of the Divine kingdom on earth. The two are not mutually exclusive, but are two alternative aspects of one and the

---

[1] Dan. xii. 12, 1 sqq.
[2] Dan. vii. 18, 21, 22. Charles says, somewhat curtly, "There is no Messiah." This would imply, what is not the case, that a Messiah is not only not named, but excluded. And Enoch (B.C. 90, see Charles, p. 214 sq., and Driver, *l.c.*) already understands the "Son of Man" in Dan. as the Messiah.

same general expectation. In Daniel it must be said that the thought of universal dominion predominates over the other. The book contemplates conversion by means of dominion rather than dominion by means of conversion. And this gives the keynote for the hope of the Kingdom of GOD as we see it in possession of men's minds at the coming of Christ. The circumstances of the times—of the last two centuries before Christ, made dependence upon a heathen power more than ever intolerable to the Jews. The Pharisees, who were above all else religious loyalists, became the spiritual leaders of the people. And in foreign dominion the Pharisees saw a direct menace against the purity of the national religion. Only, in the higher minds, the aspiration for political independence was strictly subordinated to that for religious purity. · To be rid of hostile domination was a means, not an end in itself. The aim was at bottom spiritual—the free and unhampered service of GOD: " That we, being delivered from our enemies, might serve him without fear: in holiness and righteousness before him, all the days of our life."

This was the hope that had sustained the sons of Matthias and their followers in their devoted, and on the whole successful, struggle against Greek domination and influence in the second century before Christ; and the same hope, kept alive by the zeal of the Pharisees, sustained the faith of the people through the depressing days of Roman and Herodian power.

The purity of motive which at first marks out the family of the Maccabees begins indeed from a very early date to suffer from earthly alloy. The last surviving brother, Simeon, united the office of High Priest with the functions, though not with the express title, of king.[1]   Under him priesthood practically merges in royalty. The indirect result is to increase the importance of the Scribe and the synagogue as factors in popular religion, at the expense of the temple and the priest. Simeon's son, Hyrcanus the first, destroyed the Temple of Gerizim and vainly endeavoured to force the Samaritans into ecclesiastical conformity. With the Edomites he was more successful. Political aims and methods more and more displace the spirit in which the family had first attained their power. Judas Aristobulus I., the eldest son of Hyrcanus, formally assumed the style and title of king; his brother, Alexander Jannaeus,[2] gradually relapsed into a mere head of the Sadducees. Involved in civil war and bloodshed, he left his widow to break with the Sadducees and rule justly during the minority of their sons. The rivalries of these sons, the weak devotee Hyrcanus II. and the more spirited Aristobulus, the intervention of Pompey, the bloody siege and capture of Jerusalem, and the profanation of the Temple, need not be recalled at length. As a result, Hyrcanus was left as High Priest but not as king. His granddaughter and sole surviving representative, the unfortunate Mariamne, married the son of his Edomite major-domo Antipater, and by the favour of Mark Antony the monarchy founded upon the purest movement of intense religious zeal passed into the hands of Herod the Great.

The Maccabean house had in fact followed up self-sacrifice by self-aggrandisement; they began as

[1] From his reign date the first known Jewish coins (B.C. 139).
[2] B.C. 106–79.

defenders of a purely spiritual cause, but ended by usurping both the high-priesthood and the throne. In both ways they violated the principle of legitimate succession which had become so sacred in Jewish eyes; they set it aside not for any more spiritual principle, but merely as political opportunists. No wonder then that this relapse from their first purity cost them the whole-hearted support of the religious purists who had at first carried them to power. No consistent Pharisee could wholly accept a High Priest who did not represent the legitimate line of Aaron, or tolerate, as an embodiment of his hope of the Messianic kingdom, a king who had no pretence to descent from David. That some did not share this attitude of strict protest, and rallied to the *de facto* dynasty, was a matter of course. Such is always apt to be the case, and the tendency accounts for the existence in gospel times of the party of Herodians. But it is not in such quarters that we must look for the hope of the Kingdom of GOD to which our Lord made his first appeal. The deeper religious feeling to which I have just referred found expression, in the very generation which ushered in the Christian era, in the Psalms of Solomon of which I will speak in the next Lecture.

IV

Meanwhile, let us briefly gather up the results of our survey of the Messianic expectation in its growth and modification to the close of O.T. times. The idea of the Kingdom of GOD took shape at first as a virtual philosophy of history, and a philosophy of history pre-

JEWISH ESCHATOLOGY 33

supposes a philosophy of life and existence. In other words, faith in GOD himself lies behind the idea of his purpose for his rational creation—*i.e.* behind the idea of a kingdom of GOD. A GOD who is not supreme over nature can have no effective purpose for beings whose bodily constitution and surroundings are at the mercy of nature's forces. Now whatever rearrangements may be necessary in the order of the documents of the O.T., or in the inferred order of religious development, it must, I think, be allowed that the idea of GOD presented to us in the Old Testament is distinctive from the first in this very respect. Anthropomorphic and anthropopathic language and thought there is,—limitations from which the mind, especially the popular mind, was only gradually cleared. That the personal name[1] of the national deity of one small nation, coupled with the early experiences in which that nation saw the arm of their national God, should have supplied the real and absolute point of contact between the human race and the Personal Existence, which underlies the boundless seen and unseen universe, and guides its every movement from the greatest to the least, is a thing hard at first sight to conceive. But when we see the fact in all its context, and realise that *there* is the beginning of every advance that religion has made in the world, the original starting-point of all Christian prayers and hopes and efforts, the fountain-head of all that is

---

[1] Justin Martyr, resting upon the LXX rendering κύριοσ for יהוה, makes it a proof of the purity of O.T. religion that, unlike heathen deities, the God of Israel lacked a personal name (θετὸν ὄνομα, *Apol.* I. x., cf. *Cohort. ad Graec.* xxi.). This of course cannot now be maintained, but the essential difference, as stated in the text, remains.

3

noblest in thought, word and action around us to-day, he would indeed be rash who should dismiss it as incredible. If the sequel has been on such a momentous scale, we cannot doubt that some consciousness of what it meant was present in the minds that first received the tender seed of divine revelation. Men set out on the first stages of their journey toward the hope of GOD'S kingdom with a belief, implicit if not formally expressed, that the GOD in whom they trusted was able to perform all that he promised. The Israelites, then, from time immemorial, thought of their God in a way that implied a lofty and exclusive moral allegiance, —their earliest political unity was that of a kingdom of GOD. And then by a series of national experiences which we are partly able to trace in detail, and into which the institution of monarchy and the work of the prophets entered as leading factors, they were led to realise how little their actual condition corresponded with this great idea, and to look for a time to come when the ideal would be realised in the future, as it had never been in the past, of a righteous people reigned over by the GOD of all the universe. This future was conceived in the form of a perfect Kingdom, and its realisation hung upon the coming of a King in whose person the reign of GOD should find its final and absolute expression. In the great prophets who saw and followed the downfall of the Monarchy, this hope reached its most spiritual conception, and embodied a principle which left no room for the distinctive privilege of the Jew, but included all nations on a common basis of spiritual regeneration. Later on, in response to a crisis which called for concentrated and warlike action,

JEWISH ESCHATOLOGY 35

this world-wide range of sympathy was somewhat narrowed, and the kingdom was figured in terms more distinctively Jewish. But the faith itself was the more intense and keen, and after burning now more dimly, now again brighter in the century and a half which preceded the birth of Christ, now once more popular expectation watched with feverish anxiety for the Person of the predestined King. It has been said of late, by one whose moral earnestness has left its mark upon this place, that the Messianic hope is a Jewish dream, the creation of national vanity, and without importance or interest to the modern mind.[1] As long as the best men and women, the very salt of human society, pray Thy kingdom come,—as long as the command, to seek first the Kingdom of GOD and his Righteousness, awakes in us the strongest aspirations for good of which our poor nature is capable, this will remain a singularly unsympathetic and shortsighted pronouncement. Our Lord certainly set aside much that entered into the hopes and aspirations of his followers, and taught them much that seemed to give the lie to their most sacred convictions. But in doing so he was interpreting to them what their own prophets had taught,—the inmost secret of the hope they had faithfully in their ignorance kept alive, and to that hope he assured the future of the world.

[1] Goldwin Smith, *Guesses at the Riddle of Existence* (1897), p. 117 f.

LECTURE II

THE KINGDOM OF GOD IN THE NEW TESTAMENT (I.)

Καὶ οἶμαι νοεῖσθαι Θεοῦ μὲν βασιλείαν τὴν μακαρίαν τοῦ ἡγεμονικοῦ κατάστασιν καὶ τὸ τεταγμένον τῶν σόφων διαλογισμῶν· Χριστοῦ δὲ βασιλείαν τοὺσ προϊόντασ σωτηρίουσ τοῖσ ἀκούουσι λόγουσ, καὶ τὰ μὲν ἐπιτελούμενα ἔργα δικαιοσύνησ καὶ τῶν λοιπῶν ἀρετῶν· λόγοσ γὰρ καὶ δικαιοσύνη ὁ υἱόσ τοῦ Θεοῦ.

Origen.

LECTURE II

THE KINGDOM OF GOD IN THE NEW TESTAMENT (I.)

That we being delivered out of the hands of our enemies might serve him without fear: in holiness and righteousness before him all the days of our life.—LUKE i. 74.
The kingdom of God is within you.—LUKE xvii. 21.

THE Gospel of St. Luke, in many respects the most purely Greek of the writers of New Testament history, preserves, taken evidently by the author from some native Palestinian source, four canticles of marked beauty and loftiness, and of very marked correspondence with the poetical style of the Old Testament. This is specially true of the three longest of them, known to the modern Churchman as the Benedictus, the Magnificat, and the Nunc Dimittis. They appear to come to us from the very heart of the original Hebraic nucleus of the Christian Society,[1] and from a time when the language and thoughts of the Old Testament still suffice for the expression of a devotion which was potentially Christian, but was exulting as yet but in the first daybreak of the Messianic advent.

The Lucan canticles are the immediate historical

[1] Materials bearing on this question have been collected by Resch, the well-known compiler of *Agrapha*, in his *Kindheits-evangelium* (*Texte u. Untersuch.* vol. x. part 5). His critical judgment is not quite equal to his enthusiasm, but the latter gives to his work the interest of a labour of love.

sequel of a collection of psalms, much inferior to them in poetical form, separated from them by that indefinable but to us Christians surely very perceptible difference of spiritual savour which so often distinguishes books outside the Canon from those included in it—the difference between Clement of Rome and St. Paul, of Ignatius from St. John. But allowing, as I think we must, for this difference, the Psalms of Solomon have many phrases and other characteristics in common with the canticles of St. Luke, and give them a historical context in which they take a natural and convincing place. In B.C. 65 the Romans had extinguished the Seleucid kingdom of Syria: the two rival claimants to the Jewish throne,[1] and a third party in protest against both, appeared at Damascus to seek the aid of the new sovereign power. But Aristobulus, the nominee of the Sadducees, was at the same time preparing to fight; as soon as he learned this, Pompey at once marched his legions upon Jerusalem. After a three months' siege in which twelve thousand Jews perished, he took the Temple. The building had no special sacredness for the victorious Roman, and in curiosity rather than with the intention of trampling upon the most sacred feelings of the conquered, Pompey entered the Holy of Holies. Though, as the Psalms of Solomon expressly allow, the sin was one of ignorance,[2] the pious Israelite regards his tragic end as the vengeance of GOD.

> I delayed[3] not until GOD showed me that insolent one lying pierced upon the high places of Egypt . . .
> Even his dead body tossed upon the waves in great contempt: and there was none to bury him.

---

[1] See above, p. 31.   [2] Ps. Sol. xvii. 15.
[3] ii. 30. Von Gebhardt suggests ἐφρόντισα for ἐχρόνισα.

This allusion, with others nearly as clear, appears to bring the completion of the Psalms of Solomon down later than B.C. 48, the year of Pompey's death. The absence of any allusion to the reign of Herod the Great is good evidence that the collection was completed before his accession in B.C. 39. The psalms are wholly Judean in reference and interest; they can hardly have originated outside Jerusalem, and it appears probable that their original language was Hebrew.[1] They breathe the spirit of the Pharisees who had sided with Hyrcanus II.—these are "the just," "the holy," of the psalmists—against Aristobulus and his Sadducean followers, who appear as "the sinners," "the transgressors," "the men-pleasers."[2] The Pharisees sided by preference with Hyrcanus, but in reality they rejected the claims of both princes to kingdom and high-priesthood alike. Of both factions alike they speak, when they say[3]—

"The holy things of God they took for spoil: and there was *no inheritor* to deliver out of their hand," and predict[4] that the true King, the Son of David, "shall thrust out the sinners from the inheritance." The watchword of these psalms, directed both against the Roman overlordship and the Hasmonean monarchy, is "The LORD is King."

"Blessed be the glory of the LORD: for he is our

---

[1] The above is the view of Ryle and James, and is substantially held by von Gebhardt (*T. u. U.* vol. xiii. 2) and most modern scholars. Of course the psalms may be by different authors, but there is no evidence for assigning them to different *periods*.

[2] Ps. Sol. iv. 8, 21. This psalm gives a vivid sketch of the high-placed Sadducee.

[3] vii. 12.

[4] xvii. 26, cf. ver. 6, where see note of Ryle and James.

King." "O LORD, thou art our King henceforth and even for ever more, for in thee, O GOD, our soul exulteth."[1]

The interest of the psalmists is not primarily political. Even the Roman rule is taken as a chastisement for the sins of the nation, expressly sent by God. This is in marked contrast with the spirit of the "zealots"—the Pharisaic extremists of the next generation. The Messiah is to restore the kingdom to Israel, but not by fleshly weapons:—

"For he shall not trust in horse and rider and bow, nor shall he multiply unto himself silver and gold for war, nor by many people[2] shall he gather confidence for the day of battle."

From the restored kingdom the "hypocrites" are to be shut out. It will include only those who fear and love God in sincerity. The latter will be marked with a sign, which will protect them in the Day of Judgment—ἡμέρα κρίσεωσ κυρίου.[3] This judgment, which is apparently adopted from Daniel, seems to precede the coming of the perfect kingdom. The Kingdom is depicted especially in the 17th and 18th Psalms. It will consist of Israel, after the Romans are expelled and the Sadducees put down, not of Judah only, but of the dispersed tribes as well, and its seat will be at Jerusalem, its centre a restored temple worship. The Gentiles will bring in their tribute and will learn the true faith. The kingdom will be spiritual, holy, wise, and above all just. The King is—for the first

---

[1] Ps. Sol. v. 22, xvii. 1 (and cf. vers. 38, 51).
[2] xvii. 37. The MS. reading πολλοῖσ gives no sense. Ryle and James conjecture "ships," πλοίοισ; Gebh. would insert λαοῖσ as above.
[3] ἡμέρα κυρίου in Amos (*supra*, p. 19), ἡμέρα κρίσεωσ in Judith xvi. 17. The phrase here seems to combine the two.

time, for Dan. ix. 25[1] is not an exception—called the Messiah or Christ:—

"There will be no iniquity in his days in their midst, for all shall be holy, and their King is Christ the Lord."[2] "The LORD cleanse Israel for the day when he shall have mercy upon them and shall bless them: even for the day of his appointing when he shall bring back[3] his Christ. Blessed are they that shall be in those days: for they shall see the good things of the LORD which he shall bring to pass for the generation that cometh, under the rod of the chastening of the Lord Christ[4] in the fear of his God"[5] . . . The Christ-King is moreover a son of David, he reigns as God's vicegerent. The Christ of these psalms is man not God; a true son of David, an idealised, sinless, unworldly Solomon. To share in the joys of the kingdom, the faithful dead will be raised to life—this life will be eternal and joyful;[6] its realisation is in the "generation to come."[7] Coupled

---

[1] See Westcott, *Epistles of St. John*, p. 118. But perhaps Enoch, *Sim.* xlviii. 10, lii. 4, is an exception (Charles, *Esch.* p. 214).
[2] Ps. Sol. xvii. 36.   [3] See Ryle and James' note on the passage.
[4] *Or* the Lord's Christ.   [5] Ps. Sol. xviii. 6–8.
[6] See iii. 16, xiii. 9, x. 9, xiv. 7, xv. 15. On the raising of the dead see Ryle and James, p. li. But Charles (*Eschatology*, p. 223 sq.) understands the kingdom in these psalms as not eternal, but earthly, and limited to the lifetime of the (human) Messiah; whereas the faithful are to be raised to an *eternal* life, *i.e.* not to life on earth, the scene of the Messianic reign. But while these psalms do not clearly define the relation of the Messianic reign to Eternity, I see nothing in them incompatible with the idea of a reign *eternal on earth* (on which see below, p. 53, note 3, and Charles, pp. 82, 83, 188, 189, 230, 288, etc.); if the psalmist's eschatology is thus far indefinite, Charles' argument hardly holds good.
[7] xv. 14. The *expression* ὁ αἰὼν ὁ ἐρχόμενοσ does not occur in these psalms, but the *idea* of an "age to come" (whether to be inaugurated by the Messiah's advent or to follow upon his Reign) is presupposed (see below, p. 52, n.).

with this is the doctrine of the Day of Judgment, referred to above, which is still conceived in the undeveloped form which meets us in the book of Daniel.

On the whole, as compared with Daniel, our psalms show a distinct limitation of view. As in Daniel, a definite historical crisis is the theme, but it is treated in and for itself, and not as part of a scheme of universal history. Our psalmist looks passionately for a "son of David"; Daniel looks for a "Son of Man." The Psalms of Solomon are didactic but not apocalyptic; they bring very definite religious and moral principles to bear upon their subject, and they comprise an eschatology, but hardly a philosophy of history. Even the familiar Hebraic thought of "the world to come" is presupposed rather than expressly appealed to.[1] It is presupposed, in so far as the Advent of the Christ-King is to bring about a perfect kingdom on earth, beyond which the prophetic vision of the psalmists does not travel. The following passage contains the express phrase "Kingdom" or "Reign of God" in the sense which furnishes the starting-point for our Lord's teaching :—

"O Lord thou art our King henceforth and even for evermore . . . and the kingdom of our God is unto everlasting over the heathen in judgment. Thou O LORD didst choose David to be king over Israel and didst swear unto him, touching his seed for ever, that his throne should not fail before thee. . . . Behold O LORD and raise up unto them their King, the son of David, in the time which thou O GOD knowest, that he

[1] See previous note.

may reign over Israel[1] thy servant; . . . and he shall not suffer iniquity to lodge in their midst; and none that knoweth wickedness shall dwell with them. . . . He shall judge the nations and the peoples with the wisdom of his righteousness. Selah. . . . And there shall be no iniquity in his days in their midst, for all shall be holy, and their King is the Lord Christ."[2] The eternity of the kingdom comes from Dan. vii. 27, "and his kingdom is an everlasting kingdom," compare Ps. cxlv. 13, "Thy kingdom is an everlasting kingdom, and thy dominion endureth throughout all generations." The imagery of Ps. lxxii. is apparent in the universality and beneficence ascribed in detail to the Messiah's reign, and the Sibylline Oracles reecho or anticipate[3] this feature, with a clear reference to the house of David—

βασιλεία μεγίστη
'Αθανάτου βασιλῆοσ ἐπ' ἀνθρώποισι φανεῖται
"Εστι δέ τισ φυλὴ βασιλήϊοσ, ἧσ γένοσ ἔσται
"Απταιστον . . . .
Καὶ τότε δὲ ἐξεγέρει βασιλήϊον εἰσ αἰῶνασ
Πάντασ ἐπ' ἀνθρώπουσ.

The coming of Christ, therefore, found in existence a cycle of beliefs and hopes concerning the Kingdom of GOD, founded upon the Old Testament, and echoed in the literature current among the Jewish people outside[4] the official schools. These beliefs and hopes took shape, no doubt, to many minds as crude and political aspirations. But among the stricter

[1] Cf. Ps. Sol. v. 21. [2] xvii. 1-36.
[3] Sib. iii. 47, 288, 766 (see Ryle and James, p. 129). The passage is dated by Charles (p. 176) before 100 B.C.
[4] Stanton, *The Jewish and Christian Messiah*, p. 39 sqq.

Pharisees—or at least the more spiritually-minded of them, they comprised the following elements:—

1. Israel was ideally the kingdom of GOD, and destined to become really what it already was in idea.[1]

2. Israel as it was was not the kingdom of God, for it contained unworthy elements. The existing faithful Jews are the *nucleus* of the future kingdom.

3. The future kingdom was to be on earth, with Jerusalem as its seat and centre.[2] It was variously conceived as (*a*) eternal, or (*b*) of limited duration.

4. It was to include the faithful who are dead, and will be raised again.

5. It was to be inaugurated by a Day of Judgment, which appears to be identified with the day of the Messiah's appearance.[3]

6. It was to be an embodiment of all elements of national well-being—social, ethical, spiritual.

7. It was to embrace all peoples, who would come to worship at Jerusalem.

II

It will aid us to pass at once, for the sake of contrast, to the generation which preceded the final and hopeless destruction of the Jewish state, and with it of all hopes which involved its continuance under however purified a form. A band of teachers had arisen to whom no such catastrophe could come as a surprise, but who still hoped for and preached the Kingdom of GOD.

---

[1] Ps. Sol. v. 21.   [2] xvii. 33-55.
[3] xv. 13-15, comparing xvii. 24-31, 41-51.

SAINT PAUL

Even after the Risen Lord had during the great forty days spoken to his apostles of the things pertaining to the Kingdom of God,[1] they can still ask him: "Lord, wilt thou at this time restore again the kingdom to Israel?" But the Ascension, and Pentecost in its train, make it plain that the Restoration is not yet. The hope of it is now centred upon the promised Return of Christ with which[2] the Kingdom of God is primarily associated in the Apostolic age. The Apostles are at first rather concerned to win their Jewish hearers to the allegiance of Jesus as the Christ-King than to define the nature of his kingdom. But, as hitherto the popular hope of the Kingdom had hung entirely upon the Advent of the King, a change in that hope was inevitable, in view of a change in the view of the Advent itself. To the Christian, there was no longer one advent only, longed for as future. He still passionately looked for a future advent which would bring the Kingdom of GOD with Power. But his confidence in its coming now largely rested on the certainty of an Advent already accomplished in fact. To convince a Jew that Jesus was indeed the Christ, was to convince him that in a sense the Kingdom of GOD was already come, and present on earth.

---

[1] Acts i. 3–6.

[2] Ἀνάψυξισ (Acts iii. 20) correlative with ἀποκατάστασισ (*ibid.* 21) and therefore with ἀποκαθιστάνεισ (i. 6). The "refreshing" is the Messianic "Regeneration" which (Mal. iv. 6) is associated with the coming of Elijah, and therefore (Matt. xvii. 11 ‖ Mark ix. 12) with the Baptist; but (as he is "not the Christ" but his forerunner) finally only with the Return of Christ. The antecedent of ὧν in Acts iii. 21 is doubtful. Probably it is χρόνων, πάντων (which, however, Dalman, *Worte Jesu*, 146, makes the antecedent to ὧν) being absolute, as in Matt. xvii. 11 (cited above). See also Matt. xix. 28 (παλιγγενεσία) and below, p. 51. A somewhat different view is taken of the passage in Charles, *Eschatology*, p. 373 sq.

This in itself meant the abandonment of much that had hitherto entered into the web and fibre of the popular expectation of GOD'S Kingdom,—except in so far as all such realistic elements were capable of being transferred from the kingdom of the First Advent to the kingdom of the Second. That this was to some extent the case, the sequel appears to show. But the whole change of which I speak must have been somewhat gradual. Apart from the slowness with which men habitually realise the full consequences of acquired knowledge, we must remember that it was long before the impossibility of an entire conversion of Israel became manifest, and with it the destination of the gospel for all nations without distinction or condition. The twelve Apostles are to evangelise the twelve tribes, and they will not have accomplished this task until the Son of Man be come.[1] His coming will be hastened [2] by the repentance of Israel. Prophecy had of course prepared them for a hardened and intractable section,—but apart from these, to work for the kingdom is to work for the conversion of Israel; to the Christian-Jewish mind, the conversion of the Gentiles is to bring them into a Christendom still loyally obedient to the law of Moses.[3]

It will be needless in this place to trace through the earlier section of the Acts the process of gradual de-judaisation which paves the way for St. Paul. It has been commonly objected to the chapters in question that St. Peter and the minor characters of the story are unhistorically made to forestall the distinctive work

---

[1] Matt. x. 23, see also Mark ix. 1. [2] Acts iii. 19 sq. ($ὅπως$).
[3] Acts xv. 1 sqq. and especially xxi. 21.

of St. Paul by the removal, as in the case of Cornelius, of Jewish restrictions which he was the first to set aside. But when we remember that in fact great historical changes do not obey in every detail the strict logical succession which critical analysis rightly exhibits in the process as a whole, and when we take just account of the conditions under which each important forward step is recorded as having occurred, we shall I think be struck with the general consistency of the narrative and its harmony with what the historical circumstances of the time justify us in regarding as probable. Thus much I have been obliged to say of a period of which, especially for the purpose of this enquiry, our materials for knowledge are the slightest, —in order that we may realise that great and distinctive as was the work of St. Paul it was not wholly without antecedent developments which prepared for it.

In St. Paul's treatment of the idea of the Kingdom of GOD three things strike us at once. (1) The complete exclusion of the realistic eschatology of a visible reign of the Messiah upon earth;[1] (2) the twofold application of the idea, corresponding to the two Advents of Christ; and (3) a distinction, discernible side by side with the fundamental unity of the two, between the Kingdom of Christ and the Kingdom of GOD.[2]

To begin with the second and fundamental point, St. Paul's primary conception of the Kingdom of GOD is eschatological. In itself, it is nothing short of the final consummation of the divine purpose for the rational creation, GOD all in all. For the individual

[1] Pp. 52, 54, note. [2] P. 53 sq.

Christian, it stands as the goal of life and endeavour. Like the correlative phrase δόξα τοῦ Θεοῦ, it connotes, with infinite richness of meaning, all that is implied in the word "Salvation." In this Kingdom and Glory redeemed mankind is to share, "to be glorified together" with Christ, "to reign with" him.[1] This sense meets us in St. Paul's earliest and latest Epistles, "that ye should walk worthily of GOD, who calls you into his kingdom and glory"—"that ye should prove worthy of the kingdom of GOD, for which ye also suffer"—"or know ye not that the unrighteous shall not inherit the kingdom of GOD"—"this I say brethren that flesh and blood cannot inherit the kingdom of GOD."[2]

But the Kingdom of GOD is not only future. It is present here and now as the sphere of all the work of an Apostle and of all the life of a Christian. "The kingdom of GOD," he writes with direct references to present concerns, "is not in word but in power"—Aristarchus, Mark, and Jesus Justus are his "fellow-workers for the kingdom of GOD," *i.e.* in building up the body of Christ now.[3]

The two senses are distinct, and yet one. They are linked by such a passage as Col. i. 11, where in a context coloured by hope of the eternal inheritance St. Paul speaks of himself and his readers as already translated by GOD from the power of darkness into the kingdom of his dear Son. That kingdom then exists to

---

[1] 1 Cor. iv. 8; Rom. viii. 17, and elsewhere.
[2] 1 Thess. ii. 12; 2 Thess. i. 5; 1 Cor. vi. 9, 10, and Gal. v. 21; Eph. v. 5; 1 Cor. xv. 50.
[3] Θεοῦ σύνεργοι, 1 Cor. iii. 9, cf. 2 Cor. vi. 1; see also 1 Cor. iv. 20, cf. Rom. xiv. 7; Col. iv. 11. On this sense see also Sanday in *Journal of Theological Studies*, July 1900, p. 483.

St. Paul already wherever man is in a state of salvation, wherever Christ is king. But its complete realisation is still hindered by men's sin and the hardness of their hearts, by the activity of mysterious powers which are still permitted to range themselves in hostility to GOD and his people, and by the still more mysterious corruption which attaches to flesh and blood, and to all created things, which, as St. Paul holds, is the accompaniment of man's fallen condition, and with man awaits the hope of final restoration.[1] The reign of Christ, which began potentially with his coming in the likeness of sinful flesh, and the condemnation of sin in the flesh which that coming *ipso facto* involved, dates in its actual exercise from the resurrection and exaltation of Christ. By the former he is declared to be the Son of GOD with power, by the latter he takes the preordained place of the Messiah at the right hand of GOD, whence he reigns until all the Enemies, whose power retards the consummation of his Kingdom, are placed under his feet. This subjugation of the Enemies is the specific work of Christ's Mediatorial reign at GOD'S right hand, and it culminates in the Return of Christ which delivers the sons of GOD, and with them the whole creation, from the bondage of corruption and death, and directly ushers in "the end," the re-delivery of the kingdom to the Father, the perfect and absolute Kingdom of GOD.[2] In the passage, familiar to us all from its use at the Burial of the Dead, which is St. Paul's only express utterance on this mysterious theme, the contrast with the Jewish eschatology of the Psalms of Solomon is extraordinarily sharp. The

[1] Rom. viii. 20.   [2] Cf. Rom. viii. 21 with 1 Cor. xv. 26.

"world to come"[1]—the eternal Kingdom of GOD which will follow when all earthly history has run its course—which hardly enters into the view of the Jewish psalmist, is clearly placed before us by St. Paul as the ultimate goal. Again, the relation between its inauguration and the second coming of Christ is so close, so direct, that all thought of an earthly and visible reign of Christ, begun by his second coming and ended by the Redelivery, is manifestly excluded.[2] Thirdly, the kingdom of Christ as Mediator and Messiah synchronises, in St. Paul's thought, with the interval between the First Advent and the Second. With the consummation of its functions, with the final deliverance of GOD's creation, the kingdom of Christ is merged in the perfect Kingdom of GOD,[3] that GOD may be all in all.

The history of the world, therefore, from the Resurrection of Christ,—virtually from his coming in the flesh, is viewed by St. Paul as the Reign of Christ. Wherever that reign is effective, there is Christ's king-

[1] Not in so many words (except perhaps Eph. i. 21, τῷ μέλλοντι). St. Paul it is true often speaks of ὁ αἰὼν οὗτοσ, but he contrasts with it not ὁ ἀ. ὁ ἐρχόμενοσ, but the "kingdom of God." (See Dalman, *Worte Jesu*, p. 120.)

[2] The contrary view has been maintained, *e.g.* (to mention very dissimilar writers), by Godet and by Schmiedel in their notes on 1 Cor. xv. 24, and by St. John Thackeray, *St. Paul*, p. 120 sqq. But the view in the text is capable of something like conclusive proof, and I am glad to find myself here confirmed by the disinterested judgment of Professor Charles (*Eschatology*, pp. 387-396).

[3] This must be carefully distinguished from the doctrine of Marcellus of Ancyra, against which the words of the "Nicene" Creed are directed: "Whose kingdom shall have no end." The system of Marcellus (see Nicene and Post-Nicene Library, series 2, vol. iv., *Athanasius*, p. xxxvi) involved the return of the Son into the Being of the Father, so that His *distinct personal existence* was to cease,—a thought wholly foreign to St. Paul.

dom; outside his kingdom lie sin and Satan, and all that St. Paul would include under the head of "Enemies." The Apostle looks, as many passages of his Epistles show us,[1] for a final catastrophe of all these "enemies" at the return of Christ. But meanwhile this is being prepared for by the increase of Christ's kingdom, both in its extent and in its intensity, through the Christian centuries; by every victory of good and every form of warfare against evil.

But let us take note, before passing on, of St. Paul's distinction between the Kingdom of GOD and of Christ. On the one hand the distinction is real. It corresponds to the distinction, faint but discernible in contemporary Jewish thought, between the Messianic age and the "age to come." In the Fourth Book of Esdras and in the Apocalypse of Baruch, and in some Rabbinical utterances, a clear distinction is made between the two,[2] the resurrection of the faithful being placed at the beginning of Messiah's earthly reign; and that reign has a definite conclusion[3] which is followed by the birth of the new world. But another view made

[1] 2 Thess. ii.; 1 Cor. xv. 24. On the antecedents of this factor in the Apostle's eschatology, see above, p. 26, note 2.

[2] Stanton, pp. 315 and 317 note; Dalman, *Worte Jesu*, p. 123.

[3] The Psalms of Solomon, as we have seen (p. 43, note 6), are indefinite as to the duration of the Messiah's earthly reign; but in the Apocalyptic and Apocryphal literature the thought of a Reign of limited duration on earth is widely held; *e.g.* Ethiopian Enoch xci.-civ. (Charles, *Esch.* pp. 201-204); *Sib. Orac.* iii. 1-62 (*ibid.* 226); *Jubiles* and *Assumpt. Mos.* (*ibid.* 248, 250); Slavon. Enoch (*ibid.* 261); *Apoc. Baruch* (*ibid.* 270-275); 4 Ezra (*ibid.* 286). This idea, possibly the outcome of the disillusionment of the Maccabean period (Charles, p. 172), is the historical root of the belief in a Millennium (on which see below, Lect. IV.). The Messianic age is conceived of in most of the above-cited passages as giving place to the new world, and as closed by the universal judgment and the final destruction of evil.

the Advent of Messiah the immediate inauguration of the world to come. Now St. Paul appears to adopt both views,—the former with reference to our Lord's First Advent, the latter being applied to the Second.[1] Again, as we shall see, the same distinction may be traced in some words recorded of our Lord himself.

On the other hand the distinction between the Kingdom of GOD and of Christ is not complete. The one is the process, the other the complete result. Perfection is, throughout the Bible, the note of the Kingdom of GOD; the kingdom of Christ has perfection as its goal, but its mediatorial character, the gradual conquest of sin in the individual heart, the gradual conversion of men from the power of darkness to the kingdom of Christ,—the fact that the powers of evil are still at work, and that corruption still holds in bondage the whole realm of material life, marks the kingdom of Christ with imperfection. It *is* the Kingdom of GOD in its idea,—in potency and in promise; but visibly and openly not yet. This is St. Paul's well-known paradox of the Christian life. Our whole task as Christians is to become what we are. The Christian is, in one sense, now what he is truly to be hereafter,—the son or child of GOD. The assurance of access to GOD, the spirit of sonship, the filial spirit, the Holy Spirit, which is vouchsafed to him in this life, is

---

[1] This appears to be more correct than to say, with Professor Charles (*Esch.* p. 390), that in 1 Cor. xv. 27 sq., the Apostle conceived of Christ's Reign as temporary and ended by the Judgment, but afterwards abandoned this view. But St. Paul of course associates the Resurrection of the Just ἐν τῇ παρουσίᾳ αὐτοῦ (1 Cor. xv. 23) with the *Second* Advent and with the Redelivery. The language of the passage can hardly be harmonised with the doctrine of two resurrections (*supra*, p. 52, note 2).

an instalment—ἀρραβών—of the destiny promised to him hereafter. That which is to come at the end *ipso facto* exists now, but in *growth* and therefore in imperfection; "it doeth not yet appear"—it is held down in bondage,[1] its glory is veiled. And what is true of the individual is true of the kingdom into which he is called. The kingdom of Christ is the Kingdom of GOD in reality, but in the making. It is an instalment of the perfect which is to come; imperfect as an instalment is, but a sure pledge of the perfect kingdom for which we look.

St. Paul nowhere expressly states the relation between the Kingdom of GOD and the visible society of Christians—the Church of GOD. But from the above points of his teaching it is possible to bring his doctrine on the two subjects into relation. Obviously the relation is close.

If what has just been said of the individual Christian life represents the mind of St. Paul, then the Christian brotherhood is necessarily, in respect of its true members, the sphere of Christ's reign—the kingdom of Christ on earth. That kingdom finds its visible

[1] "The bondage of corruption." Φθόρα is in St. Paul a purely physical, not an ethical, conception (see Lightfoot on Gal. vi. 8); his use of it may be indirectly derived from its use by Aristotle as the correlative of γένεσισ, both alike characterising the phenomenal in contrast to the πρῶτον κινοῦν (*Phys.* v. 1, viii. 6, etc.). But St. Paul regards physical φθόρα as the "vanity" to which the creature is subjected in consequence of sin (Rom. viii. 20, cf. v. 12 sqq.). The dependence of physical death (even before man's appearance on earth) upon sin, and the liberation of the κτίσισ from its vanity as a result of the final redemption of man from sin, are conceptions which modern physical knowledge renders doubly difficult, but they are unquestionably factors in St. Paul's view of existence. The difficulty is however part of the wider problem of the relation of matter to spirit, and, I would add, of time to reality. (Cf. Illingworth, *Divine Immanence*, p. 116.)

expression in a society of men united by the bond of personal faith, and living a heavenly life.[1] And this the Church is in its essential idea. The "Body of Christ"—and the "Kingdom of Christ" are expressions which suggest somewhat different ideas, but whether they cover precisely the same field or not, their centre is at least one and the same. And if there is close correlation between the two conceptions, —if without going outside St. Paul's world of thought we may say—not perhaps "the kingdom of Christ is the Church",·but certainly—"the Church is the kingdom of Christ," then according to St. Paul the Church is the pledge and latent germ of the Kingdom of GOD in the full and final sense. But St. Paul never expressly equates the two ideas, and for this—closely related as they obviously are, there must be a good reason. The phrase ἐκκλησία τοῦ Χριστοῦ (or Θεοῦ) does not, as directly as ἡ βασιλεία τοῦ Χριστοῦ (or Θεοῦ), suggest, what to St. Paul is of vital moment, the *effective reign* of Christ. The Church is *becoming* the kingdom of Christ,[2]—and the Church in her glory to come, the ἔνδοξοσ ἐκκλησία,[3] would seem to rise to the full height of the Perfection of GOD'S kingdom. But the Kingdom of GOD appears to range, in its ultimate completeness, as wide as all creation; and although the Church plays a mysterious though indispensable part in the consummation of this final reality,[4] it would be going beyond St. Paul's language, and his apparent thought, to speak of the Church even in her glory in the world to come,

---

[1] Phil. iii. 20; Eph. ii. 6, cf. i. 20.
[2] ὑποτάσσεται, Eph. v. 24, cf. 1 Cor. xv. 27, 28.
[3] Eph. v. 27.   [4] *Supra*, p. 55, note, and next note.

SAINT PAUL 57

as fully coextensive [1] and convertible with the Kingdom of GOD.

The kingdom of Christ, then, is partially distinguishable in St. Paul from the Kingdom of GOD, as the means from the end, or the imperfect and growing from the mature and perfect realisation of the Divine Will. The completion of the one is the beginning of the other, Christ sits at GOD'S right hand until [2] he has made his Enemies his footstool.

Christ is reigning now, and the Church on earth represents his visible reign over sinful men. To claim perfection for the Church as she is on earth, or on the other hand to attempt to realise ideal perfection by the ruthless and premature extirpation of every person and thing that offends, are two opposite, and, as experience has shown, fatally easy directions in which we may drift away from St. Paul's conception of the kingdom of Christ.

Christ is reigning now, and as each conquest over sin and evil brings his Enemies under his footstool, his reign

---

[1] Indirectly we approach most nearly to this identification in Eph. i. 22. In ver. 10 the Apostle has spoken of the destined *summing up of all things in* Christ; here he speaks of Christ as *filling* ("with himself," *mid.*) all things (*i.e.* heavenly, earthly, and καταχθόνια). The Church is the πλήρωμα—almost "the instrument"—of this purpose. Christ's purpose is to "fill all things" with himself; he must first, as a step toward this end, fill the Church. The Church is therefore (ideally, for the μέτρον τῆσ ἡλικίασ τοῦ πλ., Eph. iv. 7, is not realised as yet) the πλήρωμα—vessel or vehicle, Col. ii. 10—of Christ, and as such carries out his work for man (and so for all creation, Rom. viii.). All creation is in its origin and destiny (Eph. i. 10) GOD'S kingdom. Meanwhile the Church is the visible embodiment (σῶμα, ver. 23) of Christ, and in proportion as she is "filled" with him she is bringing about the supreme end. Of that end, the ultimate Kingdom of GOD, the ἔνδοξοσ ἐκκλησία will be a part only, but the central part. (See Lightfoot, *Coloss.* p. 261).

[2] On the "Enemies" see above, p. 53, note 1; and below, pp. 109, 110.

on earth advances, and the Church grows nearer to the stature of the Kingdom of GOD.

Lastly, we must, before leaving St. Paul, ask a question which will recur [1] when we consider the teaching of our Lord, a question of no small importance for our general conclusion. Does St. Paul, in speaking of the Θεοῦ βασιλεία, mean by that phrase the kingdom in the sense of the *realm* over which GOD rules, or in the sense of the *reign* exercised by him? Is the Kingdom of Christ and of GOD thought of by him primarily as a Society, or as a state of things? Our account of St. Paul's conception of the kingdom has been gathered from his Epistles without any conscious reference to this question; but in the result, the Reign of Christ now, and the perfect Reign of GOD all in all hereafter, have asserted themselves irresistibly in the most prominent place. This result is confirmed if we remind ourselves of the sense in which the words were used in the pre-Christian Jewish schools in which St. Paul had been trained, and whose language would in this as in so many other respects in the first instance colour his own. On the whole the evidence seems to support the conclusion that there too the thought of the *reign* of GOD is primary. This does not *exclude* the thought of the realm; for we can as little have a reign with no kingdom to govern as a kingdom without one who reigns. But "an Oriental 'kingdom' is now as of old not a body politic in our sense, but the rule of a person embracing a particular region" [2]—the thought of the king is uppermost, that of the subjects secondary. The Old Testament passages reviewed in the first Lecture anticipate the N.T. thought

[1] See below, p. 98 sq., and Lect. V.   [2] See Dalman, *Worte Jesu*, p. 77.

of the Kingdom of GOD in so far as they speak of *Jehovah as King*. This is least evident in Daniel, but even there the "kingdom" is the everlasting reign of the Most High, which he gives to his saints to share as their possession. The society or body politic in Daniel and in the Psalms of Solomon consists of Israel purified and transformed—in a word of the saints. The kingdom is the effective reign of GOD through his Messiah, a blessed and perfect condition which gives happiness to all who are privileged to come under it. This is of a piece with the language of the Jewish schools, in which, as a recent careful enquirer assures us, "kingdom of GOD" means always "divine rule" and never "divinely governed state."[1] This does not take away from the realm of the Messiah's government the title Kingdom of GOD;—but it does define more accurately its right to that title. It is the Kingdom of GOD because in it the Reign of GOD is effective and real, and in proportion as this is less or more truly the case.

In St. Paul, we have already travelled very far from the idea of the Kingdom of GOD which, in the generation before Christ, was expressed in the Psalms of Solomon. All idea, as we have seen, of a visible earthly reign of the Messiah, all thought of a visible Hebraic kingdom or of Jerusalem as its centre, every shred of nationalism, has disappeared. On the other hand the eschatological side of Jewish hope has been deepened, spiritualised and strengthened. The Christian ἐκκλησία, in which there is "no room" for Jew, Greek, Barbarian or Scythian, supersedes the brotherhood of "Israel after

[1] See Dalman, *Worte Jesu*, p. 79.

the flesh," the Divine Christ the human King-Messiah, the glories of the earthly Christ-kingdom give place to the redemption of the body and the unveiling of the sons of GOD; the resurrection of the departed saints to share the delights of the Messiah's reign melts into the thought that flesh and blood cannot inherit the Kingdom of GOD, neither does corruption inherit incorruption. And this great transformation of Jewish thought has not failed to transform the whole present aspect of the world and of life. That GOD may be served on earth "without fear, in holiness and righteousness," it is no longer necessary that a particular nation should be delivered from its overhanging doom. The old Israel, to St. Paul, no longer exists; a new Israel, the true descent of Abraham, has taken its place.[1] And as the old Israel in reality consisted of the faithful remnant only, and that Remnant, though hard to recognise, was the present embodiment of the Kingdom that was to be,— so now the Church of Christ. Wherever Christ has disciples, wherever he reigns and lives in man, there is the Kingdom of GOD on earth, growing, being built up, ever tending to what it shall be. The work of the Christian Society as a whole,—and not only that but every good or even lawful and necessary object pursued or act done by the Christian—whether he eats or drinks, or whatever he puts on,—is an activity of the Kingdom of GOD.

No transition could be more abrupt than that from the Psalms of Solomon to St. Paul. But the transition was not wholly, nor in reality chiefly, his work. He

---

[1] Gal. vi. 16. The contrast between the two,—between the true and the "empirical" Israel, underlies the argument of Rom. ix., xi.

teaches and writes as the interpreter—as he himself says the "slave"—of Jesus Christ.

And we now have to see that as a preacher of the Kingdom of GOD he interprets truly—that the transition from the Psalms of Solomon to St. Paul is explained by the difference [1] between the hope which Christ found in being and that hope as he retaught it, purified and transformed, to his disciples.

III

The tradition of Christ's teaching was the possession of the Jewish Christians. It was committed to writing in two widely differing forms, first, about the time of the destruction of Jerusalem, in the triple record of the synoptic Gospels; secondly, about the time of Domitian, with marks of long and deep reflexion, in the Gospel of St. John. It will be necessary for the present to reserve what is to be said of the latter. We deal first with the synoptic tradition,[2] and for our purpose it will be unnecessary to deal, except incidentally, with the mutual relations of the first three Gospels.

When Jesus begins his ministry by the simple announcement, accompanied by no definition, that the

---

[1] Cf. Titius, *NTliche Lehre v. der Seligkeit* (1895), part I, p. 177 sq.

[2] The problem of the *ipsissima verba* of our Lord is placed on a fruitful basis of enquiry by Dalman, *Die Worte Jesu*, Leipz. 1898. Allowing that the first *written* form of the synoptic record may have been Greek, he starts from the fact that our Lord's converse with his disciples must have been in the vernacular Aramaic of Galilee, a fact that lies behind the tradition preserved by Eusebius as to the original language in which the "Oracles" of Christ were written down (pp. 46-48). The recovery of the *ipsissima verba* therefore depends upon successful retranslation from Greek into Aramaic. The dialectic difference between Galilean and Judean does not, Dalman concludes, seriously affect the security of the result (p. 65).

appointed time was fulfilled, and that the Kingdom of GOD was at hand,[1] we are bound to infer that he uses the words, to begin with, in the sense in which his hearers understood them.[2] What that sense was, we have learned in part from Daniel and from the Psalms of Solomon. That the Jewish people would receive as good news the announcement that their passionate hopes were so near to realisation was only natural. His teaching is the gospel,—"the good news,"—of the Kingdom,[3] and there is no solid reason for ascribing this title to the evangelists rather than to Christ himself.[4] The phrases to believe the gospel[5] and to receive the Kingdom of GOD are in meaning convertible.

St. Matthew, it is to be observed, alone among the evangelists prefers the expression "kingdom of heaven" to "kingdom of God." The former phrase has had meanings read into it both by Jewish and Christian students which are somewhat remote from the mental conditions of the time.[6] The analogy of then current Jewish language makes it almost certain

[1] Mark i. 4; Matt. iv. 23.

[2] Direct reference to existing anticipations is implied in the constant use of the formula as the short summary of our Lord's message; see Luke iv. iv. 43, viii. 1, ix. 2, 11, 60; Matt. ix. 35, xiii. 19; see also Matt. x. 7 (Luke x. 9).

[3] Matt. xxiv. 14, etc.

[4] Dalman (p. 84) doubts whether our Lord spoke of his message as "good news"; he ascribes εὐαγγελίζεσθαι to the disciples. He points out (1) that where the latter word is connected with the Kingdom of GOD (Luke iv. 43, xvi. 16; Matt. xxiv. 14; Mark i. 15) it is absent from the parallel passages; (2) that the probable Aramaic original *bassar* does not necessarily imply "good" news; (3) that the direct result of the announcement was to be *repentance*. I do not regard these arguments as convincing; (3) especially, is but half the truth. As we have seen, the kingdom expected in the Psalms of Solomon had at once rewards for the righteous, and terrors for the ungodly.

[5] Mark i. 15, x. 15. [6] Dalman, p. 76 and note.

that "heaven" in the phrase "kingdom of heaven" represents the common euphemism for GOD which meets us also in the Parable of the Prodigal in St. Luke.[1] The Mishna speaks[2] of the "fear of heaven," "the name of heaven," "by the hand of heaven," "the mercy of heaven," "the word of heaven," "heaven does miracles,"—heaven in each case meaning "GOD" simply. If St. Matthew's Gospel stands closer than the other two to the original Aramaic of our Lord's actual words, we may perhaps infer that he commonly used the phrase "kingdom of heaven," and that in the other Gospels the equivalent, which Greek readers would more readily understand, is uniformly and correctly given. We shall do well, then, to adhere to the phrase "Kingdom of God"; and when using the alternative in quotations from St. Matthew, let us remember that the difference is one of expression and not of meaning.

The Kingdom of GOD was a Jewish hope, and the Jews whom the hope had so long inspired, and who possessed it alone among men, were its obvious heirs. They are (in the expressive idiom preserved by St. Matthew alone) the "sons of the kingdom."[3] But the true "sons of the kingdom"[4] are marked out differently, not by blood but by disposition. Accordingly the Kingdom of GOD is to be taken away[5] from the Jews and given to others. What is to be

---

[1] This is probably so, but see Dalman, pp. 174, 178.
[2] Dalman, p. 179.
[3] Matt. viii. 12, cf. "a son of peace," Luke x. 6; also Matt. ix. 15.
[4] Matt. xviii. 38 (contrast Luke xvi. 8). The Talmud speaks of "sons of the world to come" (passages in Dalman, p. 94).
[5] ἀρθήσεται, Matt. xxi. 43.

taken away, is clearly the privilege of sharing the blessings of the Messianic reign. The Kingdom, as we shall see, is an inheritance, to be given by GOD, sought for by man; and what is given can be taken away.

The true "sons" of the kingdom, then, are determined by moral conditions, not by the mere accident of Jewish birth. This is already taught in Daniel and in the Psalms of Solomon, though it is contrary to general Jewish belief as exemplified in some quotations from the Rabbis, and in the appeal to descent from Abraham referred to in the Gospels.[1] But this is not all.

Firstly, the days of the chosen people are over. "The law and the prophets were until John," but from the days of John the Baptist "the kingdom of heaven suffereth violence, and the violent take it by force,"[2] while John himself is less than the least in the kingdom of heaven.[3] Combining St. Matthew's and St. Luke's version of the former saying, we see that "suffereth violence" in St. Matthew answers to "is preached" in St. Luke. The idea suggested then by βιάζεται[4] must be that of the crowd rushing in over the prostrate fences which had hitherto shut them out. The βιασταί are those who, disqualified from entrance down to the time of the Baptist, now press in from all sides. This includes a secondary thought, namely that many are pressing in who will prove unfit for it. That such

---

[1] Luke iii. 8, etc.; cf. Mark xii. 34 for the corrective principle.
[2] Matt. xi. 12; Luke xvi. 16.   [3] Matt. xi. 11 (Luke vii. 28).
[4] Dalman, pp. 113-116, prefers to refer the original meaning to *persecutions*, as in the case of John himself. But this would mean that Luke wholly misunderstood the passage, which moreover becomes reduced to an anticlimax. Neither does βιάζεται refer to the effort necessary to enter,—a thought expressed elsewhere, *infra*, pp. 66, 68, but foreign to the context here.

SYNOPTIC TRADITION

should press in is the penalty of all movements that become important or popular.

In a word, the Kingdom of GOD is here already. It was imminent when the Baptist announced its approach, and now the new reign of the Christ has begun. In this sense, our Lord's mere coming as man has brought with it the true fulfilment of the hope of Israel: the house of Israel has received in him its promised King, who is to reign over them for ever and ever, and of his Kingdom there shall be no end.[1] But this is true only to the faithful Israelite, not to the average Jew. The latter is expecting the Kingdom of GOD immediately to appear, but his observation is misdirected.[2] For the Kingdom is not to appear suddenly and palpably; it is growing secretly, but is not here in its completeness. Rather it is barely beginning; so secret are its workings that many even sincere and devout watchers for it do not see it as yet. Joseph of Arimathea, though St. Matthew speaks of him as "Jesus' disciple," is according to the two other Gospels still at the time of the Crucifixion on the outer fringe, simply waiting for the Kingdom of GOD.[3] To "receive" the kingdom, special preparation is necessary, the child's heart must be regained.[4]

For although in one sense the violent are taking the Kingdom by force, and whosoever will is pressing in, in another sense it is the exception to gain admission.

---

[1] Luke i. 33, cf. x. 9, 11; Matt. x. 7.
[2] Luke xvii. 20, xix. 11 sqq.   [3] Mark xiv. 43 (Luke xxiii. 51).
[4] Mark x. 15 (Luke xviii. 17; Matt. xviii. 3, 4). "Entrance into the future kingdom of God is dependent on a man's right attitude to the present kingdom of God" (Charles, *Esch.* p. 321. On "entering" see also Dalman, p. 95; on "receiving," p. 91).

The first are last and the last first. The recognised religious leaders not only fail to enter themselves,[1] but their influence keeps back those who would otherwise go in. Those who are most intractable to that influence are in many cases the nearest to the Kingdom. Our Lord watches as it were the entrance to the Kingdom and those who pass in, and he warns the religious world that those outside it are preceding them—προάγονται. " The publicans and harlots are preceding you into the kingdom of heaven."

So far we have hardly come in sight of the twofold aspect of the Kingdom of God which we noted in St. Paul—the present and the purely eschatological.[2] But the affirmation of a kingdom already come, membership of which depends simply upon character, and the range of which does not appear to the eye of flesh, gives the first[3] hint of the distinction between the two—between the First Advent and the Second.

But meanwhile the two classes, those who enter and those who miss the way, are watched by Jesus as they range themselves on either side—together in the field, the bed, the mill, but wide asunder in view of the kingdom of heaven, and it is character that separates them, not anything else—sin that closes the door and forgiveness that unlocks[4] it again. The Scribes and Pharisees may shut the door against men; but what they bind upon earth is not for that reason bound in heaven.

[1] Matt. xxiii. 13, cf. vii. 21.
[2] But see above, p. 65, note 4; also below, p. 69 sq.
[3] This I think is at least as true as the suggestion of Charles, *Esch.* p. 320.
[4] Matt. xvi. 19, contrast xxiii. 15 (see Lect. VIII. p. 371, note).

Light is thrown upon the *kind of* character which our Lord demands by the passages in which he speaks of entering into the Kingdom of GOD. After the departure of the rich young man, he had shocked his disciples by remarking "how hardly shall they that have riches enter into the kingdom of GOD." He meets their astonishment (according to the best attested and very convincing text in St. Mark)[1] by the simple reminder, "Children, how hard is it to enter the kingdom of GOD." The thought clearly is that it is hard in any case to be born again—hard to escape or to get rid of that sophistication of character which is in the New Testament[2] the peculiar note of "the world," hard to clear the ground of the heart from the thorns which are always growing up when we are most truly face to face with the realities of life, very hard to preserve or recover the child's heart,—and that wealth, or its pursuit, makes what is hard in itself doubly difficult. But hard in itself, even without wealth, it remains; and the central and radical condition of the task is to become as little children:—"*of such* is the kingdom of GOD"[3]—that is the standard type of character;—not childish in mind but childlike in heart, the type of Mary Magdalene, who with all her grievous sin "loved much," of the twelve, who left "their own" to follow Jesus;[4]—not negative freedom from sins that "needs no repentance," but that truth of instinct which distinguishes real morality from mere propriety, loyalty from "respectability," love from worldly, or even other-

---

[1] Mark x. 24 (ℵ B) ‖ Luke xviii. 24.
[2] Not in the Synoptics, but in SS. John and James, and partly in St. Paul.
[3] Matt. xviii. 3 (Mark x. 14).   [4] Luke vii. 47, xviii. 28 τὰ ἴδια.

worldly, self-regard. It is the secret reserve which we make for our personal aims—the calculating instinct, cynical at its core, and incapable of whole-hearted devotion—that makes a man unfit, not εὔθετοσ, for the Kingdom of GOD.¹ Our Lord demands of us the lovable character rather than the admirable. "The violent take it by force"—there are many who call Christ Lord, many who are now in his kingdom in its present imperfection, who will prove not to be of it. The warning is of terrible import to all who are "called." But as to the qualification, he has left us in no doubt.

It is now time to ask more particularly as to the nature of the kingdom which is guarded by these conditions. To enter into the Kingdom of GOD is, in many passages of the synoptic record, placed in equivalence with entering into Life. To enter into the Kingdom of GOD we must become as little children, and to this end we must often surrender what has become as necessary to us as hand or eye ²—for it is better to enter *into Life*, even maimed and halt. "How hard is it to enter into the kingdom of GOD"—strait is the way that leadeth unto Life.³ To enter into Life, again, is to be an heir of Eternal Life," ⁴ to have treasure in the heavens,—in one word, to be "saved." ⁵ Now the conception of Life doubtless covers, in the N.T. generally, the spiritual life of the present time; but in the synoptic Gospels at any rate the principal reference is to Life in the World to come,⁶ brought to the true

---

[1] Luke ix. 62.   [2] Matt. xviii. 3, 8 (Mark ix. 47).
[3] Matt. vii. 14, cf. Mark x. 24.
[4] Compare Matt. xix. 6, 7, 21 (Mark x. 17, 21; Luke xviii. 18, 22).
[5] See the disciples' question, Matt. xix. 25.
  Always either ζωὴ αἰώνιοσ or ἡ ζωή. See Dalman, pp. 137-142.

Sons of the Kingdom of GOD by its complete realisation. But to pray for the realisation of that kingdom is not merely to ask a personal reward; to make the Kingdom of GOD and his Righteousness the goal of their lives was not, for Christ's disciples, to live simply for their own interest, however spiritual, however remote, at however great present cost.[1] Rather it is the Father's settled will that these things should be the Reward of those who do and suffer all things simply for *the name*[2] of Christ. The Kingdom of GOD as the supreme goal of Christian endeavour is the absolute reign of GOD,— the selfless pursuit of the will of GOD as revealed for man's well-being and salvation. Its worth to the individual is founded upon absolute trust in GOD as Father. If that trust is ours, we find in his Kingdom the only secure object of desire,—find what is worth all the world beside, the pearl[3] of great price for which alone we can give our very life and soul. "For whosoever will save his life shall lose it; for what shall it profit a man if he gain the whole world and lose his own life; for what must a man give as ransom for his life."[4]

And now to consider more closely the eschatology of the Kingdom of GOD in our Saviour's teaching. "The violent take it by force"—many are now in Christ's kingdom who will not be in the kingdom of the Father. This is plainly laid down by him in the passage where

---

[1] Matt. vii. 33 (Luke xii. 31, 32); and see Lect. VIII. p. 381 sqq.
[2] "For my name's sake," Matt. xix. 29, explaining "for the kingdom of God's sake" the parallel in Luke xviii. 29. Mark x. 29 appears to combine the sense of the two other parallels.
[3] Matt. xiii. 44 sqq., cf. xix. 2.
[4] Mark viii. 35, 37 (Matt. xvi. 26; Luke xvii. 33, xiv. 26).

the two are most clearly distinguished.[1] "The Son of Man shall send forth his angels, and they shall gather out of *his kingdom* all things that offend, and them which do iniquity, and shall cast them into a furnace of fire, there shall be wailing and gnashing of teeth. Then shall the righteous shine forth as the sun in the kingdom of their Father." The kingdom of the Son of Man here most directly represents the Kingdom of GOD, as the kingdom towards which all Jewish hope has been directed, "the kingdom that cometh, the kingdom of our Father David."[2] Its moral characteristics are exhibited, though not perfectly nor without admixture, in the Society which Christ gathers round him, a new ἐκκλησία continuous with, but superseding, the ἐκκλησία of GOD that has subsisted up till now, a congregation which he has built up upon the eternal rock, and which will never disappear from earth.[3] But its true character will never wholly appear, its glory, its identification with its heavenly counterpart the Kingdom of GOD is reserved for the Day when the Son of Man will come again "in his kingdom."[4] The kingdom of Christ, now a reality but hidden, will then be manifest to friend and foe alike, and will reach its complete and final consummation. It was possibly of the triumphant return[5] of their Master as Messiah that the disciples were thinking when they asked[6] "who should be greatest in the kingdom of heaven," certainly

---

[1] Matt. xiii. 41.   [2] Mark xi. 10 (ℵ B).   [3] Matt. xvi. 18.
[4] Luke xxii. 30 (ℵ B; D reads "in the day of thy coming," an early and correct gloss). See Matt. xvi. 28.
[5] Compare Matt. xx. 21, βασιλείᾳ, with Mark x. 37, δόξᾳ.
[6] Matt. xviii. 1, cf. xix. 28; the final award, however, is οὐκ ἐμὸν δοῦναι, Matt. xx. 23 (Mark x. 40).

it is the direct object of the faith of the dying malefactor, "Jesus, remember me when thou comest *in thy kingdom.*"¹

In our Lord's teaching we distinguish three respects in which his coming will affect his kingdom. Firstly, it will complete it: he will sit enthroned as "the King" in the universal judgment of mankind.² Secondly, it will purify his kingdom by judgment. He will send his angels to gather out of it all things and all persons that offend,—the foolish virgins will find too late that they are unready for the Bridegroom's coming. Thirdly, it will inaugurate the kingdom of the Father,³ the Kingdom of GOD in its complete and final realisation, the Kingdom of GOD as it comes with Power,⁴ the Kingdom of GOD in the absolute sense,⁵ the Kingdom of GOD whose approach, bringing with it the complete redemption of the elect, is announced by the signs which usher in the consummation of the ages.⁶ This kingdom is free from all impurities; in it the saints⁷ will find their lasting reward and reign with Christ.

---

¹ See above, p. 70, note 4.
² Matt. xxv. 34; Charles, *Esch.* p. 337 sqq.
³ Matt. xxvi. 29, xiii. 43.
⁴ This expression occurs Mark ix. 1, in a context to be compared carefully with Luke ix. 27; Matt. x. 23, xxiv. 34, xxiv. 30, μετὰ δόξ. κ. δυν. ‖ Mark xiii. 26; Luke xxi. 27. To refer the "kingdom of God coming with power" to the first Pentecost, or to anything short of the Return of Christ, appears like flinching from the plain and inexorable reference of this group of passages. That the disciples believed the Lord to have foretold his return within the lifetime of some then living is a conclusion hard to gainsay. But with reference to our Lord himself, all such passages must be read in connexion with Matt. xxiv. 36; Mark xiii. 32, where οὐδὲ ὁ υἱόσ is too unlikely an addition not to be original. See also Charles, *Eschatology*, pp. 330-332, 339.
⁵ Luke xxii. 18.   ⁶ Luke xxi. 31, cf. 27, 28, ix. 27.
⁷ Matt. xiii. 43, contrasting 41.

To them it will be an inheritance[1] prepared from the foundation of the world,—but not only for those who have appeared to belong to it on earth—many from strange and remote countries will come in to share it while "sons of the kingdom" are cast out.[2]

The kingship of Christ, then, is manifest to all only when he comes in his kingdom, when the Kingdom of GOD comes with power.[3] In other words we have here the manifest origin of the thought that we met with in St. Paul. By completing his kingdom Christ in a sense supersedes it, by visibly beginning his reign he ends it. But yet it is not ended so much as merged. For in one well-marked group of passages he still speaks of the Father's kingdom as his own. "And I appoint unto you a kingdom as my Father hath appointed unto me, that ye may eat and drink at my table in my kingdom, and sit on thrones judging the twelve tribes of Israel."[4] This passage, if compared with the words used[5] by Christ of the eucharistic cup at the Last Supper—which as reproduced by St.

---

[1] Matt. xxv. 34, cf. Luke xii. 32.

[2] Matt. viii. 11 (Luke xiii. 28, 29). Compare St. Augustine, *Ep.* 102, and other passages referred to below, Lect. V. p. 199.

[3] Matt. xvi. 28; Luke xxiii. 42.

[4] Luke xxii. 30. The passages which speak of eating and drinking in the future Kingdom of GOD (Matt. viii. 11; Luke xiii. 28, 29), and those referred to in the text, certainly are in direct relation to then current ideas; see Luke xiv. 15. With them we may class the passage Matt. xix. 28, 29 ‖ Luke xx. 30 as above (but contrast Mark x. 30), and possibly Matt. v. 5. The passages, taken literally, are less in keeping with the drift of Christ's teaching than with Jewish and early Christian realistic eschatology (see below, Lect. IV.). But "it is impossible," as Stanton says with justice, "to speak of a state so removed from our present earthly conditions except by the aid of symbolism." See Charles, *Eschatology*, p. 339 fol.; Schürer, *Gesch.*³ ii. 290-292; and Dalman, p. 90.

[5] Matt. xxvi. 29; Mark xiv. 25; Luke xxii 16, 18.

Matthew expressly refer to the kingdom of the Father—certainly seems to bear the interpretation I suggest. But in view of our Lord's reply to the mother of Zebedee's sons it is just possible[1] that the reference here may be to the judgment and its attending circumstances rather than to the eternity that follows it.

We cannot then, either now or in eternity, deduce from our Lord's words a real separation between his kingdom and the Kingdom of his Father. But a distinction—as real and as evanescent as the distinction of eternity and time—is manifestly present to our Saviour's mind. The kingdom of Christ is the kingdom of the Messiah, and is in its essential character mediatorial. It *is* the Kingdom of GOD, for the Kingdom of GOD is proved by Christ's divine power to have arrived;[2] but it is the Kingdom of GOD in conditions adapted to time and space, and to the actual state of mankind; and that in three respects.

(1) In accordance with the whole tenor of prophecy, and with the expectation which prophecy had nursed and formed in the minds of the people, the Kingdom of Christ is the Kingdom of GOD delegated to Jesus as the Christ, the Messiah or anointed representative of GOD's reign over his people.[3]

(2) The kingdom of Christ is the Kingdom of GOD in its making—in its imperfection—in its invisible growth.

(3) The kingdom of Christ is thrown like a net to include as many as can be brought inside it, fit or

---

[1] See above, p. 70, note 6.   [2] Matt. xii. 28; Luke xi. 20.
[3] "He is the Mediator of GOD's continuous and present judgment of the conduct of men." Charles, *Eschatology*, p. 336.

unfit [1]—*until* the coming of the Kingdom of GOD with power. Then at last the Baptist's conception of the first coming of the Christ—in which he is the spokesman of the same thought as we traced in the Psalms of Solomon—will be verified : " his fan is in his hand, and he will throughly purge his floor "—he will have reigned, as St. Paul formulates what Christ had in substance taught—" until his enemies are made his footstool." In a sense then the kingdom of Christ, so far as it is visible on earth, is wider in its range than the Kingdom of GOD. *Out of it* they will gather at his coming all *things* that offend, and them—those *persons* —that work iniquity. For the present the kingdom of Christ comprises in it persons and things also—ideas and institutions—which will ultimately prove not to belong to it, though they may in many cases have served its purpose in their time.

To gather up what has been said so far, our Lord is more explicit as to the spiritual meaning of his coming for ourselves than he is as to its material conditions [2] or surroundings. That GOD will reign in a sense in which he does not now appear to reign, that the disorders which now perplex us will be overcome and righteousness come by its own, is involved in the whole idea of GOD which permeates the Bible and in particular permeates the teaching of Christ.

---

[1] See above, p. 64, note 4.

[2] Taking the record of our Lord's words as it stands, we are left in some doubt as to (*a*) whether the Return is to be absolutely sudden, or preceded by definite and recognisable signs, and (*b*) whether in "this generation," or at the end of a long and slow historical development. As to the latter point see above, p. 71, note 4; also consult the discussion in Charles, *Eschatology*, pp. 322-334.

Our Lord's eschatological teaching simply emphasises this great truth, adding to it the assurance that he will himself return to inaugurate GOD'S Kingdom. But in his descriptions of his personal reign as Messiah and of his return, all the earthly Judaic elements which even the Psalms of Solomon retain, are laid aside, although language is still used to which later on crude realism did not fail to appeal.[1]

The Kingdom of GOD, as our Lord preaches it, is at once present and future,[2] to be received now[3] to be entered into hereafter,[4] at once actual and ideal. In this respect it corresponds to the idea of Salvation, the *summum bonum* of the individual, as the whole to the part. It is to be found now, to be fully realised hereafter,—like the goodly pearl, or the treasure hid in the field,[5]—to be acquired, when found, only at great cost: "Children, how hard is it to enter into the kingdom of GOD."[6]

Our Lord nowhere simply identifies his kingdom, or the Kingdom of GOD, with the Church which he came to found. As we have seen, his kingdom is visibly represented in his Church; but there are insuperable obstacles to treating the two things as convertible. Our Lord founded a society which was to be visible like a city seated on a hill that cannot be hid;[7] but the Kingdom of GOD is visible only to faith—the Kingdom of GOD is within you[8]—the Church is

---

[1] See above, p. 72, note 4.   [2] Matt. v. 20, vii. 14, xxiii. 3.
[3] Mark x. 15; Matt. v. 3, 10.
[4] But, in a real sense, also in the present, Matt. xxi. 31, xi. 11 (Luke vii. 28).
[5] Matt. xiii. 44.   [6] Mark x. 24.   [7] Matt. v. 14.
[8] Luke xvii. 21 ἐντόσ has been variously translated "among" or "within." But the latter is the only rendering admissible on grounds of Biblical Greek; this alternative is confirmed by Dalman, p. 119.

present and actual, the Kingdom of GOD is present and yet future, actual and yet ideal. The Kingdom of GOD is the supreme end, the visible Church a means and instrument to that end. The Kingdom of GOD is in its essential idea the Reign of GOD: those over whom he reigns, and who answer to that reign by loyal allegiance, constitute a kingdom in the sense of a body of subjects, and this is the ideal toward which the Church must ever be advancing;—moreover in this kingdom there can be diversities of rank—some greater some less. But whereas the diversities of rank in the Church are diversities of administration—of function and office,[1] those in the Kingdom of God are degrees of spiritual character only—he that has become as the little child is greatest in the Kingdom of Heaven. The Kingdom of GOD is as it were the idea, the transcendent reality, of which the Church is the visible, but necessarily imperfect copy; the more the Church rises towards perfection, the more truly her every act has its eternal counterpart in the sphere of transcendent reality—the more surely what she binds and looses on earth is bound and loosed in heaven. So far as the mediatorial reign of Christ can be distinguished in his teaching from the absolute and final reign of GOD, so far as the Church does really and truly embody in her members the reign of Christ in his redeemed, so far we can go beyond the letter of our Lord's words, and in conformity to their spirit speak of the Church as the kingdom of Christ. So far as the authoritative acts of the Church or her ministers are true to the known

[1] See below, Lect. V. p. 178.

will of her Master,[1] we must recognise in them the mandate of Christ from his throne: He that heareth you heareth me, and he that despiseth you despiseth me. But the Reign of Christ is in itself invisible still, and its seat is in the heart and will. It is not exhaustively embodied in anything visible, even in his visible Society. What it really includes and excludes is kept to be revealed with the perfect Kingdom of the Father. That kingdom is with us in this life as an inspiration and an ideal, comprising all that is really akin to GOD'S Kingdom, all that embodies, in this world, any eternal principle. Understood thus—and no more limited range is worthy of it—the Kingdom of GOD is within us in so far as things eternal are with us now as things unseen.

[1] See below, Lect. V. p. 221, and Hinkmar's comment on the words of Leo the Great (Serm. 2. ii.): "'manet ergo Petri privilegium ubicunque fertur ex ipsius aequitate iudicium.' Qua sententia constat quia non manet Petri privilegium ubi ex eius aequitate non fertur iudicium."

LECTURE III

THE KINGDOM OF GOD IN THE NEW TESTAMENT (II.)

Gloria Dei uiuens homo, uita autem hominis Visio Dei.
IRENAEUS.

Salvation according to Scripture is nothing less than the preservation, restoration, or exaltation of life: while nothing that partakes or can partake of life is excluded from its scope; and as is the measure, grade, and perfection of life, such is the measure, grade, and perfection of salvation.
HORT.

LECTURE III

THE KINGDOM OF GOD IN THE NEW TESTAMENT (II.)

Things new and old.—ST. MATT. xiii. 52.

THE ideal character which belongs, in our Saviour's teaching, to the Kingdom of GOD,—present yet not of this world, coming down from the past, yet bringing novel resources to meet new needs; the natural sequel of all that in the order of GOD'S working has gone before it, yet destined inevitably to burst the old wine-bottles, to break up existing forms of thought and life, and to cast men's life in fresh and more plastic moulds, —involves the consequence that the most qualified and trained interpreters of the past have to go through a transformation before they can be fit—εὔθετοι—for the Kingdom. They have much to unlearn, but they must not be "offended"—shocked into looking back from the plough. Much to unlearn, but not all—they will rather learn over again what they thought they had known before. Such a man, the "discipled scribe" γραμματεὺσ μαθητευθείσ, will be like a householder, bringing out of his storehouse things new and old.[1] The ideal is a special application of the general and fundamental condition of re-birth—of receiving the

[1] Matt. xiii. 52, cf. Lev. xxvi. 10.

Kingdom of GOD as a little child. The Scribe when made a disciple may be abhorred by his fellow-scribes as a renegade, he may be accused as St. Paul was accused of teaching "apostasy from Moses"[1]—but such misjudgment will not disturb the serene loyalty of his discipled heart. The true convert differs from the renegade above all in this, that his change is not from love to hate, but from love to love: he has learned the higher without coming to despise the lower; the old, through which he has passed, is not disloyally cast aside, but is still his; the time has come, as it had come to Paul the servant of Jesus Christ, when he can "bring forth the old because of the new,"—he is the householder who dispenses from his store things new and old.

It was said by Newman[2] that "Christianity, though represented in prophecy as a kingdom, came into the world as an idea rather than as an institution." If we must choose between the two alternatives suggested, the statement has an element of paradox. It might be maintained, on the contrary, that our religion first entered into the experience of mankind less as a speculative suggestion, like the philosophy of Plato or the word of some profound religious thinker or inspiring poet, than as an organisation actually at work, in the hands of a definite body of men, among whom alone could the specific lesson of Christ be learned, or his specific benefit to man be experienced. To treat Christianity simply as an idea, and to explain its history by laws supposed to govern the development

---

[1] ὅτι ἀποστασίαν διδάσκεισ ἀπὸ Μωσέωσ, Acts xxi. 21.
[2] *Development of Christian Doctrine*, p. 77 (ed. 1878).

of thought, was the presupposition of the famous school of Tübingen two generations ago. Their work has not been unfruitful; neglected facts have been once for all set in clear light, and historical theology is the richer for many illuminating suggestions. But the one-sidedness, and in many respects the pedantry, of the resulting view of early Christian history has long since convinced students on all sides of the inadequate perception of the nature of a religion upon which the whole process of investigation rested.[1] If we are to choose between the two conceptions as alternatives, there would be weighty grounds for preferring the concrete view to the abstract, for reversing Newman's *dictum*, and for saying that Christianity, represented, not in prophecy only but by its Founder, as a kingdom, came into the world as an institution rather than as an idea.

But are the terms mutually exclusive? Institutions are the creation and vehicles of ideas, and have no vitality except as far as they embody ideas. If the

[1] Westcott justly remarks on the "persistent forgetfulness" of many writers of this school,· "that Christian literature is from the first one product of the Christian life"; neglecting "what I may venture to call the vital relations of literature . . . they treat books, for the most part, as if they belonged wholly to the region of speculation, and were not products and reflections of social activity" (*Canon*, ed. 4, p. xxxv sq.). The modern critical school have practically superseded this *Tendenz-kritik* by a more inductive method of *Quellen-kritik* which has in many important respects reversed the verdicts of Baur and his followers. Without claiming more authority for Harnack's famous utterance (*Chronologie d. Alt.-Christl. Literatur*, 1897, pp. 8, 10) than he would claim himself, it may fairly be regarded as a weighty sign of the times. But the sincerity and courage of the Tübingen school must be cordially recognised. Not only were the facts emphasised by them, however exceptional, important and unduly neglected: not only did they do justice to the ideal which underlies the concrete; but truth, and therefore piety, can permanently only be the gainer by the results of free investigation, with ample consideration of the strength and weakness of every rational hypothesis.

religious conception of the world is a valid one,—and no rival conception has yet succeeded in displacing it, —ideas are the ultimate realities, not only in human society but in the whole universe of matter animate and inanimate. Our limited minds can indeed with difficulty spell out the ideas which are embodied in the uniformities and correlations of Nature, but every fresh conquest of human knowledge confirms us in our belief that wherever in the universe we shall at any time succeed in penetrating, there we shall realise that Mind has been beforehand with us, and that blind unreason has nowhere a realm of its own. Revelation comes from GOD to man, not in abstract but in concrete form; but the institution, and the facts of our creed, embody ideas, embody a central idea. It is not given to us to co-ordinate these ideas in a perfect and flawless system, yet we are encouraged to exercise our mental faculties in the attempt to do so in some degree. The task of deciphering — the path of ἐπίγνωσισ—is marked out for us by our own constitution and by the promise of GOD'S Spirit, and it is not faith, but "little faith," to flinch from the work. Not an idea merely, nor an institution merely, but an institution embodying an idea, and to be administered by constant recurrence to its informing idea, is a truer formula, if those are the terms to which we are bound, for the characterisation of the Christian Religion.

But it may be questioned whether, when tried by the touchstone of the "Kingdom of GOD," the alternative we are considering touches the underlying reality at all. The Church is an institution more obviously than an idea; the Christian religion is an institution

SYNOPTIC TRADITION

the vehicle of an idea, or an idea expressing itself in an institution; the Kingdom of GOD may be called an idea whose reality is a hope assured in the future, and a fact which faith affirms to be a reality now, rather than an institution in the sense of something tangible, organised, and patent to the eyes of all. The Church, as an institution, embodies imperfectly the Kingdom of GOD as an idea. But as we weigh the two alternatives in the balance and seek a place for the Kingdom of GOD in either scale, we find the scales too small. Our categories fail us, we have missed the category which really and alone applies—the category of Life. That the kingdom of GOD is Life, we have already seen [1] and shall see. That life embodies an idea is axiomatic for the Christian—for any Theistic—view of the universe, it is the postulate of organic teleology, and for that very reason—that it is no blind product of mindless forces, but embodies the divine idea,—life is organised, systematised, proceeds upon definite laws of wonderful constancy coupled with as wonderful plasticity of adaptation. An institution, as we commonly use the term, borrows some of these characteristics from life, of which it is the feeble copy. And if the Kingdom of GOD was rightly placed by the founder of the Christian religion as the head and summary of that Religion which he brought into the world, we shall speak more worthily if we rise above the alternative of idea and institution, and say that the Christian religion came into the world as a LIFE.[2]

---

[1] See Lecture II. p. 68.
[2] That is not merely a course of life ($\beta\iota\omega\sigma\iota\sigma$, Acts xxvi. 4, or $\beta\iota o\sigma$, Luke viii. 14; 1 John ii. 16, iii. 17), but an animating principle, distinctive of life as against death ($\zeta\omega\acute{\eta}$ as in almost every book of the N.T., especially in St. John and the Ep. to the Romans).

The Kingdom of GOD is within you; so far as the Kingdom of GOD is a fact of present experience, it consists, so we gather from the tenor of the gospel record, in the reign of Christ within the heart and conscience of those who receive him—and where he reigns, there is Life. To enter into the kingdom, as our Lord saw the publicans and harlots enter it, *now*, is to enter into life now, and to enter the kingdom *at the last day* is to enter into life eternal.

By the words "kingdom of GOD," then, our Lord denotes not so much his disciples, whether individually or even as forming a collective body, as something which they receive, a state upon which they enter.[1] For its ultimate fulfilment the term indicates an *order of things* final and absolute, in which GOD is all in all.[2]—But the Kingdom of GOD is also spoken of in another[3] sense, descriptive of the *order of events*, the sum total of the methods and processes which, under the guidance and rule of GOD, go to bring about that final state of Perfection. Our Lord came not to destroy but to accomplish, and a man's rank in the Kingdom of GOD[4] will correspond to his truth to that vital principle. The Kingdom of GOD is advancing by means to which we are often blind; we may hinder it by ignorance or perverseness, by lack of sympathy with its subtle and secret principles, by ill-judged anxiety for its advancement in what may seem to us obvious and necessary ways, by

---

[1] See Luke xii. 32; Matt. xxi. 43, xxv. 34.

[2] We may, for the sake of contrast, distinguish this as the "statical" sense of the words; but we must not think of the Kingdom of GOD, even in this sense, as a motionless state of equilibrium, an idea for which Nature supplies no analogy.

[3] Or "dynamical."   [4] Matt. v. 18 sq.

impatience at what look to us like obstacles to its progress, though they may be in truth essential factors in the counsels of GOD for our good and the cause of his kingdom. For—

> GOD fulfils himself in many ways,
> Lest one good custom should corrupt the world.

The Kingdom of GOD in this sense is to be distinguished from God's general rule over all creation, which it presupposes; and also from his general moral government, of which it may be viewed as a central but special part. In the kingdom of GOD he is not merely controlling the issues of human conduct, which is supposed in the bare idea of moral government, but is bringing his rational creatures into conscious dependence on himself on the ground of the redemptive work of his Son. This GOD does, so we must believe, in many ways, some obvious and marked out, some hidden and apt to elude our appreciation. But Christ wills that his disciples should, for others' good and for their own, be on the alert for the inward principles which exhibit themselves in the boundless variety of particular cases. Such principles are secrets—μυστήρια [1]—of the Kingdom of GOD, and it is to give hints of some of them that many of the Parables are spoken—especially those introduced by express reference to the Kingdom of GOD. Sometimes the bearing of the parable is obvious. The dealings of GOD with Jew and Gentile in history is brought under a broad and deep principle in the Parable of the Labourers in the Vineyard,[2] and again in part in the Parable of the Marriage Feast in St. Matthew.[3] The Parable of the

[1] Matt. xii. 11.   [2] xx. 1 sqq.   [3] xxii. 1 sqq.

Mustard Seed, of the Leaven, and of the gradual growth of the corn,[1] illustrate equally the growth of the Christian Society and the growth in grace of the individual soul. Those of the Net and of the Tares,[2] and in part again St. Matthew's parable of the Marriage Feast, throw light upon the Reign of Christ in the Christian Church, that of the Unmerciful Debtor[3] brings out the relation of the Kingdom of GOD to the forgiveness of sins. That of the Wise and Foolish Virgins relates specially to the return of Christ "in his kingdom."[4]

It is not very easy in all cases to trace a generic difference between Parables which are introduced by the formula "the kingdom of GOD is likened"—or its equivalent—and those which are given without the formula. But it appears to be designedly omitted in many instances where types of character which have no place in the Kingdom are described. For example, in St. Luke's parables of the Unjust Judge, the Rich Fool, the Unjust Steward, and the Barren Fig-tree, and the Parable of the Wicked Husbandmen, which all three Gospels give without the characteristic formula. Again, some parables of contrast lack it; for example, St. Luke's parables of the Rich Man and Lazarus, of the Pharisee and the Publican, of the Two Debtors, and St. Matthew's of the two sons sent by their father to work in his vineyard. But it is difficult to assign a reason for its absence from St. Luke's parables of the Prodigal Son,

---

[1] Mark iv. 30; Matt. xiii. 33; Mark iv. 26. "The kingdom must spread extensively and intensively: extensively till its final expansion is out of all relation to its original smallness . . . intensively till it transforms and regenerates the life of the action and of the world" (Charles, *Eschatology*, p. 333).
[2] Matt. xiii. 47, 36.   [3] xviii. 23 sqq.   [4] xxv. 1 sqq.

the Lost Coin, of the good Samaritan, the Great Supper, and the Pounds, St. Matthew's parable of the Talents, and from that of the Lost Sheep, common to SS. Matthew and Luke. It should be noted that the Parable of the Sower, though not introduced by the formula, is expressly referred to the Kingdom of GOD in our Lord's comment as given by all three evangelists.[1] Further, we must observe that as a rule where more than one evangelist record the same parable, the formula is present in all or absent in all, even in variants like the Parables of the Pounds and of the Talents; the only exception I can recall is that of the Marriage Feast in St. Matthew, which has the formula, while the very similar Supper-Parable in St. Luke omits it. We cannot fail to notice, again, that the omission of the formula is specially frequent in St. Luke.

I cannot more fitly conclude a survey of the teaching of our Lord on this subject as recorded by the synoptic Gospels, than by a brief consideration of the Beatitudes. The relation of the individual to the Kingdom of GOD depends, nothing in our Lord's teaching is more clear than that, upon his character. This is the principle which the Beatitudes enforce, and in them one fundamental type of character is throughout in view. The poor, not merely that is to say those actually badly off, but those who as St. Matthew adds are poor τῷ πνεύματι,[2] the afflicted, the sufferers for righteousness' sake, the meek, those who are conscious of personal sin but long to be better—who hunger and thirst as St. Matthew again convincingly adds "after righteousness,"—those who face unpopularity in all its forms and

[1] Matt. xiii. 11; Mark iv. 11; Luke viii. 10.   [2] Luke vi. 20; Matt. v. 3.

with all its consequences for the Son of Man's sake—the merciful, the peace-makers, the pure in heart. All these are so many manifestations of the childlike temper [1] which turns to Christ with no secret reserve, no hankering back,[2] the loyal children of GOD—the type of the Hasidean loyalists of the Maccabean time raised to a higher spiritual plane—one to which all men, Jew or Gentile without distinction, are summoned to rise. And as the type of character—many and beautiful as are its forms—is at bottom one, so also the promised reward is one. Theirs is the Kingdom of GOD—theirs now, as a present possession. They shall inherit the land—though obscure and oppressed they really rule its destinies and are the promise of its future—they shall obtain mercy, be fed, be comforted, shall laugh, shall enjoy the great reward in the heavens; they shall earn the name of Sons of GOD—shall see GOD. The kingdom of GOD is to see GOD—both now and hereafter. Now, as sons by faith, then as sons in possession of their inheritance.

We have been thus brought by the synoptic record within the range of thought characteristic of the Fourth Gospel, to which we must now turn.

II

The Kingdom of GOD is not often referred to by name in the Gospel of St. John. For example in our Lord's words to Pilate, "my *kingdom* is not of this world,"[3] the reference is at most indirect. What is

---

[1] Matt. xix. 14 (Mark x. 14; Luke xviii. 16).
[2] Luke ix. 62. [3] John xviii. 38.

there in question is our Lord's βασιλεία in the sense of his personal royal rank, "Art thou a king, then?"—"My kingship is not from this world." I am a king—that is, but in a sense which rises above the world's idea of kingship, in the sense that "all who are of the truth hear my voice." We can bring this use of the word into relation with the thought of Christ's *reign* as King,[1] but not quite to the extent of identification. Here the kingship of Christ is asserted as his personal claim, generally when his kingdom is spoken of his royal rank is presupposed rather than asserted *de novo*. With "kingdom" in the sense of realm the passage has no direct concern. But in the Fourth Gospel as in the Synoptics, the Kingdom of GOD meets us at the outset of Christ's teaching. In the colloquy with Nicodemus to "see" or "enter into" the Kingdom of GOD is assumed as the chief good upon which man's ultimate well-being depends.[2] But generally in St. John the chief good of man is conceived as Life, or Eternal Life, as in the passage[3] which, as we have just seen, sums up the thought of the Kingdom of GOD as expressed in the several Beatitudes:—" And this is Life Eternal, that they know thee, the only true GOD, and Jesus Christ whom thou hast sent."

And since the expressly announced[4] purpose of the Fourth Gospel is to bring out the value of Christ's work for the individual soul, it follows that where the synoptic Gospels speak of the Kingdom of GOD, St.

---

[1] See for example Mozley's University Sermon on this text.
[2] John iii. 3, 5. In the latter verse the variant τῶν οὐράνων is a corruption, though apparently an early one. For "seeing" the Kingdom of God compare Luke ii. 30 with John iii. 36.
[3] John xvii. 3.   [4] xx. 31, ταῦτα δὲ γέγραπται ἵνα, κ.τ.λ.

John speaks of Life. In his telling, "the Gospel of the Kingdom becomes the Gospel of Life."[1] It is important here to remind ourselves that this is not a substitute but a true equivalent, not simply due to the idiosyncrasy of the Fourth Evangelist. The synoptic record has already shown us[2] that Life, Eternal Life, was an equivalent term for the Kingdom of GOD in their tradition of Christ's teaching. Here however, as in some other respects, a vein of his teaching traceable though not emphasised in the triple record is placed by St. John in the forefront and centre. We have, it would seem, in his Gospel a tradition of one and the same Personality, character,[3] and teaching as that portrayed by the Synoptics, but passed through a psychological medium different in kind, and coloured by experience and reflexion of a generation longer's duration. How then does the Johannine tradition of Christ's teaching present this "Life" to us?

On the one hand it is, in its full and final sense, eternal and reserved for the future.[4] "For this is the will of my Father, that every one which seeth the Son and believeth him may have everlasting life; and I will

---

[1] This side of Christ's teaching, like the gospel of the kingdom, left its mark on the early preaching of the Apostles. Compare John vi. 69 with Acts v. 20. See also Charles, *Eschatology*, p. 368.

[2] See above, p. 68. The same equivalence in many passages of St. Augustine, see Reuter, *Augustinische Studien*, pp. 19, 124, note.

[3] Without at all minimising the differences of presentment in the Fourth Gospel as compared with the synoptic tradition, it must be insisted that to the non-theological reader the human character of Christ in the two records is wholly homogeneous; see for example the traits taken without any prepossession from both sources, in Hazlitt's fine passage on the character of Christ in his introductory essay on Elizabethan Literature (Ireland's *Selections from Hazlitt*, p. 175 sq., ed. 1889: Warne & Co.).

[4] John vi. 40, and often elsewhere.

raise him up at the last day." It is unnecessary to multiply quotations to illustrate the thought, here so clearly expressed, which saturates the Gospel according to St. John. But on the other hand the life which Christ gives is a present possession, "he that believeth on the Son *hath* everlasting life,"[1] a possession of which death cannot rob us; "he that believeth in me, though he be dead yet shall he live"; "if any man eat of his bread he shall live for ever,"—"except ye eat, ye have no life in you,"[2]—the Life is not only prospective but *in us* now, "If a man keep my saying, he shall never see death," "whosoever liveth and believeth in me shall never die," *i.e.* the mere fact of physical death cannot destroy the Divine Life possessed in this life. "Whosoever seeth the Son and believeth in him,—eateth my flesh and drinketh my blood,—hath eternal life, and I will raise him up at the last day";[3] the future life, that is, is the unfolding of a seed already quick with energy in this life, the salvation realised then is organically linked with the state of salvation to be experienced now: "verily, verily, I say unto you, he that heareth my word and believeth on him that sent me, hath everlasting life and cometh not into condemnation, but *hath passed* out of death into life."[4] Again, to "see God" is an equivalent, not only as we have seen from the Beatitudes in the synoptic tradition, for possessing the Kingdom of GOD, but also as we have seen and shall see, in St. John's Gospel for *Life*. *Vita hominis visio Dei* is a voice from the direct spiritual

[1] John iii. 36, vi. 47, and perhaps 54, xx. 31.
[2] xi. 25, vi. 50, 53.   [3] viii. 51, 52, xi. 26, vi. 40, 54.
[4] v. 24, cf. 1 John iii. 14. "Eternal life in the Fourth Gospel is not a time-conception, but a purely ethical and timeless one" (Charles, p. 370).

lineage[1] of St. John. This vision of GOD is reserved for the future, "when he shall appear, we shall be like him; for we shall see him as he is"[2]—this alone absolutely satisfies the verse[3] which I quoted at the outset of this part of our enquiry; but it is a present possession to faith. It is remarkable that the word "faith,"—πίστισ,—with the simpler meaning which it bears in the first three Gospels, disappears entirely in St. John. But in his writings, more than in the whole of the New Testament outside them, the profoundly suggestive πιστεύειν εἰσ—"believing in" (lit. *into*) is prominent and frequent.[4] "He that hath seen" Jesus "hath seen the Father";[5] and to believe in him is to live.[6]

The conception of Life, then, in St. John, corresponds to that of the Kingdom of GOD, both in St. Paul and in the synoptic record of Christ teaching, in this respect, that its full and fundamental reference is to the consummation of all things at the last day, but that it is "timeless," and therefore has also a preparatory and partial, but real place in present experience, a fact of real experience in so far as the eternal is the real which underlies the temporal. St. Paul,[7] St. John, and the first three evangelists are here at one.

---

[1] Irenaeus, *Haer.* IV. xx. 7, cf. xxxviii. 3, ὅρασισ δὲ Θεοῦ περιποιητικὴ ἀφθαρσίασ.

[2] 1 John iii. 2 (cf. Matt. v. 8). I quote the First Epistle of St. John as of one piece with the Gospel, which it appears written to supplement, 1 John i. 1, 2.

[3] John xvii. 3.

[4] The phrase πᾶσ ὁ πιστεύων is peculiar to St. John and St. Paul.

[5] John xiv. 9; cf. Ign. *ad Polyc.* 3, τὸν ἀόρατον τὸν δι᾽ ἡμᾶσ ὁρατόν, and Iren. *Haer.* IV. iv. 2, "Mensura enim Patris Filius quoniam et capit eum."

[6] John x. 26.

[7] Rom. xiv. 17, and above, p. 54 sq.; the correlation of "Kingdom" and

In the synoptic Gospels Jesus is King, and his advent brings with it a kingdom in which he reigns as vicegerent of his Father; and as he has received his kingdom from his Father, so he appoints it to his disciples that they may reign with him. In St. John he is charged with divine Life, which his Father has given him to possess in himself, and which he has power to give to others. "And this is the record, that GOD hath given to us eternal life, and this life is in his Son,"[1]—"that whosoever believeth should in him have eternal life."[2] He is the Resurrection and the Life, the Way, the Truth, and the Life, "For as the Father hath life in himself, so hath he given to the Son to have life in himself." "As the living Father hath sent me, and I live by the Father, so he that eateth me, even he shall live by me."[3] The mediatorial Reign thus appears as a mediatorial ministry of divine Life, of personal knowledge of God: "If ye had known me, ye should have known my Father";[4] "If ye had known me, ye should have known my Father also."[5] He who has seen him has seen the Father. And here we are brought face to face with all the moral qualifications for that Life which consists in the knowledge of GOD, and which answer to the more simply formulated qualifications[6] we have gathered from the other Gospels for entering into the Kingdom of GOD—for entering into Life, "He that saith I know him, and keepeth not his commandments, is a liar, and

---

"Life," Rom. v. 17. The "Johannine" idea of life already in Rom. vi. 4, cf. viii. 12.

[1] 1 John v. 11.
[2] John iii. 15, ℵ B.
[3] John xi. 25, xiv. 6, v. 26, vi. 57.
[4] John viii. 19.
[5] John xiv. 7, cf. 17.
[6] *Supra*, p. 67 sq.

the truth is not in him"; "whoso sinneth hath not seen him neither known him"; "he that loveth not knoweth not GOD, for GOD is love"; "we know that we have passed from death unto life, because we love the brethren."[1]

Our survey, brief and inadequate as it has necessarily been, of our Lord's teaching concerning the Kingdom of GOD, has sufficed, I think, to explain fully the great transition from the hope of the Jewish people, as formulated in the Psalms of Solomon, to the hope of redeemed mankind which centres round the Kingdom of GOD in the writings of St. Paul. The former was intense and, in its highest expression, noble and sublime. But its appeal was so bound up with national experiences and national feeling as to be incapable of awaking a spontaneous response in the deep and universal aspirations of the human soul thirsting for salvation. Statesmen and political writers languidly noted that oracles were afloat in Judea to the effect that some would arise in the East and gain supremacy over the world; or again reaction from the emptiness of Greek and Roman religion filled the synagogues of the Jewish Dispersion with Gentile adherents; but there was no gospel for sinful humanity. Whereas, in St. Paul, the hope of Israel has become the hope of mankind, and all without distinction of birth, blood, or culture are called to the Kingdom and Glory of GOD as fellow-citizens of the saints.

This change we have now traced in its origin, in the preaching of the Kingdom of GOD by Jesus Christ. Beginning with the announcement, essentially a "good

[1] 1 John ii. 4, iii. 6, iv. 8, iii. 14.

spell"—a εὐαγγέλιον, that the hope of GOD'S people was now to be fulfilled, he uses the conviction, already impressed upon them from of old, that the unworthy would be excluded from the fulfilment, and that the children of the Gentiles were to be blessed in the reign of the Messiah; and proclaims, to minds already in part prepared to receive it, that character alone will be the qualification for entrance into the promised kingdom. This entrance, again, is entrance into Life, life to be enjoyed as an eternal activity of the soul in the completed Kingdom of GOD, but to be experienced now as a renovation of the inner self, as the reign of Christ in our hearts and wills and character. We see, accordingly, that the Kingdom of GOD is, in our Lord's teaching as in St. Paul's, primarily associated with the consummation of GOD'S ultimate purpose for his rational creation, a goal but dimly apprehended by the Jews in their belief in a world to come, but clear and dominant in the view of the world inculcated by our Lord. This is especially true of the perfect kingdom of the Father, and wholly true of the kingdom in which Christ is to return at the last day. But whereas the Jewish hope of the kingdom had looked for its inauguration by the advent of the King Messiah, our Lord distinctly taught that his advent as Messiah was twofold; and there resulted a twofold conception of the Kingdom of GOD of which he is the Mediatorial Head. In the future he is to come, in the last day, "in his kingdom"; but with his entrance into the world his Kingdom has also come. From thenceforward he is King, and reigns. His Kingdom in this sense is within, and consists in his reign in the hearts of his true disciples. What is true of life in the Fourth Gospel applies with equal truth to the Kingdom of GOD in the Synoptics; it is present and future, and its present existence is in preparation for the future which precedes it not in time but in the purpose of GOD. The Society of Christ's disciples—his Church—is therefore not to be identified with GOD'S Kingdom in the sense of a realm or body politic; rather it is a body of men,—a little flock,—to whom that Kingdom is promised as their divinely destined possession.[1] The Church stands in a more direct relation to the Mediatorial Kingdom of Christ; but here, too, the two things are not convertible; the Church is an instrument, the chief instrument, of the Reign of Christ, it is its principal sphere, and aims at worthily embodying it in the sight of men. The Kingdom of GOD is not simply an idea, nor simply an institution, but a Life, and of that Life —the Christian Life—the Church is the nurse and home. Finally we have seen that while the Kingdom of GOD is most properly the final and perfect state in which GOD'S will is fully accomplished, the name is also applicable to the complex and manifold process which is leading to that state, and how this application is made in a large number of our Saviour's Parables. And coming back to our starting-point, the fundamental condition of character, we saw the character which makes a man fit for the kingdom summed up, both in its unity and in its diversity, in the Beatitudes, in which moreover the synoptic conception of the kingdom begins to converge with that of Life, its equivalent in the writings of St. John. Here the

[1] Luke xii. 33.

universalisation of the originally Jewish and nationalist hope of a Kingdom of GOD reaches its culminating point. Our Lord, starting from the position that "salvation is of the Jews," has widened it out till it embraces human nature as a whole. The national longing for the "sure mercies of David" has become in his hands the desire of all flesh for the salvation of GOD, and the assurance that that desire has not been implanted in our hearts in vain.

Our Lord then, from his first Advent, has begun a Reign on earth, the seat and sphere of which is in the inward spiritual life of man, a reign within us, and therefore, though visible by its effects, having a range whose limits are not visible to the eye nor definable like those of a temporal kingdom by ascertained frontiers. He has also instituted a Society, with a definite rite of admission, and entrusted its extension and its government to disciples selected and trained in the first instance by himself. During his personal and visible presence this Society needed no other provision for its guidance than his Eye and Hand and Word. When his visible presence was to be removed, as it was expedient that it should, he promised that his followers should not lack guidance as real as that which his personal presence had supplied. He would be with them still, not visibly, but by the Spirit which would "take of his and show it to them." Clearly then, if we have rightly interpreted our Saviour's words in regard to the relation between the inward and spiritual Kingdom of Christ and the visible Church of Christ as its nurse and home, then the personal reign of Christ in which his Kingdom consists,—represented in the first instance by the direct dependence upon his look and his word of his disciples during his life upon earth, will from his Resurrection and Exaltation to the Right Hand of the Father be realised in the guidance of his followers, collectively and individually, by the Holy Spirit.[1] In the Church of New Testament times this is abundantly verified in both respects. And, when we bear in mind that the only "positive" laws bequeathed by our Saviour to his visible Society— over and above the general commission to the Apostles —had relation to the visible Society as such, namely, the rite of admission to the fellowship of his Body and the rite by which that fellowship was to be asserted, maintained, and strengthened, it does not surprise us that it is in the collective action of the Society [2]—as a whole or in its parts—that the guidance of the Spirit is most especially counted upon. But clearly there remain many possible alternatives in the application of these general principles. When the first intensity of spiritual fellowship and spiritual life has become weakened, partly by time and custom, still more by the increasing diffusion of the Body—when our Lord's saying that the violent take the Kingdom of GOD by force becomes verified on a scale incomparably beyond anything possible in its first beginnings; when experience has begun to remind men how much more possible it is to mistake the utterances of the Spirit than the audible words of a visible

[1] The Spirit accordingly was, to the primitive Church, the "Vicar of Christ," see Tert. *de Praescr.* xiii., who says that Christ "*misisse uicariam uim Spiritus Sancti, qui credentes agat,*" cf. John xvi. 13, etc.

[2] For instance Acts xiii. 2, xv. 28, xvi. 6, 7 (cf. v. 3, 4), xx. 23, 28; 1 Tim. i. 18.

Master; when last but not least the Christian Society becomes, if not coextensive, at any rate commensurate with the organisation of government and the sphere of the civil ruler: then the Christian Church is confronted with problems of which no appeal to the recorded word of Christ furnishes a solution ready to hand. To begin with, how is the true voice of the Spirit to be distinguished amid conflicting utterances which claim to be his? what and where is the authority finally to adjudge between alternative interpretations of the Words of the Lord? is the Reign of Christ exercised, in default of a clear direction of the Spirit acknowledged by all, by some visible representative, collective or singular? And again if the Church is in some sense to be identified with the Kingdom of Christ, how far does that identification carry us? Is the Church a body politic as completely equipped for all purposes of government as a temporal state πάσησ ἔχουσα πέρασ τῆσ αὐταρκείασ?[1] And if so, what is her relation to the civil government which has been accustomed to regulate many matters which are essential to the self-completeness of the Church as a Perfect Society? In a word, what precise consequences lie in that mission of the Christian Church to all the world with which Christ left her entrusted?

These questions were some of them long in coming to an issue,[2] very long in receiving a practical answer,[3] and their answer in explicit thought [4] has been slower still. But if the religion of Christ was assured from

---

[1] Arist. *Polit.* I. ii. 8; see below, Lect. VII. p. 344, note 2.
[2] Lect. V. p. 219.   [3] Lect. VI. p. 227 sq., 252 sq.
[4] Lect. VII. pp. 337 sqq.

the first of a world-wide and age-long history, they were every one of them inevitable. Were the solutions of these inevitable questions given by our Saviour in advance? To claim this is either to make extravagant demands upon the theory of secret tradition, or to torture into our service passages from the Gospels which, before the questions which they are supposed to decide became urgent, received interpretations different in kind—the true reply is, surely, that they were designedly left by our Lord, in his supreme Wisdom, to the test of Christian experience. Had a ready solution of them been a necessity for his followers, a necessity for his Reign on earth, it would have been furnished, and would have been known from the first. Whether this was so, we shall endeavour to see. But the Holy Spirit was promised to guide the Church into all truth, —not *in* but *into*,—not along a single groove well-marked out from the first, but through the difficult ways of experience, devious and disappointing at times, with many a triumphant forward rush in directions which have proved to be mistaken, but never without resulting light and gain, never without the Spirit, interpreting the one fundamental experience of Redemption " in many parts and in many manners "—always and everywhere the same Kingdom of Christ, the Christian life in its infinite variety; but in its essence, first and last, true to type. The question which lies behind appears to be this. Granting that the mediatorial reign of Christ, which is the Kingdom of GOD in its progressive realisation between the first Advent and the second, is in itself invisible, it must still produce visible effects, and tend toward a condition of things on earth which corresponds to it. Well then, what condition of things, what state of human society and what relation of the Church to the civil organisation of human society, satisfies the true conception of the Reign of Christ? how is the Kingdom of GOD to receive its truest realisation possible in this world? This is the question, the answer to which is to be read from the experience of Christian history. It can at best be answered imperfectly, because we know only a part, perhaps as yet only the beginnings, of that history. But it is of vital moment to read, as truly as it is given us to do, that part which has so far unfolded itself to our view.

It has been necessary to say thus much by way of epilogue to the consideration of the gospel record, for it is from the recorded words of Christ, alone, that we gain an insight into the idea of the Kingdom of GOD in its essence, in its subtle connexion with its historical presuppositions, and its multiple complexity of application. Even St. Paul's letters, invaluable for their sidelight upon the gospel record, add, as we now see, but little to the substance of our Saviour's words—what St. Paul taught on the subject was what he had received from the Lord.

III

With one exception, the remaining New Testament books add little to the results now before us. St. James and St. Peter make reference to the Kingdom of GOD, but their few allusions serve principally to show that it was the eschatological idea—primary as we have seen in our Lord's own teaching—that was mainly associated with it in the mind of the Apostolic age. St. James, in language which seems in part to echo a verse of St. Paul's, speaks of the "poor in respect of the world" chosen by GOD as "heirs of the kingdom which he hath promised to them that love him."[1] St. Peter's language about the incorruptible inheritance[2] reserved for the saints is of the same kind, and the same may be said of the reference in the Second Epistle.[3] In the Epistle to the Hebrews, in which we have in so many ways an earlier parallel to the thought of the Fourth Gospel, but with marked Pauline influence, two points, both secondary to St. Paul, require our notice. Firstly, here as in St. Paul, the 110th Psalm supplies the terms[4] in which the exaltation of Christ is described; but in the words "for ever sat down at the right hand of GOD" we are struck by the absence of the difficult Pauline thought of the Redelivery of the Kingdom.[5] Secondly, the writer, in conformity with the words of the Gospels, speaks of our "receiving a kingdom which cannot be shaken"—$\beta\alpha\sigma\iota\lambda\epsilon\iota\alpha\ \dot{\alpha}\sigma\dot{\alpha}\lambda\epsilon\upsilon\tau\sigma\sigma$.[6] This kingdom, the reward of Christ's followers, is spoken of, in words for which St. Paul[7] furnishes a precedent, as "the heavenly Jerusalem,"[8] which is ours by the assurance of faith, though the earthly one be overthrown. This is the first trace of a special modification of the thought of the Kingdom of Heaven which we shall meet with in the immediate sequel, and again later on—the thought of a *City of GOD*.

---

[1] Jas. ii. 5; cf. 1 Cor. ii. 9 fin., cf. i. 26-28.   [2] 1 Pet. i. 4.
[3] 2 Pet. i. 11.   [4] Heb. x. 12.   [5] 1 Cor. xv. 24-28.
[6] Heb. xii. 28   [7] Gal. iv. 26.   [8] Heb. xii. 22.

IV

The Apocalypse of St. John remains for consideration. It is needless to enumerate the numerous conflicting theories as to its interpretation, many of which lie in directions widely divergent from that of our historical enquiry. The broken Greek in which it is written detracts little or nothing at all from the deep poetical power of the book, inspired by passionate desire for the Kingdom of Christ and passionate devotion to his Person. As the first Christian philosophy of history, it forms a monumental landmark in the development we are tracing. In this respect it sums up a development begun[1] by Daniel, and continued in the less known Jewish Apocalypses. As Daniel places the vicissitudes of the Church of the Old Testament in context with the unfolding of the great drama of World-History as he saw it, and unveils the meaning of the trials which the contact of the Church with the World-Power brings forth, and their issue in the everlasting Reign of the Son of Man and of the Saints, so the seer of the Christian Apocalypse portrays for us not the Kingdom of GOD only, but the throes of its birth in the midst of the turmoil of battle, physical and spiritual, and its vicissitudes under the World-Power,—now embodied in the Roman State,—over which it is destined in the end to triumph. We must take note of the interval of time or sympathy or both which separates the seer from St. Paul. St. Paul had not, when he wrote the great bulk of his letters,[2] known the Roman power as a

[1] See Lect. I. p. 27.
[2] Philippians is hardly an exception. The first clear traces of this experience are in the Second Epistle to Timothy.

persecuting power. On the contrary, as it seems,[1] he had hoped great things of the Roman Empire, of which he himself was a citizen, as a vehicle for the readier diffusion of the gospel,—in Rome itself he had felt a deep interest[2] for years before he was able to visit the Christian Church there. The Roman State is apparently that which hinders the outbreak into lawless violence of fanatical hatred to the cause of Christ,—τὸ κατέχον,[3]—and in fact the protecting arm of the Roman magistrate had, not once nor twice, shielded him from the ferocity of his Jewish compatriots. The heathen magistrate is indeed no proper court of appeal to which Christians should resort for justice in civil disputes,—that were to seek righteousness from the unrighteous,[4]—but in the administration of the criminal law they are the ministers of GOD, and to be obeyed as a matter of conscience.[5] Therefore we are to pray for emperors "that we may lead a quiet and peaceable life in all godliness"[6]—perhaps a hint of coming danger in St. Paul's latest years. From St. Paul, the Roman citizen, the instinct of good citizenship flows down to the Apologists of the next century and prepares the way for the later alliance between Christianity and civil life. But the conditions of the primitive Church were such as to retard this tendency. The attitude of Daniel toward the cruel empires of the East and the sacrilegious encroachments of the Seleucids, of the Psalms of Solomon toward the Roman who had dared to profane the Holy of Holies, was retaken up

---

[1] Ramsay, *The Church in the Roman Empire*, p. 148, etc. (ed. 1), and *St. Paul the Traveller*, p. 139.
[2] Rom. i. 14 and Acts xxiii. 11, etc.   [3] 2 Thess. ii. 6, 7.
[4] 1 Cor. vi. 1 sqq.   [5] Rom. xiii. 1–5.   [6] 1 Tim. ii. 2.

in a less restrained form in the minor apocalyptic writings which fed the Jewish hopes of a coming downfall of the enemies of the people of GOD.[1] And to many Christians of the first three centuries, either actually under official persecution, or without security against a renewed outbreak at any moment, the civil power appeared mainly as a persecuting power, the Empire of the world hung over the followers of Christ as Babylon, the devastator of GOD'S inheritance. Of this attitude of Christians toward the Imperial Power, to which it will be necessary to recur in the following Lecture, the keynote is struck by the Apocalypse. Its way of regarding the heathen power is characteristically Jewish. The Christians are figured as a New Israel. The writer, profoundly Christian, but most deeply saturated of all New Testament writers with Jewish sympathies, sees, either as accomplished fact or in the immediate future, the fall of Jerusalem.[2] But more than this, he knows—whether in the first shock of the terrible announcement or over a retrospect of a whole generation—of the official persecution of Christians; Rome to him is "drunk with the blood of the Saints."[3]

[1] *E.g. Orac. Sibyll.* iii. 668 (μιαροὶ βασιλῆεσ); Enoch lxii. 11 (Charles, *Esch.* 218)

[2] Rev. xi. 1, 2. The measured temple may perhaps signify the Christian Jews.

[3] It is beside the purpose of these Lectures to discuss the date or composition of the Apocalypse; the position taken up by the writer in a review of Völter (*Critical Review*, Jan. 1895) is still held by him. The difficulty of reconciling the indications which point respectively to the Neronic and Domitian dates may be due to the use by the seer, writing under Domitian, of earlier materials. This is too thoroughly in keeping with the phenomena of apocalyptic literature to be set aside as very improbable. But the book as it stands is too entirely the work of its final author to encourage us to hope that the derivative passages can be disengaged with any certainty from their present context. In particular, the hypothesis of a non-Christian

The book is written in expectation of the imminent Return of Christ. The keynote "Behold I come quickly" persists from the beginning to the end of the prophecy.[1] Accordingly, the outlook of the seer is primarily upon the events of the present or immediate future,—upon the events passing or which " must shortly come to pass."—" The time is at hand "—so the book begins and so it ends.[2] The structure of the book merits attention at this point as bearing on the question of its interpretation. After the prefatory admonitions of the Spirit to the seven Churches the vision of what is to come to pass hereafter begins, in the form of the opening by the Lamb of the Book and of its seven seals.[3] As each is opened an angel of vengeance upon the earth rides forth. At the fifth[4] the voices of the slaughtered saints are heard crying for speedy vengeance for their blood; at the sixth there is a pause,[5] amid terrifying signs of thickening doom, while the hundred and forty-four thousand are sealed against the destruction impending upon the earth, and the multitude of the redeemed from every nation appear before the Throne in Heaven. At the seventh seal,[6] a new series of seven trumpets begins, each bringing woe to the earth. Again the sixth trumpet marks a pause,[7] and seven thunders utter their voices, but the seer is forbidden to write then.[8] The seventh trumpet appears to usher in the End. Voices announce the Messianic Reign over all the

---

Jewish original document appears quite gratuitous. Nor can it be said that the Neronic date for the whole book, in spite of the present tendency to revert to the tradition of Irenaeus, is wholly argued out of court.

[1] See Rev. iii. 11, xxii. 7, 12, 20, and compare ii. 25 and 26.
[2] i. 1, 3, xxii. 6, 10.   [3] Chaps. iv., v.   [4] vi. 9 sqq.
[5] vi. 12.   [6] viii. 1.   [7] ix. 13.   [8] x. 4.

REVELATION OF ST. JOHN 109

earth; the vision of the Ark of the Covenant,[1] the Wonder of the Man-child, the war of Michael against the Dragon—the appearance of the Beast and the False Prophet, the vision of the Lamb upon Mount Zion, pass before us in quick succession.[2] Three angels fly forth in mid-heaven, the angel of the Eternal Gospel, the angel of the fall of Babylon, and the angel of the Judgment.[3] The blessing upon those who die in the Lord introduces the vision of the Son of Man upon his white cloud, the harvest of the earth is reaped, and its vintage gathered for the winepress of the wrath of GOD. But now begins yet another series of seven, the bowls in which the wrath of GOD is accomplished.[4] The plagues fall upon the earth, the sea, the rivers, the sun; upon Rome, on the Euphrates —which is dried up that the kings may pass to the war of the great day of Armagedon. The last bowl[5] is poured upon the air, and with the judgment of Babylon the Harlot all is finished, and preparation is made for the marriage feast of the Lamb.[6] But first the Word of GOD goes forth to battle and overthrows the Beast and the False Prophet and all the kings of the earth.[7] Then the Dragon, Satan, is bound,[8] and the abyss sealed over him, for a thousand years. The martyrs and confessors come to life, and reign with Christ a thousand years. "This is the first resurrec-

---

[1] Rev. xi. 19; contrast Jer. iii. 16.   [2] Chaps. xii.-xiv.
[3] xiv. 6-12.   [4] Chap. xv.
[5] xvi. 17.   [6] Chap. xix.
[7] xix. 11-21. The Beast and False Prophet are cast into the lake of fire. This shows that Satan, here as before, is not to be identified with the Beast. See xx. 10.
[8] xx. 3.

tion," in which they are priests of GOD and of Christ. At the end of it Satan is loosed, and the innumerable hosts of Gog and Magog are rallied by him to besiege the Beloved City. Fire falls from heaven and consumes them, Satan is thrown into the lake of fire, to be tormented with the Beast and the False Prophet for ever and ever, and the Universal Resurrection and Judgment follow.[1] Then the new Creation and consummation of all things are described, the heavenly Jerusalem, the bride of the Lamb, is revealed, and the Vision reaches its end, as it began, in the form of an epistle to the saints of Asia.

Clearly, the End is reached repeatedly.[2] Again and again all seems to begin *de novo*, and with each new beginning much is repeated. The course of the world is viewed as a preparation for the Return of Christ; the plagues are the summons addressed to the world to repent, the trial of the Faithful whether they will endure to the end. The persecuting power, the Beast, is apparently the Empire, the False Prophet is the embodiment of all that tempts to apostasy,—possibly, if the Domitian date be adopted, the Provincial Governor moving men to worship the Image of the Emperor. The Empire, or throne of the Beast, is struck with darkness by the fifth bowl;[3] but its final judgment appears to merge in that of the Harlot[4] which again has been anticipated many chapters back.[5] The inference which the structure of the Book suggests as to its character is unfavourable to any realistic scheme of continuous prediction. The whole arrangement of

[1] Rev. xx. 11-15.   [2] Chaps. vi., xi., xvi., xix.
[3] xvi. 10.   [4] Chap. xviii.   [5] xiv. 8.

its contents defies literalism. All is figurative, interprétative; presupposing facts rather than "writing history before the event." But its interpretation for that very reason is not exclusively bound to the facts primarily under contemplation; it finds its application to the various phases which are assumed in the course of the centuries by an antithesis which is for all time.

It is now necessary to consider some details directly bearing upon our subject.

1. The Christians are a kingdom of Priests.[1] We noticed [2] this conception at the outset of our survey of the Old Testament antecedents of the Christian conception of the Kingdom of GOD. With the partial exception of a phrase in the First Epistle of St. Peter,[3] this is the only recurrence of the Old Testament thought in a New Testament book. It is to be noted that the thought is placed by the seer of the Apocalypse in the closest relation with Christ's reign on earth for the thousand years, "thou hast made them unto our GOD a kingdom and Priests, and they shall reign on earth,"[4] and again, "they shall be priests of GOD and of Christ, and shall reign with him the thousand years."[5] That they who are Christ's shall reign with him when he comes in his Kingdom we have learned from the Lord himself and from St. Paul;[6] but the priesthood is a new feature; it has in common with the passage where it occurs in Exodus the thought of unbroken

---

[1] Rev. i. 6, v. 10, xx. 6.   [2] Lect. I. p. 12.
[3] 1 Pet. ii. 9; see the latter part of Hort's very interesting note on the words, pp. 125, 126.
[4] Rev. v. 10.   [5] xx. 6.
[6] Rev. i. 9 refers to the *present* reign "in patience."

attendance upon GOD, and the closest access to him.

2. The utterance,[1] familiar by frequent quotation from the English Version, that "the kingdoms of this world are become the kingdoms of our Lord and of his Christ," has suggested to some the early certitude of the eventual conquest by the Church of the powers which then seemed likely to crush her by force of persecution, and in particular the conversion to Christ of the Empire of Rome. Or in modern times men have seen in the passage the promise of a sanctification of human life, and of the reign of Christ in a purified and ennobled civil and political society. But text and context alike forbid us to read into the passage before us ideas which however true and inspiring in themselves, are apart from its direct reference. The Revised Version correctly renders the true Greek Text: "The kingdom (singular) of this world is become [the kingdom] of our Lord and of his Christ," in other words the "dominion over" this world has passed into his hands. The context[2] refers this to the Return of Christ "in his kingdom"; the underlying thought is that of the Messiah at GOD's right hand, whose enemies are made his footstool, and who rules the nations with a rod of iron.[3] The verse is strongly and exclusively eschatological, and it belongs to the immediate antecedents of the great judgment.[4]

3. Prominent in the imagery of the book, alike at its beginning and ending,[5] is the Heavenly City, the New Jerusalem, which here, as in the Epistle to the

---
[1] Rev. xi. 15. [2] See ver. 17, and xii. 10.
[3] Ps. cx. 1, ii. 9; Rev. xii. 5. [4] xi. 18. [5] iii. 12, xxi. 2, 10.

REVELATION OF ST. JOHN 113

Hebrews, is the embodiment of the completed Kingdom of GOD. It belongs to the regeneration, the new Genesis, in which the new heavens and new earth take the place of the old.

4. But before the appearance of the Heavenly Jerusalem, which is the final Kingdom of GOD, the reign of Christ has had a full realisation of its own. Between the Harmagedon of the seventh Bowl[1] and the final victory over the hosts of Gog and Magog,[2] between the first Resurrection of the just[3] and the final resurrection of all mankind to Judgment,[4] comes the reign of Christ on earth, with its centre in the Beloved City,[5] for a thousand years during which Satan is bound. To share in this the faithful dead are raised: "this is the first resurrection." The latter thought we have already met with in the Jewish eschatology of the visible reign of the Messiah. The thousand years occur in the Slavonic book of Enoch which is ascribed to a date slightly earlier than the earliest probable date of the Revelations, and more vaguely in the contemporary Apocalypse of Baruch.[6]

It is hard to answer satisfactorily the question of the true meaning of the passage. The general disposition in the first centuries of the Church was, as we shall see, to understand the passage quite literally. Those who rejected the authority of the book did so largely on the

---

[1] Rev. xvi. 16, 17.   [2] xx. 8.   [3] xx. 4, 6, cf. v. 14.
[4] xx. 11, 13.   [5] xx. 9.
[6] See Charles, *Eschatology*, pp. 201-204, 349-352, 270-275, 286. It is very doubtful what parts of Slavonic Enoch, Apoc. Baruch, and 4 Ezra are of earlier date than the Apocalypse of St. John, more especially if the Neronic date for the latter is a possible one.

ground of this passage. But it may be questioned whether, taking the Apocalypse simply as it stands, the literal interpretation is necessarily the true one. To begin with, as we have said, the general arrangement of the book defies literalism in detail. It is urged [1] moreover with reason that a thousand years is a round number, lending itself readily to figurative use. In any case, if we can distinguish the thousand years' reign from the reign of GOD Almighty proclaimed [2] *before* the thousand years begin, it constitutes a more marked distinction than we find anywhere else in the New Testament between the Kingdom of Christ and the Kingdom of GOD.[3]

The full realisation of GOD'S Kingdom was not to be looked for on earth, so the Lord had taught, and St. Paul and St. John had but followed his teaching. In this life, the reign of Christ was spiritual, inward; visible in the realisation of that character which springs from a life hid with Christ in GOD, the character which ideally the Body of Christ exhibits in all his members. Is the millennial reign of the Apocalypse, as Augustine holds, but the expression in a concrete image of this spiritual truth? or is it no image at all, but to be taken, as Justin and Irenaeus accepted it, in literal realism? or in a semi-realistic sense as the prophecy of the imperial power of the Catholic Church? These

---

[1] Dr. Stanton argues (1) that Christ does not leave GOD'S right hand to reign for the thousand years. But xix. 11, 21 and xx. 4, combined with v. 10, make this very doubtful; (2) that it is not said where the thousand years' reign has its scene. But it is on earth (v. 10) and in Jerusalem (xx. 9).

[2] Rev. xix. 6. But xix. 11, 21 lead on to the picture of Christ's return to reign on earth.

[3] See above, Lect. II. pp. 53 sqq., 71-4.

were the alternatives imposed by the authority of the Apocalypse upon all who shared the seer's faith that the Christ must set up a visible Kingdom on earth, a Kingdom in which should accumulate the divine power by which good should finally triumph over evil.

LECTURE IV

THE KINGDOM OF GOD IN THE FIRST FOUR CHRISTIAN CENTURIES

And no one asks his fellow any more
"Where is the promise of His Coming?" but
"Was He revealed in any of His lives
As Power, as Love, as Influencing Soul?"
                                                    BROWNING.

Μανθάνω, ἔφη· ἐν ᾗ νῦν διήλθομεν οἰκίζοντεσ πόλει λέγεισ, τῇ ἐν λόγοισ κειμένῃ, ἐπεῖ γῆσ γε οὐδαμοῦ οἶμαι αὐτὴν εἶναι. 'Αλλ', ἦν δ' ἐγώ, ἐν οὐράνῳ ἴσωσ παράδειγμα ἀνάκειται τῷ βουλομένῳ ὁρᾶν καὶ ὁρῶντι ἑαυτὸν κατοικίζειν. διαφέρει δὲ οὐδὲν εἴτε που ἔστιν εἴτε ἔσται· τὰ γὰρ ταύτησ μόνησ ἂν πράξειεν, ἄλλησ δὲ οὐδεμίασ.
                                                    PLATO.

LECTURE IV

THE KINGDOM OF GOD IN THE FIRST FOUR CHRISTIAN CENTURIES

Son of man, what is this proverb that ye have in the land of Israel, saying, The days are prolonged, and every vision faileth?—EZEK. xii. 22.

THE Kingdom of GOD has, in the course of Christian History, received three principal interpretations. It has been identified firstly with the perfect reign of GOD in heaven after the Last Judgment, secondly with a visible reign of Christ on earth between his second coming and the Last Judgment, thirdly with the Visible Church on earth between the first and the second coming of Christ. Of these three, the first has been the most persistent, and even when partially set aside in favour of one or of the other two, it has been recognised, not only in theological thought but in popular language and the unstudied utterances of hymns and prayers, as ultimate and supreme. But in the period which we are to consider to-day, the Christian imagination was in many quarters and for long periods held spellbound by the second.

The belief in a visible earthly reign of Christ to be inaugurated by the Second Advent and a "first resurrection,"—the belief known, from one detail which was a common element in it, as Millenniarism or Chiliasm, but which is better designated simply as Realistic Eschatology, was closely associated with belief in the imminence of the Second Advent. The two beliefs were in themselves quite independent, and either was tenable without the other. St. Paul for instance held, at any rate when he wrote his earlier Epistles,[1] that the return of Christ would certainly come in the lifetime of many who were then living. But as we have seen, not only is there no trace of Millennarian belief in his writings, but his belief as to the Kingdom of Christ is so formulated as to positively exclude the supposition that a millennium of any kind was part of it.[2] We may in fact go so far as to say that belief in the early return of our Lord was quite universal in the Church of the Apostolic age, and was only very slowly and reluctantly surrendered. But we are by no means justified in inferring that belief in the Visible Reign prevailed to the same extent. Our materials for knowledge of the beliefs of the Christians of the first two centuries are not exhaustive, and what generalisations we may found upon those materials must be made with caution and held subject to the probability of fresh light being thrown upon the premises of our inference by further discovery. But subject to these warnings against hasty generalisation, it may safely be said that the Eschatology which prevailed in the early Church was realistic in a very high degree. The realism in question was in part due to a common and

---

[1] 1 Thess. ii. 19, iv. 15; 1 Cor. xv. 51, 52, i. 8; Rom. xiii. 12; Phil. iii. 21; in 2 Cor. v. 3, 4 there is uncertainty as to the Advent occurring in the lifetime of the Apostle; see Waite's note in *Speaker's Comm.*

[2] *Supra*, Lect. II. pp. 52, 53.

APOCALYPSE AND MILLENNIUM 121

legitimate religious instinct, which prompts men to clothe spiritual truths in concrete and tangible form, and to accept authoritative words in their literal meaning unless some strong and clear reason compels them to set it aside in favour of a less obvious sense. This tendency was very strong in the Jewish mind, which was especially marked by its tendency to the concrete. And although the cleft between Jew and Christian widened rapidly, and became by degrees impassable, nearly every Christian Church had originally formed round a nucleus of Christian Jews or proselytes,[1] and it is difficult exactly to estimate the extent to which popular Christian thought was leavened by ideas derived from this source. At any rate, the Christian additions which are traceable in much Jewish apocalyptic literature prove that Jewish books of this kind were widely read and copied among Christians, and that Jewish eschatology was not without influence upon popular Christian expectations of the Last Things.[2] The prevalence of Realistic Eschatology, therefore, is not exclusively to be set down to the influence of the Revelation of St. John. But certainly

[1] Ἰουδαίῳ πρῶτον, Rom. i. 16, ii. 9, 10, is the principle on which the Apostle uniformly proceeds in the Acts (xiii. 46). The synagogues of Antioch in Pisidia, Iconium, the proseucha of Philippi, the synagogues of Thessalonica, Beroea, Athens, Corinth, Ephesus, were the point of departure in the principal Churches founded personally by St. Paul. Jewish influences were strong in Galatia and Colossae. St. Paul assumes that the Roman Christians were grounded in Jewish knowledge (Rom. vii. 1, 4; see art. ROMANS in Hastings' *Dict. of the Bible*). See also Rev. ii. 9, 20, iii. 9.

[2] The *Sibylline Oracles* and the *Testaments of the XII Patriarchs* are perhaps the most conspicuous examples : but for the whole subject, which is too vast to be more than alluded to here, see the references in Stanton, *Jewish and Christian Messiah* ; Charles, article "Apocalyptic Literature" (in *Encycl. Biblica*) and his *Eschatology*, etc.

its hold upon the mind of the early Church was very greatly strengthened by the literal and realistic interpretation of the imagery of the Apocalypse, and especially of those passages in it which speak of the "first resurrection" and of the reign of Christ and his saints upon earth for a thousand years.[1] The question of Realistic Eschatology was accordingly closely connected, though not quite to be identified, with that of the authority of the Apocalypse itself. The general history of the New Testament Canon, or at any rate of those books whose authority was for a time in dispute, is one of widespread doubt at first, gradually settling down into universal acceptance.[2] Or to put the matter differently, the number of books accepted by some Church or other was at first considerably larger than the number eventually accepted by all.[3] As the Churches compared notes, certain books, originally known and read in some Churches only, came to be either accepted by all, or rejected by all. To this general process the Apocalypse forms a singular exception. Apart from the Syrian Church, which apparently did not receive it, its original reception in the Churches of the Greco-Roman world was general.[4]

[1] See Lect. III. p. 113 sq.

[2] For the general history of the Canon, and of the New Testament "Antilegomena," I must be content to refer to the standard Introductions, to Westcott on the *Canon*, Sanday's *Bampton Lectures*, etc.

[3] For example, the Epistles of Clement and Barnabas, the *Didache*, the *Shepherd of Hermas*, the Gospels according to the Hebrews and the Egyptians, the Apocalypse of Peter, all enjoyed local reception for a time. See Sanday (*ut supra*), p. 26 sqq. Of the oldest MSS. of the Greek Bible, ℵ contained Barnabas and the *Shepherd*, A the First and "Second" Epistles of Clement. But see Westcott, *Canon*, Appendix B.

[4] I must refer for details to Westcott on the *Canon*, esp. p. 241 (ed. 4); Zahn, *Geschichte d. N.T. Kanons*, i. pp. 220-261.

APOCALYPSE AND MILLENNIUM 123

The rejection of the book by the so-called Alogi of Asia Minor was apparently doctrinal in its motives,— and in part due to the high value set upon it by the Montanists.[1] But although Origen himself received it, as the influence of his theology spread, objections to the book increased in the Greek Church. Origen's great pupil Dionysius of Alexandria[2] was unable to believe that it could be the work of the same John who had written the Fourth Gospel. Of the fourth century theologians, Eusebius vacillates on the subject.[3] Cyril of Jerusalem (348) passes it over, as also does the Council of Laodicea (perhaps about 362), and Gregory of Nazianzus.[4] His fellow-countryman Amphilochius of Iconium says, "Some insert it, but most class it as spurious." This statement is certainly surprisingly strong; we may compare it with that of Sulpitius Severus,[5] "A *plerisque* aut stulte aut impie non recipitur." His horror contrasts strangely with the fact he records, but at any rate guarantees his freedom from colouring bias. Athanasius (in 367),[6] who accepts it without question, shows the decline of Origen's influence in his native Egypt; Epiphanius shortly afterwards leads a reaction in its favour, and Basil, Gregory

---

[1] This would also go to explain their hostility to the Gospel of St. John, the mainstay of the doctrine of the Paraclete. On the Alogi see Sanday, *Bampton Lectures*, pp. 15, 64 sq., and reff., also Zahn (*ut supra*). On Gaius of Rome see below, p. 127, note 1. The "Alogi" were a party rather than a sect. The name was invented for them by Epiphanius.

[2] Euseb. *H. E.* III. xxviii., VII. xxiv., xxv.; see also M'Giffert's note (19) on III. xxiv. (in *Nicene and Post-Nicene Library*, series 2, vol. i.).

[3] *H. E.* III. xxv., xxxix. 6, etc.

[4] *Carm.* xii. 31. This, and the other passages referred to in the text are brought together by Westcott, *Canon*, Appendix D.

[5] *Hist. Sacr.* ii. 31 (*c.* A.D. 403).

[6] Letter 39 (in *Nicene Library*, vol. iv.).

of Nyssa, Didymus, Cyril of Alexandria, and others follow. Chrysostom however makes no use of the book, nor does even Theophylact as late as the eleventh century; but with that exception, its authority has stood firm in the East since the year 500.[1] Briefly then the volume of pre-Nicene testimony is strongly on the side of the Apocalypse; the remarkable fact is the growth of a strong reaction against it in the later third century and in the fourth. The main disturbing cause was unquestionably the growing discredit of Realistic Eschatology, and the support which that Eschatology derived from a literal construction of certain parts of the Apocalypse. The objections to the book were gradually overcome in proportion as its literal interpretation gave way to a figurative. The early attitude of Churchmen toward the Apocalypse is, accordingly, to be understood by reference to their eschatological prepossessions — in short to the more or less realistic way in which they conceived of the Kingdom of Christ.

II

Briefly, it may be said that the Realistic Eschatology prevailed in the Church generally for two centuries and a half, and in the Western Church for four centuries—that is until the time of Augustine, who shared it himself, until, as he expressly tells us, reflexion led him to a different mind on the subject.[2] His vast

---

[1] The influence of Dionysius the Areopagite (about A.D. 500) doubtless helped to clinch the reviving authority of the book in the East.
[2] See Lect. V. p. 170 sq.

PRIMITIVE CHURCH AND MILLENNIUM 125

influence coupled with other more general causes, carried the Church's mind in a new direction; Millennarianism quickly lost ground, and ceased to be even a tolerated doctrine. The general causes to which I have referred operated in the East before they much affected the simpler mind of the Western Church. In the East, Millenniarism received its first shock in the battle against Montanism. Its final extinction was the work of the spiritual and philosophical theology which owed its great stimulus to Origen. Till about the last third of the second century, then, was its time of unchallenged strength. It is possible to cite prominent writers who show no trace of it in their extant writings. Clement of Rome, who regards the Apostolic succession as a precaution *in case* the existing successors of the Apostles should fall asleep, evidently believed in the probability of a speedy return of Christ. But of his millennial or earthly Reign he says nothing.[1] Ignatius, in his seven epistles, says nothing of it, nor does Polycarp. But we cannot, in view of the extreme brevity and occasional character of their writings, be sure that their silence was intentional. On the contrary, we must allow some weight to the connexion of Polycarp with Papias and with Irenaeus, and to the possibility that the belief which the two last-named held so strongly was shared by other prominent Asian Christians as well. Barnabas expects the sixth day, that is the sixth millennium, of the world's history to be followed by the Sabbath of

---

[1] Clem. Rom. *Ep.* xliv. 2, ἐὰν κοιμηθῶσιν. See however xlii. 3, where the Apostles after Pentecost go forth preaching τὴν βασιλείαν τοῦ Θεοῦ μέλλειν ἔρχεσθαι.

Christ's power.[1] The Roman visionary Hermas is saturated with realistic expectations of the Last Things. The prayer of the Διδαχὴ τῶν ιβ' ἀποστόλων, "Let grace come and this world pass away,"[2] would at any rate come naturally from the lips of those who hoped for a Reign of Christ on earth—more naturally than the prayer "pro mora finis" comes from the intensely millennarian Tertullian. The second epistle (so-called) of Clement[3] bears traces of the same influence. Justin himself holds to the millennial belief, though recognising that some Christians disbelieve it.[4] Papias holds it in its fulness; Cerinthus the Jewish-Christian syncretist expresses it in a crassly material form, yet hardly more crass than that of Irenaeus himself. The opinion of Cerinthus is quoted by the Roman presbyter Gaius who says, in his tract against the Montanists:—

"But Cerinthus also, through Revelations written, as

---

[1] Barn. xv. This Sabbath will be followed by the eighth day—*i.e.* the new world. The scheme of seven days, answering to those of creation, for the course of earthly history is, if not a fundamental, at any rate a nearly constant element in all forms of Chiliasm. The first division of the kind is the *ten* weeks of Ethiop. Enoch xci. (see Charles, *Esch.* 205), of which seven "embrace all events from the creation till the Advent of the Messianic kingdom." But in the Slavonic Enoch, dating from before A.D. 50 (*ibid.* p. 261 sqq.), we have the six "days" of history, each of a thousand years (see Ps. lxxxix. 3, LXX, and various readings), to be followed by the Messianic Sabbath of the seventh thousand. Compare below, Lect. V. p. 170, and Lect. VII. p. 298, on Abbot Joachim.

[2] The phrase alone (*c.* x.) would be inconclusive. But combined with the prayer (ix., x.) that the Church may be gathered from the ends of the earth into the Kingdom of GOD, and with the reference to a first resurrection (xvi. 6) it points decisively to the thought of a future reign of Christ on earth. Tertullian's prayer, *Apol.* xxxix.

[3] §§ 5, 12, 17. There is no express reference to a millennium.

[4] *Tryph.* lxxx., lxxxi. Compare his attitude toward Ebionites, *ibid.* xlviii.

PRIMITIVE CHURCH AND MILLENNIUM 127

he would have us believe, by a great Apostle, brings before us marvellous things which he pretends were shown him by angels; alleging that after the Resurrection the Kingdom of Christ is to be on earth, and that the flesh, dwelling in Jerusalem, is to be subject to desires and pleasures. And being an enemy to the Scriptures of GOD, writing to deceive men, he says that there is to be a space of a thousand years for marriage festivals."

Apart from doubtful questions which have been raised here, it would appear from this passage that Cerinthus pressed the language of the Apocalypse in its most literal and material sense.[1] But he is only treating the Apocalypse as Irenaeus himself treated the prophecies of the Old Testament. Irenaeus quotes elders—that is Papias and his authorities—as reporting the following, on the authority of John, as the teaching of Christ himself :—

"The days will come when vines shall grow, each having ten thousand branches, and on each branch ten

---

[1] Eus. *H. E.* III. xxviii. The preponderance of modern opinion is that Gaius refers to the Apocalypse of St. John, which he accuses Cerinthus of fabricating under the name of the Apostle. This is supported by the words of Dionysius (*supra*, p. 123, note), who, however, dissociates himself from a view so repellent to Christian instinct. Gaius was answered by Hippolytus, who, although opposed like Gaius to the Montanists, shared in a less crass form their millenniarist beliefs (see his *Heads against Gaius*, vii., in Berlin ed. of Hippol. 1, n. p. 247. He repudiates the idea that Satan was bound at the first Advent; but treats the thousand years as "one perfect day." Lightfoot's doubt of the existence of Gaius is no longer tenable: *S. Clem. of Rome*, ii. 387, etc.). Zahn (*Kanon*, i. 230 sqq.) endeavours to show, from the silence of Irenaeus, etc., that Gaius was wrong in attributing these views to Cerinthus. But Irenaeus would hardly have included Chiliasm among the *errors* of Cerinthus. Into the relation between Gaius and the "Alogi" it is beside our present purpose to enquire.

thousand twigs, and on each twig ten thousand shoots, and on each one of the shoots ten thousand clusters, and on every one of the clusters ten thousand grapes, and every grape when pressed will give twenty-five firkins of wine. And when any one of the saints shall lay hold upon a cluster, another shall cry out, 'I am a better cluster; take me; bless the Lord through me!' (And in like manner) that a grain of wheat will produce ten thousand stalks and each stalk ten thousand ears . . ." and so forth.

He identifies his source as Papias "in his fourth book"—and Papias adds, he tells us, "now these things are credible to believers."

"For if," he continues, "the lion, that fierce animal, is to feed upon straw, of what quality must the wheat itself be, whose straw shall serve as suitable food for lions?"[1]

The cycle of beliefs we are considering is clearly a survival of the Jewish inability to realise ideas except by the aid of concrete forms, as we see it exemplified in the Apocalyptic literature which, as we have said, the Christians borrowed and adapted from Jewish sources. Jewish imagery therefore, and Jewish expectations of the Messianic Reign, fired the Christian imagination, while the Christian Church took the place of the Jewish people as the heirs of the promised Kingdom.

The essential elements of the Realistic Eschatology were mainly the following :—

[1] Iren. *Haer.* v. xxxiii. 4, cf. 1. This is a pre-Christian picture of material felicity. It appears in substance in Ethiop. Enoch x. (second cent. B.C.), and in the Apocalypse of Baruch xxix. See Charles, *Esch.* pp. 189, 271. Its adoption by Papias illustrates by contrast the absence of this kind of credulity from the pages of the New Testament.

PRIMITIVE CHURCH AND MILLENNIUM 129

1. A final, presently impending, and terrible array of the World-Power in all its strength against the Church of Christ.

2. The imminent return of Christ.

3. That Christ will overcome the World-Power, and establish a glorious kingdom on earth.

4. The First Resurrection of the saints to share in this kingdom.

5. The close of the kingdom to be followed by the universal Resurrection and Judgment.

Among the more variable and to some extent subordinate elements we may mention:—

6. The conception of the world's history as made up of seven days, typified by the seven days of Creation.[1]

7. The enemies of the kingdom of Christ, and specially the Antichrist who is to lead them.[2]

8. The place, duration, and extent of the kingdom of Christ.[3] Justin, who holds that it will be set up at Jerusalem and last a thousand years, follows the prevailing view, as did Cerinthus. But Montanus looked for its establishment at Pepuza and Tymion in his own country.

This Realistic Eschatology was favoured by the conditions of the first Christian centuries. Firstly, there was as yet no comprehensive theology to bring to bear upon it any reasoned principles of exegesis, or

---

[1] See above, p. 126, note 1.
[2] See Lect. I. p. 26, note 2, and Lect. II. p. 57, note 2, etc.
[3] The pre-Christian tradition was either indefinite as to the duration, or specified four hundred years (4 Ezra vii. 28 sq.; see Charles, *Esch.* p. 286), a number founded on the years of captivity in Egypt, Gen. xv. 13 combined with Ps. xc. 15, or a thousand years (see above, p. 113, note 6).

to place Eschatology in context and analogy with a consistently framed Christian view of life and existence. Theology of course there was, in the sense of profound religious reflexion upon the facts of the Christian Religion; Ignatius and Irenaeus are examples that will occur to all. But before the rise of the Alexandrian school and its great teacher Origen, no one had endeavoured to reach a "unified consciousness" in which the best attainable knowledge, and the best philosophical method then available, should be applied to interpret Christian truth, and correlated with its principles. To a theology in this sense, the greater Christian minds have always aspired at the creative and vigorous periods of the Church's history. Origen was the first of these. He had no doubt predecessors, partly in the Gnostics, partly in the Apologists. Both of these in their way aimed at a union of Christian with philosophic thought. And it may be remarked in passing that, while naturally we neither expect nor find among the Gnostics any millennarian eschatology, the Apologists of the second century, as a class, give it very little prominence in their writings.[1] But neither they nor the Gnostics were likely to exercise much influence in weakening its hold upon the Church. The Gnostics as a class had in common the tendency to express in Christian language non-Christian—what passed for philosophic—ideas. They were too obviously out of sympathy with the inmost convictions of the Church to affect its prevalent belief

---

[1] It was hardly within their purpose to do so. Had we only his *Apologies*, we should not have known of Justin's Chiliasm. His pupil Tatian betrays no trace of it.

PRIMITIVE CHURCH AND MILLENNIUM 131

on the kingdom of Christ. The Apologists had in common the task of proving that the Christians were good citizens and that theirs was the most reasonable religion. In discharging this task they aimed at expressing Christian ideas in philosophical language. But both as philosophers and as theologians they failed to sound the full depth of the questions they handled, and except prospectively, as precursors of Origen and his school, they did not leaven or modify the convictions of the average Christian. There was then before A.D. 200 no widespread influence in Christian thought to counteract the realism of early Christian Eschatology.

But secondly, outside the Church, the circumstances of the time were such as to foster it. Far more than the Middle Ages, the pre-Nicene centuries deserve to be spoken of as the "Ages of Faith." The Christians, though daily increasing in numbers, were still a minority, and to become a Christian meant a wrench from many social ties, often great personal sacrifice, sometimes imminent risk of life. Each convert as he entered the Church felt that he was joining a body united by a strict standard of conduct, the members of which were under close mutual observation; a body in which the standard of conduct was enforced in extreme cases by formal discipline, in all cases by the discipline of a severe public opinion. The Christian body was compact and keenly conscious of itself, in face of a suspiciously hostile public, of a government never friendly, and not infrequently active in measures of suppression. That the little flock thus placed should look passionately for the kingdom promised them by Christ, that they should hold tenaciously to the graphic and definite descriptions of its glories which they had received, and expect its realisation not at the far off consummation of a historical process in continuous development, but as the result of a convulsive breach with history which would by a sudden catastrophe reverse the existing supremacy of the powers opposed to Christ, was surely but natural and to be expected. Persecution at once braced the faith of the early Christians, and kept alive their realistic conception of the kingdom of Christ. Crude realism is, in short, incidental to naïve and vigorous faith. It may be directed to different objects, but where the faith of the simple crowd is deep and strong, some alloy of the kind will almost always accompany it. A well-known modern critical historian, who is distinguished among critics by his keen perception of religious character, observes that nearly all great religious personalities, in whom the essence of Christian faith has been strong, have been apt to combine with it some element which other Christians, perhaps of equal spiritual calibre, pronounce incongruous. He mentions as examples the neo-Platonic mysticism of some of the great Greek theologians, the predestinarianism of Augustine; instances which some here present will be less likely to dispute, whether it be the anthropomorphism of the early monks of Egypt, the sabbatarianism of the Puritans, the extravagant devotion to the Blessed Virgin of many of the best minds of the Middle Ages and of modern Roman Catholicism, the *furore* of the Crusades, the ultramontane enthusiasm, or the proscription of even moderate use of wine as sinful, will occur variously to different minds. The pure essence of the Christian religion, he continues, does not "occur free in nature," its isolation is the work of the theological laboratory. What we have to learn is that although, if we strip off the bark, the sap will cease to flow, the external element is now one, now another, but that the essence remains always one and the same.[1]

The ages of persecution were the ages of faith, and their faith, in its strength and intensity, carried along with it the incongruous element of millenniarism, an element whose realism we may see to be grotesque, but which, in however grotesque a form, enshrined a genuine religious perception.

In their realistic picture of the coming kingdom of Christ, these simple Christians asserted their conviction that in spite of appearances, this world is God's world, and its history is in his hands: their conviction that the Church of Christ is to inherit the earth, that the chequered and unsatisfactory course of its affairs is to culminate in the triumph of the holy Will of GOD, and that in whatever way, at any rate in some way the temporal will be organically linked on to the eternal.

None the less, millenniarism was certain, sooner or later, to fade out of the Christian consciousness. To begin with, it lacked adequate authority in the New Testament as a whole. Apart from the Apocalypse, the interpretation of which was not beyond question, while influential teachers were ready to concede the millennial interpretation only at the expense of the authority of the book itself, the most clearly formulated eschatological scheme in the New Testament,

[1] Harnack, *Dogmengesch.* iii. 213 sq. note 1.

that of St. Paul, left no place for it.[1] The Jewish features which characterised the belief were increasingly felt to be alien to the spirit of the Greek Churches, and to the spirituality of the Gospel itself. When persecution no longer kept it alive,—when the active hostility of the State no longer counteracted the natural Christian instinct of good citizenship, exemplified in St. Paul,[2]—the old Realistic Eschatology silently melted away.

Once again, intense as was the Christian instinct to which Chiliasm gave articulate form, it was in some respects in latent antipathy to the ecclesiastical spirit, and waned as that spirit gathered strength. This side of millenniarism is apparent in more ways than one. Its rejection by rational theology, and by the trained theologians who filled the more important places in the Greek Churches in the third and fourth centuries, had practically the effect of ranging the clergy in opposition to it. In fact millennarianism, by virtue of its direct appeal to minds of crass simplicity, was a creed for the lay-folk and the simpler sort, and when the religious interest was concentrated upon it, it would indirectly undermine the interest felt in doctrines requiring a skilled class to interpret them. The Apocalyptic spirit is in fact closely akin to the spirit of unregulated prophesying, and the alliance has been apparent, not only in the second century, but in the Middle Ages and in modern times as well.

Once more, a cycle of belief which centred round the imminent return of Christ was essentially out of sympathy with a Church order and organisation calculated for a lasting and permanent state of things.

[1] *Supra*, Lect. II. p. 52.   [2] *Supra*, Lect. III. p. 105 sq.

Finally, whatever causes tended towards the identification of the Kingdom of GOD with the visible Church, for that reason tended to render Chiliasm superfluous by satisfying in another way the fundamental instinct upon which it was founded, — the desire for the realisation on earth of the Kingdom of GOD.

These tendencies were of course not always, perhaps were seldom, present to the minds of the persons through whom they took effect. But men seldom understand fully all that is implicit in their actions, words, or thoughts. And that the tendencies were such as I have stated, the experience of the Christian centuries forbids a doubt.

Now during the second century, in face of the presence of dangerous separatist movements, the organisation of the Church was perfecting itself rapidly; and all who laboured together in this cause,—Chiliasts though they might be, like Irenaeus himself,—were the conscious or unconscious enemies of Chiliasm.

Of the two great dangers which were, by their pressure, hastening the consolidation of the Churches, Gnosticism has already been mentioned incidentally, and it is hardly necessary for our immediate purpose to say much more. But this is not so with the other separatist movement of the second century, known to us as Montanism.

The character and history of the movement are well known, but it may be permitted to recall them briefly. It originated about the year 160 in Western Phrygia, near the country towns of Pepuza and Tymion. The Greek Church knew the movement as that of the people in Phrygia—τῶν κατὰ Φρύγασ—hence the name

"Cataphrygian," the Eastern equivalent of the Latin "Montanist." The latter name was derived from that of the leader Montanus,[1] who with two ladies of good social position, Priscilla and Maximilla, came forward to proclaim and prepare for the approaching Advent of Christ. They protested vehemently against the increasing assimilation of the lives of Christians, and the discipline of the Church, to the standard of the heathen world. Possibly they also complained of the supersession of Prophecy by the organised Ministry; on this point we are not clearly informed. In doctrine they were perfectly orthodox.[2] The extravagant personal claims of Montanus must be ascribed not to any heretical principle, but to a tendency not infrequently seen when religious enthusiasm overthrows mental balance. They were " schismatics," not " heretics."

The main features of Montanism were three. Firstly, the "new prophecy." They proclaimed that the immediate prelude to the return of Christ was to be a signal outpouring of the Spirit, tantamount to a new dispensation, and guided no doubt by the words of Joel, they looked for its fruits in visions, especially

[1] The Latin cast of these names suggests (not Western extraction but) freedom from Greek culture. On the Montanists see Euseb. *H. E.* v. xiv.-xix.; Hippol. *Philos.* x. 21, 22 (*al.* 25, 26); Tertullian, *adv. Prax., de corona, de Pudic.*, etc., and the later heresiologists from Epiphanius onward. Also Bonwetsch, *Montanismus*, and Salmon in *Dict. Chr. Biog.* Montanus is stated to have been a recent convert, and a mutilated ex-priest of Cybele (cf. Catullus, *Atys*). The latter statement, which is not contemporary, we have no means of verifying; the former is not improbable in itself.

[2] Hippolytus can only accuse them of monarchianism (which may have as much foundation as his similar charge against Zephyrinus and Callistus), and of paying excessive heed to the prophecies of Montanus, etc., which was doubtless true.

PRIMITIVE CHURCH AND MILLENNIUM 137

during the assemblies for public worship, and in a revival of the languishing gift of prophecy. Montanus is said to have carried his belief in his inspiration to the pitch of claiming to be identical with the Paraclete; "I am the Father and the Son and the Holy Spirit" are the words ascribed to him by his opponents. The pathology of religious mania makes the accusation just short of incredible.[1] The word "dispensation" is used, but the prophetic outpouring was to be but temporary —the Advent was so near. "After me," cried Maximilla, "there shall be no prophetess more, but the Consummation."[2] Secondly, the Montanists were marked by Puritan Rigorism in morals. They are said to have used the strictest discipline, to have enjoined strenuous fasting, they forbade second marriage, and allowed no lapsed penitent a second place of repentance, should he again fall into grievous sin. They are said to have broken down under persecution in some cases: but this is not to be magnified into an indictment against the whole body.[3] The movement was the first of an unending series of similar movements of protest, some of which we shall have to notice in the sequel; they are all alike in their demand for a

[1] Montanus certainly believed that he was indwelt by the Holy Spirit, and doubtless appealed to passages like John xiv. 17, 23. Such extravagant utterances as ἐγώ εἰμι ὁ πατὴρ καὶ ὁ υἱὸσ καὶ ὁ παράκλητοσ may be invented for him by his opponents, but the transition from indwelling to identification would be possible in so ill-balanced a mind.

[2] The principal phenomena of Montanism are strikingly reproduced in the Abbot Joachim of Fiore. See below, Lect. VII. p. 298.

[3] Their bitterest enemies even when taunting them with having suffered nothing for the Name, admit in the same breath that they have many martyrs (Eus. *H. E.* v. xvi. 20, cf. 12). The evidence for the breakdown of Montanists under persecution belongs to the reign of Decius, when the first zeal of the movement was spent (see below, p. 143, note 1).

more visible enforcement of the Holiness of the Church. The Holiness of the Church must be seen, not in the sacredness of the ordinances but in the lives of her members. The demand of these movements is for a Holy Society, a " spiritual Church-Membership." " The Church," writes their most eloquent spokesman, is strictly and primarily the Spirit: "and accordingly the Church will remit sins, but the Church in the spiritual sense, by the spiritual man, not the Church in the sense of the bench of bishops" (*numerus episcoporum*).[1] The Montanists in fact stand up for ruthless strictness of principle as against the necessities of government, which weighed with the greater Churches in their judicious relaxations of disciplinary severity. Thirdly, the Montanists were, in relation to the coming kingdom of Christ, intense realists. Their entire system was dominated by belief in the close approach of the Second Advent; and they held fast to the conviction that it would inaugurate the Millennial Reign. Montanus himself looked for its establishment in Phrygia. Tertullian, whose Montanism was free from the personal eccentricities of Montanus, speaks of " the kingdom promised to us on earth,—before heaven—in a different state, namely after the resurrection, for a thousand years in the God-created City Jerusalem brought down from heaven."[2]

---

[1] Montanus, expecting the immediate establishment of the Millennial Reign at Pepuza, aimed at gathering all the true Church thither, and appears actually to have organised a food-supply for the purpose (Eus. *H. E.* v. xviii. 2). But this was a feature which was naturally dropped as the movement spread.

[2] *Adv. Marc.* iii. 24. It will be noted that, with an inconsistency common to other millenniarists (cf. Hippol. *de Antichr.* 44), Tertullian here transfers to the Millennial Reign features which in the Apocalypse belong to the *general* Resurrection.

The influence of the Montanist movement spread very wide. Outside Phrygia, indeed, it appears to have laid aside some of its original extravagances; there is no evidence, for example, that the alleged identification of Montanus with the Paraclete was adopted by his followers outside his own region. But we find traces of the movement far and wide. In Gaul its activity is said to have been the occasion of a visit of Irenaeus to Rome, as some think in the cause of toleration, but as others hold to warn Bishop Eleutherus against its danger to the peace of the Church.[1] In Rome itself it seems to have had a not unfriendly reception for a time. Its most prominent representative there, Proclus, was followed from Asia Minor by Praxeas, who succeeded in obtaining its condemnation by the bishop— either Victor or his successor Zephyrinus, but whose own Monarchian teaching, according to Montanist evidence, did more injury to Roman orthodoxy than the teachers whom he successfully opposed.[2] In Africa Montanism made its most brilliant conquests.

---

[1] The relation of Irenaeus to the Montanist movement is very obscure. He would certainly have no sympathy with its desire to found a new schismatic communion (see *Haer.* IV. xxxiii. 6, 7). But his polemic (III. xi. 9) against those who "ut donum Spiritus frustrentur, quod *in nouissimis temporibus* secundum placitum Patris effusum est in humanum genus . . . *propheticum repellunt Spiritum*," etc., is hardly anti-Montanist in its tone. It is probably neutral as regards the new prophecy, and directed against the party known later as "Alogi" (see above, p. 123, note 1). Irenaeus would probably favour treatment of the prophets as gentle as circumstances allowed; and this may well have been the tendency of the representations of the Gallican Christians to Eleutherus (Eus. *H. E.* v. iii. 4; note the terms of their recommendation of Irenaeus, chap. iv.). On the passages in Irenaeus, see Zahn, *Kanon*, i. 240-242.

[2] Tertull. *Adv. Prax.* i.: Duo negotia diaboli Praxeas Romae procurauit, prophetiam expulit et haeresin intulit; Paracletum fugauit et Patrem crucifixit.

Here also, it would seem, many who were in full communion with the Church were deeply influenced by the "new prophecy." The Acts of Perpetua, who suffered with her companions about 202, show unmistakably Montanist features. They are probably from the hand of Tertullian the most eminent Churchman of Africa, and an ardent Montanist.[1] At what date he formally seceded from the Church is uncertain, but eventually he became convinced of the corruption of the official Christianity, and formed a Montanist schism in Africa. His latest writings—*de Pudicitia* for example—are full of bitterness against the laxity of the Church's rulers in dealing with moral offences.

Montanism lasted longer as a schismatic sect than might have been expected from the evanescent nature of its predictions. The last Tertullianist church at Carthage had returned to Catholic unity in the memory of St. Augustine[2]—not therefore much before 390. But clearly this was a late survival. In the East the movement died harder. About A.D. 260 Montanists were still common in Asia Minor.[3] The Edict of Constantine was fatal to many weak sects, and Montanism appears to have survived it only in its native Province. Here, under Justinian, it was stamped out with the cruelty of that degenerate age; the bones of Montanus and the prophetesses were dug up and burned.

[1] See Robinson's edition (*Texts and Studies*, i. 2, 1891), pp. 47-58. That Montanist influence should thus permeate members of the Catholic Church is perhaps less surprising than the fact that Irvingites, the modern antitype of Montanists, in many cases find it possible to remain in communion with the Church.

[2] *De Haer.* lxxxvi.

[3] See Firmilian of Caes. Cappad. in Cypr. *Ep.* 75 (p. 814, Hartel), and p. 137, note 3, above.

PRIMITIVE CHURCH AND MILLENNIUM 141

But its decline was in reality due to its spent vitality. Its one permanent strength, the rigorist demand for a Holy Society, passed into other hands. Novatianism and Donatism satisfied the persistent instinct in the West, in the East it began to find a new channel in the growing attractions of Monasticism. Montanism was left without special recommendations. Prophecy in due time faded away, and Millenniarism was enfeebled by the repeated falsification of its prophecies of the approaching end of the world.

In Montanism, the latent anti-ecclesiastical leaven which we noticed in Millenniarism came conspicuously to the surface. And the campaign against the movement necessarily tended to discredit crassly realistic eschatological hopes. An interesting example of this in the West is the difference between the eschatology of Tertullian and that of Cyprian. Cyprian generously acknowledged Tertullian as his master in theology. Tertullian had in fact taught theology to use the Latin tongue,[1] and Cyprian was in this respect at least his spiritual heir. But Cyprian never speaks of the Millennial Reign of Christ; and where he speaks of the Kingdom of GOD, it is exclusively in the eschatological sense [2] which we have distinguished as primary, and dominant

[1] "The lamp which all runners in the sacred race have received is that which Tertullian lit and Cyprian trimmed" (Benson, *Cyprian*, p. 531). Jerome had met an old man who when very young had seen at Rome Cyprian's secretary, then of advanced age. The latter related "solitum nunquam Cyprianum absque Tertulliani lectione unam praeterisse diem, ac sibi crebro dicere *Da Magistrum*! Tertullianum uidelicet significans" (*de uir. illustr.* liii.). The name of Tertullian does not occur in Cyprian's extant writings.

[2] Cyprian uses "regnum" without the addition "Dei" or caelorum. It is contrasted with the Church on earth; see *De Op. et Eleem.* ix. : Eos Dominus, *cum iudicii dies uenerit, ad percipiendum regnum* dicit admitti

in ecclesiastical tradition,—the sense of the perfected Kingdom of the Father in heaven, after the universal Judgment. And in the East, the decline of Montanism coincided with the rise of that philosophical theology which gave Chiliasm its deathblow in the Greek Church.

Montanism has been at times a subject of controversial debate, and although the controversial interest directly turns upon matters somewhat apart from the present enquiry, it may assist our purpose to consider for a moment a question upon which diametrically opposite opinions have been maintained. Was then Montanism essentially a conservative movement, or was it on the contrary marked by a spirit of reckless innovation? For the latter alternative, appeal is made above all to the " new prophecy "—*nova prophetia*—which was its most conspicuous feature, and to the claim that as the Old Testament represented the dispensation of the Father, the New Testament that of the Son, so the New Prophecy, an advance upon both, signalised the dispensation of the Spirit. On the other hand, and with equal *a priori* reasonableness, it is urged that prophecy was an institution of the Apostolic and of the post-Apostolic age,[1] that the rigorous insistence

qui fuerint in ecclesia eius operati. Also *de Unit. Eccles.* xiv.: Ad regnum peruenire non poterit qui *eam* (sc. ecclesiam) *quae regnatura* est dereliquit. Cf., for the general idea of the kingdom, *de op. et el.* viii. ; *de Dom. Orat.* xxiv., xxxvi. ; *de mortal.* xxvi.

[1] The belief in the continuance of prophecy was kept alive till well into the second century. The daughters of Philip (Acts xxi. 9) were supposed to have ended their days at Hierapolis in Asia, and we hear of a prophet Quadratus (apparently not the Apologist) and a prophetess Ammia in the same region about the reign of Hadrian (Eus. *H. E.* III. xxxvii., v. xvii.). The *Didache* assumes that genuine prophets still exist, and Irenaeus (*supra*, p. 139, note 1) will not hear of prophecy being banished from the Church.

upon the note of Holiness in the Church was in correspondence with the spirit of St. Paul and of St. John, and that the prominence of the perceptible guidance of the Holy Spirit is a marked feature of the Apostolic Church as we see it in the Acts of the Apostles and the Epistles of St. Paul.

The truth appears to be partly on either side. In its motive power, Montanism was intensely conservative and even reactionary. But the movement had its original home in a population little influenced by Greek culture, among a rude and impressionable mountain people. It had something of the character of revivalism; and the tendency of sectarian enthusiasm in such a medium is to overleap established rules and to set aside standards and precedents. That such a movement, reactionary in its first impulse, should develop extravagances and innovations, is not without probability nor without historical parallels.[1]

Certainly, then, its Chiliasm was a highly conservative feature. As the expectation of Christ's Coming was deferred, it could not but grow fainter in men's minds. "The days are prolonged and every vision faileth" was the feeling that irresistibly spread, and as it spread men rested more and more upon an organisa-

The gravamen against the new prophecy was its irrational, ecstatic character (on which see below, p. 144, note 1).

[1] No inference either way can be drawn from the Acts of Bishop Achatius or Acacius in the Decian persecution (A.D. 250), in which the heathen magistrate says to the confessor, "Cataphrygas aspice, *homines religionis antiquae*, ad mea sacra conuersos," etc. (Ruinart, *Acta Sincera*, p. 154, ed. 2). The pagan is not appealing to their conservatism as Christians (as to which he could know nothing), nor to their return to the old gods (which would hardly be likely to move the bishop), but to their character for old-fashioned integrity; cf. Cicero, *pro Caecin.* x., "exemplar *antiquae religionis.*"

tion that would stand the test of indefinite duration. But the Montanist could not brook the thought of the Church settling down peacefully to a tenancy of the present world. "The days are at hand and the effect of every vision" was the protest of an instinct, however narrow and one-sided, yet aboriginally Christian.

Montanism, then, was in certain fundamental respects tenaciously conservative. But clearly those elements of primitive Christian life and conviction which it most jealously conserved were precisely those which were becoming most inevitably outworn. Unlike Gnosticism and many later heretical tendencies which consisted in the fusion of extraneous matter with Christian tradition, Montanism was a movement intensely and exclusively Christian;[1] but it neglected many elements of the original Christian teaching which in the Catholic Church balanced the eschatological realism which at that time still possessed the Christian mind.

[1] The only heathen feature alleged against the Montanists was the "ecstasy," which some of their opponents pointed to as distinguishing their prophets from Christian prophets (Eus. v. xvii. 2, etc.). This was true in itself (1 Cor. xiv. 32); but the exercise of abnormal gifts of utterance in the Church had never in fact been without features of this kind, see 1 Cor. xiv. 14 sq., and St. Paul's warning, *ibid.* xii. 2, 3. And for the legitimacy of ἔκστασισ *per se* the Montanists might have appealed to the precedents of among others Adam, Abraham, David, and Daniel (see Gen. ii. 21, xv. 12; Ps. cxv. 2; Dan. vii. 28, all in LXX). But as the Montanist prophecies were written down and circulated, they can hardly have been wholly incoherent. The claim of Montanus really was that he was but the passive instrument of divine inspiration; this was what Athenagoras held to be characteristic of inspired writers (see Epiph. *Haer.* xlviii. 4; Athenag. *Apol.* ix. οἱ κατ' ἔκστασιν . . . ἐξεφώνησαν, κ.τ.λ.). If Montanus had been, as fourth-century authorities say, a heathen priest, it might no doubt go to explain the type of Christian zeal which he developed; the same might with as much, or as little, justice be said of Pachomius (*supra*, p. 136, note 1, and *infra*, p. 163, note 3).

PRIMITIVE CHURCH AND MILLENNIUM 145

This is specially true of the Puritan rigorism with which the Montanists sought to enforce the ideal of a Holy Church. Nothing, certainly, is clearer than that our Lord established, and the Apostles sought to build up and maintain, a Society whose visible note should be that of Holiness, a holiness not satisfied by mere adherence to sacred and inviolable doctrine, nor by the carrying out in its perfection of a system of rites charged with divine efficacy, but consisting above all in the character and lives of its members. "The temple of GOD is holy, which temple ye are"; "In this the children of GOD are manifest, and the children of the devil: whosoever doeth not righteousness is not of God, neither he that loveth not his brother"; "My little children, these things write I unto you, that ye sin not."[1] And St. Paul expects the Christian community to show their sense of what is due to a holy Society by prompt sentence of exclusion against those who compromise and threaten its character.[2] But the eye of man does not see into the secrets of conduct nor into the depths of the heart. And even where evil is visibly present, its ruthless extirpation must involve the risks of inquisitorial tyranny and of irremediable harm to the soul of the offender. The Lord's parable of the Wheat and the Tares is part of a whole side of his teaching which sets the Church on her guard against replacing the inhuman pedantry of the Scribes and Pharisees by a new legalism,[3] equally inhuman but more dangerous because more insidious.

---

[1] 1 Cor. iii. 17; 1 John iv. 10, ii. 1. [2] 1 Cor. v. 1 sqq.
[3] This side of Montanism is brought out by Harnack, *Dogmengesch.* vol. i. p. 325 sq. and notes (1st ed.).

The problem of the Christian Church, to guard the holiness of the body without transgressing the limits which are incident to all exercise of spiritual authority by frail flesh and blood, is one which calls for infinite tact, infinite wisdom and love, for its beneficial solution. To say this is to say that the problem has never been perfectly solved; at times the solution has erred on the side of severity, more often, especially as the numbers of the Church have increased, on that of leniency. And recollecting the fallibility of man, even when guided by the Spirit of GOD, that surely is the safer side on which to err. But if so, the visible holiness of the Church must suffer the risk of dilution. This is inevitable; the only remedy is to beware of lowering the ideal to the level of the attainable, and not, by transferring the Note of Holiness too entirely to the institutions of the Church, to admit the spirit of legalism by one door in excluding it at another.

The difficulty of this complex but vital problem has been consistently forgotten by all Puritan movements in the Church. One and all have been inspired by a zeal for GOD, but a zeal not according to full knowledge — οὐ κατ' ἐπίγνωσιν.[1] One and all have entered with ardour upon the work of weeding out the tares, one and all have broken the bruised reed and quenched the smoking flax, and in rooting out the tares have rooted out the wheat also.

Had Montanism had its way, it would have made all Christian progress, all durability of the Church impossible; the Christian body would have been

[1] Rom. x. 2.

narrowed down to a fanatical sect at war with reason and civilisation,—and with Christian charity.

The defeat of Montanism was not the annihilation of Millenniarism. But it was the result of a campaign in which the organisation of the Church joined its ranks in the struggle against a separatist movement whose inspiration was rooted in the Chiliastic hope. As a result the party which most energetically asserted the crassly realistic Eschatology was discredited and unchurched; and in the East at any rate men were henceforth set looking for the Kingdom of GOD elsewhere than in the visible reign of Christ over his saints on earth. The Second Advent, it was now increasingly recognised, was to usher in no such reign as Montanus imagined, but the Universal Judgment and the reign of the saints with GOD in Heaven.

And if a reign of Christ on earth was an idea which still demanded satisfaction, was there not the Catholic Church in its advancing empire over the lives and thoughts of men — going forth conquering and to conquer? The identification was obvious, waiting only for one to proclaim it. But the moment was not yet come.[1]

III

But meanwhile the theological activity of the Greek Church was setting in a direction which was inherently hostile to the crude realism hitherto unchecked by any strong counter-tendency within the Church. To the general character of the theological movement of the

[1] See Reuter, *Augustinische Studien*, p. 106 and reff., and below, Lect. V. p. 173 sq.

second century I have already referred.¹ It is impossible to hold or impart the simplest knowledge on any subject, especially in the presence of opposition, without some admixture of theory, and this is especially true of religion. We find then the earliest theology in the form of an interpretation of these elementary facts of Christian belief which were taught as the prerequisite of baptism and which formed the basis of mutual recognition by Christians of different Churches and Provinces—in a word theology grows up as a commentary upon the Regula Fidei,² the creed in its simplest form. This creed is, before all things, a confession of what Christ has done for us. That he died for our sins and rose again the third day are the two articles of the earliest creed of which we know.³ That is to say, the first steps in theology are determined by the way in which men think of the primary need of man and the satisfaction of that need by Christ. The great divergent theologies of later times, orthodox and unorthodox, go back when analysed to distinctive appreciations of what Salvation really consists in. The earliest reflexion upon the Christian creed brought out two prominent thoughts. On the one hand man's mortality, and the disease of sin, in contrast with the immortality which GOD possessed and bestowed through Christ, who as the physician of life

---

¹ *Supra*, p. 130.

² The expression "Rule of Faith" is commonly used nowadays for the criterion, or formal authority, which guides us to the true belief (*e.g.* the authority of Scripture, of the Pope, or the Vincentian canon "quod ubique," etc.). But the ancient Church invariably uses it of the Creed itself: the change is significant of much.

³ 1 Cor. xv. 3, 4 ; cf. Rom. iv. 25.

THEOLOGY AND THE MILLENNIUM 149

could alone heal our disease, and whose flesh and blood were the medicine of immortality. On the other hand, man's need of moral guidance, met by the New Law of Christ, who had superseded the ceremonial law of the Old Testament, and supplemented its moral code by his own higher teaching. The typical representatives of this simple theology are Ignatius and Irenaeus; they are fervently Christian, realistic in their presentation of doctrine, full of profound reflexion, and little coloured by philosophical ideas. It is a theology which aims rather at making intelligible, and defending against current misstatements, the deposit of teaching received from Scripture and tradition, than at correlating it with the knowledge derived from nature or with the intellectual heritage of the time. The same may be said of the one-sided and unorthodox theologies of Marcion and of the second century Ebionites. Marcion is only to a limited extent to be classed as a Gnostic. His theology is rather a caricature of St. Paul. His docetism exaggerates St. Paul's depreciation of a knowledge of Christ after the flesh, and St. Paul's doctrine of the Spiritual Body. His rejection of the Old Testament is a one-sided insistence on the absolute newness of the Christian religion.[1] The Ebionism of the Clementines, on the other hand, is an extreme anti-Pauline form of Jewish Christianity, with elements of Gnostic origin, but probably borrowed through a Jewish channel. But neither Marcion nor the party represented by the Clementines were

---

[1] His doctrine of the "Demiurge" or evil creator of the material world, formed a substructure of dualism for this antithesis. He probably borrowed it from the Gnostic system of Cerdo.

psychologically possible except as aberrant forms of Christian belief.

The Gnostics proper, both in Syria, Egypt, and the West, were on the contrary the product of tendencies with which Christianity had nothing to do.[1] The Syrian Ophites, whom Hippolytus regards as the earliest Gnostics, would appear to have grafted upon a stock of serpent-worship an eclectic admixture of Biblical elements chosen on the strength of superficial coincidences with their essentially Oriental and barbaric theosophy.

The Western Gnostics derived their primary impetus from Basilides, whose system, to judge by the conflicting accounts of it, was a profoundly pantheistic philosophy of the universe, with elements directly or indirectly borrowed from Buddhism.[2] Stripped of its popular and fantastic dressings, the system appears as essentially "monistic," the evolution being imagined as from below upwards. The system of Valentinus differs in greater indebtedness to Greek thought, especially to Plato whose "ideas" it disguised in the mythological forms of Pleroma and Aeons. It is dualistic in contrast to the system of Basilides, the cosmic process being held to consist in an emanation of "Sophia" from the highest Being, involving a fall, and a subsequent return through a process of purification. It was the latter systems, especially that of Valentinus in its many variations, that lent themselves to some degree of semi-Christian syncretism. But throughout,

---

[1] Lightfoot, *Colossians*, p. 78.
[2] On the possibility of this, cf. Lightfoot, *Colossians*, p. 388 sq.; the doctrine of "the great Ignorance" (*Philosophum.* VII. i. 27, Cruice) must be an echo of Nirvana.

THEOLOGY AND THE MILLENNIUM 151

the fusion consists in the taking up, under the theosophic categories of Gnosticism, of words symbols characters and incidents from the Scriptures, often in a purely fanciful way, rather than in any attempt to allow the native meaning of the Bible to work unhampered upon the soul of the reader.[1]

Moreover the Gnostics were not mere speculative teachers; their schools were religious organisations, analogous to the mysteries of ancient Greece.[2] Practically they were from the first rival Churches committed to competition with the Christian Churches; their aim was to convince the doubter that with them he would find whatever healing for his soul the Christian Church had to offer, and in addition satisfaction for the deeper intellectual needs which the simple faith of the Church wholly failed to satisfy. It is therefore only part of the truth to define the Gnostics as "the first Christian theologians," or their position as the "acute Hellenisation" of Christian thought.[3] They represented a tendency which had never been regarded with favour by the representative philosophers of Greece, and which was only now beginning to infect Greek thought in the lower forms of neo-Platonism. Again, it is only by a slight stretch of language that the Gnostics can be spoken of as Christian theologians.

---

[1] It must, however, be remembered that Heracleon, the earliest of commentators on St. John, was from the school of Valentinian. Nor do the extant fragments of his Commentary (Brooke's ed. in *Texts and Studies*, i. 4, 1891) wholly lack the genuine exegetical spirit.

[2] On the religious propaganda of the Mysteries, see Jevons, *Introduction to the History of Religion*, p. 327 sqq., also Anrich, *Das antike Mysterienwesen in s. Einfluss auf das Christentum* (1894), pp. 47, 74-105 (relation to Gnosticism).

[3] Harnack.

They attempted, it is true, a cosmic scheme of thought which should include the Christian creed, but the scheme itself was not Christian, nor properly even theistic, and to include the facts of the Christian creed in such a scheme was to transform their native character. But in their attempts at a comprehensive system of religious thought, grotesque and repellent as those attempts often were, they were in a sense the precursors of the great Alexandrian school; not only does Clement habitually use the term "Gnostic" for the fully instructed Christian, but the theology which appears in its developed form in Origen is an endeavour to satisfy, on the basis of the Rule of Faith, the real needs which Gnosticism professed to meet, and to apply in a rational and purified form whatever genuinely philosophical ideas Gnosticism embodied.[1]

As Christian theologians, however, the Alexandrians were the successors of the Apologists. But while the Apologists had set out to defend the Christian Society, and so incidentally were led to interpret the Christian Faith, the Alexandrians began by study and teaching, and on the basis of their results, turned to attack and defence. Pantaenus was first a teacher, finally a missionary.[2] Origen's *de Principiis* came early in his career, his refutation of Celsus seven years before his death at the age of sixty-nine.

To describe at length the influence of Platonic thought upon the school of Alexandria, and through it upon the Christian Church of all time, is happily

[1] The fundamental difference was that between the *esoteric Church* of the Gnostics, and the *esoteric perception* of the meaning of the *common faith*, at which Clement and Origen aimed.
[2] In "India," *i.e.* probably Abyssinia.

THEOLOGY AND THE MILLENNIUM 153

unnecessary in a Lecturer who can appeal to expositions of this subject by predecessors who speak with authority far beyond his own.[1] I shall be content to specify the particular directions in which the Alexandrian theology appears to have affected the conception of the Kingdom of GOD.

To begin with, the Christian Religion—except in the sense in which belief in GOD as creator and ruler of the world, and of man as a responsible but sinful being, the subject of divine redemption, involves a certain implicit view of existence and life—neither is nor contains a philosophy;[2] yet on the other hand the very limitations under which this fact has been stated suffice to show the impossibility of a consistent statement of all that our faith implies—in other words the impossibility of a system of Theology, without regard to philosophical questions. This being so, every great attempt at a comprehensive scheme of Christian Theology has been necessarily made with the aid of a philosophical method and philosophical categories, independent of the sources of specifically Christian knowledge. The *Summa* of Thomas Aquinas, the characteristic philosophical Theology of the Middle Ages, had as its intellectual basis the theology of Aristotle. Modern systems have been founded on the philosophy of Kant or of Hegel. In the ancient Church, with the exception of the Antiochene schools,[3]

---

[1] Bigg, *Christian Platonists of Alexandria*; Inge, *Christian Mysticism*, Lect. III.

[2] 1 Cor. i. 22, 23, ii. 6 sqq.

[3] This includes the (in many respects widely differing) schools of Lucian (and the Arians), Apollinarius, and Diodorus (see Harnack, *Diodorus*, p. 233 (*T. und U.* xxi. 4, 1901).

whose philosophical apparatus was mainly Aristotelian, the great theologies were Platonic. This is true of the Eastern Church as a whole; it is equally true of the early Western Church, whose first and last great creative thinker was preceded, in the appropriation of Platonic categories as the philosophical instrument of Christian thought, by Victorinus, Hilary, and Ambrose.

Firstly, then, the practical recognition of this necessity involves a sympathetic attitude toward the pursuit of truth, and a belief that it is never carried out in good faith without some degree of Divine aid and benediction. The Alexandrians were the heirs of those Apologists who had proclaimed that either the Christians were now the philosophers or the philosophers had been Christians.[1] However energetically the attacks of hostile philosophers might be repelled, or false philosophies combated, there is something in the genius of higher theology which can hardly live with that indiscriminate scorn for all products of non-Christian thought and life [2] which sustains the longing hope for their destruction in a sudden and divinely-wrought catastrophe. Moreover, it is impossible to carry out any synthesis between philosophy and faith without more or less distinguishing, as the result, between the primary and the secondary elements of Christian conviction. This cannot but be unfavourable to crude Realism, in proportion as the synthesis is sincere.

Now, secondly, the philosophy which the Alex-

[1] Minuc. Felix, *Octav.* xx. See also Justin, *Apol.* I. xlvi., II. viii., xiii. But contrast the vehement condemnation of Philosophy and specially of Aristotle, in Tertullian, *Apol.* xlvi., *de test. anim.* i., *de Praescr.* vii.

[2] See the passages of Tertullian referred to in the previous note.

THEOLOGY AND THE MILLENNIUM 155

andrians pressed into the service of Christian thought emphasised the contrast between the Real, the Absolute, whose sphere was in the region accessible to thought alone, and the material and contingent in which sense finds contact with a faint and far-off copy of the Real. Applied to theology, this tendency may, if unbalanced by other and not less truly philosophical tendencies, have the effect of disparaging the importance of what is conditioned by time and space in comparison with eternal and transcendent realities; in other words of loosening the grasp of faith upon the historical facts of redemption.[1] But even if not pushed thus far, the idealism of Plato predisposes men to distrust whatever belongs to the sphere of the contingent, and to estimate the importance of material facts past, present, or future according as they more or less directly embody eternal truth. When once theology has become imbued with this instinct, eschatological Realism, at any rate in the form in which it prevailed in the second century, is resented as an earthly intrusion into the sphere of things spiritual.

Thirdly, millennarianism derived and retained its hold upon the minds of Christians from the supposed plain and literal sense of Scripture. But the Alexandrian school inherited the exegetical tradition of Philo, in whom Jewish Faith two centuries earlier had joined hands with Platonic philosophy. With his philosophy Philo had learned a method of exegesis, already applied by men of culture to the Greek

[1] This tendency of the Platonism of Alexandria is emphasised by Dr. A. S. Farrar, *Critical History of Free Thought* (Bampton Lectures for 1862), p. 62: " religious facts [lost] in metaphysical idea." But see also Inge, *Mysticism*, pp. 91, 112, etc.

poets,[1] but which Philo systematised and applied with unbridled ingenuity to the interpretation of Scripture itself. We are accordingly prepared to find, and in fact do find, allegorisation in the Exegesis of Scripture before Origen. But it was Origen who gave it a permanent home in the Church as an exegetical method. In no respect did the influence of his school cut more directly at the roots of Millenniarism than in this. For it loosed its sheet-anchor,—naïve literalism in the interpretation of Scripture. And although the principles of Origen found a formidable rival in the exegetical methods of Antioch, the time had gone by when any return to the literal sense of Scripture was likely to restore Millenniarism to the credit it had for ever lost in the Eastern Church.

Origen hardly came into direct conflict with it;[2] but his successor as head of the theological school,[3] Dionysius, who in 247 became the first really illustrious bishop of Alexandria, marks an epoch in the history of the question. He refuted the Millenniarism of one of his suffragans, Nepos, bishop of Arsinoe, and he criticised adversely the internal evidence for the received authorship of the Apocalypse. It could not, he argued, from its style and character, be from the pen of the author of the Fourth Gospel, and as the latter was not doubtful, he concluded that the ascription of the Apocalypse to St. John the Evangelist was due to a confusion of names.

[1] See Hatch, *Hibbert Lectures.*
[2] In *de Prin.* II. xi. he combats grossly materialistic Chiliasm by St. Paul's doctrine of the spiritual body.
[3] A.D. 232. On the friendly controversy with Nepos, see Euseb. *H. E.* VII. xxiv.

THEOLOGY AND THE MILLENNIUM 157

The theology of Origen was hotly attacked, but made its way in spite of all opposition. Certain elements, necessary perhaps to the completeness of his system, but too evidently incompatible with the traditional belief of Christians, were generally abandoned.¹ But relieved of their unwelcome burden, the theology of Origen became the prevalent theology of the East, and Basil and Gregory, the founders of the new orthodoxy of the outgoing fourth century, circulated a manual of Christian doctrine composed of extracts from Origen's writings.² The name of Origen was the battleground of acrimonious debate, and fell into increasing disrepute, but through the Cappadocian fathers his theology in an expurgated form retained its influence upon Greek theological thought. Meanwhile, by the end of the third century, Millenniarism was scarcely treated by Greek theologians as a serious subject. The typical representative of the dominant theology, both in its learning and in its weakness, is Eusebius of Caesarea. The contemptuous way in which he refers,³ on the score of his eschatological realism, to Papias, is a fair measure of the extent to which the millennial hope had now become impossible to the average Greek theologian. Commodian, Victorinus, and Lactantius,⁴ among the chief Latin Church writers of

---

¹ Especially the view of the Universe as destined to return to GOD from whom it had proceeded, and the view of matter as the negation of the Real and Good. The doctrines of universalism, of the pre-existence of Souls, and of the eternity of the Universe, were founded upon this presupposition.

² The *Philocalia*.

³ *Hist. Eccl.* III. xxxix. 13, σφόδρα σμικρὸσ τὸν νοῦν.

⁴ Commod. *Instruct. adv. Gent. deos*, 43, 44 ; Lactant. *Inst.* IV. 12, VII. 24, *Epit.* 71, 72 ; cf. Victorin. Pet. *in Apoc.* and *de Fabrica Mundi.*

this period, show that the West is still largely Chiliastic. Apollinarius (*c.* 370) is an example of the survival of Millenniarism in anti-Origenist circles in the Greek Churches. His ground was adherence to the literal sense of Scripture. But Athanasius, who in some respects is free from the theological spell of Origen, has no trace of Chiliasm in his writings. To him, the Kingdom of GOD is purely and simply the heavenly state to which the saints look forward after the Last Judgment.[1]

IV

One more great factor in the dissolution of Millenniarism remains to be taken account of,—the Christian Empire of Constantine. The events of 311–313, beginning with the edict of toleration by the dying Emperor Galerius, and ending with the edict of Constantine in 313, in which the Emperor practically announced his conversion to Christianity, convinced the Church that her time of suffering was over, and that henceforth the Imperial Power would be the protector, not the destroyer, of her Faith. Constantine, whatever the extent of his conversion,—however superficially he may have grasped the meaning of his new faith, at any rate recognised the Christian Religion as the great Power of the Future, and if only in the interest of his Empire, desired that the Church should be one and powerful. Under his sons the religious equality proclaimed by him was superseded by the establishment of the Church as the State Religion. In the fourth

---

[1] It may suffice to quote *c. Gent.* xlvii. 4, *de Incarn.* lvi. 3, and *in Matt.* vi. 33 (*P. G.* xxvii. 1376).

A CHRISTIAN WORLD 159

century, the Church further assimilated her organisation for purposes of general government[1] to that of the Empire, and the Empire became officially a Christian institution. This meant the collapse of another great support to Realistic Eschatology. The antithesis of the suffering Church and the cruel godless world-power was exchanged for the co-operation of a Christian Empire with an imperial Church.

The illusion of the Christian Empire did not last very long, but while it lasted—and its remains died very slowly—men were necessarily less disposed to long for a visible reign of Christ and his saints on earth. It might well appear for the time that Christ, in the new power and splendour of the Church, was now at last reigning on earth, and Satan bound. Eusebius in his life of Constantine[2] describes to us the entrance of the Emperor in all his splendid array at the Council of Nicea. As the doors were thrown open, and that almost superhuman presence passed between the lines of awestricken bishops to the imperial chair, a thrill passed over the assembly as at the sight of an angel of GOD. The modest and almost cast-down demeanour of the Sovereign subtly enhanced the effect. The scene is typical of the momentary illusion of the Churches. All difficulties were referred to the Emperor for solution, and it was his statesmanlike instinct that conceived the Council of Nicea, as but a few years before he had by a like expedient on a somewhat lesser scale, appeased what threatened to be an equal danger

[1] I refer to the groupings of episcopal dioceses into provinces, exarchies, and patriarchates corresponding to the administrative divisions of the Empire. On the extent of this see Sohm, *Kirchenrecht*, pp. 350-377.

[2] III. x.

to the Churches of the West. But already, at that first imperial intervention in Christian questions, an undercurrent of misgiving was felt. *Quid imperatori cum ecclesia?* was not the utterance of the Catholic and victorious majority, but it gave expression to a feeling which had to be reckoned with in the future.[1]

And indeed the Empire soon began to show its untrustworthiness. Constantine, as long as he lived, would endure no departing from the decision of his great council, but practically he did much to undermine its authority. His sons were not of one mind, and Constantius, who survived to reign over the undivided Empire, was a patron of the Arian cause and persecuted the Catholic bishops. It did not, then, follow that the Emperor, if Christian, would be a Catholic. And there was no certainty that he would be a Christian at all. The illusion of the Christian Empire was but poorly sustained by Constantine himself, it was discredited by Constantius, and destroyed by Julian. We stand here at the parting of the ways. The revival of an actively Christian Empire under Theodosius was the beginning of a new development in the Greek Church, which more and more settled down from the end of the fourth century in the direction of Byzantine "erastianism." The West, on the contrary, never wholly went back to the illusion of the Christian Empire as an embodiment of the kingdom of Christ. From the middle of the fourth century the outlines of a rival and grander ideal begin to gather shape and substance. The papal ideal was very

---

[1] I may be permitted to refer here to the Prolegomena to Athanasius (*Nicene and post-Nicene Library*, 1892), pp. xvii, xlii (cf. lxxvi).

A CHRISTIAN WORLD

many centuries in reaching maturity, but its roots are in the first tentative steps toward centralised ecclesiastical rule which date from the year 343.[1]

In the Western Church, then, the drift of events was setting strongly in the direction of an ecclesiastical, as distinct from an eschatological interpretation of the idea of the Kingdom of GOD. The tendency was practical rather than explicit in thought. In fact it was in the West that the Millennial interpretation, which had died down in the Greek Church, still held its ground till the end of the fourth century.[2]

But the general tendency to its abandonment by the Church is unmistakable; and the Christian instinct, however ardent the faith and hope which looks in patience for the perfect Kingdom of GOD in the world to come, will not forego some ideal which enlists the enthusiasm of effort for the realisation of GOD'S Kingdom on earth as the highest object of personal aspiration. In the West, where Christian religion was already most practical and energetic, and where it was destined to receive the whole-hearted allegiance of races more gifted and virile than any whose life it had

---

[1] The reasons for regarding the Sardican canons as marking an epoch have been stated in a short essay on *Roman Claims to Supremacy* (S.P.C.K. 1896, for Church Historical Society), part iv. (and part iii. on the claims of Julius I.).

[2] We trace it in Pelagius (*c.* 410), who held that unbaptised infants, though not deprived of eternal life, were excluded from the Kingdom, and more strongly in Tyconius the Donatist (*c.* 370, *Reg.* v. in Burkitt's ed., *T. and S.* iii. 1, 1894, pp. 56, 61). But in Primasius (*c.* 540), who used Tyconius' commentary on the Apocalypse, it has disappeared, doubtless under the influence of Augustine. Possibly this process had begun in Tyconius himself; for his commentary, *as it reached Gennadius* (*de vir. ill.* xviii. *c.* A.D. 495), shows strong traces of the new view stated by Augustine (see below, Lect. V. p. 171 sqq.).

up till now controlled, the immediate future was assured to the ecclesiastical ideal of the Kingdom of GOD in the form of an omnipotent Church.

A movement was already in full progress which at first made in a contrary direction, but which very soon lent to the new direction of men's hopes and efforts an indispensable element of organisation and leadership.

When the wonderful development of the monastic life in the Egyptian deserts had begun to be the talk of Christendom, a Gallican Churchman, John Cassian, visited the fathers of the wilderness in order to see for himself what this thing might be. In reply to one of his first enquiries, as to what had led these men out into the desert, he received the answer: "We have come to seek the Kingdom of GOD."[1] The answer is significant of much. The earlier hermits had fled from a cruel world, from the persecutions of the heathen, from the responsibilities of worldly possessions, from the temptations of social life; they went to seek GOD in solitude, their search was for the Kingdom of GOD within them. The movement toward the hermit life was not merely a condemnation of ordinary human society, but of life in the ordinary brotherhood of Christians, as no fit sphere for the earthly reign of Christ. Isolated from the common offices of the Church, and sharing but rarely either in common Christian teaching or in the ordinary means of grace, the first and obvious tendency of the μονάζοντεσ was towards an individualistic conception of the Kingdom

---

[1] Cassian, *Collat.* I. iii., iv. But in II. vi. the kingdom of heaven is taken by Abbot Chaeremon simply of Reward in the Life to come.

A CHRISTIAN WORLD 163

of GOD diametrically opposite to that toward which Western Christendom was moving. But the hermit movement soon diminished in importance beside the growth of monastic societies; and even an Antony, separate as his life was from the visible organised Church, was united to that Church by the strongest ties of veneration on the one side, and of spiritual sympathy on the other.[1] And the influence of later solitaries shows that their aloofness from ordinary Church life was compensated by immense power on the exceptional occasions when they deigned to intervene in its affairs.[2] On the whole then, the hermits as a factor in the history of our question, merge in the broader and stronger current of organised Monachism.

The beginning of monastic societies appears to have been nearly as early as that of solitary Monasticism, and to have sprung from a parallel and independent source.

Pachomius founded societies of monks in Upper Egypt as early as the time of Constantine,—upon what model, if any,[3] it is not easy to say for certain. The foundation of such a society was inspired in part by the same ideal as that of Antony or of Cassian's in-

---

[1] See Preface to Life of Antony in *Athanasius* (Nicene Library), pp. 190-193; cf. also p. 503, X.

[2] *E.g.* Symeon the Stylite's correspondence with the emperor, Euagr. *Hist*. II. x.; cf. I. xiii. (p. 266), v. xxi. fin. (the younger Symeon), VI. xxiii.; Aphraates in Thdt. *H. E.* IV. xxiii.

[3] It has been held that Pachomius had been a monk of Serapis, and that he modelled his new institute upon the Serapeum. If the former fact were certain (and the evidence for it appears somewhat slender), the latter would not follow of necessity. See *Athanasius* (*ut supra*), p. 193, sub fin., and works referred to *ibid.* p. 188; Krüger in *Th. Literaturzeitung*, 1896, p. 620; Grützmacher, *Pachomius*, etc. (1896); Ladeuze, *Étude sur le Cénobitisme Pakhomien*, p. 157 sq. (Louvain, 1898. Strongly against any connexion of P. with Serapeum).

formant, the ideal of the perfect life, of the Kingdom of GOD within. But it added to the inspiration of Antony the perception that the perfect life is hardly to be obtained in solitude. It was a great and real advance to substitute for the dream of solitary perfection that of a perfect society. The vision of a perfect society to be realised on earth is fertile of noble effort, and it has had a long and varied history. If our Lord's teaching is borne in mind, we shall not dare to count upon its actual realisation here below, but none the less our effort, if true to his inspiration, will never swerve from that direction. And Monasticism has this further true spiritual perception, that the ideal of perfection towards which Christ directed our aim is perfection of character rather than mere institutional completeness of organisation.[1] It may be that, equally with the hermits, the monastic communities made a mistake in their despair of the holiness of the visible Church, in seeking a holy Society not in the Church as such, but in a special enclosure within it. That mistake was at any rate natural in an age when the world, hitherto contentedly heathen, was transferring itself in mass to the Church, where it went on contentedly Christian. Be that as it may, the double standard [2] of Christian life—one for the monk, another for the laity, with the clergy hovering between the two, some on one

[1] Cassian's *Collations*, and, I would add, the Sermon in the Life of Antony, are witnesses to the strong moral aim which, however mingled with heterogeneous elements, penetrated early Egyptian Monachism.

[2] See the letter of Pope Siricius, A.D. 385, to Himerius. He enforces clerical celibacy on the ground that "they who are in the flesh cannot please God" (Rom. viii. 8; compare with the context in Romans the two ominous assumptions (1) that the married life is "in the flesh," (2) that to "please God" is a distinctively clerical obligation).

A CHRISTIAN WORLD

side some on the other, became established just at a time when the general level of Christian morality was becoming imperilled [1] by the rapid absorption of the degenerate population of the Greco-Roman world. Moreover the monks, who by the action of Cassian, of Augustine, and of many others rapidly became acclimatised as an institution of the Western Church, proved a much-needed reinforcement to the zeal of the Latin West in dealing with the Teutonic races that soon were to become its masters. The monks of the West were by their numbers, their organisation, their devotion, to play a primary part, first in preserving the ecclesiastical hierarchy from total secularisation and discredit in the storms of the dark ages, and then, when order began to emerge from confusion and learning from utter barbarism, in enabling the popes of the eleventh century to turn into reality the ideal—dimly perceived by the greatest thinker of early Latin Christendom—of the Kingdom of GOD upon earth in the form of an all-powerful Church.

[1] This comes out, for example, in Augustine's letters to Count Bonifatius. Practically the alternative to a lax morality is the monastic state. Marriage is treated as a step in the former direction (*Ep.* 220. 4. See also the article on Augustine referred to in the next Lecture, § 15).

LECTURE V

THE KINGDOM OF GOD IN ST. AUGUSTINE

This is Christianity, a spiritual Society, not because it has no worldly Concerns, but because all its Members, as such, are born of the Spirit, kept alive, animated, and governed by the Spirit of GOD. It is constantly called by our LORD the Kingdom of GOD, because all its *Ministry* and *Service*, all that is done in it, is done in Obedience and Subjection to *that Spirit*, by which Angels live and are governed in Heaven. The Kingdom of CHRIST, is the Spirit, and Power of GOD, dwelling and manifesting itself in the Birth of a new inward Man; and no one is a member of this Kingdom, but *so far* as a true Birth of the Spirit is brought forth in him.

W. LAW.

    And then at last our bliss
    Full and Perfect is,—
    But now begins; for from this happy day
    The old Dragon under ground
    In straiter limits bound,
    Not half so far casts his usurped sway,
    And, wroth to see his Kingdom fail
    Swinges the scaly horror of his folded tail.

MILTON.

LECTURE V

THE KINGDOM OF GOD IN ST. AUGUSTINE

> We know in part and we prophesy in part. But when that which is perfect is come, that which is in part shall be done away.—1 COR. xiii. 9.

OF the three alternative conceptions of the Kingdom of GOD distinguished in the previous Lecture,[1] the primary and ultimate one has dominated the thought and the prayers of the Church at all times without distinction. The other two have prevailed side by side with it, and in acknowledged subordination to it; but to an unequal extent, and for unequal lengths of time. The history of the conception of the Kingdom of GOD relates mainly to these more variable elements. Its history in the early Church is the history of the prevalence and decline of Millenniarism. It ends with St. Augustine. The history of the medieval idea of the Kingdom of GOD and of its more modern interpretations is, mainly, the history of the theology and constitution of the Church. It begins with St. Augustine.

Augustine, as a Western Churchman, inherited a refined and spiritualised Millenniarism, which later reflexion led him deliberately to abandon. Preaching

[1] *Supra*, p. 119.

on a certain first Sunday after Easter,[1] he dwells on the significance of the "Octave" of the feast. The eighth day, he says, symbolises the final rest of the saints in heaven, whereas the Sabbath, or seventh day, corresponds to the coming millennial rest of the saints on earth. "The Lord will reign on earth, as the Scriptures say. . . ." There have been, from the Creation to the first coming of Christ, five *millennia* or week-days of history. "Ab adventu Domini sextus agitur,—in sexto die sumus."[2]

But reflexion on the events of his time, and the pressure of controversy, especially with the Donatists and the Pelagians, led him, as he tells us, to a change of mind. Writing about 420,[3] he distinguishes the "first resurrection" from the second, as the resurrection of the soul, under grace, from the resurrection of the body at the Universal Judgment.

"Of these two resurrections," he continues, "John the evangelist, in the book called Apocalypse, has spoken in such a way that the first resurrection has been misunderstood by some of our people and turned into certain ridiculous fables. . . . Those who, on the strength of the above words, have surmised that the first resurrection would be a corporal one, have, among other reasons, been mainly moved by the number—a thousand years—as though there were destined to be a Sabbath rest of that duration for the saints, a holy vacation after six thousand years of labour, . . . as it is written 'One day is with the Lord as a thousand years,

---

[1] *Serm.* 259. The date of this sermon is unknown, but it is evidently prior to Augustine's change of mind (*infra*, p. 171).

[2] On this scheme see above, pp. 125, 126, note 1, 129.

[3] *de Civ. Dei*, xx. vii.

ST. AUGUSTINE AND MILLENNIUM 171

and a thousand years as one day'[1] . . . and that the saints are to rise again to keep this Sabbath. Which opinion would be at least tolerable, if it were understood that the saints would enjoy certain spiritual delights from the presence of the Lord. *For we ourselves were formerly of this opinion.* But when they say that those who then rise again will spend their time in immoderate carnal feastings—in which the quantity of food and drink exceeds the bounds not only of all moderation but of all credibility,[2]—such things cannot possibly be believed except by carnal persons." Accordingly, he now explains the first resurrection as the resurrection of souls from the death of sin to faith in Christ, the binding of Satan as the limitation of his power to the hearts of the wicked, and the thousand years as the interval between the first and second Advent. During this period the true saints, even on earth, reign with Christ:[3]—

" Excepting, of course, that kingdom, of which he will say at the last: Come ye blessed of my Father, possess the kingdom prepared for you,—unless in some manner, of course far inferior, his saints, of whom he says: 'Behold I am with you even to the consummation of the world,' were even now reigning with him, certainly the Church would not be spoken of,[4] even now, as the

---

[1] See above, p. 125, note 1.   [2] See above, p. 127 sq.

[3] *de Civ. Dei*, xx. ix. For the details of Augustine's exegesis here, see Reuter, p. 114 sqq.

[4] *I.e.* by our Lord in the sayings and Parables to which he proceeds to refer. Augustine is *arguing for an interpretation of the Gospels, not appealing to language current in his day.* This is overlooked by Reuter, *August. Studien*, p. 111 and elsewhere. In this Lecture my obligations to Reuter's most accurate and impartial investigations will be apparent to every student. I cannot overstate them; but I have never followed even Reuter blindly or without verification.

kingdom of Christ, or kingdom of Heaven. For of course it is *in the present* that the scribe, of whom we spoke above, is instructed in[1] the kingdom of Heaven ... and it is *from out of the Church* that those reapers are to collect the tares ... 'the Son of man shall send his angels and they shall gather *out of his kingdom* all things that offend.'" He goes on to draw the same inference from the passage "whosoever shall break one of the least of these commandments and shall teach men so, the same shall be called least in the kingdom of heaven,"—as contrasted with the warning that "except your righteousness exceed the righteousness of the Scribes and Pharisees ye shall in no case enter into the kingdom of heaven." He continues "accordingly the kingdom of heaven is to be taken in two senses. In one sense it contains both,—him who breaks and him who keeps,—but the one least, the other great. In the other sense there is the kingdom of heaven into which only he enters who keeps the commandment. The kingdom which contains both is the Church as it now is. The other is the Church as it shall be, since there will be no evil person there. Accordingly even now the Church is the kingdom of Christ, and the kingdom of heaven. *That is to say even now his saints reign with him*, not indeed in the same way as they will reign then. Nor yet do the tares reign with him, although in the Church they are growing with the wheat. . . . Lastly, *they* reign with him, who are *in* his kingdom in the sense that they *are* his kingdom. For how are *they*

---

[1] But the Greek is εἰσ not ἐν (T.R.), or the virtually equivalent dative, without ἐν. On the passage see above, Lect. III. p. 81.

ST. AUGUSTINE AND MILLENNIUM 173

the kingdom of Christ who, to say nothing of other points, although they are there until all things that offend are gathered out of his kingdom until the end of the world, yet, while there, seek their own, and not the things of Jesus Christ?" Augustine, then, has abandoned Millenniarism even in its most refined form, and has adopted in its place, on the basis of the biblical distinction between the reign of Christ now and the reign of GOD hereafter, an identification of the kingdom of Christ with the Church as it now is.

It is very commonly said [1] that Augustine identified the visible Church with the Kingdom of GOD, and that he was the first to identify the two. The two statements are both correct only under certain limitations.

As to the latter point, it will have appeared from what has been said in former Lectures [2] that the identification of the Church with the kingdom of Christ was no invention of Augustine. It was prepared for by the whole course of Christian thought on the subject, and the decline of Millenniarism simply removed an obstacle from a development which was certain to come about. The close relation of the Church to the kingdom of Christ, which we found both in our Lord's teaching and in that of St. Paul, must above all be borne in mind here. But the fact that neither our Lord, nor St. Paul, nor any early Christian writer

---

[1] *E.g.* Hort, *Christian Ecclesia*, p. 19; Ritschl, *Unterricht*, § 11, note: "Am meisten falsch ist, sie *wegen einer bestimmten rechtlichen Verfassung* als das Reich Gottes zu bezeichnen, was die römisch-katholische Kirche *seit Augustin* für sich in Anspruch nimmt." The italics are mine. This is apparently what is spoken of (*e.g.* by Hatch, *Bampton Lectures*, Preface to ed. 2) as the "Augustinian idea" of the Church.

[2] See Lect. II. pp. 55 sq. and 75 sq.; and Lect. IV. pp. 147, 161.

before Augustine[1] is known to have stated in so many words the identification between the two, is important, both in itself, and as bearing upon the question of St. Augustine's influence. Assuming, as we must assume, that the eschatology of Justin Martyr, Papias, Irenaeus, and even of Augustine himself in his earlier days as a Christian, was the inevitable, but mistaken and transitory, outcome of a realism natural to simple faith in the absence of corrective experience, and that its disappearance left unsatisfied a genuine Christian instinct, the demand for a tangible interpretation of the Kingdom of GOD as an object of present effort and as a now living fact,—it was a problem imposed upon serious Christian thought to bring the conception of the Church into relation with that of the Kingdom of GOD. It only surprises us that the formal attempt to do so was so long delayed. But the activity of Christian thought had been, by the tendency of speculation and by the presence of controversies, so far directed to the objective and transcendent, to the relation of GOD and the Universe, of the historical Christ to the eternal Father, the relation of the Unity of GOD to the Trinity of Persons.

Belief in the Catholic Church was, it is true, among the articles early incorporated in the baptismal creed;[2] this was necessary in order to guard the catechumens

---

[1] "Erst er ist—wie man *vermuten* darf—der Producent der Formel geworden," Reuter, p. 110. An ingenious Roman correspondent of Augustine's friend Casulanus, about A.D. 397, furnishes the only exception I can recall (*Ep.* 36. 17).

[2] See Swete, *Apostles' Creed*, p. 73 sqq. It is interesting to note that among the Valentinian "Aeons" *Ecclesia* occupied a prominent place (Hipp. *Philos.* VI.).

against the pretensions of rival bodies. But in the East, the questions in controversy had been discussed upon their merits; authority was invoked, but it was the authority of Scripture, and of the Apostles as exhibited in the Rule of Faith.[1]

The schismatic movements, however, had early begun to concentrate interest upon the Church and its distinguishing marks—its "notes." But at first the process was practical and implicit, not formally theoretical. Montanism even more than Gnosticism sharpened the Catholic self-consciousness of the Church in contrast to particularist movements. But even in Cyprian, who felt the pressure of the still more formidable Novatian schism, there is still no identification of the Church with that Kingdom of GOD for which it is the preparation. "He cannot," so Cyprian writes,[2] "hope to reach the kingdom, who deserts her (the Church) who *is destined* to reign."

The relation between the two is close and defined; but it is one of preparation, not of identity. Cyprian's thought is substantially, as we shall see, identical with that of Augustine himself. The difference is simply that Augustine, on the basis of a systematic exegesis of the New Testament, subordinates to Cyprian's simple eschatological conception of the kingdom a historical reference, and places the resulting conception in relation with a wide and deep doctrinal context and with a far-reaching religious philosophy of history.

It was schism, then, rather than heresy, that first

---

[1] On this *supra*, p. 148, note 2. On the general principle see August. *c. Maximianum*, II. xiv. 3; cf. also Athanasius (*ut supra*), pp. lxxiv, lxxv.

[2] See above, Lect. IV. p. 141, note 2.

presented to the mind of Churchmen the issues that are involved in the analysis of the idea of the Church, and it was mainly in Africa, the province of Augustine, that the first formal answer was given by Christian theology to the challenge of pure and simple schism, disengaged from any doctrinal issues. Cyprian, and a century later Optatus, deal with this question; they enforce the principles of unity and of catholic communion against separatist pretensions, and Cyprian in particular dwells upon the authority of the collective Episcopate. But their interest is practical,[1] not theological; they have not gone back to the essential conception, not laid the foundations of a systematised theology of the Church.

This was reserved for Augustine. Although therefore we cannot say, in the face of the strong drift of converging tendencies of thought, and of the notorious risks [2] of an argument from silence, that no one before Augustine, in writing or in speech, spoke of the Catholic Church as the Kingdom of GOD, the fact remains that extant literature records no instance of such language, and this fact becomes intelligible when we notice that Augustine grounds the identification upon a revision of received exegesis, and that it is with him part of a new theological analysis—the analysis of the conception of the Church.

But the question which is really more important and difficult than that of the pre-Augustinian use of the words is that of Augustine's own thought on the sub-

[1] As to Cyprian, see the excellent passages in Reuter, p. 233, and Benson, *Cyprian*, p. 530.
[2] Reuter, p. 109.

ST. AUGUSTINE AND MILLENNIUM 177

ject, and of his influence upon Christian posterity. That he identified the Kingdom of GOD with the Catholic Church is a commonplace of popular theology; and it is commonly assumed as a matter of course that this identification involved the conception of the Kingdom of GOD as identifiable with the hierarchically organised body,[1] whose authority, canons, and discipline are all thereby conceived of as the authority, the laws, and the administration of a kingdom, differing from earthly kingdoms in this respect, that while they and their laws are human, this kingdom is divine, and its laws divine laws. Possibly it was this conception of the Kingdom of GOD to which, in the circumstances of the immediately succeeding centuries, Augustine's influence supplied the intellectual stimulus. But the way in which, in the passage quoted above, Augustine elaborates his identification, suggests at least a doubt whether his real meaning was that just suggested. It is true that, in working out the details of exegesis of the Apocalypse, when he comes upon the words "I saw thrones (*sedes*), and they sate upon them, and judgment was given unto them," he interprets them of "what, during those thousand years, the Church is doing, or what is done in her.... This is not to be taken of the last judgment, but we must understand it of the thrones of the officers (*praepositi*) or of the officers themselves by whom the Church is governed ... [and the 'judgment' probably of the power of binding and loosing, cf. 1 Cor. v. 12]." But he says nothing to specially connect these *sedes* with the thought of

[1] See p. 173, note 1, *supra*.

reigning. On the contrary, the reference to the "sedes" comes in, in passing, as a detail of minor exegesis,[1] whereas in the entire context before and after, the Reign of Christ is referred not to any rank or office in the Church, but to truth of Christian character. The Church is now the kingdom of heaven and kingdom of Christ, *because* Christ is reigning in his true saints, and because they are in a real, though not in the perfect sense, reigning with him. The unworthy members of the Church, the tares, are not reigning in any sense, they are *in* the kingdom "donec colligantur," but not of it. Clearly then the "*reign*" with Christ, in so far as it is a present fact, is what constitutes the existing Church the kingdom of Christ, and this reign with Christ is the lot of all true Christians, whether *praepositi* or not; and if *praepositi* belong to the tares, as they may, they are not "eo modo in regno eius ut sint etiam ipsi regnum eius." It is important to enquire, then, whether the interpretation which pervades St. Augustine's exegesis of the millennial passage in the Apocalypse, or that which refers the Church's character as "regnum Christi" to her government by *praepositi*, to the exercise in her of organised authority, on the whole represents the mind of Augustine. Is the Church identified by him with the Kingdom of GOD because in her the saints reign with Christ, or because she is hierarchically governed?

To begin with, we must notice that even in the act of superseding the crude eschatological interpretation of the Reign of Christ in favour of what we may provisionally call the ecclesiastical conception of it, he

[1] See Reuter, pp. 111 sqq., especially 118-120.

ST. AUGUSTINE AND MILLENNIUM 179

makes a large reserve in favour of the primary and ultimate sense, the sense alone known, as we have seen, to Cyprian. The contrast which Cyprian draws between the Church as present and the Kingdom of GOD as future is maintained by Augustine, and colours his language in an important class of passages, in which the Kingdom of GOD is spoken of as future simply. It is hardly necessary to quote examples.[1]

Secondly, the contrast marked, in his comment on the Apocalypse as quoted above, between the "ecclesia qualis nunc est" and the "ecclesia qualis tunc erit" is characteristic of a class of passages, of which the following from the *Retractations* may serve as a sample:[2]—

"Wherever in these books I have mentioned the Church as not having spot or wrinkle, it is not to be taken as now existing, but of the Church whose existence is being prepared." Again, to anticipate a subject to be discussed below, he distinguishes, in a third class of passages, between the *civitas Dei* on earth, and on the one hand the *civitas superna*, its counterpart now in heaven, on the other hand the completed *civitas* in the eternity to come.[3] In a fourth class of passages[4] he more or less definitely

---

[1] See quotations already made, and, for example, *de s. Virginitate*, vi. 6, "ecclesia uero in sanctis regnum caelorum *possessuris.*" Also the numberless passages in which the "Regnum" is equated with "Vita aeterna." The classification is Reuter's.

[2] *Retract.* II. xviii.; cf. *de Civ. Dei*, XX. ix.; *Serm.* 259. 2, 3, etc.

[3] *de Civ. Dei*, II. xxix. : Superna ciuitas . . . ubi uita aeternitas. XV. ii.: Umbra sane quaedam ciuitatis huius. . . . seruiuit in terris. . . . *Serm.* 214. 11 : sanctam quoque ecclesiam matrem uestram *tamquam* supernam Ierusalem sanctam ciuitatem Dei honorate. *Serm.* 223. 9; *Enchirid.* xix., xx.

[4] *de Civ. Dei*, XXII. xix.; *de pecc. mer. et remiss.* II. i. 1, III. xii. 21; *c. duas Epp. Pel.* I. xxi. 40; *Serm.* 71. ii. 4, and elsewhere.

and directly identifies the Church on earth with the Kingdom of GOD. The difficulty of reducing all passages of these four classes to a single consistent sense is in part due to the alternation in his mind of two conceptions of the Church itself, to be referred to hereafter, which Augustine never completely synthesised. But the general sense is sufficiently clear from the following passage:[1]—

"What resource have they left, but to assert that the kingdom of heaven itself belongs to the present life in which we now are? For why should not their blind presumption proceed to this madness also? And what could be more senseless than such an assertion? For although even the Church now existing is sometimes called the Kingdom of the heavens, it is of course so called because it is being gathered for the future and eternal life."[2] In other words the Church as it now is may be called the Kingdom of GOD, in so far as it consists of those of whom the true Kingdom of GOD is being made up.

So far, then, the thought of Augustine seems clear and consistent. His conception of the Kingdom of GOD as existing now on earth is determined by, and subordinated to, his conception of that Kingdom in its perfection hereafter. The same applies to his conception of the Church. The Church "qualis tunc erit" is primary, and the real nature of the Church in her present imperfection is to be understood by reference to it. Moreover the Church "qualis tunc erit" is identified by him with the Kingdom of GOD in its perfection, which shall include all good and exclude all

[1] *de Virginit.* xxiv.   [2] Cf. *in Joann. Tr.* lxviii. 3.

evil. The Church and the Kingdom are there perfect, and the identification is correspondingly perfect. But it would naturally follow that there should be a corresponding but imperfect identification—" alio aliquo modo longe quidem impari "[1]—between the Kingdom of Christ in its imperfection and the Church " ut nunc est in terra." So far we have included, in a simple statement, with one exception (namely, the relation between the *civitas Dei* on earth and the now existing *civitas superna*), the gist of the four classes into which Augustine's language on the Church and the Kingdom of GOD may be disposed, and it remains to enquire whether the indeterminate relation—" aliquo modo "— between the Kingdom of GOD and the Church of Christ on earth is more clearly brought out by Augustine elsewhere.

II

But this enquiry involves a more comprehensive survey of St. Augustine's religious and intellectual development, and of his outlook upon the theological and historical problems of his time.

To gather up into a single and at the same time a just impression the many sides of a many-sided thinker is never an easy task. When the special distinction of that thinker is religious genius the task is doubly difficult. And in no instance is it less easy than in the case of Augustine, the most commanding religious personality of the ancient Church,—perhaps of the Church in any age. To the subtle philosophical perception of an Origen,[2] he added a concentration of

[1] *de Civ. Dei*, xx. ix.   [2] See Reuter, p. 101.

interest upon the realities of life and a sense of the immanent reason of historical development which kept him in heartfelt sympathy with the practical life of the Church, and assured Churchmen that whether or not they understood him,[1] he understood them, and was at one with them. If he lacked the naïve picturesqueness and practical power of a Francis of Assisi, he added to all his love of GOD and of GOD'S creatures a command of thought to which Francis made no claim, and an intellectual influence which is hard to measure. If he falls below Luther in the freshness and reality of his grasp of some vital elements of New Testament religion, is he not incomparably above him in humility and refined self-discipline, in versatile intellectual sympathy, and in the universality of his appeal to the spiritual nature of man?

If it is impossible, without unduly emphasising or suppressing here and there, to state Augustine's convictions in strictly harmonious coherence, it is perhaps because he perceived, as none had perceived before him, consequences of axiomatic truths which inevitably lead the finite mind of man into insoluble oppositions —oppositions synthesised in his case in the harmony of a rich personality, but destined to reveal their antagonism under intellectual analysis, or when in the course of history men have endeavoured to act them out.

(*a*) Augustine, then, is before all things an intensely experimental Theist. The thirst for the living GOD

[1] Cf. *Ep.* 214. § 6 ; *de dono Perseu.* xvi. : "Sed alia est ratio uerum tacendi, alia uerum dicendi necessitas . . . quantum tamen est et haec [causa tacendi] una, ne peiores faciamus eos qui non intelligunt, dum uolumus eos qui intelligunt facere doctiores."

runs through all the restless tossings of his soul in earlier life, and his Christian experience is that of one who has drunk deep and is satisfied, but yet thirsts again.[1] *Bonum est mihi adhaerere Deo.* He cleaves to God not merely with heart and will but with the reasoned conviction of the intellect as well. Many, before and since, have reached a philosophic idealism as absolute as that of Augustine; but never, surely, was philosophical idealism [2] more completely absorbed into living religious experience than it was by him. That absolute reality belongs to GOD alone, that the reality of things in time and space, of the whole order and course of this world, is derivative and in a sense illusory, that the Phenomenal is but a faint reflexion of the Real and incapable of altering the unchanging Reality which centres in GOD himself, that in finding GOD the soul finds her only stable foundation in Reality, —all this was to Augustine not merely a philosophical creed, but the persistent foundation of his personal religion and of much of his theological thought as well. As applied to history, it leads Augustine to the thought that all religions are but more or less imperfect expressions of one essential religion,[3] now known to us as the Christian religion, by which the members of the *civitas superna* have ever been guided to their divine home by the Christ whose presence has never been wanting in the world. As applied to the Church, it tempers his strong insistence on the preroga-

---

[1] *Conf.* x. xxvii. : "Gustaui, et esurio et sitio" (cf. Ecclus. xxiv. 21).

[2] I would refer the reader to an article on Augustine in the forthcoming one-volume edition of Smith and Wace's *Dictionary of Christian Biography*, § 16*a*. I shall in the sequel refer to the article in question as "Aug."

[3] Aug. § 16*a* fin. (and see below, p. 199).

tives of the visible organised body by setting over against it the heavenly and eternal Church, the reality of which the society on earth is the shadow. And in the doctrine of grace, it accounts not wholly but unquestionably in part for his increasing insistence upon the eternal predestinating Will of God to which the salvation of man is in the ultimate resort carried back.

Augustine's idealism was rooted in his personal religious history. The Platonic philosophy had, by destroying his early materialism, brought him intellectually within range of the appeal of the Catholic Church,[1] which had always found an echo in his heart of hearts; it had been supplemented rather than superseded by the preaching of Ambrose who was the chief human instrument in his conversion; and it remained as the philosophical substratum not only of his theology but of his intimate spiritual conviction, of his communion with GOD. There is then, in reserve, throughout Augustine's utterances on doctrinal and even practical questions, this element of abstract idealism,—the appeal to transcendental reality, to the aspect of things as viewed *sub specie aeternitatis*.

(*b*) But secondly Augustine did not live in the atmosphere of abstractions. On the contrary, no Christian has ever given himself with more single-hearted allegiance to the Church as he found it and to the course of practical Church Life.[2] He does not need to arrive at an ideal Church by *a priori* construction. What has made him a Christian is the appeal of the Church as it actually is: "The grandeur of her

---

[1] See *Conf.* VII. ix. etc.; *de vit. Beat.* i. 4, and Aug. § 5.
[2] Aug. § 16*b*.

ELEMENTS OF AUGUSTINIANISM 185

organisation, the ordered ranks of her Episcopate, the authoritative tradition, superseding individual enquiry, the uniformity of her dogma in the face of all error and variations of opinion, the majesty of her mysterious rites, the rich resources of her means of grace." [1] Augustine's was not a nature to be satisfied with abstract idealism, imagination and devotion demanded a satisfaction which he found in the practical life of the Church. His personality found its necessary freedom of scope for action, and its equally necessary limitation, in the environment of a life which he felt to be immeasurably greater than his own. When he says [2] that he should not be a believer in the gospel unless the authority of the Catholic Church moved him to believe, he is not insisting on dogmatic or hierarchical authority as a court of appeal on doctrine; what he has in his mind is the immanent authority of the Church, as seen by him, as a witness to the truth of the Christian Religion.[3] In other words Augustine was in a sense a Catholic before he became a Christian. This being so, his Catholic Churchmanship was not only a matter of intellectual conviction but of deep habitual emotion. He owed his whole self to his conversion, and his conversion he owed to the silent argument of the Catholic Church. By the Church is inspired all that incomparable warmth of love, grati-

---

[1] Reuter, p. 98. [2] *c. Ep. Fund.* 6 (written in 397).
[3] *Conf.* VI. xi. 19: Pereant omnia, et dimittamus haec uana et inania; conferamus nos ad solam inquisitionem ueritatis. . . . Non uacat, non est inane quod *tam eminens culmen auctoritatis Christianae fidei toto orbe diffunditur.* Nunquam talia pro nobis diuinitus agerentur, si morte corporis etiam uita animae consumeretur. Quid cunctamur igitur relicta spe saeculi conferre nos totos ad quaerendum Deum et uitam beatam.

tude, compunction, ineffable yearning of the inmost soul, which speaks to GOD in the *Confessions*. This passion of devotion[1] to the Catholic Church, then, was inspired in Augustine not by an idea, but by a visible fact, by the life of a visible society, which worked upon him at first from without, but afterwards as an inward personal experience. It would be difficult to overstate Augustine's influence in this respect upon the tone and expression of Catholic feeling for the Church, as it is difficult to overrate the deepening and enrichment which personal religion in the whole Western Church owes to him. But just as our unreserved recognition of this latter fact would gravely mislead, were it to blind us in any way to the reality and depth of individual religion in the three centuries before Augustine, as it stands revealed to us in the innumerable memorials of Christian life enshrined in the deeds, the words, the sufferings, of those of every rank, class, age, sex, date, and country who lived and died for Christ; so it cannot be too often insisted upon that the belief in the Christian Church as the one visible Society, to which the work of Christ's Kingdom is confided and its promises are expressly attached was in no sense "Augustinian," as if originated by Augustine or under his influence.[2]

That we believe "in remission of sins through the Holy Church," that "he cannot have GOD for his Father who has not the Church for his Mother," that salvation is in the Church alone, "extra ecclesiam nulla salus," were ideas in full currency very long before

---

[1] *Enarr. in Psa.* lxxxviii. 14.
[2] See above, p. 174, note 2, and Cyrill. Hier. *Catech.* xviii. 26.

ELEMENTS OF AUGUSTINIANISM 187

Augustine's time, and he simply entered upon them as part of the traditional heritage of Catholic belief.[1] Diverse shades of interpretation no doubt there were, especially the theoretical limits of the Church had not been satisfactorily laid down; but while it was still possible for the plain man to distinguish without hesitation between the general Christian body and the sectional and separatist movements which from time to time broke away,—while "securus iudicat Orbis Terrarum"[2] was available as a ready test, such theoretical questions were of minor urgency. Broadly speaking, it was agreed that the Church, outside of which there was no salvation, was the obviously visible general body of Christians, the καθολικὴ ἐκκλησία, as to the identity of which there could be no *bona fide* mistake. "Whatever novelty there may have been in Augustine's presentation of the matter, at least he did not originate the idea of a visible Church."[3] It would be truer to one side of the facts, to say that he originated the idea of an *invisible* Church. The suggestion of such an idea was present, as we have seen, in the background of transcendent idealism which qualified his intellectual appreciation of all visible things.

(*c*) But its application to the idea of the Church comes out in connexion with a third side of his mind and work which remains to be noticed,—his contribution to the doctrine of Grace.[4] Augustine was, in relation to this subject, unconscious of any desire or tendency to do more than uphold the traditional

[1] See references in Gore, *The Church and the Ministry*, p. 13 sq. and notes.
[2] *c. Ep. Parmen.* III. iv. 24.   [3] Gore (*ubi supra*).
[4] Aug. § 10, and § 16*c*.

teaching of those who had gone before him, he was unconscious of any even implicit divergence between his own instincts and those of Greek-speaking Christendom.[1] But in spite of this, the fact remains that he stamped upon Latin theology a character markedly different from that of the Greek Fathers, and naturalised in the Latin Church itself conceptions which had been either absent from or unfamiliar to its earlier thought. Augustine had to formulate and develop his doctrine of Grace under the stress of an acute theological controversy. But it is now recognised that his characteristic convictions were in all essentials fully formed long before Pelagius came forward to oppose him. This was in 411, and Pelagius was roused to protest by the language of the *Confessions*, published ten years before. In fact Augustine had formulated his doctrine of Grace as the result of his studies in St. Paul's Epistles, especially those to Romans and Corinthians, as early as the year 396.[2] His earlier view, he tells us, had been that man was indeed dependent upon divine grace for his salvation, but that faith, without which Grace could not be received, was man's own spontaneous act. But St. Paul's question: What hast thou that thou hast not received? had given him pause, and had gradually worked a revolution in his mind. If man contributes anything,—if the difference, between the effectual operation of Grace in the case of one man and its frustration in the case of another, ultimately goes back to the different response of the will in the two

[1] Aug. § 11, and Reuter, pp. 153-170.
[2] The two books *ad Simplicianum*, published in 397, mark the change. See *de Praedest.* iv., *de dono Pers.* xx., and Loofs' article on Augustine in the new edition of Herzog (Hauck).

ELEMENTS OF AUGUSTINIANISM 189

cases, then it is with Free Will, not Grace, that the crucial decision rests which determines whether Grace is to act or no; Free Will, not Grace is the ultimate turning-point of a man's relation to GOD. To the Augustine of the *Confessions*, conscious of nothing but self-will and self-deception on his own part, deeply convinced that nothing but the grace of GOD had set his own will free, nay, had moved it, to believe, to repent, such a conclusion was impossible to rest in. And as, in the years following his conversion, he gradually exchanged the methods and temper of the Platonic dialectician for the results of deeper study of St. Paul, the assumption appeared to him not only impossible but irreligious also. In utter self-condemnation and self-abasement before GOD, in unreserved whole-hearted gratitude of self-surrender to His Will, nothing could satisfy him but the unqualified reference of everything that had made him what he now was, that had made him other than what he once had been, to the *gratia Christi*,[1] the free gift of GOD in Christ. *Domine da quod iubes.* This strong and genuinely religious predisposition was clinched, and crystallised into an unalterable theological conviction, not only by the text to which I have already referred, but by the general tenor of St. Paul's doctrine. In particular, the ninth chapter of the Epistle to the Romans fitted his own spiritual experience with startling exactness. "It is not of him that runs or wills, but of GOD that showeth mercy." In argument, at the end of his life, with the brethren of Southern Gaul who rejected his

[1] On the centrality of this in Augustine's thought, see Reuter, pp. 45, 49, 51, 52, 19–25, 97.

three characteristic doctrines of the total depravity of man, of the irresistibleness of Divine Grace, and of absolute predestination, he refers them with perfect right to his two books addressed in 397, fifteen years before the Pelagian controversy, to Simplicianus, bishop of Milan,[1] as proof that his convictions on these points, derived from his study of St. Paul, were of no recent standing.

All alike were agreed in building the certainty of personal salvation upon the divine election of individuals. But where Augustine differed from the Massilians, and we may add from Jerome also and from general Catholic opinion before his own time, was as to the basis of this election itself.

It was generally assumed, and the assumption has the apparent support of St. Paul in one passage,[2] that GOD, foreseeing those who would be faithful, predestined them to eternal life—" whom he foreknew, he predestinated." But Augustine will not allow the fundamental assumption. To GOD, to predestine is to foreknow, and to foreknow is to predestine. If election is determined by any merit, whether of works or of faith matters not, then the old impossible result comes back, Free Will not Grace is the pivot upon which salvation turns. GOD'S purpose, on the contrary, is *secundum electionem*;[3] the call of grace follows election, does not, even in divine foreknowledge, determine or precede it—election, then, is absolute, prior to and independent of anything in the history of the elect. It may be allowed

---

[1] *Supra*, note 2.
[2] Rom. viii. 29, ὅτι οὓσ προέγνω, καὶ προώρισε, κ.τ.λ.
[3] Rom. ix. 11.

ELEMENTS OF AUGUSTINIANISM 191

that the elect must be holy, be baptised, be members of the Catholic Church; but all these things will be not the conditions but the results of their election, upon which alone the question of all questions depends. Many fulfil all these conditions, but if they are not of the elect they will avail nothing: they will fall away either openly or secretly, either in life or in death, for they lack the supreme gift which is the crucial sign of election, the *donum perseverantiae.* This gift may be in store, again, for many who are now ungodly and alien from the Church; in life or death, but surely as a rule visibly to others as to the Church, they will join the body of Christ; the *donum perseverantiae*, the gift of final reconciliation, is theirs already assured to them by GOD whose gifts and calling are without repentance. Meanwhile, no doubt the call of Grace comes to all, "many are called"; but not all are called "congruenter"[1]—in such a way, that is, as to ensure that they will answer to that call. To the non-elect the divine appeal comes as a *vocatio non congrua*, they will disobey from the first, or perhaps they will respond for a time,—for a lifetime; but to no purpose, for they are not marked out for the gift of perseverance, the number of the predestined is known to GOD, and unalterable; the *vocatio congrua* comes to the elect alone, and to the rest it can never come. Terrible as is the doctrine of predestination, terrible as is its elaboration in the doctrine of the *donum perseverantiae,* surely the doctrine of the *vocatio non congrua* is

---

[1] *Ad Simplic.* I. xiii. fin. See also what he says of the final grace of perseverance: "multi enim possunt habere, *nullus amittere,*" *de don. Pers.* vi.

the culminating point of all that is terrible in his system.¹ Yet how, on Augustine's principles, could the case be conceived otherwise? At any rate, conscious as Augustine was of the advance of his own mind on these subjects, he remained wholly unconscious of what was none the less the fact, that he had effected a revolution in Catholic opinion.² For in face of the personal influence of Augustine, the counter-efforts of the Churchmen of Southern Gaul could effect nothing. The antithesis of Pelagianism, with its patent breakdown on the crucial point of infant baptism,³ was perhaps needed to secure the adhesion of Western Christendom to Augustine's doctrine of grace; at any rate Augustine as the leader of the movement against Pelagius carried the Church with him, practically to all lengths. Africa was steadily with him from the first. Rome, where Pelagius was more powerful than elsewhere, proved teachable in the person of her bishops, first of Innocent, then with a moment of hesitation in that of Zosimus,⁴ — finally with the unreserved adhesion of Caelestinus, Leo, Hilary. Italy

---

[1] Reuter, pp. 57, 67 sq., 81 sq., follows out with painful exactness the life-history of a convert who, under Augustine's guidance, passes through the catechumenate, baptism, and the successive *beneficia gratiae* of which the Church is the home (see below, p. 201, note 3), only to learn that there is after all no certainty that he is a member of the Church in the true sense, or that his prayers (*fides orans*, see Reuter's reff. p. 79) for the one decisive *beneficium*, the *donum perseverantiae*, have any prospect of being heard. But he fully allows (p. 72 sq.) that Augustine, while holding in theory the absolute secrecy of the divine Election, practically treated it as sometimes recognisable, *e.g.* in the Church's martyrs: "Er hat nie ernstlich daran gezweifelt, das alle Martyrer der Kirche zu den *electis*, d. h. den *definitiv* Heiligen, gehörten; darum nicht gezweifelt, *weil* sie jene als Heilige verkündigte und verehrte." This, however, is compromise, not synthesis (see Reuter, p. 73).

[2] Aug. §§ 10*d* fin., 16*c*.   [3] Aug. § 10*d* init.   [4] Aug. § 10*a* fin., *b*.

ELEMENTS OF AUGUSTINIANISM 193

rallied in the person of Paulinus of Nola, drawn more perhaps by instinctive sympathy with Augustine's Catholic piety than by profound interest in his cause, —in Gaul itself Augustine found his most ardent supporters.[1]

But the ecclesiastical instincts of average Catholic Churchmanship had grown up in an atmosphere of Free Will equipped with sacraments, to which the Augustinian doctrine of Grace was not, nor ever could become, wholly congenial.[2] Augustine himself, as we shall see, never reached a real synthesis of the two, and in the sequel, the latent incompatibility of the two makes itself persistently felt. True, Augustine left a permanent, an indelible stamp, upon ecclesiastical life and thought. The conception of Grace was thenceforth never in the West so nearly limited to sacraments as it practically remained in the Greek Church. The sacraments were held in a deepened sense, with a context of Grace, preventing, predisposing, concomitant, which conditioned the grace of the sacrament itself. This was largely Augustine's work. But from the first, it began to be evident that Augustine's characteristic paradoxes must be modified if Augustinianism was to remain the standard of ecclesiastical thought. This was apparent at Orange in 529,[3] still more so in the

---

[1] Especially Prosper of Aquitaine and the monk Hilarius (on whom see *Dict. Christ. Biogr.* vol. iv. p. 493*b*).

[2] Reuter, pp. 30–38.

[3] The twenty-five Canons of the small Council of Orange consist mainly of extracts from Augustine and Prosper. They assert the powerlessness of man, even if unfallen, for good without prevenient grace (3, 4, 12, 19, 21, 22), which is, however, as a rule assumed to be *baptismal* grace (see 13, and conclusion); but they are silent as to irresistible grace and as to predestination, except that, in the conclusion, the supposition that "any are by divine

controversy of the ninth century,[1] and we have hardly yet seen the final issue of the questions which Augustine bequeathed for solution to the Church of after times.

III

I have said that Augustine himself never succeeded in effecting a synthesis between his working conception of the Catholic Church and his theological doctrine of Grace. The difficulty was a very real one. Taking first the mere question of extent, what was the real Body of Christ, the true Bride of whom the glorious things of Holy Scripture are spoken? Was it the Church as it appears on earth, the organised hierarchical body, or only those members of it who were worthy of their calling? The parables of Christ, the experience of Puritan schisms,—Montanist, Novatian, Donatist,—might seem to decide this question. The visible Church is the Body of Christ, in spite of the "hypocrites" whom she may for the present include. Their presence belongs to the present imperfection of the Church, but does not diminish her essential prerogative as the Body and Kingdom of Christ. But yet, as we saw at the outset of this Lecture, it is those

power predestined *ad malum* [*i.e.* "to sin"?] is repudiated, and those, "if there be any such," who hold it are anathematised. The reconciliation of the Augustinian and "semi-Pelagian" parties was therefore effected by shelving (perhaps wisely) the insoluble difficulties of "perseverance" (10), of free will (13), and of predestination. See the text of the Canons in Hahn, § 103; also Seeberg, *Dogmengesch.* i. 323, 4.

[1] Harnack, *Dogmengesch.* iii. 261-270, in a very interesting account of the Gottschalk controversy, points out that Southern Gaul (Council of Valence, 855), the former stronghold of semi-Pelagianism, now maintained the stricter Augustinian view against the "kirchliche Empirie" of Raban, Hinkmar, and the Council of Quiercy-sur-Oise (853).

ST. AUGUSTINE AND THE CHURCH 195

who are truly living members of Christ and they alone, not any organisation or government, that gave the Church, in Augustine's eyes, the character of the Kingdom of GOD. And not only so; behind and above the present distinction of the sincere Christians and the hypocrites, the "fideliter et pie viventes," the "temporaliter stantes," and the at present unworthy members of the visible Church, there is the vital and eternal distinction between those who belong to the *certus numerus*[1] of the predestined, though they may be at present outside the Church or unworthy members of it,[2] and the non-elect, who may be living faithfully and piously now, but who have no hope of salvation, no true part or lot in the *communio sanctorum*. The elect is inwardly and outwardly indistinguishable from the non-elect; "nonne utrique vocati fuerant, utrique ex impiis iustificati?"[3] There is then on earth a visible Church of Christ containing good and bad, elect and non-elect, and there are also a number, unalterably known to GOD, of those predestined to Life, some within the visible Church, some outside it. Which of these two, the *communio externa* or the *communio sanctorum*,[4]

---

[1] *de corrept. et Grat.* xiii. 39, "ita certus . . . ut non addatur eis quisquam, nec minuatur ex eis"; 40, "numerus praedestinatus"; 42, "istum certissimum et felicissimum numerum"; and see the whole context, especially in § 40.

[2] *Ibid.* vii. 16: "Aut si qui sunt quorum [fides] deficit, reparatur antequam uita ista finiatur."

[3] *Ibid.* ix. 21.

[4] The *communio sanctorum* will from time to time include those who are sincere Christians, but not of the *certus numerus* (*supra*, note 1); so that in strictness it is not identifiable with the latter (Reuter, p. 66 sq.). But bearing this in mind, we may, for convenience, without departing very far from Augustine's usual language, treat the *communio sanctorum* as practically representing the *electi* (cf. *de Bapt.* VI. iii. 5, xviii. 23).

is the real Church identifiable with the kingdom of Christ on earth?

We must remember that to Augustine the Real is the timeless, the immaterial, the Good.[1] The historically conditioned partakes of Reality only in the second or in a still remoter degree. The Real again is the Good; imperfect goodness means a lower degree of Reality. Augustine's predestinarianism certainly grew upon him in the last twenty-five years of his life,[2] the period to which his most mature writings belong; and this fact must be set down not merely to the pressure of the Pelagian controversy, but to the steady influence of his metaphysical theory of being which led him to fall back in thought upon things as viewed *sub specie aeterni*, and which tended to neutralise, from this point of view, the value of all institutions which belong to space and time. We have to deal then with a very delicate analytical problem, that of disengaging two really disparate strains of thought in Augustine's mind, with a view to assign to them their relative predominance.[3] The result may be tentatively stated in this way: In estimating the significance of the Church as the Body of Christ, in investing the Church with all the attributes which command the devotion of a Christian and belong to the idea of the Kingdom of God, Augustine builds upon the conception of the Church as the *communio sanctorum*, the total number of GOD'S Elect. In this sense [4] he

---

[1] Aug. § 16*a*; see also Reuter, pp. 360, 58, 84, 461, 464 sq. etc.
[2] Reuter, p. 102.   [3] *Ibid.* p. 70 sqq.
[4] Certainly in the sense that not all who "tenent ecclesiam sunt in ecclesia," *de unit. eccl.* 74; *de Bapt.* VII. lii. 100: "illi qui sic sunt in domo per communionem sacramentorum ut extra domum sint per diversitatem morum." How far Augustine held that those who were outside the

ST. AUGUSTINE AND THE CHURCH 197

makes his own the saying which the Church had inherited from Cyprian, *extra ecclesiam nulla salus*. But in *applying* this ideal doctrine of the Church, Augustine is very apt to pass to the Catholic Church as it was; the *externa communio* is simply invested with the ideal attributes evolved from the consideration of the *numerus praedestinatorum*.[1] This is no synthesis but a simple transference of predicates from one subject to another; Augustine is not always unconscious of the transition, but he speaks rather frequently as though the subjects were the same.[2] Yet he nowhere identifies them expressly, on the contrary he expressly and carefully distinguishes them.[3] That many belong to the visible Church who are not in the transcendent *communio sanctorum* he has of course no difficulty in admitting,— he insists upon it. But practically he not infrequently seems to assume that all the predestined now on earth are to be thought of as included in the *communio externa*.[4] If this is his true thought, the Church on

Church might yet be "in ecclesia" in the ultimate and real sense is a more difficult question, and will be considered below (see also Reuter, p. 64, note 4).

[1] There is also, to some slight extent, a converse transference. Reuter, p. 65.

[2] Reuter, pp. 68, 69, 98-100; *Serm.* 213. 7, 214. 11; *Enarr. in Psa.* cxxvi. 3.

[3] *de Bapt.* IV. ii. 4: [Merely nominal Christians] non sunt in Ecclesia de qua dicitur Una est columba, etc. Cf. *ibid.* VII. li. 99. In treating of the fundamental doctrines in the *Enchiridion*, he has in view the Church as *communio sanctorum*; see chaps. v., lvi., lxii., lxiv. (Migne).

[4] *de corrept. et Gratia*, ix. 22. Reuter (p. 64, note 4) has in vain searched Augustine for a clear statement that "qui non sunt in sacramentorum communione cum ecclesia non sunt in ecclesia" (the nearest are *de Bapt.* VII. xvi. 21, "non autem habent Dei caritatem qui ecclesiae non *diligunt* unitatem," etc., and *Ep.* 185. 50: "Non est autem particeps diuinae caritatis qui hostis est unitatis; non habent itaque Spiritum Sanctum, qui sunt extra ecclesiam," or stronger still, *Ep.* 141. 5: "Quisquis ergo ab *hac catholica*

earth is bounded by three concentric circles,—first that of the visible Society, containing wheat and tares alike; within that the inner circle of consistent and faithful Christians, not all of whom however are truly vessels made for honour, *i.e.* elect, or destined to persevere; then inmost of all the elect members of the true Church, the Church of eternity, whose presence in the heart and core of the visible Society distinguishes that Society as the Body and Kingdom of Christ. But this is not quite Augustine's view. For firstly there are the elect outside the Church, who are destined to come in and to persevere, while many now within will fall away, the last first and the first last. This will take place,[1] Augustine assumes, before death;—so that although at no given moment the Catholic Church contains the whole of the elect living on earth, yet none of the elect die outside the Church. This thought certainly depreciates the paramount necessity of the *correptio*[2] and other means of grace which the Church supplies, but perhaps not more so than is demanded by the Parable of the Labourers called at the eleventh hour. But there is a further side of Augustine's teaching to be considered here. Augustine does not limit salvation through Christ to believers in the historical Christian

---

ecclesia fuerit separatus . . . non habet uitam, sed ira Dei manet super eum." The question is whether *external* separation is compatible in some cases with real though internal "esse in ecclesia."

[1] *de dono Pers.* 8 : "Perseuerantia quae in aeternum saluos facit, tempori quidem huius uitae, non tamen peracto sed ei quod usque ad finem restat, necessaria est"; and see *supra*, p. 195, note 2.

[2] For the idea of *correptio* see Matt. xviii. 15 (Vulg.), "corripe eum." Augustine applies the word to sum up the Church's resources of moral appeal and discipline. On the statement in the text, see Reuter, pp. 32, 83.

ST. AUGUSTINE AND THE CHURCH 199

Religion. On the contrary he believes that it has never been inaccessible to those who were worthy of it. What we now call the Christian Religion, he says in a well-known passage, is as old as the world—the same faith, the same salvation, in diverse forms corresponding to the times, has been always, now more clearly now more obscurely, made known to men.[1] This thought of Augustine's at first reminds us of that of some of the Apologists and of the Alexandrian Fathers, that all who in every age lived in accordance with reason were really Christians, because they shared in the presence of the Logos, the light which lightens every man that cometh into the world.[2] Moreover the apparent divergence of the idea of the " worthy ":—" Nulli unquam deficit cui dignus fuit "—from Augustine's view of man's helpless bondage to sin, and his well-known condemnation of the virtues of the heathen as splendid vices,[3] inclines one to detect here a strand of heterogeneous influence in Augustine's thought, derived neither from his ecclesiastical loyalty nor from his analysis of the Pauline doctrine of Grace,—rather an isolated suggestion followed up without relation to other lines of thought and conviction. But the view under consideration is too persistent[4] in Augustine's writings, especially those of the last twenty years of his life, to permit us to dispose of it in this way. On the

---

[1] *Ep.* 102 ; see especially § 12, and cf. *de pecc. mer. et rem.* II. xxix. 47 ; *de Civ. Dei*, XVIII. xlvii. (other reff. Reuter, p. 91, note).

[2] *Supra*, Lect. IV. p. 154.

[3] *de Civ. Dei*, XIX. xxv., XXI. xxv. He allows, however, that Fabricius is "minus malus" than Catiline, and will be more mildly punished ;— rejecting the "Stoic" view, that all vices are equal. Cf. *de Civ. Dei*, XXI. xvi. fin. ; *Ep.* 138. 17 ; *de Sp. et Litera*, 48.

[4] See above, note 1 and reff.

contrary, it appears to hang very directly together with his theory of reality referred to above, and to have been brought into conscious correlation with his doctrine of predestination. Reviewing the question in the latter connexion,[1] he explains that the "digni" to whom salvation through Christ has in all ages been accessible were not "worthy" from their own merit, but because they were marked out as such by God's predestinating grace. Primarily no doubt this applies to the saints of the Old Testament. *To them* was revealed, obscurely indeed but truly, the grace of Christ which to us is revealed more plainly—*prius occultius postea manifestius*. But Augustine does not limit the application of the principle to them. There are cases like Job and Melchizedek, who were not members of the sacred commonwealth, and the Sibyl, who was remoter still from all contact with it. There was indeed never more than one *society* identifiable with the *civitas Dei* on earth, but that does not preclude us [2] from believing that *individuals* may have been within the number of the elect, though never visibly included in the "external communion" of GOD's people. In a sense then Augustine's narrow Predestinarianism led him directly to the widest of Universalism. Practically no doubt he makes very sparing use of these premises. The number of the elect is a secret known to God alone, no man can be sure of his own election, much less can we be certain of that of others; cases of this abnormal kind lie *ex hypothesi* beyond our powers of ascertainment, and to argue from them is impossible. But the

[1] *de Praed.* 17.
[2] Augustine makes this distinction, but I have mislaid the reference.

ST. AUGUSTINE AND THE CHURCH 201

principle remains, and makes it impossible to hold as a formal theory the necessary inclusion in the visible Church on earth of the whole number of the predestined.

As the result, then, Augustine's transcendentalism and his predestinarianism on the one hand, and on the other his practical working churchmanship, his insistence on the visible Catholic Church as the exclusive pale of salvation, remain unreconciled; they lie side by side as disparate elements in his mind, incapable of any true synthesis. The synthesis we have been discussing,—that the visible *externa communio* is the wider body, which, until it is purified of its unworthy elements, contains as its inmost core the *communio sanctorum*, the elect, the body of whom now living on earth must for practical purposes be assumed to be identical with the *externa communio*,[1] rests upon no inward principle at all. The teaching, worship, and sacraments of the Church are means to an end, namely, the salvation of souls; but between that end and the means there is not in Augustine's theory a true causal connexion.[2] The Church with all the means of *correptio* at her command unquestionably purifies men's lives, enlightens their minds, heals the spiritually sick, and assures the benefits[3] of grace to their souls. But all

---

[1] "Appellamus ergo nos et electos et Christi discipulos et Dei filios quia sic appellandi sunt quos regeneratos pie uiuere cernimus," *de corrept. et Grat.* ix. 22; cf. *Serm.* 214. 11.

[2] Reuter, p. 82.

[3] By the term *beneficia gratiae* Augustine denoted the graduated course of spiritual stages through which the Christian was expected to pass. He probably found this scheme traditionally established, but he certainly modified the traditional significance of some of its stages—*e.g.* that of Final Perseverance. (See the careful note of Reuter, p. 584. The passage he cannot identify, "Distat, et quod distet Deo notum est," etc., is from *Serm.* 295. xix. 18.)

the while, unless they are marked out for the last and crowning *beneficium*, the gift of perseverance, they are not *in reality* separated from the "mass of perdition."[1] Salvation really has its single root in the eternal election of GOD, elect and non-elect pass it may well be through the same earthly history; in faith, baptism, the *correptio* of the Church, the eucharist, they are together side by side, and apparently with the same immediate result; both alike pray for the crowning grace of perseverance, but one is taken and the other left, while the sinner whom a deathbed repentance brings into the Church, and who has never passed through the discipline of the Christian life,[2] may all along have been of the number of the elect from which the other, his faith and piety notwithstanding, has all along been excluded.

Augustine's predestinarianism, then, is at issue with his conception of the visible Catholic Church, known as such to all mankind by her organisation, teaching, and worship, as the body which administers the grace of Christ with the sure promise of salvation to those who belong to her in heart and soul, and faithfully use her means of grace. His lofty appreciation of the Catholic Church is in no small part the transference to the *externa communio* of the eternal and indestructible prerogatives of the *communion of saints* in the sense of the predestined, the only real Church in the

---

[1] This stated with terrible clearness *de corrept. et Grat.* 16.

[2] *Ibid.* v. 8: "Nullo homine corripiente," and vii. 13. The Church is a place of preparation for the elect; but the preparation is no condition of the election. The elect are distinguished (*discreti*) from the *massa perditionis* by the *lavacrum regenerationis*; but no one can *really* be *discretus* unless he has the *donum perseverantiae* (*de corrept. et Grat.* vii. 12, 16).

ST. AUGUSTINE AND THE CHURCH 203

Augustinian sense of Reality; and it is in so far as the visible Church corresponds to this transcendental idea, in so far as "even now"—on earth—"his saints reign with him," in so far as the wheat is now "being gathered" for the eternal harvest, that Augustine identifies the visible Church with the Kingdom of GOD.[1]

It is possible to accept the identification, but to set aside the ideas to which it is correlative in Augustine's mind; and this was in fact the course substantially taken by later ecclesiastical development. But this is to give the identification a new meaning, foreign alike to Augustinian and to pre-Augustinian thought.

Or, again, it is possible, especially in an age when there is no searching and inevitable problem confronting men as to the conception and functions of the Church, to combine Augustine's predestinarian convictions and his ecclesiastical enthusiasm much as Augustine did himself, without pressing them to their inherently divergent issues. This was done in the generations which immediately followed Augustine, when the great teacher's authority had enlisted in his following all the most active Churchmanship of the West, especially the support of the Apostolic See, while the semi-Augustinianism of the school of Vincent and Cassian and Faustus was branded with the somewhat harsh label of semi-Pelagianism. For the moment, the Church was carried away partly by the recoil from Pelagianism, partly by the character and earnestness of Augustine, and it was no time to analyse critically the inward logic of his doctrine.

[1] See above, p. 172.

But in truth Augustine had left a heritage of difficulty for the ages to come. We may recognise that the doctrine of predestination exercises a spiritualising influence on Augustine's conception of the Church, but was not the cost a heavy one? To us, accustomed by Butler to view life as a probation, does not a doctrine which logically excludes any true idea of probation seem to uproot the base of sober morality,—to neutralise even the thought of GOD's moral government of the world? And yet the problem which is at the root of all this apparent paradox defies theoretical solution. To affirm moral responsibility without allowing human merit, in other words to satisfy the demands of the moral sense without infringing those of the religious sense, was the task lightly taken in hand by Pelagius, more cautiously attempted, but without any real success, by the semi-Pelagians. If they were wrong, it is hard to resist the alternative conclusion that Augustine was right. He set out from the demand of the religious sense for absolute self-abasement in GOD's sight as the very first elementary necessity of religion. But very soon he had virtually undermined the truth—which he yet did not cease to affirm in words—of man's moral responsibility.

It is indeed easy to content oneself with half-solutions,—in fact it is necessary to forego any complete solution. But if so, let us at any rate not delude ourselves with the appearance of a solution without the reality. A facile naturalistic determinism, which surrenders responsibility and merit alike, affronts morality with no corresponding gain to religion; by

ST. AUGUSTINE AND THE CHURCH

lowering human nature in its own eyes it surrenders the problem of even stating the facts adequately to human nature as it knows itself to be. Pelagianism, the vulgar doctrine of Free Will, the shallow appeal to things as they seem, has never appealed to the religious instinct. The naïve pre-Augustinian doctrine of Grace, the assumption of Free Will equipped with sacraments, contained virtually, as Augustine saw, the refutation of Pelagianism;[1] Augustine's claim throughout was that he was simply vindicating the traditional belief of the Church. This was not literally true,—especially as regards predestination,—but it is virtually true in so far as on the Pelagian theory the need of even sacramental grace has no foundation in principle. Augustine, from this point of view, simply extended to Grace in general, prevenient and crowning grace as well as concomitant grace, the principle involved in infant baptism, that man can make no step to Godward except GOD be beforehand with him. But in doing so, logic carried him further than it had carried St. Paul. The dilemma of responsibility without merit was unsolved, as it is insoluble; St. Paul had offered no solution, he had simply contented himself with affirming responsibility while denying merit. Augustine's difference from St. Paul was one of proportion and balance, which he sacrificed by carrying his premises to their conclusions in a subject-matter where logic is no safe guide.

But our purpose is not to discuss the question on its merits so much as to record what Augustine actually held, and of this there is no doubt at all.

[1] See Reuter, p. 40.

IV

Augustine's great influence in moulding the Western theory of the Church is best understood if we consider what is on the whole his greatest work, the *de Civitate Dei* upon which the last twenty years [1] of his life were to a great extent employed.

In the year 410, for the first time for eight hundred years, Rome had been taken and sacked by a barbarian force. But in the year 410 after Christ the impression produced by the catastrophe was very different from anything that was contemplated in B.C. 390. The capture by the Gauls of an important Italian town left its deep impress upon local tradition, but the world at large was little concerned. But the capture of the Eternal City by Alaric caused men's hearts to fail them for fear.[2] The imperial might, the invincible sovereignty of Rome, was accepted as part of the established order of nature; when Rome fell, men felt the solid earth giving way beneath them, and the powers of heaven were shaken. Roman and barbarian, Christian and pagan alike, were filled with something of religious terror. Christians saw the bowl of wrath poured out upon the seat of the Beast, and looked for the end of the world to follow forthwith; pagans saw in the fall of Rome the vengeance of Rome's neglected gods, or the effect of a new and enervating religion. Rome had perished " temporibus Christianis."

[1] Strictly the years 412–426. Augustine died August 28, 430. But the idea of the two *civitates* occurs in *de catech. rud.* written in 400. The Church is spoken of by Epiphanius (*c.* A.D. 377) as πόλισ Θεοῦ, *Exp. Fid.* ii.

[2] Dill, *Roman Society in the Last Century of the Roman Empire*, p. 61.

In Africa the shock was felt with all its force. Carthage, which seemed at that time to lie safely out of reach of the barbarian, was crowded with refugees of the educated and ruling class, full of harrowing details of the horrors from which they had fled, loud in their denunciation of the religion by whose rising influence the disaster was to be explained. These complaints were not confined to the unthinking multitude. Thoughtful men detected in the very core of Christian teaching principles incompatible with the maintenance of States. If the dominant religion forbids resistance to evil, and bids us turn the cheek to the smiter, how can the barbarians fail to carry all before them? Rome grew great under the training of the old Religion: it has perished in Christian times. The distinguished official Volusianus, son of a Christian mother and the intimate friend of Augustine's spiritual son Marcellinus, was kept back from the Christian faith by doubts of this kind, and it was from Augustine's correspondence [1] with him that the conception of his work *de Civitate Dei* originated. His original object was simply to show that it was not the renunciation of the old gods that had ruined Rome, but that on the contrary the Christian religion, if duly carried out, produced the best not only of soldiers, but of husbands, sons, officials, debtors, creditors, citizens, while the decay of Rome as appears from Sallust and other authors of the republican period had set in long before Christian times. But Augustine's work expanded into a constructive theory of history. He had long pondered over the problem of human history in the light of the

[1] *Epp.* 135-138 (see Aug. § 9).

fundamental relations between man and GOD,—the two *civitates* had as early as the year 400 taken shape in his mind as the ultimate factors in the story of mankind. He now works his account of the rise and fall of Rome into a comprehensive survey of history, in which the contrast between the *civitas Dei* and the *civitas terrena* furnishes the key to the significance of the whole. Augustine writes under the stimulus of a terrible actuality. The antique world was, in serious truth, breaking up to make way for a civilisation cast in new moulds and not to be born without long and terrible sufferings; and the fall of Rome was but the beginning of sorrows,—a symbol rather than an efficient cause of all that was coming. Lesser men felt that momentous changes were in progress. Augustine's friend Orosius at his suggestion wrote a history [1] of the world in refutation of the heathen view of history; Salvian a generation later [2] brought the downfall of the degenerate Christian civilisation under the scheme of the Divine Government of the World. These efforts, especially the latter, are of interest and importance; but they are altogether dwarfed by the decisive work of Augustine. The *de Civitate* was published at intervals, book by book, as Augustine's manifold engagements gave him leisure to work at it. The 22nd and last book appeared in 427, fifteen years after the first lines of the work were penned. The work bears the traces of interruptions; it would have gained by a compression which more continuous com-

---

[1] A.D. 417.
[2] A.D. 451, four years before the sack of Rome by Gaiseric and his Vandals.

THE *CIVITAS DEI*

position would probably have secured for it. But Augustine put into it the very best that he had to give, and nothing that he ever wrote gives us a deeper insight into the manifold workings of his mind and soul.

The first ten books are polemical, and directed to proving the inutility of the pagan religion of Rome, both for the purposes of this world and of the world to come. In the remaining twelve books Augustine treats constructively of the two *civitates*, in respect of their origin, their history, and their destiny. He interprets the whole history of the world as the product of these two fundamental factors. The *civitas terrena* began with the fall of the angels, and was continued by that of man. Its course is traced through the descendants of Cain, the tower of Babel, and the great Empires of Nineveh, Babylon, Persia, Macedonia, and Rome. The *civitas Dei* on the other hand began with Creation. Its history is drawn out in the descendants of Seth, Noah, Abraham, and the choice and training of Israel, culminating in Christ.

The two *civitates* represent diametrically opposite principles. The one is founded upon the love of GOD, *usque ad contemptum sui*, the other upon the love of self, *usque ad contemptum Dei*.[1] In other words the *civitas terrena* is in principle the embodiment of evil; the kingdom of the devil[2] in contrast to that of Christ.

---

[1] See *de Civ. Dei*, XIV. xxvii. This is the ultimate moral distinction which divides angel from devil (*de Gen. ad Lit.* I. xiii. 26).

[2] *Enarr. in Psa.* lxi. 6: "una ciuitas tamen et una ciuitas; illa rege diabolo, ista rege Christo . . . omnes qui felicitatem terrenam Deo praeferunt, omnes qui sua quaerunt non quae Iesu Christi, ad unam illam ciuitatem pertinent quae dicitur Babylonia mystice et habet regem Diabolum."

They differ in their inherent purpose. The *civitas Dei* pursues the *pax caelestis*, while the *civitas terrena* pursues merely the *pax terrena*.[1] But the latter is but a futile pursuit so long as the two *civitates* are viewed strictly and apart. For the earthly *civitas* has no resources of its own commensurate with its purpose. It can use worldly wisdom and worldly power, but has no command over the moral life. In a word it works its way by force or fraud. Apart from justice—which the earthly *civitas* can only possess by borrowing from the *civitas Dei*,[2] the great Empires of the world have been—nay the earthly Commonwealth, the State *per se*, is simply—a great brigandage, *grande latrocinium*. So far, then, as the separation between the two *civitates* is absolute, and embodied in distinct societies[3] of men, the State is Babylon, the *civitas* or *regnum diaboli*, the Church the *civitas Dei*.[4] So far, then, as the *civitas Dei* corresponds to the *regnum Dei*,[5] the reader of this treatise will infer that Augustine simply identifies the Church, over which the bishops keep watch, with the Kingdom of GOD, and the secular power with the kingdom of the devil.

But this is far from doing justice to Augustine's full complex of thought. We have already seen how profoundly his enthusiasm for the Catholic Church was

---

[1] *de Civ. Dei*, XIX. xiii.   [2] *Ibid.* IV. iv.

[3] A *civitas* is defined as "a society of men," *de Civ. Dei*, XV. viii.

[4] See *Enarr. in Psa.* cxxvi. 3, where the "City" is the Church, which includes, indeed, all faithful, past, present, or to come, but its "watchmen" are the bishops. That is, the hierarchically governed Church is *civ. Dei*. But this is only so in so far as individuals are built into Christ. The true Jerusalem is not a literal *civitas*, but is "built *as* a city," *Enarr. in Psa.* cxxi. 4 sqq.

[5] See preceding note, and p. 209, note 2.

THE *CIVITAS DEI*

coloured, or rather modified in principle, by his predestinarian convictions. The *de Civitate* was written during the years in which the predestinarian idea was taking more and more complete possession of Augustine's mind. As the argument proceeds, the contrast between the two *civitates* shows signs of merging into that between *electi* and *reprobi*.[1] But apart from this consideration, Augustine does not forget that the visible Church is at most but the fragment of a kingdom which embraces, not only the departed and the unborn, but the angels.[2] And it is not merely a fragment, but it exists in conditions which give it the external form of the *civitas terrena*.[3] Again, while outside the *civitas Dei* no good can be said to exist, so that virtues themselves are but vices,[4] Augustine does not deny the possibility of individuals outside the Church belonging to the *civitas Dei*, though no *Society* other than the Church can be allowed to share the name.

But above all, it is impossible, in the face of history, to view the two *civitates* as absolutely and visibly separate. As a matter of fact the two interpenetrate, as the elect and reprobate are commingled in civil as well as in ecclesiastical societies. And not only so, the two *civitates* depend upon one another. On the one hand the *civitas Dei* can secure no earthly good, not

---

[1] *de Civ. Dei*, XX. ix. (*supra*, p. 171 sqq.); *Retract*. II. xviii.: "ubicunque in his libris commemoraui ecclesiam non habentem maculam . . . non sic accipiendum est quasi iam sit, sed quae praeparatur ut sit."

[2] *de Civ. Dei*, XI. vii.: "sancta ciuitas in ss. angelis," etc.

[3] He goes so far (*ibid.* XV. ii.) as to speak of the Jewish Church as "pars quaedam terrenae ciuitatis," fashioned to foreshadow the heavenly *civitas*.

[4] *de Civ. Dei*, XIX. xxi., xxiv., xxv., and *supra*, p. 199, note 3.

the *pax terrena*, no possessions or buildings of any kind, —in a word it lacks the means of taking shape as a visible Church—without the aid of the *civitas terrena*. *Iure regum possidentur possessiones*; the civil authority alone can confer property rights, the Church enjoys them on the sufferance of the State,[1]—that is Augustine's clear doctrine, diametrically opposite to that of Ambrose, as the circumstances under which Augustine fashioned his theory of property differed diametrically from the conditions at Milan a quarter of a century before. Practically, for all purposes not contrary to religion or morality, the Catholic must obey the law; the Donatist, indignant at the employment of civil force to confiscate his churches and property, must learn that the State may resume the rights which it alone has conferred; the Catholic may be called upon to suffer the same thing; but he will recognise in it merely a trial of his faith.

But still more important is the dependence on the other side. We have already noticed the inability of the *civitas terrena* to effect its own end, the *pax terrena*, by its own resources, or without the aid of moral forces which only the *civitas Dei* can supply. A *civitas* is defined by Augustine as *concors hominum multitudo*;[2] and no such association is possible without mutual goodwill, in fact without some degree of friendship or love.[3]

---

[1] *In Joh. Tra.* vi. 25 sq.; see more fully Aug. § 15. Augustine in his doctrine of property is the forerunner of Arnold, Francis of Assisi, etc. See Lect. VII. p. 324, etc.

[2] *Ep.* 155. 9.

[3] *Caritas*, or *dilectio*, or *concordia*; see *de Civ. Dei*, XIX., xiv., xv., xvii. Cf. Aristotle's treatment of φιλία as the correlative of justice in the maintenance of society, *Eth. Nic.* VIII. ix. sqq.

But this again is impossible without justice. Without justice then, no society of men can hold together; the earthly *civitas* is only a *civitas* at all by virtue of some approximation, however slight, to the heavenly. As all things exist by participation in GOD, the only true Reality,[1] so every *civitas* is such only in so far as it partakes to some degree of the *civitas Dei*, which is the only *civitas* in the ultimate and real sense. Here Augustine's transcendental idealism asserts itself; and here as elsewhere he readily transfers the attributes proper to the ideal to its empirical counterpart. The Church, the ecclesiastical Society, takes the place of the *civitas superna*,[2] and becomes the only true *civitas*[3] which exists on earth. The State, in so far as it is Christian,—*i.e.* in so far as it is other than a *grande latrocinium*,—merges, *qua civitas*, in the Church,[4] and the civil power becomes the weapon of the Church, the legislator and the magistrate are but sons of the Church, bound to carry out the Church's aims. Optatus, Augustine's immediate predecessor in the Donatist controversy in Africa, had still occupied the old standpoint of the Apologists and of the Nicene age. The Church, he said, was " in the Empire,"[5] *i.e.* the Empire secured liberty and the common rights of citizens for

---

[1] *In Joh. Tra.* xxxix. 8.   [2] Cf. *Serm.* 214. 11.

[3] See the moral drawn from the decay of Rome, *Ep.* 138. 16, 17; cf. *de Civ. Dei*, XIX. xxi.

[4] See *Ep.* 105. 5, 6. The power of the State is the *ordinatissima potestas* which "Deus secundum suam prophetiam subdidit Christo" . . . "et ideo *hac Ecclesiae potestate* utimur, quam ei Dominus et promisit et dedit."

[5] The Donatists had asked: "Quid est Imperatori cum ecclesia?" Optatus replies (*de schism. Don.* III. iii.): "non respublica est in ecclesia, sed ecclesia in republica, *i.e.* in imperio Romano."

Churchmen, who in return were bound to show themselves good citizens and obedient subjects: *Ecclesia in Imperio*. Augustine reverses the relation, making the Empire, in so far as it can be reclaimed from the *regnum diaboli*, the instrument and vassal of the Church: *Imperium in Ecclesia*. In the contrast between this side [1] of Augustine's philosophy of Church and Crown and the view of Church property alluded to above, we have one more example of that unreconciled antithesis between his practical Churchmanship and his religious Idealism which runs through the whole of Augustine's theory of the Church. But clearly the side we are now considering is the more significant in respect of its immediate and continuous influence. Here for the first time in history we are confronted with the interpretation of the Kingdom of GOD on earth as an omnipotent Church, which so powerfully moulded the central ecclesiastical development of the medieval system. Here, it is hardly too much to say, we have in germ the Counter-Reformation theory of the Church as a *Societas Perfecta*,[2] an institution equipped with all that is necessary to a self-contained body-politic, perfect not indeed in the moral character of its members, but in organisation, institutions, and the

[1] *Ep.* 35. 3 (A.D. 396): "Dominus iugo suo *in gremio Ecclesiae* toto orbe diffuso omnia terrena regna subiecit." Augustine is, in this and similar passages, a disciple of Ambrose (*Serm. c. Auxent.* 36, Imperator intra Ecclesiam, non super ecclesiam est). This line of thought is disparate with that indicated *supra*, p. 212, note 1 (see context of passage there cited). Both, however, are suggested by the fanatical antagonism of the Donatists to any State interference with religion. Augustine replies—(1) the Church in any case depends on the law to protect its property rights; (2) in the case of Christian emperors (cf. *de Civ. Dei*, v. xxiv.), the secular arm becomes the weapon of the Church (*supra*, note 4).

[2] See Lect. VII. p. 344, note 2.

THE *CIVITAS DEI*

divine right to everything necessary to the carrying out of its temporal ends. That this is in complete harmony with the deeper side of Augustine's theory of the Kingdom of GOD can hardly be maintained; that it brings the conception of the Church into collision with imperishable Christian instincts the after-experience of the Church has I think made plain. But it is certain that Augustine to a large extent held it and was prepared to apply it in practice. One conspicuous instance of this application is in relation to the treatment of heretics and unbelievers.

In his earlier days, Augustine held that the appeal of the Church, spiritual in its nature, must be addressed to the spirit only, and must be restricted to the methods of persuasion by warning, entreaty, and argument.[1] His personal experience had impressed upon him the difficulty of the process by which man arrives at spiritual truth,[2] and the uselessness of angry or violent methods to force the process. Moreover the experience of the Church under persecution had taught him that while persecution breaks the feeble and half-hearted, it nerves and braces the conviction of the nobler spirits. But the opinion of some of his colleagues, instances of coercion successfully applied,—arguments of a purely opportunist character,—and the precedent of imperial legislation against paganism, overbore his scruples.[3] "I yielded," he tells us; and once he had given way, he was able not only to refute the Donatists by an effective appeal to their own law-

---
[1] "*Neminem ad unitatem Christi esse cogendum*; uerbo esse agendum, disputatione pugnandum, *ratione uincendum*" (*Ep.* 93. 17).
[2] *c. Ep. Fund.* 1-3.
[3] Cf. *Epp.* 23. 7; 93. 5, 17; 185. 25; *Retract.* II. v., *Ep.* 50.

less violence in contrast to the *ordinatissimae potestates*[1] employed to put them down, but to bring the result, in which he had against his better judgment acquiesced, into relation with his theory of the *Imperium in Ecclesia*. He yielded himself without further reserve to the principle "cogite intrare."

If then we eliminate from our consideration of Augustine's theory of the Church all elements directly traceable to his transcendental philosophy of religion, or again to his distinctive doctrines of grace and predestination, we are left with a conception of the visible Church, and of its relation to human society and government which is prophetic of the coming development. That the medieval conception of the Kingdom of GOD as an omnipotent Church was consciously derived from Augustine, or was even due to any conscious analysis of the idea of the Kingdom of GOD itself, is true only within very narrow limits.[2] The process by which a conception of the Church, and of the Church's relation to the State and Society, grew up, was unconscious, determined not by theoretical but by practical conditions. In Augustine the organic, subconscious process rises for a moment into consciousness. Here is his importance. He registers for us the beginning of a process the full nature and destiny of which he could not fully realise, a process which could only be embodied in fact in conditions which Augustine neither knew nor foresaw,[3] but which were none the less even then on their way to fulfilment.

[1] *Supra*, p. 213, note 4.
[2] But see below on Gregory VII. (Lect. VI. p. 252, note 1).
[3] Augustine's view of the general government of the Church, and the seat of sovereignty within it, is fully discussed Aug. § 12.

V

To understand Augustine's relation to the characteristic medieval idea of the Kingdom of GOD, we must, as I have said, for the moment eliminate from our survey certain elements of his many-sided range of thought. These were in fact the very elements which were least deeply rooted in the minds of contemporary Churchmen, least congenial to the mind of the age that followed Augustine, and were in fact eliminated by it.[1]

But to Augustine himself they were no unessential accidents which could be dropped without affecting his general religious position. They were on the contrary part of his innermost core of religious certitude. And in more ways than have been alluded to above Augustine's most inward convictions made it impossible for him to reach a rounded-off and consistent theory of the Church and her authority. That absolute Reality and Truth are in GOD alone, that Truth and Goodness are inseparable, that we can, even under GOD'S grace, possess Goodness and Truth only relatively, that absolute Truth is not within our grasp in this life, not until faith and knowledge are one in the vision of eternity, all this was Augustine's habitual conviction. Infallible authority, then, belongs to the Church in that degree in which knowledge of Reality is possible to man: it is her ideal attribute, but the Church as known to us is but the visible shadow of the *civitas superna*. She has truth, trustworthy for all practical purposes, *Catholica veritas*, but never in the

[1] *Supra*, pp. 193, 203.

sense that it is accessible to the bare-handed grasp of reason;[1] never as *ultimate* truth. *Credo ut intelligam* is the ideal order, but is never adequately realisable in this life.[2] Here the Church, collectively and in all her members, is and remains a *seeker*. Authority is, ideally, but the door through which the soul passes to the knowledge of GOD; practically we are all dependent on it, all "stulti"; the authority of the Catholic Church is, negatively and in contrast with other pretenders, to be followed and trusted. But positive finality it cannot possess or claim. This is most probably the reason[3] why we look in vain to Augustine for any indication of an infallible, irreformable *organ* of Church authority. He discusses this question more than once, or rather he is on the point of discussing it but never actually grasps it. Councils, he appears to hold, are the supreme organs of authority in matters of doctrine; occasionally he attaches high importance to their acceptance by the Apostolic See of Rome. But the decisions of councils can be amended; local by more general, these by ecumenical, and of these again earlier by later. This latter is precisely the point reached by Pope Julius I.[4] more than seventy years before Augustine; evidently Augustine knew, no more than Julius, any final organ of Church authority. But with Augustine, the liability of councils to indefinite revision can hardly be separated from the unreconciled

---

[1] Cf. Aug. § 16*b*.

[2] *de util. Cred.* 34. The "stulti" cannot complete the process, but must be content with authority. Only, ideally, they do not constitute the standard of Christian perfection.

[3] See Reuter, p. 350 and following, and his reff.

[4] See Lect. IV. p. 161, note 1.

antithesis in his mind between faith and knowledge, the transcendent and the empirical.

It need not then surprise us that Augustine, as has been remarked, bequeathed to the medieval Church three unsolved questions, all of vast importance, which were certain, with time, to demand a practical answer.

Of the first question, the relation between the ecclesiastical and the predestinarian ideals of the Church, I have already said[1] what is necessary for my present purpose. The second question was a more external, but not less vital one. Augustine in the *de Civitate Dei* had dimly but unmistakably outlined a new ideal of the Kingdom of GOD on earth, in which the Empire should take its place within the Church, and the Church through it should govern the world. With the Church as then constituted, such an ideal could not be realised even approximately. For it to become, not an unpractical dream but a living fact, the Church must be able to act promptly and habitually as a whole, it must possess a normal, a central, a supreme organ of authority, such as Augustine never even faintly conceived.[2] To give effect to the ideas of the *de Civitate Dei*,—if only to put them to the test of practical application,—an episcopal federation, working together only by conciliar action, was wholly powerless; a papacy was needed, and Augustine knew of none. What then,—this is the second great question which Augustine raised, but left it to posterity to settle,—what is to be the constitution of the Catholic Church? Episcopal in Cyprian's sense, conciliar in the sense of the Nicene age, or papal in the sense already

[1] *Supra*, pp. 194-205.   [2] *Supra*, p. 216, note 3.

implied in many utterances and acts of Roman bishops, and presently to be still more vigorously formulated by Leo the Great?[1] The constitution of the *local* Church, the Diocese, had been settled from time immemorial; the bishop was its head, the *sacerdos* in the unique sense. But during the hundred years of which Augustine's life saw the close, the question had been forced upon the Church by terrible experience:— who is to judge when bishops are in conflict? Councils no doubt, but what if they also differ? is there no constitution for the Church Catholic as a whole? or a constitution so incomplete as to provide no finality in the Church's decisions, no authority to which, in the ultimate resort, all Christians are bidden to look? In a word, it was agreed that the Church is governed by an organised hierarchy of bishops, but the *form of the hierarchy* was a question for the future. Augustine, as we have seen, has no answer to this question; but an answer on a magnificent scale was preparing and was assured at least of trial, and in part of success.

The third question seems one of lesser magnitude, but it is a vital one, and to some extent links together the other two. It is this: Have the spiritual censures, the excommunications, the reconciliations, of the Church an absolute, unconditional validity, or is there an appeal open from the judgment of man to the justice of GOD? To us the question may seem to answer itself; but we must remember the terrible sternness of Augustine's view of heresy and schism,[2] the ruthlessness with which in some places he insists upon the obvious sense of the

[1] See Gore's article on Leo in *Dict. Chron. Biography*.
[2] Reuter, p. 501.

axiom *Extra ecclesiam nulla salus*,[1] the awful significance attached then and later to exclusion from the Church, as a "binding on earth" which would not fail to be ratified in heaven. Yet how could Augustine, with his inward certainty of the lack of finality inherent in all that takes place on earth, Augustine with his conception of the true Church as the "numerus praedestinatorum," refuse to allow that sometimes the reprobate might be absolved by the ecclesiastical tribunal, the elect condemned and excommunicated? He never expressly discusses the question in this form. But here and there he betrays some consciousness of it. There may be those, he says, who are regularly, but by a miscarriage of justice, excluded from the visible society of the Church. "Such men the Father, who seeth in secret, crowns in secret."[2] If they accept their unjust sentence in a Christian spirit, and without stirring up schisms, they set an example to the rest of mankind. Such cases are, he continues, rare, but not unknown; in fact they are probably much commoner than might be supposed.

To sum up, then, the complex question we have been discussing to-day: Augustine, in common with all who had gone before him, finds no adequate embodiment of the Kingdom of GOD short of the world to come; the Kingdom of GOD is perfect, and

---

[1] *Serm. ad Caesareensis ecclesiae plebem*, cf. Aug. § 8c.

[2] *De vera relig.* 11. This is faithfully reproduced in Quesnel's theses (condemned in the Bull *Unigenitus*), 91, 92: "Excommunicationis iniustae metus nunquam debet nos impedire ab implendo debito nostro; nunquam eximus ab ecclesia, etiam quando hominum nequitia uidemur ab ea expulsi, quando Deo, Iesu Christo, atque ipsi ecclesiae per caritatem affixi sumus," etc. For other expressions of Augustine's view, see *Ep.* 78. 4; *de Serm. in Mont.* II. xviii. 62; see also below, p. 257, note 1.

in its full reality is reserved for the eternity when that which is in part shall be done away. On this fundamental point he never wavered. But for that great harvest the seed is being sown on earth, and shock after shock of corn is being gathered in. There is therefore an inchoate and imperfect, but still a true embodiment of the Kingdom of Christ on earth. In this sense the Church is the Kingdom of Christ. The Church may be regarded in two ways, either as the external Society bound together by the sacraments, the *correptio*, and the hierarchy, or else as the sum total of those now on earth who are predestined to eternal life. It is the latter aspect of the Church, accordingly, that alone satisfies the Augustinian identification of the Church with the Kingdom of Christ on earth. But Augustine is constantly passing from the ideal to the phenomenal, and he is constantly applying, ideally, to the *externa communio* of the Church conceptions derived from the consideration of the *communio sanctorum*, the unalterable number of the elect. Hence the visible hierarchically organised Church acquires in his thought and language much of the ideal character of the Kingdom of GOD. It was only required to slightly change the significance of the latter idea, to substitute for the Reign of the saints with Christ, for the Reign of Christ in the soul, the familiar thought of a kingdom in the sense of an organised government, to make Augustine's doctrine of the Church the foundation for the ecclesiastical superstructure, raised by Gregory VII. and Innocent III., of an omnipotent hierarchy set over nations and kingdoms, to pluck up and to break down and to destroy, and to overthrow and to build and to plant.

LECTURE VI

THE KINGDOM OF GOD IN THE MEDIEVAL THEOCRACY

> Surely he sought thy praise—thy praise, for all
> He might be wedded to the task so well
> As to forget awhile its proper end.
>
> BROWNING.

> Quid est ergo Ecclesia nisi multitudo fidelium, universitas Christianorum? Hoc itaque nomen signat membra Christi participantia Spiritum Christi.
>
> HUGO DE S. VICTOR.

> Diuitiae habitae difficile contemnuntur: sunt enim uisco uiscosiores.
>
> ST. JEROME.

LECTURE VI

THE KINGDOM OF GOD IN THE MEDIEVAL THEOCRACY

See I have this day set thee over the nations and over the kingdoms, to root out and to pull down and to destroy, and to throw down, to build, and to plant.—JER. i. 10.

WHEN St. Augustine points to the Kingdom of GOD as our chief good and as the goal of all endeavour, he is thinking of it as realised in the next world, as the Eternal Life which GOD has prepared for them that love him. In this, he is giving utterance to the common faith and hope of all Christians of all times, and marks no epoch in the history of Christian thought on the subject. But in the definition of the Kingdom of GOD on earth he stands at the beginning of a new historical development. His change of conviction in this respect arose, as we have seen, from the felt necessity of a comprehensive religious interpretation of the course taken by human affairs as a whole, in a word from the need of a religious philosophy of history.[1] Such a philosophy of history, implicit rather than consciously argued out, the earlier Church had found in the old Realistic Eschatology, in the expectation of the imminence of the second Advent with the

[1] *Supra*, Lect. I. p. 27 sq., III. p. 105, V. pp. 206–214.

earthly reign of Christ in its train. But in the East, Origen had made this Eschatology impossible; in its place he had offered a subtle emanationist theory of the universe which the Church never accepted nor could accept. The Eastern Church accordingly was left without a philosophy of history, and remains without one to this day. The illusion of the Christian empire, fossilised in Byzantinism, was but a feeble substitute for the inspiring ideal of an earthly kingdom of Christ.[1] But Augustine who, nearly two centuries after Origen, superseded Millenniarism in the West, replaced it by a profound historical idea which fertilised and ennobled [2] the merely hierarchical interpretation of the Kingdom of GOD, and secured for it a long and fruitful influence in the life of nations as yet unborn. The *de Civitate Dei* lays the foundation for the characteristic medieval conception of the Kingdom of GOD, that of an omnipo-

---

[1] The Greek Church of to-day reproduces the Church of the Greek Fathers in the absence from its theology of any complete theory of the Church. (*a*) The Russian Church is the modern embodiment of Byzantinism, *i.e.* the original illusion of the Christian empire (*supra*, Lect. IV. p. 159) hardened down into the *de facto* supremacy of the emperor which dates in principle from Theodosius I. (*b*) The Patriarchal theory, which is that of the Greek Church proper, erects into a constitutional principle of the Church what is merely a late and incidental result of history,—the superior eminence of certain particular Sees. This is not all loss. That "the Church is in her structure not a State," while "the Church of Rome is a State and has a right to act as a State" (Khomiakoff in Birkbeck, *Russia and the English Church*, i. 7 sq.), is a far-reaching criticism, resting on a genuinely archaic conception of the Church. (Contrast the reff. in Gierke, *Political Theories of the Middle Ages*, notes 49, 51.) But the Roman Catholic conception, in contrast to the Greek, represents a principle (whether rightly or wrongly applied) which goes back to the teaching of Christ, and not merely to an incidental development of Church history.

[2] John VIII. (A.D. 872–882) set the precedent of dating documents issued during vacancies of the imperial throne "imperatore domino nostro Iesu Christo."

AUGUSTINE AND HIS SUCCESSORS 227

tent Church. Till that is realised,—until the Church can not only inspire, educate, and admonish, not only baptise and nourish with sacraments, nurse up and show forth to the world the Christian life, but can also control the actual legislation and administration of kingdoms, and enforce obedience to her laws and decisions, something is wanting to Augustine's ideal of the *civitas Dei*,[1] to the kingdom, the complete reign of GOD on earth. But the elaboration of this ideal as a working system took many ages; nearly twelve centuries had passed before its theoretical completion was achieved.

The conception of the Kingdom of GOD as an omnipotent Church, in the form, indispensable to its practical effect, of papal absolutism, was in large measure realised in the Middle Ages, and it is still in theory maintained by the Roman Catholic Church.[2]

In principle it was the legacy of St. Augustine. On the theology of the Church, both in its inherent character and in its relation to the civil Society, he said the last word for many ages to come. But he never considered the problem as a practical one, never analysed the means which were necessary if his theory was to take effect, above all, never conceived of its first indispensable prerequisite, namely, a central authority

---

[1] That is, as explained later on, to one side of it. See Reuter, *August. Stud.* 499, and Gierke, *Political Theories of the Middle Ages*, pp. 112, 109.

[2] Pius IX. on August 22, 1851, condemned the statement that "doctrina comparantium Romanum Pontificem Principi libero et agenti in universa ecclesia, doctrina est quae medio aevo praevaluit" (*Syll. Error.*, 1864, No. 34). What is condemned is of course not the truism that the doctrine of papal absolutism prevailed in the Middle Ages, but the suggestion that it was *merely* medieval.

capable of wielding the prerogatives of the *civitas Dei*.[1]

It was not, indeed, necessary that any such analysis should be made in theory; what was essential was that the Institution should take shape as an accomplished fact; the need was not for Theology but for organisation.

The dying eyes of Augustine were hardly closed when his native Africa ceased to be a Roman province, and passed into the hands of the Teutonic conqueror. The Roman times were passing away, the time of the new peoples had come.

The circumstances of the earlier Middle Ages, the difficulty, in the face of untamed barbaric passion, of maintaining any right or enforcing any principle that could not appeal to force or fear, the decay almost all over the West, but especially in Italy under the Lombard conquest, of letters and learning, the increasing divergence and consequent controversies between the Latin and Greek Churches, all in different ways impelled the Western Church in one direction, that of closer organisation and reliance upon resources other than spiritual. Theology had outlived its constructive period, and was in fact hardly alive. The utmost of which it was capable was to preserve the heritage of dogma handed down from the constructive age;[2] to

---

[1] See above, Lect. V. pp. 216, 219.

[2] The essay of Vincent of Lerins, on the criteria of Catholic truth, heralds in this tendency, which is also indicated by the new interest in heresiology (Augustine, Philaster, Praedestinatus), and in compendia of Church doctrine, *e.g.* Gennadius, *de eccl. dogm.* (about 500), Fulgentius, *de fide* (*c.* 510). See Seeberg, *Dogmengesch.* i. 327, n. Of Gregory I. Harnack (*DG.* iii. 233) goes so far as to say: "Gregor hat nirgendwo einen originellen Gedanken ausgesprochen ; er hat vielmehr überall den überlieferten Lehrbegriff conservirt, aber depotenzirt," etc.

AUGUSTINE AND HIS SUCCESSORS 229

the working out of the idea of the Church it devoted no attention. But practical urgency, and as time went on the growth of ecclesiastical Law,[1] were building up the system of the future: precedents which favoured the general process were carefully used up, in some cases were fabricated.[2]

In Gregory the Great (590–604) we see the process of building up a central authority in a transition stage. Gregory takes for granted, certainly, the papal position as decisively formulated by Leo I. a century and a half before. He claims without misgiving to have inherited the custody of the universal Church committed to St. Peter, and to act as the ultimate judge of appeal in the concerns of all Churches, even of that of Constantinople, whose patriarchal rank he did not in theory recognise. But it must be noted that he claims no dogmatic authority. He professes his absolute homage to the four General Councils; on entering upon office he sends his confession of faith to the four patriarchs, including even Constantinople; he recognises that the bishops of Alexandria and Antioch are, like himself, heirs of St. Peter, he protests that he would never make the sacrilegious claim to be "universal bishop." To a patriarch who addressed him with this title, he replies that he is best honoured if honour is paid to all the Church, "honor meus est

---

[1] Rashdall, *Universities of Europe*, i. 232 : "It was not by Theology so much as by Law—by her inheritance of those traditions of Imperial Jurisprudence which had subtly wound themselves round the common Faith of Europe—that Rome established her spiritual monarchy." Cf. Bp. Stubbs' Lecture *On the Characteristic Differences between Medieval and Modern History*, Lectures, ed. 3, p. 240, etc.

[2] See below, p. 238, note 2.

honor totius ecclesiae."[1] The great blot upon his fame is his obtaining from the murderous usurper Phocas an edict recognising his supremacy, which the murdered emperor Maurice had refused. But apart from this, Gregory combined with the unflinching assertion of the papal claims as he had inherited them an exemplary personal modesty and charity. On the whole, his high personal character recovered for the Roman See the loss of prestige which it had suffered at the hands of the popes of Justinian's reign, especially at those of the weak and unprincipled Vigilius. And not only so. The political necessity which had withdrawn the imperial viceroy of Italy to Ravenna left the Pope the only really important public functionary in Rome. Upon him fell the responsibility for warding off the Lombards from Rome, of negotiating peace first with the Lombard duke of Spoleto, then seven years later with King Agilulf himself, and Gregory not only won Spain, and England, and the dreaded Lombards themselves to the Catholic Church and to the spiritual allegiance of Rome ; but he laid the first foundations of that temporal power without which the spiritual empire of his See, and its position at the head of the medieval political system, could never have been securely founded.[2]

[1] This dictum of Gregory, nobly used by him in disclaiming episcopal jurisdiction over all Christians, is rather cynically incorporated into the decree of the Vatican Council of 1870 as a reason for claiming it (c. iii.). But whereas Gregory means "if you would honour me, honour the Church," his modern successor means " if you would honour the Church, honour me." On Gregory generally, see the article in *Dict. Chr. Biog.*, one of the best of the masterly and judicial articles on Roman bishops from my friend Dr. Barmby (*in pace*). See also his work in *Nicene Lib.* vols. xii., xiii.

[2] A very interesting anticipation of future development is the threat in a letter to an abbess of Gaul (Greg. M. *Ep.* 9) : " Moreover, if any one,

II

(*a*) The four centuries and a half which separate Gregory the Great from Gregory the Seventh are of fundamental importance in the development now under review. They are collectively spoken of as the "dark ages," and with reason. It is true they were never wholly dark. In the darkest age of all, which extends from Gregory I. to the reign of Charles the Great, the lamp of learning and study, quenched in Italy and in most parts of the Continent, was burning brightly in scattered monastic societies north of the Alps, nowhere more brightly than by the banks of the Wear and the Tyne in our own country, whence it passed to the coast of the great Frankish king.[1] The Mahometan power, which swept away more than half of the Eastern empire poured over Africa and Spain and threatened to overpower Europe, was beaten back by Charles Martel in 732. And if the Church was intellectually weak, the great missions of the eighth century, the work of a Willibrord and a Boniface testify to her spiritual vitality. The papacy was active and respected, though in the hands of comparatively obscure men. Honorius, Martin I., Leo II., Gregory II. are not the peers of Leo or of Gregory the Great, yet they com-

whether king, priest, judge . . . etc., let *him be deprived* of the dignity," etc. etc. But Gregory is rather momentarily forgetting the limits of his authority than formally asserting the later right to depose (see below, pp. 232, 252, notes).

[1] Bede, A.D. 673-735 (at Wearmouth and Jarrow); Egbert, archbishop of York, 732-766; Alcuin, b. in Yorkshire about 735, 782-789 at Court of Charles, 796-804 abbot of Tours. Among his pupils Prudentius of Troyes, Ratramn of Corbie, Remigius of Lyons, Raban Maur (see Stubbs in *Dict. Chr. Biogr.* i. 74).

pare favourably with the popes of the age of Justinian. But the age was a dark one, and political confusion weighed heavily on the intellectual life of the Church. "Our countries," writes a pope of the seventh century, "are incessantly harassed by the fury of divers nations; there is nothing but battle, unrest, and rapine. In the midst of these barbarians our life is full of disquiet. We live by the labour of our hands, for by divers calamities the ancient possessions of our Churches have little by little been destroyed."[1] "For more than three centuries," to quote Dean Church, "it seems as if the world and human society had been hopelessly wrecked, without prospect or hope of escape."[2]

But beneath all the misery and confusion the seeds of a new world were quick with life, and the new races were founding a civilisation higher and more enduring than that which they had destroyed. After the age of Charles the Great, with whom the reign of pure barbaric force is ended,[3] the dark ages were never, not even in the dismal tenth century, quite so dark as they had been in the seventh and eighth.

The light, which political disorder had quenched, was fanned to temporary splendour with the renewal of strong and organised rule. That Pope Zachary was appealed to by Pipin the Short to sanction the deposition of Chilperic the last *fainéant* king of the Franks,[4]

[1] Agatho to the Council of Constantinople under Constantine Pogonatus, A.D. 681.
[2] *Beginning of the Middle Ages.*   [3] Oman, *Europe*, 476-918.
[4] Eginhardt, *ad ann.* 749 (*PL.* civ. 373): "Burchardus Wirziburegensis episcopus et Folradus presbiter capellanus missi sunt Roman ad Zachariam papam ut consulerent pontificem de causa regum . . . per quos praedictus Pontifex *mandauit* melius esse illum uocari regem . . . dataque auctoritate sua *iussit* Pippinum regem constitui"; and *ad ann.* 750: "Hoc

that his successor Stephen II.[1] anointed Pipin and Charles as kings at St. Denis in 754, are facts more significant perhaps as omens of what was to come than as expressive of any then formally recognised authority of the Roman See to make or unmake kings. More important was the transaction by which Pipin, after finally putting down the Lombard supremacy in Italy, presented the territory, which the Lombards had wrested from the Greek emperor, to the successor of St. Peter.[2] The possession of a formally recognised territorial sovereignty, for the present no doubt under the theoretical suzerainty of the Frankish crown, was a far more concrete thing than the " uncrowned kingship " of Gregory the Great. Coupled with the record— which now appeared for the first time—of the donation of Constantine,[3] it committed the Roman See to the

anno secundum Rom. Pontificis sanctionem Pippinus rex Francorum appellatus est . . . Hildericus uero qui falso regis nomine fungebatur tonso capite in monasterium missus est." This was a precedent appealed to from Gregory VII. onwards (Gierke, p. 116, n. 30 ; p. 117, n. 34).

[1] See on the question of coronation at this period, Fisher, *Medieval Empire*, vol. i. p. 30 sqq. It may be worth noting that the first hint we have of the coronation of kings by bishops is in the dream of Theodosius (Thdt. *H. E.* v. vi.). The first pope to crown an emperor is supposed to have been John I., who on his visit to Constantinople (525), is said to have crowned Justin (for the *second* time). By the eighth century the emperors were always crowned by the Greek patriarchs ; the coronation referred to in the text is the first example of a pope crowning a German king. The next is the famous coronation of Christmas Day, 800. (Cheetham in *Dict. Chr. Antiq.* 466 ; see next page, note 1.)

[2] *Dict. Chr. Biogr.* iv. 403 and reff.

[3] This is not the place to unravel the complicated strata of forgery which enter into the "Donation." The substratum of truth is that Constantine aided in the building and enrichment of churches both in Rome and elsewhere. The superstructure of error is that he (1) was healed of leprosy and baptised by Silvester, bishop of Rome ; and (2) in gratitude for this, granted to Silvester the Lateran Palace, sovereignty in Italy and the West, and the insignia of Empire. The forgery, which was accompanied by a personal

principle of the temporal power, at first as a mere Church endowment, later on as the indispensable condition of effective spiritual dominion, and in the inevitable result as an inalienable political right.

The work of Charles the Great[1] marked an all-important epoch, both in the renewed Church-life of Western Europe and in the great question of the future, the function of the Church in relation to Government. The ecclesiastical and theological literature of the Caroline age is in compass, quality, and importance superior to any that appeared between the periods of the two great Gregories. But the immediate effect of the revival of the Western Empire was rather to retard than to further the building up of papal power. The illusion of the Christian empire momentarily reappears in Charles, the new Constantine—or rather the new David or Josiah.[2] He had already, with the support of his clergy, and in the teeth of papal ratification, set aside the decision of the Greek council which made a dogma of iconolatry.[3] His office, as he conceived it, was one of religious and moral, as well as political supremacy. True, Leo had placed on his head the imperial crown,—adding to the feebler precedent set

---

letter to Pipin from the Apostle St. Peter, was designed to give the Donation of Pipin the character of a restoration. (See G. Krüger in *Theologische Literaturzeitung*, 1889, nn. 17, 18; Mirbt, *Quellen zur Gesch. des Papstthums*, No. 60; Duchesne, *Lib. Pontif.* I. ccxxxix.; Döllinger, *Papstfabeln*, and *Papsttum*, 28, 370; Richardson on Euseb. *V. C.*, Nicene Lib. vol. i. p. 442; Dante, *Inf.* xix. 115 sqq.

[1] A.D. 768-814. Crowned emperor of Rome by Leo III., Christmas Day, 800. See Döllinger, *Kaiserthum Karls des Gr.* in his *Akad. Vorträge*, vol. iii.; Fisher, *Medieval Empire*, chap. i.; and Bryce, *Holy Roman Empire*.

[2] "David" was Charles' name in the literary circle of Alcuin.

[3] On the Council of Frankfort and *Libri Carolini*, see Möller, *Kirchengesch.* ii. 116; Milman, *Lat. Christ.* iii. 94-103.

by Zachary all the pomp and symbolism of a world-historical ceremony. But no one in that age was ready to draw the deduction—

> Homo fit Papae sumit quo dante coronam.[1]

The Pope had "adored," in the sight of the assembled crowd in St. Peter's, the Emperor whom he had crowned. He had renounced his allegiance to the distant Empress, to the distrusted throne of Byzantium, with no idea but that of transferring it to a Catholic and Western prince who had protected him against his foes and to whom he might look for protection for the future. Leo frankly accepted the position of a subject, Charles that of the head of Western Christendom, the supreme Lord of Rome, the guardian of popes and the guarantor of papal elections. Practically this meant a feudal government of the Church. The ordinary diocesan bishop was subject to the great metropolitans, who as prince-bishops were the vassals of the imperial throne. The relations of Pope and Emperor were tolerable and even cordial; but in changed conditions they might soon become intolerable.

(*b*) And with the death of Charles, conditions rapidly changed. The confusion, in which the Carolingian empire soon lost its unity and its power to command respect, left the great Sees of the empire in a position of independence dangerous to the papacy, oppressive to their suffragans.

---

[1] See below, p. 259. Leo's behaviour to Charles is that of a subject; Eginhardt, *ad ann.* 800: "Occurrit ei pridie Leo papa et Romani cum eo apud Nomentum, xii^{mo} ab Urbe lapide, et summa eum humilitate summoque honore suscepit, prandensque cum eo ad Urbem praecessit"; and *ad ann.* 801: "post quas laudes" [*i.e.* post imperatoris salutationem] "ab eodem pontifice more antiquorum patrum *adoratus* est" [Carolus].

To this state of things was directly due a momentous step toward the goal of papal autocracy, the forgery of the pseudo-Isidorian Decretals. Composed in Gaul, possibly in the chapter of Le Mans, they were designed in the interest of the suffragan episcopate, who looked to Rome for protection against the metropolitans and the civil power. The main part of the forgery consisted of nearly a hundred papal decretals, of which fifty-nine were ascribed to popes from the apostolic age down to Siricius (385), who was the first Roman bishop to issue letters of this kind.[1] The forgery was momentous in its consequences,—not because it greatly extended the claims of the popes, but because it so completely imposed on an uncritical age, and because it bequeathed to the centuries which followed, centuries in which a growing importance was attached to legal precedent, a wholly false conception of the constitution of the earlier Church. It represented the popes from the days of the Apostles onward as doing what for four centuries they never had done,—as legislating for the universal Church by edict and rescript, in the manner of the popes of the ninth

---

[1] They grew out of the correspondence with foreign bishops who wrote to consult their most influential colleague. Siricius (see above, Lect. IV. p. 164, note 2) was the first to date his replies by the Consulate, after the style of an imperial rescript. The forger incorporated in the second of the three parts collections of genuine canons already in existence, *e.g.* in Dionysius Exiguus and in the Spanish Corpus. The latter fact, and the name "Isidorus Mercator" which he assumes in the preface, suggested that the collection was the work of St. Isidore of Seville. He incorporates some existing forgeries, *e.g.* the letter of Clement to James, the *constitutio Silvestri*, and the Donation of Constantine. But nearly all the early papal letters are of his own invention. See the monumental edition by Hinschius (1863); Möller, *Kirchengesch.* ii. 149 sqq.; Döllinger, *Papstthum*, 35-40, 375, 377.

century. This was the most important thing which the Isidorian forgery effected; it effectually stifled any attempt that might have been made to appeal to the constitution of the early Church, and it contributed powerfully to displace the old conciliar basis of canon law in favour of the principle of papal legislation, upon which medieval Canon Law substantially rests.

The forgery is first heard (862) of in connexion with the appeal of Rothad, bishop of Soissons, against his deposition by the famous Hinkmar, archbishop of Reims. Into the details of the case there is no need to go. What is important is the part played by Pope Nicolas the Great in vindicating his right to set Hinkmar's sentence aside. In reply to Hinkmar's demurrer to the authority of the decretals alleged by Rothad, Nicolas rebukes him for refusing to be bound by decrees, preserved in the *scrinia* of the Apostolic See, which his predecessors in the papacy had sealed "with their rosy blood," *roseo cruore*.[1] These words make it clear that the Forged Decretals are in question, for the few martyred popes[2] belong to the age previous to any genuine decretals. Nicolas therefore asserts that these, the False Decretals, were preserved in the *scrinia* of his See. Whether he had had the archives examined, and was speaking in contravention of ascertained fact, or merely assumed their genuineness without caring to verify his words, he cannot be cleared from a moral blunder of the gravest kind.

---

[1] Mansi, *Concil.* xv. 694 sqq.; Hinschius, ccv. sqq.; Mirbt, *Quellen*, No. 62.

[2] Telesphorus (*c.* 135), Pontianus (confessor, 235), Fabianus (250), Xystus (258); the last is one hundred and thirty years earlier than the first genuine decretal.

The Decretals, then, were not a Roman forgery. They were fabricated neither at Rome nor by Rome nor for Rome. But they were with indecent eagerness greedily exploited by Rome; and for many centuries, from Nicolas himself down to St. Alfonso Liguori in the eighteenth century,[1] they were the weapons of those who sought to maintain or increase the prerogatives of the papal throne. The papacy has made itself " an accessory after the fact." We need not dwell too severely on the moral aspect of the question as affecting Nicolas personally. But as it affects the cause, the case is different. The papacy has been in GOD'S hands an instrument which has accomplished much for Christianity and for civilisation. But it cannot be acquitted of conscious fraud in many of the vitally necessary steps by which its power has been built up. The assertion by Nicolas of the genuineness of the False Decretals was but a link in a long series[2] of

[1] And Bishop Roskovány in the nineteenth. Quotations from them are still made by minor controversialists; I have seen one in a letter to the *Guardian* this year.

[2] Of these we may mention: 1. The repeated attempts in the fifth century to pass off Sardican canons as Nicene (*DCB.*, new ed. AUGUSTINE, § 12 (*c*). 2. The false heading to the sixth canon of Nicea produced at Chalcedon. 3. The story of Lucius, king of Britain (Duchesne, *Lib. Pont.* l. ciii., sixth century). 4. The story of pope Marcellinus and the Council of Sinuessa (sixth century, Döllinger, *Papstthum*, p. 23, and *Papst-fabeln*). 5. The Cyprianic forgeries (Rome, about 600; see von Hartel, *Cypr. Opp.* III. xliii., and Benson, *Cyprian*, p. 527; the interpolations are still often quoted as genuine). 6. The Donation of Constantine (*supra*, p. 233, note 3). 7. The letter of St. Peter to Pipin (*ibid.*). 8. The False Decretals. This and No. 6 were of vast importance, and believed throughout the Middle Ages. 9. The collection of extracts from Greek Fathers, especially from Cyril of Alexandria, forged by a Dominican in the Levant, about 1250. It was sent to Thomas Aquinas by Urban IV. (formerly Latin patriarch of Jerusalem) about 1261, and was used by him as the basis of his work *contra errores Graecorum*. But Thomas (who used the forgery of

falsifications which had begun in the tampering with the canons of Nicea more than four centuries before, and which continued until the fabric of which these frauds were the scaffolding was solidly established.

But the leaven of the False Decretals worked slowly, and the period which immediately followed upon their appearance was one of retrogression rather than advance in the history of papal power.

The period between Charles the Great and the Ottos marks a pause in the movement toward the medieval realisation of the *civitas Dei*. If Boniface, the first transalpine bishop who had sworn fealty to Rome (722), had preached the papacy along with the Gospel to the German nations, and brought the whole Frankish Church into subjection to the pope; if Charles had unified the Western Church by comprehending in the unity of an empire the Italian and the Germanic world; if Nicolas, by his complete rupture with the Greek Church,[1] had got rid of every living tradition of the pre-papal constitution of the Church Catholic, and had thus cleared the way for the pseudo-Isidorian principles to work their way unchecked in the civil disorganisation left by the break-up

course without suspecting its nature) had seen it before this, for a quotation from the false Cyril is used in his work on the *Sentences*, as well as in the *catena aurea* on Matt. xvi.; see *Summ. Theol. Suppl.* Q. 40, a. 6. This forgery, which gave Thomas a wholly false idea of the tradition of the Greek Fathers, occurred at the critical period when the constitution of the Church was becoming incorporated for the first time in the framework of Dogmatic Theology, and is perhaps the most glaring and momentous of all. (See Reusch in *Transactions of the Royal Bavarian Academy*, class 3, vol. xviii. 3, pp. 624-742, a full and apparently final investigation.)

[1] The story of this, which lies outside the scope of these Lectures, is worked out by Card. Hergenröther in his great work on Photius with admirable thoroughness and fair impartiality.

of the empire of Charles,—yet the papacy lacked both the moral power and the material resources which were necessary if the result of all these various processes was to be gathered in. Moral power, above all, was conspicuously and increasingly wanting. At one time, indeed, it seemed as if, in spite of all the tendencies that set in the direction of a papacy, the crowning development would after all fail of effect.[1] In the night of the tenth century the candle of the Roman See all but went out. It was rekindled by the transalpine Church, and by the hand of its Imperial Chief.

Nicolas had died in 867, and his successor Hadrian II. found his hand already weaker against opposing forces both in East and West—against the Macedonian emperor, against Lothair and Charles the Bald, and especially against Hinkmar. Then, as we follow the troubled pontificate of John VIII. (872–882), we feel in spite of ourselves that all the grandeur of Nicolas has slipped away.[2] From the reign of Formosus (891) to that of Sergius III. the papacy is the prize of bloody faction-fights; each pope exhumes and insults the body of his predecessor, and reordains all clergy upon whom he had laid his sacrilegious hands.[3] From

---

[1] I would refer to the strong language of Gerbert, archbishop of Reims (afterward Pope Silvester II.) in *Patr. Lat.* vol. cxxxvii., or in Havet, *Lettres de Gerbert* (983–997); see Möller, ii. 169 sq., and Milman, *Lat. Christ.* v. xiii. (vol. iii. pp. 338–345).

[2] Yet see above, p. 226, note 2, and Fisher, vol. ii. p. 137 (also i. 34).

[3] See Hergenröther, *Photius*, vol. ii. p. 321 sqq. "*Die Reordinationen der alten Kirche*," especially p. 352, (Stephen III. and Constantine) p. 365, (Formosus, etc.) p. 369 sq. With every wish to minimise the anomalous facts, the cardinal candidly allows that ordinations were treated as null, and repeated; and that the "Augustinian" principles which clearly distinguished invalidity from irregularity were first finally established by the theologians and canonists of the thirteenth century.

EARLIER MIDDLE AGES 241

Sergius (904) till John XII. († 963) the depth of degradation is lower still. This is the period of pornocracy; into its squalid details it is quite unnecessary to descend.[1] The one strong man whose career and policy binds the formless criminality of the time into an intelligible story is Alberic, count of Tusculum,[2] a typical Italian despot, who aimed at securing the prize of the high-priesthood as the heirloom of his family. With all his vices, Alberic was a strong ruler, and where family ambition did not conflict with it, a promoter of religious work. He it was that invited the monastery of Cluny to establish on the Aventine their branch house of St. Mary, the future nursery of Hildebrand. But after his death in 954, his son Octavian succeeded him, and in the following year assumed the papal chair as John XII. (955–963). The character of John shocked even that age, accustomed as it was to unworthy popes. He lacked every element of Christian, even of clerical, character. But in his secular capacity he had redeeming qualities. Without honour or scruple, he was fearless, farseeing, and resourceful. His immediate object was the consolidation of his feudal supremacy in Central Italy; his dangerous rival was Berengar, whom an imperial settlement (952) had left with the title and power of king

---

[1] The main authority is Liutprand, *Antapodosis* in *Monum. Germ. Scr.* v. See Loescher, *Gesch. d. Mittleren Zeiten*, etc. (1725); the general reader will find all that he can wish to know in Milman, *Lat. Christ.* Book v. chap. xi.

[2] Ruler of Rome, A.D. 932-953. He was son of Marozia and of the Marquis Alberic, and collateral ancestor both of the consul Crescentius, son of the younger Theodora, whose family were Lords of Tibur (see for genealogical information Milman, vol. iii. pp. 319, 351; Tout, *The Empire and the Papacy*, p. 35) and of the great Roman family of Colonna.

of Italy. Twice John appealed to the Saxon emperor for aid, and the second appeal brought Otto in person (961).

The empire of Charles the Great had practically died out with Charles the Fat in 888. In Italy all was feudal chaos, in Germany first Arnulf (896), then Conrad (911) reigned as kings without the imperial style. But the victories of the Saxon Henry the Fowler[1] over the Hungarians, Danes, and Slavs, showed that a man of imperial calibre was once more king of the East Franks and Saxons. His son Otto was crowned king at Aachen in 936, and after many an arduous and successful struggle for the consolidation, defence, and extension of his kingdom, he made his second appearance in Italy, to put down the pretender Berengar at the invitation of John XII. In 962 Otto was crowned Emperor at Rome. He is the true founder of the Holy Roman Empire, German in its seat of power, Roman in its consecration, its idea, its claim to Italian supremacy.[2] His coronation marks the religious significance of his imperial function. Pope and Emperor joined in a solemn oath: the Emperor was to protect the Pope, Rome to consecrate no pope without the Emperor's approval, the civil government of Rome was to be supervised by Emperor and Pope jointly. To Otto, the settlement was of vital importance. His hold over Germany was rendered precarious by the power of the great feudal chiefs, who always tended, however carefully chosen in the first instance, to drift

---

[1] Henry was, through the female line, a descendent of Charles I.
[2] Fisher, ii. 137 sqq.; Bryce, chap. xii. pp. 193-203. The title "holy" was first used by Barbarossa,—although it occurs frequently enough in the *Notitia* of the old Roman Empire.

into hereditary antagonism to their overlord. To balance them there was the spiritual nobility, whose offices could never pass by heredity, and whose ranks the emperor could always hope to recruit by persons on whose loyalty he could depend. But to secure this, it was necessary to keep all the higher Church patronage in imperial hands, and to retain every possible check upon the great prince-bishops; and for this purpose the support of the Pope was all-important. Accordingly, while the Pope confirmed the new ecclesiastical organisation of Northern Germany, he received, but always as the liegeman of the emperor, the confirmation of his title to the States of the Church. Here then we have the second stage in the developing relations between pope and emperor; a Kingdom of GOD on earth founded upon a strict apportionment between the things of Caesar and the things of GOD. The Pope is absolutely supreme in things purely spiritual. But in things secular, in all rights of government and property, he is like the popes of the first Christian centuries, simply the subject of the Emperor.[1] John already feared and hated the protector he had invoked, and in the midst of their negotiations was inciting the Huns, whom Otto had routed at the Lechfeld in 955, to call him northwards again by a new invasion. Otto detected his duplicity, and promptly summoned a synod which deposed the Pope and consecrated in his place Leo. VIII. archivist of the See. But Otto's departure

[1] *The Privilegium Ottonis* forms a landmark in the series begun by that of Pipin in 754, and continued by those of Charles (774) and Lewis the Pious, 817. See Sickel, *das Priv. Otto's I.* (1883). No pope can be consecrated before taking the oath of fealty to the emperor; the emperor confirms, and slightly enlarges, Pipin's grant of territory.

threw all into new confusion, and until the end of the century Rome was under the sway of the Crescentii,¹ and the popes their miserable puppets. In 996 the Romans, weary of their tyranny, appeal to Otto III., who appoints, as Pope Gregory V., his cousin Bruno of Carinthia, the first of those German popes who mark the revival of the moral dignity of the See. Upon Gregory's sudden death three years later, Gerbert succeeded as Silvester II.

Gerbert was the most learned man, and in many ways the most interesting personality, of the day. Under Hugh Capet, as claimant of the See of Reims against Arnulf, he had protested boldly against papal claims. For the moment it seemed as if the learning of Northern Europe would rise in direct challenge against the whole ecclesiastical constitution of which John XII. was the living embodiment.² But the force of learning was then too weak, the need for a papacy too strong, to permit such a challenge to have lasting effect. Gerbert was deposed from the See of Reims by Gregory V., but Otto induced the Pope to pacify him with the archbishopric of Ravenna; and on succeeding to the papal throne Gerbert, like Aeneas Silvius many ages later, from the critic of papal claims became their warmest defender. But in four years he died, and once more (1003-1046) the papacy sank to its old degradation in the hands of the Crescentii. A climax was reached in the boy-pontificate of Benedict IX. (1033-1046), whose vices were as gross but not as

---

[1] See above, p. 241, note 2. The kindred houses of Alberic and of Crescentius divided the supreme power between them. Milman, v. xiv.

[2] See above, p. 240, note 1, and reff.

heroic as those of Octavian. The Crescentii set up Silvester III. to supersede Benedict; but the latter sells the papacy to Gregory VI., and then recovers it by force. The time for imperial interference had once more come, and this time the effect was lasting.

In 1046 Henry III. found three rival popes in the field; a council at Sutri deposed them all. The Constitution of Otto as to papal elections was renewed, and a German was set up as Clement III.[1] His brief reign, and the still briefer reign of his successor[2] Damasus II., paved the way for the decisive pontificate of Leo IX. This was the title chosen, upon his election in 1048, by Bruno, count of Egisheim and bishop of Toul. His pontificate is marked, like that of the last really great pope before him, by a decisive and this time a final rupture with Greek Christianity. If the papacy was to do its work the Church must be Latin, unencumbered by the traditions of a different cast of Churchmanship. Secondly, Leo brought from Cluny to Rome a man who was to be the counsellor of successive popes until he took up the succession as the greatest pope of them all—Hildebrand, afterwards Gregory VII.

The half-century which now began was a period of incalculable importance for the consolidation of the medieval Church. The papal power rose suddenly from the depth of ignominy to its greatest moral height; from subjects, the Popes became the lords of Europe and arbiters over its kings and Emperors.

Leo's great object was the reform of the clergy. In

[1] Suitger of Bamberg; he crowned Henry on Christmas Day, 1046.
[2] Poppo of Brixen. On Leo IX.'s breach with the Greek Church, see Mirbt, *Quellen*, No. 64.

many respects they were secularised; their offices were too often treated as personal possessions, bought and sold like other property, while the prevalence of clerical marriage assimilated them to the society in which they lived and worked. Such a clergy was, in the then state of the world, inevitably hampered in its power for purely spiritual good, while for the purposes of a compact army to be employed by the papacy for enforcing its will upon nations and kings, it was worse than useless. The movement against simony and "concubinatus," *i.e.* clerical marriage, into which Leo, with the powerful aid of Peter Damiani and the potent spiritual influence of the hermit St. Walbert of Vallombrosa, threw himself heart and soul, certainly enlisted the best religious minds of the age. Mainly it was directed against worldliness and laxity; to some extent no doubt wheat was rooted up with the tares. Zeal for the holiness of the Church was mingled with zeal for its power: the two were not easy to separate. The story of Leo's heroic efforts, of his repeated journeys to Gaul and Germany,[1] of his councils at Reims and Mainz, need not be told here. In Leo IX. the papacy was once more respected as a spiritual force. His energy and growing influence were not viewed with equanimity by Henry III.;[2] but the need of checking the Normans in Italy drew the Pope away from the North before any

[1] In 1049 he consecrated, at Cologne, the still famous Church of S. Maria im Kapitol. Milman compares him to "an ecclesiastical Hercules who travelled about beating down the hydra-heads of clerical avarice and licentiousness."

[2] A new Christian power had been created by the conversion of Hungary, under King Stephen (997–1038), who in the year 1000 received his crown from Silvester II. This, according to Gregory VII. (*Reg.* ii. 13), made Hungary a papal fief.

serious breach occurred. In the teeth of the protest of Peter Damiani, Leo marched against the enemy at the head of an army (1053). A crushing defeat followed, the pope was imprisoned at Benevento, and allowed to return to Rome to die (1054). The tragedy was prophetic; in the effort to realise the Kingdom of GOD as an ecclesiastical empire, the successor of Peter had taken the sword and perished by the sword. Of Leo's three shortlived successors, the third, Nicolas II., took two very important steps. In 1059 he cemented an alliance with the Normans, a distinct breach with imperial policy; and at Easter of the same year he constituted a new electoral college for the choice of the pope. This consisted of the bishops of the suburban Sees and the greater parochial clergy of Rome, those who were *incardinati* in the Roman Church. From henceforth the popes are the nominees, not of people or of emperors, but of the college of cardinals.[1]

Meanwhile, the battle against clerical marriage was carried on. It raged most fiercely at Milan, where earlier in the century the married Archbishop Heribert had triumphantly asserted the rights of his See, and ruthlessly put down the Paterini, a popular party of heretical origin, but enlisted by the party of reform as

[1] Cf. Mirbt, *Quellen*, 65. Any church with a staff of clergy formed a centre (*cardo*) to which its staff were attached (*incardinati*). Since about 748 the suburban bishops were on the staff (*incardinati*) of the Roman Church. Pope Zachary writing to Pipin, mentions *presbyteri cardinales*, *i.e.* clergy of towns, as distinct from country presbyters (*can. Neocaes.* 13). The episcopal See became the *cardo* κατ' ἐξοχήν, and the cathedral clergy the cardinals. The term is already applied by pseudo-Isidore to the Roman, as distinct from other Sees, and Leo IX. asserts that the clergy of the Roman See are especially entitled to the name *cardinales*. Their *exclusive* right to it was formally enacted by Pius V. (More details in Kreuzwald's art. in *Kirchen-Lexicon*, vol. ii.)

a fierce mob on the monastic side in opposition to the wealth of the married secular hierarchy. The heads of this party, Anselm of Badagio, Ariald, and Landulf, fortified by successive papal commissions, of one of which Hildebrand was a member, overawed Heribert's weaker successor Guido. A Roman council under Nicolas II. in 1059 condemned clerical marriage, but the bishops did not venture to promulgate the decree in Lombardy. Two years later Anselm, by the influence of Hildebrand, was elected pope as Alexander II. An antipope, Honorius II., appeared in Cadalous, bishop of Parma. For some time the issue of the struggle was doubtful. But the *coup d'état* in Germany, by which Hanno, archbishop of Cologne, seized the infant emperor Henry IV., decided it in favour of Alexander.

III

(*a*) The new pope reigned under the direction of Hildebrand: the epigram of Peter Damiani expresses their real relation:—

> Tu facis hunc Dominum, te facit ille Deum.

The pope's partisans at Milan ruled in spite of the bishop, supported by the popular frenzy of the Paterini. But the introduction (Pentecost, 1066) of the Roman rite by Ariald led to a revolution. Ariald fled to Lago Maggiore, where he was killed by a niece of Guido. The latter was seized and imprisoned by Landulf's brother Herlembald, who in turn was killed by a popular riot in 1075. But the force of resistance was spent, and Milan became by the following century the firm ally of the papacy.[1]

In 1073 Alexander died, and Hildebrand became pope as Gregory VII. In him, the influence of Cluny, which had long been a growing power in the Church, acquired its culminating strength. The reformed Benedictine abbey of Cluny, in what is now the department of Saône-et-Loire, had been founded in 910 by Duke William of Aquitaine. Odo and Maiolus, the successors of Bruno its first abbot, had been in close relation with Otto I. and Otto II. About 940 Alberic had brought Odo to Rome, and established him at St. Mary on the Aventine, which he made the head of the Roman monasteries. The influence of the order of Cluny was due to the clearness and tenacity with which they grasped their idea of Church Reform on the model of a well-governed monastery, *i.e.* by organisation in strict dependence on a single head. The zenith of their influence was in the first half of the eleventh century under abbots Odilo and Hugh. The Cluniac movement was but the chief of a number of movements of the kind in which the renewed vigour of Church life was making itself felt. In Italy there was, for example, the famous foundation of Camaldoli near Arrezzo, due to St. Romwald, of the family of the Traversari of Ravenna, which it is of interest to note furnished the order with its most illustrious and learned head in the critical times of Eugenius IV. four

[1] For the connexion of the Hildebrandine movement with the question of the marriage of the clergy, and with the disturbances at Milan, see Milman, *Lat. Chr.* vol. iii. pp. 432-479, who also describes the similar struggles elsewhere, *e.g.* at Florence between Bishop Peter and St. Walbert, ending in the triumph of the latter.

centuries later. Of the Camaldolese movement Peter Damiani,[1] the leader of clerical reform in Italy, was the child.

Gregory VII. (1073–1085), a Tuscan of humble birth, was brought up in the Cluniac house of St. Mary on the Aventine. He was in the service of Gregory VI., whom he followed to Cologne upon his deposition. From that city he betook himself to Cluny, whence, as we have seen, Leo IX. brought him back to Rome. His election[2] to the pontificate invested him with an office whose policy he had already practically directed for a quarter of a century.

The dramatic vicissitudes of his reign cannot be told here as they deserve. He was the greatest of all medieval popes, and in his person the idea of papal absolutism finds its completest embodiment. To the purely spiritual claims of the papacy, as he had inherited them from his predecessors, he made, with one exception of importance, no substantial addition. But he it was who first formulated the principle of the medieval papacy as the supreme governing power over all things and persons temporal as well as spiritual. His Cluniac training had filled him with the ideal of strict ecclesiastical obedience as the principle by which society was to be regenerated. Gregory was indeed no narrow ascetic; he lived and worked as a man among men, a man of affairs. But he was inspired through and through by the dualism which forms so marked an element in medieval religion, a dualism first applied to

[1] Born at Ravenna, abbot of Fonte Avellana, bishop of Ostia 1058–1062, died 1072. See Dante, *Par.* xxi. 121.

[2] It is noteworthy that, in spite of the settlement of Nicolas II., he was elected by popular acclamation.

HILDEBRAND AND HIS IDEAL

political theory as we have seen in Augustine's *de Civitate Dei*. Only whereas to Augustine the Church is the one divine *Society*, to Gregory it is the one divine *Government*. To Gregory as to Augustine the civil government is founded on mere force, is in its essence profane. Augustine ascribed the bond of justice, by which civil society holds together, to the inscrutable commingling of the two *civitates* in the complex web of human history. His conception of the *civitas Dei* as consisting of the elect tempered his tendency to identify the antithesis between the two *civitates* as that between Church and Realm. But Gregory, whose interest was wholly that of the ecclesiastical statesman, conceived of the State as wholly secular, the Church as wholly sacred. The *iustitia* necessary to the well-being and coherence of the state must be imposed upon it by the legislative, judicial, and administrative action of the Church. But the Church at large, *i.e.* the episcopate, was, as a matter of fact, honeycombed with secularity, dependent upon emperors and kings. This must be remedied by a clear separation between the Kingdom of GOD and the kingdoms of the world. To the former belong all persons, all offices, all possessions of the Church, which must accordingly be at the disposal of the Church's supreme head. And not only so. Every Christian man, peasant, prince, or emperor, is a citizen or subject of this kingdom. All questions of rule and possession are moral questions, to be decided by the supreme arbiter of Christian duty. It is for the Church, by her supreme ruler, to award to each his rights, to undo and punish wrong. And so the pope holds the disposal, not only of ecclesiastical but of royal and imperial dignities. He alone can confirm the emperor in his throne, and for just cause he can also depose him.[1]

So vast a power must be infallible in its exercise. Gregory lays it down that a papal decision can never be revised (*retractari*) save by a pope himself, and that the Roman Church never has erred, nor, as Scripture witnesses, ever can err. This is no doubt a vague declaration as compared with later definitions of infallibility, but it marks a very distinct advance upon previous papal claims to doctrinal authority.[2]

Gregory defined once for all the attitude of the papacy toward the civil power. Neither Alexander III. nor Innocent III. nor Boniface VIII. added or could add

---

[1] The influence of Augustine on the writers of the age of Hildebrand is the subject of an excellent monograph by Reuter's distinguished pupil, Mirbt, *die Stellung Augustin's*, etc. (1888). He shows that Augustine was very generally read and quoted. Gregory himself has only one formal quotation, but he adopts, without naming Aug., the whole theory of the *grande latrocinium* (*Reg.* viii. 21,—Mirbt, *Quellen*, 80e,—iv. 2, etc.), and treats Henry IV. accordingly. On the other hand he also speaks with enthusiasm of the *imperium* if joined with the *sacerdotium* "in unitate concordiae" (*Reg.* vii. 25 to William the Conqueror, and i. 19). He has absorbed, if not the letter, the entire spirit of Augustine's idea of the *imperium in gremio ecclesiae* (see Reuter, *Aug. Stud.* p. 500). On Gregory's claim to dispose of thrones, etc., see Gierke, *Polit. Theories*, notes 28, 30, 34, 131. On the Gregorian view of ecclesiastical property, persons, etc., as maintained by Becket, see Reuter, *Gesch. Alexanders des III.*, i. 315-319.

[2] See *Dict. Papae*, 18 and 22 (Mirbt, *Quellen*, 81). The *Dictatus Papae* are twenty-seven theses, apparently contemporary, and intended to sum up the main points of the very voluminous letters in Gregory's Register. Pagi, *ad ann.* 1022, doubts their genuineness, but on very weak grounds. See Lupus of Ypres (1725), *Synodorum decreta*, tom. v., and the more modern works referred to in Potthast,[2] vol. i. p. 377. The *Dictatus* are inserted at the end of the 55th letter of Book ii. ; they appear to stand in much the same relation to Gregory's letters as does the *Syllabus errorum* to those of Pius IX. (see Newman's *Letter to the Duke of Norfolk*, p. 78 sq. ; he speaks of the latter as an "anonymous compilation," etc.).

anything in principle to the Gregorian system. In Gregory we have the famous appeals to the two great lights that GOD placed in the firmament, to the two swords in the hand of Peter, the spiritual sword to be wielded by his successors, the secular at their command.

The collision between such claims and the civil authority was inevitable, even had Philip of France and Henry IV. been other than they were. Battle was at once joined on the famous question of "investitures." The question was a vital one to Emperor and Pope alike. The prelates of the Church were feudal princes, and not only was ecclesiastical patronage a protection to the emperor or king against the dangerous power of the hereditary nobility, but the oath of vassalage, of which the investiture with ring and crozier was the symbol, was the necessary guarantee that the new spiritual lord would be faithful to his patron. On the other hand, the disposal of spiritual office by the secular power, the vassalage of spiritual persons to an other than spiritual lord, either threatened the independence of Christian teaching, worship, and life, or at any rate interposed between the supreme authority in the Church and the lives and actions of the Christian laity a passive, or even at times an active barrier, in the shape of a hierarchy dependent on the Throne or independent of the Pope.

It appears to have been taken for granted on both sides that the secular dignity and possessions were inseparable from the spiritual office of abbey or See. The feudal system was firmly established in the Church. The question was simply whether the feudal headship of the Church was to rest with Pope or with

Emperor. The right of possession was, by custom coeval with the Frankish monarchy, on the side of the Emperor. At the coronation of Henry III. the settlement had been renewed by oath of emperor and pope alike. But Gregory saw in the custom the badge of the Church's servitude, the root of simony and of all the other flagrant abuses to the extirpation of which had devoted his life. Accordingly in his relentless crusade against all investiture by emperor or king he asserts the inalienable right of the Church, *iure divino*, to all Church property, and the principle that all such property stands at the disposal of the Church's visible head.[1]

(*b*) If Gregory is here giving organised effect to one side of Augustine's thought, he is doing so at the expense of another. Augustine's theory of property was not merely the outcome of his argument *ad homines* against the Donatists; it hangs together with that whole spiritual side of his idea of the Church for which Gregory had no receptivity. Gregory in his conflicts with Philip and Henry is unconsciously re-enacting, on a grander scale, the part, and developing the principles, of Ambrose in his defence of the basilica of Milan against Justina.[2] The Augustinian

[1] At the Roman Synod of 1075 he excommunicates all bishops and abbots who should receive their offices from laymen, and all emperors, kings, etc., who should give investiture. This opened the incurable breach with Henry IV. On the question of investiture, the suggestive remarks of Hatch, *Growth of Church Institutions*, pp. 75, 76, and 200-207, should not be overlooked.

[2] See Ambr. *Ep.* xx. in *PL.* xvi. 994 sqq. Ambrose anticipates Gregory (p. 1001): "Veteri iure a sacerdotibus *donata* imperia." In contrast to Augustine's theory of property, he tells the emperor (999): "*domum priuati nullo potes iure temerare*," etc. He maintains (*e.g.* 997): "ea quae essent divina imperatoriae potestati non esse subiecta." But he falls far

principle "iure regum possidentur possessiones" cuts no less surely at the roots of the papal theory of civil society than Augustine's doctrine of the *communio sanctorum* undercuts the theory of the Church developed in parts of the *de Civitate*, and in the Gregorian papacy as an institution. Gregory knew well, as the story of the Paterini at Milan shows, how to turn to account the popular hatred of a wealthy hierarchy. But while Arnold of Brescia saw in the wealth of the Church a departure from the principles of Christ, Gregory would condone it on the one condition, that it was held in sole strict subjection to the vicar of Christ. Had Gregory known, or attempted to apply to the problem of the age, the principle which Augustine had formulated against the Donatists; had he been content to wage a purely spiritual warfare with purely spiritual weapons; had he sharply distinguished between the Church, as a spiritual society with the Pope as its spiritual head, and the accidents of temporal position or possession which come to it or leave it in the course of history; had he accepted the position of the earlier Church, able to bear without loss of dignity alike the injustice of a hostile and the patronage of a Christian empire, in a word had his policy been that of modern Liberal Catholicism, it is interesting to speculate upon the possible sequel. Such a policy could not have cost Gregory more suffering or humiliation than followed from the course

short of Gregory's general position. He allows the imperial right to tax the clergy, or even to confiscate anything except the churches (1017): "si tributum petit, non negamus, *agri ecclesiae soluunt tributum* . . . non faciant de agris invidiam : tollant eos si libitum est imperatori ; non dono, sed non nego."

he actually pursued. He would have sacrificed the questionable triumph of Canossa, would have been spared the sack of Rome and the deathbed lament of Salerno. The papacy of the Middle Ages might have reigned less absolutely over the lives and souls of men; but possibly its rule would have been purer, more loved, more lasting. But Gregory could know little of the position of the early Church. To him and to his successors the donation of Constantine, and the decretals, which after the long night of the tenth century wore the glamour of immemorial age, counterfeited the true facts of history. Gregory claimed with a good conscience that the world should be ruled by the Church, the Church by the pope; and he was not afraid to push his premises to their legitimate conclusion, that of a claim to feudal supremacy over all the world.

And in fact, given these premises, Gregory was absolutely right. If the Augustinian relation between the *civitas Dei* and the *civitas terrena* is to be realised in the relation of the ecclesiastical to the civil organisation, and if the ecclesiastical organisation intended by our Lord is that of papal government,—and both of these doctrines were to Gregory self-evident axioms, —the temporal power, in its fullest extent, is of the Church's divine right. And the falsity of premises and conclusion alike was far from obvious *a priori*. Ideas create institutions, and until experience had tested the idea of an omnipotent Church, it was impossible for the immanent logic of the Christian consciousness to eliminate that idea from its supreme conception of the Kingdom of GOD.

Gregory's single-minded aim was that Christian

HILDEBRAND AND HIS IDEAL 257

ideas should rule the world. The Kingdom of Christ was to be manifested in the Kingdom of His Vicar. But to give effect to his aim, he could not dispense with the resources of an earthly prince: without the helping hand of Matilda of Tuscany, there would have been no Canossa. The Church as conceived by Gregory must be, to anticipate a formula of the ninteenth-century Jesuit canonists, a *Societas Perfecta*[1] dependent, that is, on no other power for the complete resources and apparatus of government. But this committed Gregory, as his predecessors had already been committed, to the ordinary means by which earthly princes hold their own. Confronted by Force and Statecraft, Gregory played the game with vigour and skill. There was some gain in immediate power—the gain of Canossa—but the spiritual force of the Church was irreparably lowered. The censures of the Church, reserved in her early days for the gravest moral and spiritual offences, soon lost their salutary terrors[2] when excommunications became incidents in territorial squabbles, or were issued on the most trivial pretext; and when the unchristian penalty of the interdict sought to coerce the guilty by robbing the innocent of the privilege of Christian worship and even of burial itself.

---

[1] See Lect. VII. p. 344. On Matilda and her Donation, Sir J. Stephen, *Essays in Ecclesiastical Biography*, p. 29 sqq. The Donation (1077) comprised "Liguria" and Tuscany. Canossa was in Matilda's dominions.

[2] See below on St. Louis of France, p. 271, note 1; on Augustine's view, Lect. V. p. 220 sq. In close conformity with Aug., Wenrich of Trier, a partisan of the emperor against Gregory VII., maintains that the author of an unjust excommunication merely excommunicates himself; so also Gregory's rival Wibert of Ravenna ("Clement III.") and others (see Mirbt, *die Stellung*, etc. p. 101 sqq.).

With Gregory, then, the great struggle began between Pope and Emperor. Its first phase ends in 1122 with the Concordat of Worms, which registered the complete emancipation of the Church from the Empire[1] in spiritual things, the emperor abandoning the patronal rights, and investiture with ring and crozier, but retaining investiture with the sceptre, the symbol of the *regalia* or temporalities, which, when exercised (as in Germany) before consecration amounted to a veto upon the election, that is, to no small voice in the appointment. The next and decisive phase, the subjection of the Empire to the Church, followed the fall of the Hohenstaufen, and was marked by the Council of Lyons (1274), when Gregory X. received the submission of Rudolf of Swabia.[2] After this, the empire becomes less and less important as a factor in the great question; the power of the papal system, before which the emperor could not but bow, is broken up by the new kingdoms.

The penance of King Henry II. of England was hardly less dramatic than that of Canossa eighty years before; but as a symbol of lasting papal victory, it was hollower still than Canossa.

The penance of Canossa was a great symbolic act,[3] but it shocked rather than impressed the conscience of the time. It represented an idea that was not, in

---

[1] Mirbt, *Quellen*, 83. Calixtus II. waives the right of investiture with the sceptre, an abatement of the full Gregorian claim. But outside Germany this was to *follow* consecration, and might easily sink to a mere formality.

[2] See below, p. 270.

[3] Gregory's letter in Mirbt, 66*a*. For the other side, references *supra*, p. 257, note 2.

COLLISION OF IDEALS

the eleventh century, a reality. But the idea was alive, and was destined at any rate to approach realisation. It was the inspiration, after Gregory's death, of the first Crusade, when Urban II. came forward at Clermont [1] as the leader of all Europe in the resolve to win back for Christ the Holy Places and to subdue the schismatic Greeks to Catholic Christendom.[2]

On the whole, however, in the generation between the death of Gregory and the Concordat of Worms the Gregorian idea made little progress. But eleven years after the Concordat, the submission of Lothair at his coronation to Innocent II. as his feudal chief was ominous of the issue of the coming struggle in which the Papacy was to contend for the completion of Gregory's aim,—not for emancipation from the emperors, but for the subjection of the emperors to itself.[3]

IV

The twelfth century, the age of the Hohenstaufen and of Alexander III., has had no more than justice done to it as an epoch of intellectual and religious

---

[1] The Council of Clermont opened Nov. 18, 1095. On Nov. 26 a speech by Urban II. decided the assembly to embark on the first Crusade (1096-1099).

[2] On July 15, 1099, Godfrey de Bouillon took Jerusalem.

[3] Lothair installed Innocent II., elected by a minority of cardinals, but supported by St. Bernard, as pope, and received from him the territories of Matilda, for which, on his coronation in the Lateran Church (the rival pope holding St. Peter's), he did homage to Innocent. This was the theme of the famous epigram :—

> Rex stetit ante fores, iurans prius Urbis honores
> Post *homo fit Papae*, sumit quo dante coronam.

revival, and of creative political thought.[1]   To the stimulus of Abelard's teaching we owe both the beginnings of the Scholastic Theology, the intellectual glory of the medieval Church,[2] and the first of the many reactions which were evoked by the temporal power and wealth of popes and clergy.   Arnold of Brescia is the first representative of the elements common to many of the most important anti-papal movements of the Middle Ages, the ideas of apostolic poverty, of the Church as a purely spiritual Society whose officers must be confined to purely spiritual functions, and of the tradition of republican and imperial Rome.[3]   Himself a man of saintly and austere life, he preached first in his native Brescia where he was a canon, then for a time in Zürich, lastly in Rome, against the lawfulness of worldly possessions for spiritual persons.   He insisted sternly on the duty of the laity to provide them with all that was necessary for their maintenance, but with equal sternness condemned those who possessed more.[4]   What attracted popular enthusiasm to Arnold

[1] The intellectual revival is strikingly characterised in the second chapter of Rashdall, *Universities of Europe*. It was also the century of St. Bernard; of the foundation of the Templars (1118), Cistercians (1098), Premonstratensians (1120), Knights of St. John (1099), the age of the Victorines, etc.

[2] Peter Lombard, bishop of Paris (1159-1164), pupil of Abelard and of Hugh of St. Victor, supplied the Middle Ages with the basis of scholastic teaching in his *Libri Sententiarum*, upon which some two hundred and fifty commentaries, including those of almost all the greater Schoolmen, were founded.

[3] See Gregorovius, *Gesch. der Stadt Rom.* iv. 452. His republican teaching merely voiced convictions which he found a living tradition at Rome; but he also embodies the rising spirit of autonomous town life, fed by the renascence of studies, industry, and trade all over Europe. As an ascetic and Church reformer he had, as has been often noticed, much in common with his great opponent St. Bernard. See *de Consid*. II. vi. 10, ix. 18; IV. iii. 6.

[4] The imperialist author of the poem, *de gestis Frederici in Italia*, treats Arnold simply as a criminal and heretic; but in spite of himself he reveals

was in part no doubt his appeal to the republican tradition which had never quite died out in Rome; but his lofty idealism and unworldliness raised him above the level of a mere tribune of democracy.[1] His contention that the clergy should forego worldly wealth and political power, that their functions and powers were purely spiritual, struck a note which runs right through the Middle Ages, and is the answer of the medieval conscience to the Gregorian papal system.[2] To the Emperor, whom Arnold idealised as the prince elected by the citizens of Rome, and after him to the magistrates of the City, he assigned the exclusive control

him as an idealist who lived and died with purest devotion, and moreover as wholly orthodox in doctrine. He carefully ("nam multos nosse iuuabit") enumerates Arnold's "dogmata" (lines 768-801). They comprise strong censure of (a) the corruption of the clergy, including the pope, (b) the refusal of the laity to pay tithes, (c) the general prevalence of simony, (d) also of usury; (e) the harmfulness of war, quarrelling, luxury, perjury, etc., (f) encouragement of litigation by the Curia, where "quod precio careat despectum prorsus haberi," lastly (g) he "thought no one right but himself," was for cutting off sound and unsound alike "ut fatuus medicus":—

"Simonisque sequaces
Omnes censebat; uix paucos excipiebat."

With hardly an exception these are the "dogmata" of Bernard's *de Consideratione*. If he also (783 sq.) maintained that no one should confess to, or receive sacraments from, simoniacal priests, he could appeal for this to excellent authority, papal and other.

[1] The description of Arnold by Walter Map, *de Nug. curial.*, Dist. i. 24, would not be unfitly applied to the founder of the Friars Minors (see below, Lect. VII. p. 296). He says "the luxury of the cardinals shocked him: in epistulis coram domino papa reprehendit eos *modeste*, set *moleste* tulerunt," etc. (Map was a friend of Alexander III., and was at the Lateran Council of 1179, twenty-four years after Arnold's death.) Gerhoh (to be quoted below, p. 262, note 2) will not assent to his "praua doctrina, quae etsi *zelo forte bono, sed minori scientia* prolata est." (But the poet calls him "vir multe litterature," and Map "secundum literas *maximus*.")

[2] The same ideas are forcibly expressed by Gerhoh, prior of Reicherspeng near Passau, a fanatical but candid partisan of the popes. See the very interesting account of him in Fisher, ii. 113 sqq., especially p. 116 sq. For their persistence in the Middle Age, see Lect. VII.

of the City and public life of Rome. The papal right to the States of the Church was condemned in principle.

For some ten years Arnold was the leader of the Roman people, and the popes could only live in Rome by avoiding any conflict with the Republic. But Barbarossa treated the Roman Republic with brusque contempt, and handed Arnold over to the Pope for execution. Had he had insight or foresight to perceive it,[1] he was sacrificing what might have proved an invaluable alliance in the struggle which was before him. Meanwhile the judicial murder shocked the Catholic conscience of Lombardy, Germany, and England.[2]

Of the two questions of the coming age, namely, the relation of the temporal power of the Pope to the Christian and apostolic ideal of life, and the relation of the absolute supremacy of the Pope to the sovereign power of the State, the former was raised in its clearest terms by Arnold. The latter was to be fought out by the emperors of the house of Hohenstaufen. Of these,

---

[1] Cf. Bryce, pp. 174 sq., 278. *Gest. Fred. in Ital.* 850, hints that this was realised by Frederick when too late:—

"Set doluisse datur super hoc Rex *sero misertus*."

[2] Map has been sufficiently quoted. Gerhoh, *de investig. Antichristi*, I. xlii., wishes either that he had been punished less severely, or at any rate "that the Roman Church or Curia had not been responsible for his death"; or if, as they allege, he was killed without their knowledge and consent, that his body had not been burned and thrown into the river (David, he says, set a better example on the death of Abner). Lastly, he will not seem to assent to his "nex perperam acta." His only motive in writing thus is "his care for the honour of the Holy Roman Church." According to the poet of Bergamo, quoted above, Arnold's serene and prayerful end, his confession of his sins to Christ, and his silent commendation of his soul to GOD, deeply impressed all present:—

"lacrimas fudere uidentes,
Lictores etiam, moti pietate parumper."

Both Gerhoh and Otto of Freisingen say that the dispersal of his remains was due to fear lest he should be venerated as a martyr.

COLLISION OF IDEALS 263

Frederick Barbarossa was the heroic figure. "Hildebrand himself," it has been justly said, "had not a more lofty consciousness of his high purpose and divine mission to establish GOD'S Kingdom on earth."[1] Medieval imperialism, in its most ideal expression, is embodied in his character and policy. He represents the claim not of mere might, but of right based on the divine source of kingly office, the consecrated precedents of the great Christian emperors, Constantine, Justinian, Charles the Great, the broad philosophical principle of government that "not man must rule, but Reason."[2] The laws of Roncaglia, inspired by the jurists of Bologna, are the last word of Christian Imperialism in the contest between Emperor and Pope for the mastery of the Christian world.[3]

---

[1] Tout, *The Empire and the Papacy*, p. 247. He adds: "With all his faults, Frederick remains the noblest embodiment of medieval kingship, the most imposing, the most heroic, and the most brilliant of the long line of German princes who strove to realise the impracticable but glorious political ideal of the Middle Ages."

[2] Arist. *Eth. Nic.* v. vi. 5: διὸ οὐκ ἐῶμεν ἄρχειν ἄνθρωπον, ἀλλὰ τὸν λόγον, ὅτι ἑαυτῷ τοῦτο ποιεῖ καὶ γίνεται τύραννοσ. The same principle, *Pol.* III. xvi. 5 (adding διόπερ ἄνευ ὀρέξεωσ νοῦσ ὁ νόμοσ ἐστίν), x. 5. But it must be allowed that at Roncaglia juristic theory trenched seriously upon existing rights. The *actual* collision was between imperial and papal absolutism rather than between personal government and constitutional liberties as such (cf. Bryce, pp. 175, 274; Fisher, ii. 160-163, 245-247, i. 150-152).

[3] The great Diet of the plains of Roncaglia, near Lodi, in 1158, is enthusiastically described by the Bergamo poet (quoted above, p. 260 sq.), lines 2597 sqq. Frederick summons:—

"ex magno sapientes undique regno
Quorum consilio leges ac iura reuoluens
. . . nouam legem promulgat, ut omnes
             . . . federa pacis
Perpetue teneant . . . nemo fera prelia temptet.
Fraus, dolus, insidie procul absint, preda, rapine.
Sic homines primi uixerunt temporis," etc. etc.

Frederick had to contend with two popes who were no unworthy successors of Hildebrand, the Englishman Adrian IV., and Alexander III. Adrian died while Frederick was at the height of his power, not many months after the Diet of Roncaglia. But he bequeathed an example and a policy which Alexander followed up with final success. The first seventeen years of Alexander's reign are marked by the chequered fortunes of Frederick's wars in Lombardy, the pope finding his principal support in the growing spirit of independence in the towns, a spirit which Adrian had been enabled by Frederick to put down in Rome itself. Gradually the Lombard league grew stronger, and at Legnano in 1176 the "Carrossa" of Milan triumphed over the imperial chivalry, and brought Frederick to a new Canossa at Venice. The Roncaglian laws were withdrawn, and for good or evil the Christian empire passed into the realm of shattered ideals. In 1179 a council at the Lateran registered the result.[1] A vote of two-thirds of the cardinals was henceforth to constitute a valid papal election; the veto of the emperor was abolished, the ordinary clergy and the people of Rome were to have no voice in papal elections. Frederick to some extent recovered his lost ground in the remaining years of his life, but they may for the purpose of this Lecture be passed over. His death by drowning on his way to recover the Holy City from

---

[1] Frederick's articles of peace with the pope at Venice in Mirbt, *Quellen*, No. 85; Decree on papal elections, *ibid*. 86. The archdeacon of Oxford, Walter Map (*supra*, p. 261, note 1), tells us (Dist. i. 31), how, asked by the pope at the Lateran Council to deal with the poor preachers of Lyons, he succeeded in raising a laugh at their expense. His contempt for these mendicants contrasts curiously with his veneration for Arnold.

the Saracens is the tragic symbol of a noble life frustrated in its devotion to a noble if unrealisable ideal.[1]

The pontificate of Innocent III. (1198–1216) ranks as the culminating point of the medieval theocracy. Innocent hardly advances, indeed, upon the claim of Gregory the Seventh. The old Gregorian claims to direct emperors and kings and to dispose of their kingdoms, the old Gregorian appeals to the two great lights in the firmament, to Peter's two swords, reappear in Innocent. But Innocent's success in asserting them is far more conspicuous, and that in the face of altered and more difficult conditions. He was, indeed, the first pope who was master of Rome itself; but in the contest for universal sovereignty, he is confronted, not indeed like his predecessors with a strong emperor, but with the rising vigour of the new kingdoms of Europe; and he more than holds his own against them all. In France and, at least for a time, in England he is the advocate of right and morality, even when immediate political advantage is risked by his action.[2] In Germany he decides between

[1] The Ghibelline idea (as contrasted with the spirit of the Ghibelline faction) is suggestively treated in the essay of Miss Rosina Antonelli, *L'idea Guelfa e l'idea Ghibellina*, etc. (Rome 1895; see especially pp. 28-30). On the names of Guelf (Welf—House of Altorf, dukes of Bavaria and then of Brunswick), and Ghibelline (House of Waiblingen and Hohenstaufen), and the transference of two Swabian territorial names to two Italian political parties, see the interesting passage in Fisher, i. 324-332, showing how "the old quarrel between Henry IV. and the Saxons broadened out into the dynastic struggle between the Welf and the Wibelin, which was but one side of the larger contest between the papacy and the Hohenstaufen monarchy," etc.

[2] Philip Augustus had thrown over his second wife Ingeborg of Denmark, and married Agnes of Meran. The French bishops allowed the bigamy,

rival claimants to the throne, and receives the humble submission of Otto the Guelfic pretender, whom a few years later he strikes with the ban of the Church.[1] Under him the Crusaders set up a Latin and Catholic empire in Constantinople,[2] and England is made a fief of the Holy See.[3] But Innocent is no longer, as Gregory and Alexander had largely been, the supporter of popular liberties against arbitrary kings. His Bull against Magna Carta is but one symptom of the growing tendency of the Papacy to arouse the suspicion and resentment, not of kings but of peoples. From Gregory onwards, the greatest popes of the earlier Middle Age had sought political power as a means to spiritual power for the good of the Church and the salvation of souls; but they were not exempt from the operation of the general law that tends to elevate the means into an end. The popes were human, and their claim to superhuman authority only made it impossible for them to recede from an inherently false position. And in Innocent the Great we see at least the beginnings of this fatal process. The year before his

but Innocent, at great political risk, maintained the cause of Ingeborg till the death of Agnes gave him the opportunity of a compromise by the legitimation of the children of the lawful and the unlawful marriage alike. The story of Innocent and King John is too well known to need citation.

[1] Otto IV. recognised against Philip of Swabia, March 1, 1201, excommunicated 1209 (Mirbt, *Quellen*, 87; Fisher, i. 332, cf. ii. 122; cf. Riezler, *die Literarische Widersächer der Papste zur Zeit Ludwigs des Baiers*, p. 19, note.

[2] The Normans had replaced the Greek hierarchy of Southern Italy by a Latin one (1096), and had captured Thessalonica in 1185. On April 12, 1204, Constantinople was carried and plundered by the Crusaders.

[3] In 1213. Innocent now supports John against all public liberties: his Bull against Magna Carta, 1215.

death Innocent [1] presided at the great Lateran Council of 1215,[2] which stands forth as the most resolute attempt of the medieval Church to stamp out the abuses which had stung to moral enthusiasm the great popes of the Cluniac movement. After a century and a half of the Gregorian system, these abuses were still as prevalent as ever. Centralised government, from its inherent tendency to condone everything that brought power and resources to the central head,[3] had failed to touch seriously evils which are more amenable to a power to which the papal system was steadily hostile, namely enlightened public opinion, especially lay opinion. The Lateran Council, by laying down the doctrine of transubstantiation as a dogma of the faith, by prescribing compulsory confession, and above all by establishing the Inquisition, and so repressing the sense of moral responsibility and stifling legitimate freedom of thought and speech,

---

[1] Innocent is believed to be the first pope who assumed the title "Vicar of Christ," a title reserved in the earlier Church for the Holy Spirit (*supra*, Lect. III. p. 100, note 1). Innocent's predecessors were content to be Vicarii (*i.e.* successors) of Peter. In the donation of Constantine (755-7) Peter is *vicarius* of Christ, the pope of Peter. But I observe in a form of petition probably not later than A.D. 800 the words "sedem quam regitis *deitatis* sorte *vicarii*" (*Lib. Diurn.*, Sickel, p. 21, 8). Innocent's claim to rule "non solum uniuersam ecclesiam, sed etiam totum seculum," in Mirbt, *Quellen*, 89.

[2] Mirbt, *Quellen*, 91-94.

[3] Even in Bernard's time the practice of appealing to Rome had become subversive of all local discipline and justice in the Church. "How long," he asks the pope (*de Consid.* III. ii. 7, 8), "will you pretend not to hear, or fail to notice, the murmuring of all the earth? How long will you sleep, regardless of the great confusion and abuse of appeals. . . . Were not they once the terror of evil-doers? Whereas now they are used by them to intimidate even the good. This is not 'the change of the right hand of the Most Highest.' The victims of appeals, despairing of justice at Rome, prefer to suffer wrong, 'We should fail at Rome,' they say, 'we can do no worse at home.'"

did more to stereotype the evils and abuses of the Church, than its direct legislation effected towards their removal.

The long struggle between Frederick II. and the two able popes Gregory IX. and Innocent IV. need not be followed in detail.[1] In part it turns upon the perplexing personality of the Emperor,[2] in part upon factors which the earlier struggles of the popes and emperors have taught us to appreciate. So far as occasion was needed for the outburst of an antagonism rooted in the characters and position of the parties, it may be traced to Frederick's breach of the twofold promise on the faith of which Innocent III. had sanctioned his taking up the German crown[3] (1210), namely that he would

---

[1] The reign of Frederick's father, Henry VI., was politically successful, but may be passed over here. He left his widow Constance of Sicily with the infant Frederick II. who was made a ward of Innocent III. The principal landmarks for our purpose are Frederick's Sicilian laws of 1231, enacting the equality of all (even the clergy) before the law, etc., and Gregory's publication of the Code of Decretals in 1234 (see below, p. 293, note 2). The two formulate a far-reaching contrast of principles of government.

[2] Frederick emphatically repudiated the saying, of which Gregory accused him, *de Tribus Impostoribus*: this disclaimer we may, with the Catholic historian Dr. F. X. Funk (*Kirchen-Lexicon*, s.v.), and against the equally impartial Protestant authority of Reuter (*Aufklärung im MA.* ii. 297), fully accept; but his alleged scepticism, combined with his fierce intolerance of heretics, his Oriental court, his occasional reconciliations with the Church, his fits of mysticism, his final confession, make up if not a consistent, yet a perfectly credible whole. Our estimate of him may fall somewhere between the widely divergent judgments of Gregory IX. and of Matthew Paris.

[3] The popes' claim to hold the imperial power in commission during a vacancy, founded upon their claim to represent Christ on earth (cf. *supra*, p. 226, note 2), led naturally to the claim to award the crown in case of *disputed* elections, and so to Innocent's claim to veto or ratify *any* election (Bryce, p. 217, note). Such cases furnished opportunities for the systematic exaction of some territorial concession as the *quid pro quo* (see the examples in Riezler, *Literarische Widersächer der Papste*, etc. p. 15, note 1). Cf. on the papal claims, Gierke, *ut supra*, p. 117, notes 30-33.

take the Cross, and would never unite Sicily to Germany. But the former of the conditions was due, on Innocent's part, to mixed motives; the conquest of Constantinople from the schismatic Greeks was insecure from the first; but it was now an accomplished fact, and its retention was at least as precious to the popes as the possible reconquest of Jerusalem from the infidel. The other promise, that relating to Sicily, was simply due to the tenacity with which the popes clung to a feudal fief, and had no directly religious purpose at all. Frederick's alienation from the papacy was therefore due to the increasing devotion of the popes to secular aims. His own exaggerated anti-clericalism, the reaction of one extreme against another, is most deplorable as a symptom of the coming break-up of the medieval ideals,—of the approach of the time when the highest moral aims would no longer unite the greatest leaders of men, but would drive them into opposing camps. So far as Frederick represents the new idea of the separation of Church and State, and so far as he enlists on his side movements [1] which herald the disintegration of the constructive ideas of the Middle Age, his reign already belongs to the subject of our next Lecture.

With Fredrick's death in 1250 the power of the House of Hohenstaufen is at an end, in 1268 the death of Conradin extinguished the line.[2] The bestowal of the kingdom of Sicily by Clement IV. upon Charles

[1] The followers of Joachim, specially numerous in the Franciscan order (Lect. VII. p. 297 sq.), were ardent admirers of Frederick, who knew how to use the appeal to evangelical poverty.
[2] But Manfred's daughter Constance, wife of Peter III. of Aragon (Dante, *Purg.* iii. 115), continued the descent: and the Vespers of 1282 led to the revival of an independent Sicily under a new Frederick.

of Anjou[1] marks the new direction in which the popes are looking for political support. In 1274 Rudolf of Hapsburg recognises Charles of Anjou, surrenders all Italian pretensions, and renewing the oath of Otto IV., subjects the imperial to the papal crown.[2] The Empire is henceforth a German institution, in Italy its memory remains for a while as an unpractical dream, but Italy and Germany alike must exchange the imperial for the national ideal,—an ideal which it has taken six long centuries for either to realise.

V

Gregory X., who received the submission of the first Hapsburg emperor, was one of the best of medieval popes.[3] The Hildebrandine ideal seemed at last fully realised, and the long struggle to have ended in the final triumph of the *sacerdotium* over the *regnum*. But in reality the empire had brought down the papacy in its fall. The papacy remained the undisputed sovereign power in spiritual things, but if it was to wield the temporal powers claimed by Gregory

---

[1] In 1265, Charles was brother, by blood though not in character, of St. Louis IX. He held Sicily proper till 1282 (see last note). Urban IV. (1261) was the first French pope; of the remaining popes of the thirteenth century Clement IV. and Martin IV. (1281) were also French. Clement, like Urban, was unable to live in Rome.

[2] See above, p. 266, note 1. This was at the Council of Lyons, in which Gregory also regulated future papal elections by the institution of the "Conclave" (Mirbt, *Quellen*, 97).

[3] With the rule-proving exception of Celestine of the *gran rifiuto*, he is the only medieval pope after Gregory VII. whom it has been found possible to canonise. Döllinger's admiration for him (*Papstthum*, p. 90) was originally due to Gregory's supposed disapproval of the Inquisition (Lord Acton in *Engl. Hist. Rev.*, Oct. 1890, p. 737).

MEDIEVAL SYSTEM AND AUGUSTINE 271

VII. and Innocent III., it must overcome a new and more formidable resistance, that of the nations of Europe with their new vernacular literature, the organ of a new power of independent thought; and this, it was already clear, it could never do. France under St. Louis, who while he was uniformly loyal and friendly to the popes, and supported Urban IV. against the cause of freedom and good government in England,[1] refused to recognise the deposition of Frederick II., or to take political advantage of his struggles with the papacy, and opposed a firm front to papal taxation and other encroachments,[2] was now the first power in Europe. England, enfeebled by the troubles of the reign of Henry III., was soon to renew her strength under Edward I., and the beginning of the English Parliament may be traced to the year 1265, the year after the death of the first French Pope.[3] Spain and Portugal, moreover, in the course of the thirteenth century, had practically expelled the Mahometans, and become powerful Christian kingdoms.

An important sign of the times appeared in the following year in the *de Regimine Principum* of Thomas

---

[1] Provisions of Oxford, 1258, denounced and their maintainers excommunicated, 1264, by Urban IV. Louis supports Henry III. against the English (award of Amiens, 1264).

[2] Louis' prelates complained to him that "no one nowadays has any fear of excommunication." They begged him to enforce the sentences of the Church by his bailiffs. The king expressed his willingness to do so, *if they would give him cognisance of the sentence in order that he might decide as to its justice.* This they refused as an infringement of ecclesiastical rights. Thereupon the king flatly refused to enforce their sentences, as "contrary to God's will and to justice" (Joinville, chap. xv.). Martin (*Hist. de France*, iv. 308 sq.) claims that Louis thus established the root-principle of Gallicanism "l'appel comme d'abus."

[3] First representation of the boroughs in Parliament of January 1265.

Aquinas,[1] the first attempt to formulate a new Catholic political philosophy with the aid of the *Politics*[2] of Aristotle. Full as the work is of wise and pious observations, it hardly sustains the reputation of the Angelic Doctor.[3] Its inconsistencies and confusion of thought may in part be due to its departure, as executed by the disciple, from the arrangement of the subject-matter as planned by the master. But the real difficulty was an incurable one, namely to satisfy the paramount necessity of justifying the universal monarchy and "plenitudo potestatis"[4] claimed for the Pope while employing the political categories of the *Politics*, which proceed on the hypothesis that the citizens are the real rulers and the source of power in the State.[5] This at once precludes any application of the Aristotelian ideas to the Pope himself, who, now[6] that the priesthood is

[1] A.D. 1266. Thomas only finished Books I. and II. i.-iv. The rest was completed before 1300 by his disciple and confessor Tolomeo da Lucca.

[2] His commentary on the *Politics* belongs to about 1264; The *Summa contra Gentiles* and *contra errores Graecorum* (*supra*, p. 238, note 2) were written in the pontificate of Urban IV. (1261-1264), the great *Summa Theologiae* between 1265 and 1271. Thomas died, aged 47, in 1274.

[3] That is in respect of constructive power, and accuracy in the definition of the leading terms employed.

[4] Thomas defines this elsewhere as possessed by the pope "quasi rex in regno; episcopi vero assumuntur *in partem sollicitudinis* quasi iudices singulis civitatibus praepositi." His conception of monarchy is that of absolute rule (see below), subject only to the superior control of the pope. Cf. Gierke, p. 144, n. 131, and p. 111, n. 17, 18.

[5] See Gierke, pp. 163, 165. Legislation belongs to the multitudo, or *to its representative*, *i.e.* to him "qui totius multitudinis *curam habet*," *Summ*. II. i. 90, art. 3. There is no idea conveyed here that would not equally apply to the position of the pope.

[6] In the Old Testament priests were subject to kings. But the Christian priesthood is the vehicle of *bona caelestia* not, as then, of *terrena*. The proper relation was providentially prefigured by the subjection of the kings in Gaul (destined to be the most Christian of kingdoms), to the Druids! (*de Regim*. I. xiv.).

MEDIEVAL SYSTEM AND AUGUSTINE 273

the vehicle of heavenly *bona*, is supreme over kings, the ministers of earthly blessings.[1] Aristotle, it is true, made *politia* the highest form of government; and this might be so for unfallen man.[2] But as things are, monarchy is best, and rebellion against the monarch unlawful. Even if he degenerates into a tyrant, he may not be murdered, but perhaps, in a very extreme case, deposed by his subjects.[3] But the monarchy must be so "tempered"[4] as to preclude the likelihood of such cases arising. This will be partly by papal guardianship, as above, partly by local self-government[5]—which distinguishes a "political" monarch from a despot.[6] But neither Thomas nor his continuator betray any appreciation of constitutional[7] government. The king differs from the "political" ruler in being free from legal restrictions. He "carries the laws in his breast."[8] The king is the soul of the kingdom, the papal power of the royal, as GOD is to the world.[9] Clearly the

---

[1] The argument that the Church, as pursuing the higher End, should control the State which pursues the lower, is the nerve of the whole curialist position. It hangs together with the metaphor of body and soul (Gierke, notes 76, 310, 311).

[2] Of whom (*de Reg. Prin.* II. ix.) the "antiqui Romani" were an approximate type; but now, "perversi difficile corriguntur et stultorum infinitus est numerus" (Eccles. i. 15). Cf. Gierke, note 137.

[3] Like Tarquinius superbus (I. vi.). But tyrannicide (in spite of the example of Ehud) "apostolicae doctrinae non convenit." See Gierke, note 130.

[4] *de Reg.* I. vi., II. viii.

[5] See above, p. 272, note 4. "Politia" is more suitable to cities, greater provinces belong to monarchs [who accordingly rule cities by the magistrates as their subordinates], *de Reg.* III. ii.; Gierke, notes, 165, 333.

[6] *Ibid.* III. xx., IV. xvi. A "despot" is not a "tyrannus," whose differentia is that he rules *for himself*, not for the Glory of God (*ibid.* I. i.).

[7] See also above, p. 272, notes 4 and 5.

[8] "Pectore defert," IV. i. Cf. Gierke, note 265.

[9] *Supra*, note 1; *de Reg. Prin.* III. x.

influence of Greek politics is very slight here. The very terms of the Aristotelian political philosophy refuse to lend themselves to the curialist axioms from which the whole scheme, in its operative parts, is really deduced.

In the century which followed, the material and moral power of the papacy declined. First the ill-success which attended the belated ambition and violence of Boniface VIII.,[1] then the Babylonish Captivity and the subservience of the papacy to France, then the Great Schism, and the conciliar movement which ended the Schism, made it plain to all that the kingdoms of Christendom must depend for their well-being on the justice and strength of their laws, and not on the power claimed by popes to set them aside or to depose their kings. From this depression, the recovery of the fifteenth century partially raised the papacy, but the aspirations of Gregory and Innocent could never again be asserted with any prospect of success. The time of "Concordats" had begun, the period when "most princes appear to regard the Church, and especially the Holy See, no longer as a mother and mistress, but rather as a distinct and rival political power, with which they were wont to enter into treaties in which they aimed at securing as much as possible for themselves, and conceding as little to the Church, in the shape of authority and advantage."[2] If the Church is to be a "Societas perfecta," these are in fact the only alterna-

---

[1] See the Bull *Unam Sanctam* in Mirbt, *Quellen*, No. 98. The famous clause at the end, *Porro subesse*, etc., is anticipated by Thom. Aq. *c. err. Graec.* 68, where it is based on one of the forged quotations from Cyril Alex.

[2] From de Smedt, *Introductio ad Hist. Ecclesiasticam* (Gand, 1876), p. 53.

MEDIEVAL SYSTEM AND AUGUSTINE 275

tives; either what Gregory and Innocent desired, a supremacy virtually destructive of the sovereignty of kings and rulers, or a position such as is described in the above words; a position which can hardly be permanently tolerable without the possession of temporal sovereignty.

The former alternative was tried in the two hundred years from Gregory VII. to Gregory X., the greatest and most characteristic centuries of the Middle Ages. Then, if ever, the Kingdom of GOD existed on earth in the form of an omnipotent Church. The period was, within the Church, one of comparative doctrinal unanimity; the controversies that there were did not produce movements that affected the peace of the world. The one religious question that did so was that of the relation between the Civil Power on the one hand, and the Church, whose power was by universal consent centred in the hands of the Pope, on the other. As between Pope and Emperor, the question could have but one issue; the empire was too precarious, too artificial, too little identified with the growing power of the future, namely, national life, to enlist on its side any element that could permanently outweigh the terrors of the next world, which were always and for any purpose at the Pope's command. Repeatedly and signally the Pope prevailed and the Emperor was abased. It is true, the victory was moral rather than substantial. To have shaken off the imperial right of interference in papal elections, to have successfully asserted a papal right to interfere in imperial elections, were achievements whose importance depended upon the importance of the Empire itself.

The contest for broader and more enduring principles remained to be fought out with antagonists whom the decay of the empire only left the stronger. But whatever success the Gregorian ideal has had in history, it achieved in the centuries in question. And that success must not be underrated. Whatever our estimate of the moral or religious character of the Middle Ages, there can be no question of their ecclesiastical character, nor of the immense influence of the papacy in impressing the ecclesiastical stamp[1] upon the civil and social life of the time. Religious people will differ as to the spiritual value of ecclesiastical organisation, institutions, and interests, in themselves, and as to the degree to which they may wholesomely predominate in the individual or the common life. But without their ecclesiastical character the Middle Ages would have been a barbarous time indeed. The Church brought the discipline of character, the summons to that absolute self-effacement which alone raises man wholly above the brute, brought comfort to the suffering,—and it was a time of suffering for the mass of men,—binding up of wounds to the penitent, terrors to the hardened and the tyrannical.[2]

Louis IX., most typical product of medieval Christianity, would do honour to any Christian age or country. It is no doubt to the Church, not to the papacy, that the credit of these and suchlike moral triumphs is due; but it may be questioned whether, at the beginning of the Middle Ages, the Church without

[1] See the beautiful passage in Bryce, *Holy Roman Empire* (ed. 4), chap. xxi. p. 373.
[2] "Volentes malignari, nonne his potissimum terreri solebant?" Bern. *de Consid.* III. ii. 7.

MEDIEVAL SYSTEM AND AUGUSTINE 277

a papacy would have had the coherence necessary for her task, the power necessary to enforce elementary Christian duties, to make head against the numberless petty tyrannies of feudal Europe. Thus much may be fairly claimed for the Gregorian system. But although the carrying out of that system was entrusted to a succession of popes of exceptional character and ability, men like Gregory VII. and Adrian IV., Alexander III., and Innocent III. and IV., Gregory IX. and X., it never really succeeded; nor so far as it did succeed did it wholly further the spiritual good of mankind. When Gregory VII. began his career, the age of brute force had already at least begun to yield to the regenerating forces of morality, law, and religion. The attempt to enforce the temporal claims of the popes filled Italy and Germany with war and misery, set Guelf against Ghibelline, city against city.[1] It imposed upon the popes the position of a territorial sovereignty inconsistent with the example of the Apostles and with the spiritual character of Church and priesthood. This again drew the popes into territorial wars and intrigues, and into growing need of money. The Crusades were at first a movement of pure idealism, headed by the Pope as the spiritual leader of Europe; but eventually they were turned against Christians, and popes were known to spend on objects of their own moneys raised for Crusades against the infidel.[2] Gregory had hoped, by the vigorous

---

[1] The curia was the den where Dante's Wolf of Avarice had her securest home. "E molte gente fè già viver grame" (*Inf.* i. 51).

[2] Compare Innocent III.'s crusade against the Albigenses, the wars against the Greek Church (*supra*, p. 266, note 2), and many other cases. See also Lect. VII. p. 303, note 2.

centralisation of power in his own hands, to cleanse the Church from simony and usury; his successors merely succeeded in concentrating both evils at Rome.[1] The papal supremacy was employed above all as a means for extorting money. At the Council of Lyons in 1245, Innocent IV., bent on hurrying forward the deposition of Frederick II. and the succour of the tottering Latin empire at Constantinople, was obliged to listen sullenly while amid painful silence the English delegates to the council represented the disasters he was inflicting on their Church. "We gave long since," they said, "to our mother the Roman Church an honourable subsidy, namely, St. Peter's pence. But she, not content with that, asked, by her legates and nuntios, for further help; and that too we freely gave. You know, too, that our ancestors founded monasteries which they richly endowed, and to which they gave the patronage of many parish churches. But your predecessors, wishing to enrich the Italians, whose number has become excessive, gave to them these cures, of which they take no heed, neither in caring for the souls, nor in defence of the houses in whose patronage they are. They do no duty of hospitality nor of almsgiving, nor think of aught but to receive the revenues, and take them out of the kingdom, to the hurt of our kinsmen who ought to hold these livings and who would do the duty in person. Now to tell the truth these Italians draw from England more than

[1] Ivo of Chartres, in reply to the Legate, in Möller, *Kirchengesch.* ii. 291; Durandus (1310), *de modo consil. generalis celebrandi*, pp. 69, 103; Bonaventura, *Opp.* (ed. 1773) ii. 729, 755, 815; Dante, *Parad.* xii. 91-94, and other contemporaries quoted by Döllinger, *Papstthum*, 107-114 and notes.

MEDIEVAL SYSTEM AND AUGUSTINE 279

60,000 silver marks a year, which is a larger revenue than that of the king himself. We hoped that at your promotion you would reform this abuse, but on the contrary our charges are increased." After giving details of the most recent extortions they conclude, " we pray you promptly to remedy this : otherwise we could not any longer endure such vexations."

At the beginning of the Middle Ages, the papacy had almost wholly on its side all that was good and true in the life and mind of Christendom. By the end of the thirteenth century this was far from being the case. The popes had, indeed, by judicious homage to an ideal of life in glaring contrast with their own practice, gained the support of the great movement of the Friars,[1] which did much to regenerate the medieval Church, and which secured to the support of the Church and papacy the ripest fruits of the new theological and speculative activity in the universities.[2] But the signs of the times :—Arnold of Brescia, Frederick Barbarossa, the growing popular liberties of England, the parishes of England and Germany suffering spiritual neglect in order that Rome might be rich,—are so many reminders that the papacy is beginning to be a disruptive force, unable to hold together all the good that belongs to Christ as of right, a force that enlists on its side much moral and religious enthusiasm, but also repels much that is noble and good and true.

The one supposed Christian duty in which an

[1] See Lect. VII. p. 295.
[2] The first great Schoolmen of the thirteenth century were : Franciscans, Alexander of Hales, Bonaventura, Roger Bacon ; and Dominicans, Albertus Magnus and Thomas Aquinas. See Little's *Grey Friars in Oxford* (Oxf. Hist. Soc.), and Rashdall, *Universities*, i. 345 sqq.

advance was made was that of persecuting Heretics. Before the end of the eleventh century, this was by no means frequent in the Church, though a few examples undoubtedly occur.[1] But Innocent III., who was the first to preach a crusade against the heretics, shed as much innocent blood as lies at the door of any human being.[2]

It is fairer, however, to award to individual popes the credit of the blessings, than to make them responsible for the evils, which attended their efforts to rule the world in Christ's name. Of the benefits they were conscious, and for them they consciously worked; the evils they either did not intend, or were not alive to the evil in them.

The medieval papacy has achieved something for the Kingdom of GOD. But it claimed more than this, namely to *be* the Kingdom of GOD on earth, the Kingdom in which Christ reigned through His Vicar. If St. Augustine's application to the antithesis of Church and Realm of the antithesis of the *civitas Dei* and *civitas terrena*, his conception of the *Imperium in gremio Ecclesiae*,[3] was to be embodied in a working system of society, we must, I think, allow that in the medieval papacy the attempt was made in the only

---

[1] See Socrates, *H. E.* VII. iii. : οὐκ εἰωθὸσ διώκειν τῇ ὀρθοδόξῳ ἐκκλησίᾳ, and Augustine's earlier and better view, *supra*, p. 215, note 1. Lecky, *Rationalism*, ii. 30-33, does justice to the earlier medieval Church in this matter: he goes so far as to allow that before 1208 there was little or no persecution of heretics (p. 30, note 1 ; contrast Innocent VIII. *ibid.* p. 28).

[2] One of his agents writes : "Nostri non parcentes ordini *sexui vel aetati* fere *viginti millia* hominum in ore gladii peremerunt . . . spoliata est tota civitas" [Beziers] "et succensa, ultione divina in eam mirabiliter saeviente" [!], Innoc. *Ep.* xii. 108 ; see Milman, *Lat. Chr.* IX. viii.

[3] *Supra*, p. 252, note 1, and Lect. V. p. 214.

MEDIEVAL SYSTEM AND AUGUSTINE 281

form in which success was probable, and that it succeeded so far as success was capable of attainment. But this success was gained at the sacrifice of Augustine's fundamental conception of the Kingdom of GOD on earth, at the cost of the inward and spiritual side of the Augustinian theory of the Church, which, however difficult in itself and to us, was very real to Augustine,[1] and prevented him from ever framing a completely externalised idea of the Church,—was gained by the aid of an ecclesiastical constitution of which Augustine had no knowledge nor anticipation, and of a theory of property which Augustine directly repudiates.[2] More than all this, it became manifest that the Church could only take up the position of a Society supreme over peoples and kings, could only assert the claim to be the only true *civitas* on earth, at the cost of assuming functions and employing methods directly in conflict with her essential character and with the injunctions of her Master. "The kings of the Gentiles exercise lordship over them, and their great ones exercise authority upon them; but ye shall not be so."

There are two alternative ideals of a Kingdom of Christ on earth and of the method of its realisation; Righteousness by means of government, and government by means of Righteousness. The latter is the real and fundamental idea of Augustine; it is that of St. Paul, and of Christ himself. There is room for the other, but in strict subordination to it. In the education of the young, in the infancy of a civilisation or of a Christendom, righteousness must come from without,

---
[1] *Supra*, Lect. V. pp. 194 sqq., 217.
[2] *Supra*, p. 254, note 2, and Lect. V. p. 212, note 1.

by means of government. But government must know its own limitations, and must realise the need for its gradual supersession, or rather transformation. External pressure, in the ideal healthy growth of individuals and societies alike, must give place to the self-government which comes with maturing character. In GOD'S providence, with much apparent retrogression and conflict and disillusion, the history of modern Christendom has run and, as we may believe and hope, will continue to run, some such course as this. Each stage of the process has its characteristic dangers and mistakes. We do not despair of freedom because its progress is beset with licence and indiscipline, nor need the record of tyranny and corruption blind us to the indispensable service which external authority has done in preparing us for the exercise of liberty. The papal monarchy in Christendom, like the Monarchy in Israel,[1] belonged to a necessary stage in the divinely-ordered history of our religion. In both cases its establishment was at once an advance and a decline; in neither case was it to remain for ever. But both alike served the will of God in their generation, and both alike have bequeathed for all time the ideal of a reign of Christ over[2] the unruly wills and affections of sinful but redeemed mankind.

[1] *Supra*, Lect. I. p. 14 sqq.
[2] Fourth Sunday after Easter, May 5.

LECTURE VII

THE KINGDOM OF GOD IN THE DIVERGENCE OF MODERN IDEALS

> The old order changeth, yielding place to new,
> And GOD fulfils himself in many ways
> Lest one good custom should corrupt the world.
>
> TENNYSON.

> I ergo tu, et tibi usurpare aude aut dominans apostolatum, aut apostolicus dominatum. Plane ab alterutro prohiberis. Si utrumque simul habere voles, perdes utrumque.
>
> ST. BERNARD.

LECTURE VII

THE KINGDOM OF GOD IN THE DIVERGENCE OF MODERN IDEALS

Then said Jesus unto Peter, Put up thy sword into the sheath.—JOHN xviii. 11.

Peter said, Silver and gold have I none.—ACTS iii. 6.

THE three great powers which guided medieval life, the Priesthood, the Empire,[1] and the School, stand embodied in the names of three great men, who in their work and character gather up the idealism of each, and ennoble its very limitations. These are Gregory the Seventh, Frederick Barbarossa, and Thomas Aquinas. But greater than any one of these powers, greater than all three together, is that which, in the Providence of God, all alike served, and by whose progress the success or failure of all the powers ordained by GOD must in the last resort be tried. Academic thought is eventually proved in the life and thought of the working world, Governments exist for the citizens, the Priesthood for the building up of the Body of Christ. To complete our review of the ideals of

[1] See Gierke, *Political Theories of the Middle Age*, note 8, for Sacerdotium, Imperium, and Studium. Regnum, when used instead of imperium, denotes rather a *regnum particulare* conceived either as under the empire (*ibid.* notes 334, 61), or as independent of it (337); in the former sense the emperor enjoyed the regnum of Germany by the mere fact of election, prior to his coronation as emperor (see below, p. 308, note 1).

the Middle Ages we must look to the layman, as citizen and Churchman. And the ideals upheld by the three great men whom I have named all meet in the name of Dante, the completest embodiment of the medieval spirit, in all its complexity and simplicity, its depth and strength, its poetry and its prose.

(*a*) In Dante, then, we see the best thought of medieval Christendom, enriched with all the secular and religious culture of the crowning century of the Middle Age, inspired with the undimmed religious fervour of the "ages of faith," keenly observant of the stirring life of Christian Europe,[1] reflecting upon the very same problem that had busied the mind of Augustine amid the wreck of a falling empire nine centuries before. The true nature, origin, sanction of secular government and of human society; the true function of the Church in relation to it; this is the theme common to Augustine's *de Civitate Dei* and the *de Monarchia* of Dante. Externally the two books are as unlike as possible; the length, variety, and loose discursiveness of the older writer contrast sharply with the conciseness and scholastic technical precision of the other. But common to the two is the profound conviction of the divine in history, and a substantially identical conception of the Church. That to Augustine the collective episcopate, to Dante the pope is the supreme power in the Church, is the accident of date. Dante has as complete a belief in the spiritual authority of the pope,[2] as Augustine has in that of the bishops;

[1] This will verify itself to all readers of the *Commedia*.
[2] See the closing words of the *de Mon.*: "Illa igitur reverentia utatur Caesar ad Petrum, qua primogenitus filius utatur ad patrem." Though he held Boniface VIII. to be no pope in the sight of GOD (*Par*. xxvii. 23), he

his belief is in fact stronger because more sharply defined. The great difference between the two books is in the fact that the one suggests an ideal relation between the ecclesiastical and the civil society, which the other judges by its actual working. The *de Monarchia* is the outcome, not of the part which its author happened to take in the strife of Guelf and Ghibelline, but of an undercurrent of thought and feeling which had been gathering strength from the twelfth century onwards.[1]

The *de Monarchia* is directed to prove the divine origin and sanction of the secular power, and its independence of the spiritual. At first sight the argument and interest of the book appear wholly relative to the time and conditions of its origin, so scholastic is the method, so artificial many of the proofs, so bound up is the whole with the assumed eternity of Rome and of the Roman Empire. But to see no further than this relativity would be to view very superficially a product of profound thought.

reprobates the outrage of Anagni as an insult to Christ in His (*de facto*) Vicar, *Purg.* xx. 87 sqq. :—

> Veggio in Alagna entrar lo fiordaliso
> E nel Vicario suo Cristo esser catto ;
> . . . Veggio rinnovelar l'aceto e il fele
> E tra nuovi ladroni essere anciso . . .

And compare his eloquent praise of St. Dominic :—

> Benigno a'suoi ed a'*nimici crudo.*

Par. xi., xii. The above are only a few of many possible illustrations.

[1] According to Witte, in his standard Edition (Vienna, 1874), the *de Monarchia* was written before Dante had reached his " mid-term " of life, before he had tasted Office or Exile, and before the Bull *Unam Sanctam*. This view is considered highly improbable by Mr. Butler, Dr. Moore, and other high authorities, who generally connect it with the advent of Henry of Luxemburg (*infra*, p. 295).

What Dante has in mind is not the rule of One as an end in itself or as a personal right, but the end or purpose of Society, as he has learned it from Aristotle's Politics, with which the thought of the book is saturated. That all mankind should, to secure this end in the highest perfection, be united under a single political head, is a thought which may be set down to the relativity of the book; but it enshrines the twofold principle of undivided sovereign power, and of some supreme arbiter of justice and right, higher than any merely national institution, founded in the nature of things, to which all rulers alike must bow. We can thus disengage from the temporary form of Dante's thought a permanent principle, which Aristotle, his master in political thought, had formulated in the words, "We allow not man to govern, but the Law."[1] "So far as we can form any clear idea of progress, does it not consist in the advancing prevalence and recognition of some such authority?"[2]

Augustine, in contrasting the goal of the two *civitates*, namely the peace of heaven and the peace of earth, struck a note of dualism which finds an echo in the medieval view of life. This dualism leads to the disparagement, as profane and tainted with associations of sin, of all that properly falls within the purview of secular government, unless brought into subservience to the spiritual power. The notion of the earthly commonwealth as a *grande latrocinium* is not far below the surface in the utterances of Hildebrand; here and there he comes very near to quoting it ex-

---
[1] See above, p. 263, note 2.
[2] Bishop Paget in *The Guardian*, March 21, 1900.

pressly.[1] The same idea inspires the simile of the two great lights. The *imperium* has no light of its own, but all is borrowed from the *sacerdotium*. Augustine himself did not consistently adhere to this dualism; he allows that no earthly *civitas* can attain earthly peace without justice, that is, without partaking to some degree in the qualities of the heavenly. Dante gets rid of it entirely, and it is here that the *de Monarchia* marks an epoch in Christian political thought. Taught by Aristotle, he sees in the *civitas* a moral as well as a material aim " bene sufficienterque vivere." What does this imply? Human society as a whole has a special " operation " or purpose of its own, which includes and transcends that of each particular unit composing it. This, the function of apprehension by the *intellectus possibilis*, the intellectual capacity or "virtue," is distinctive of man as compared with the animals below him or the angels above him. This cannot be wholly realised in "act" by the individual, nor by any particular community; its adequate realisation demands the participation of mankind as a whole.[2] This realisation, speculative in itself, becomes, "by a certain extension," practical in the moral and political sphere as well as in that of production and art. The proper work of mankind, then, is ever to realise the whole potency of the *intellectus possibilis*, primarily in thought, derivatively in action. And for this "almost divine" purpose (Ps. viii. 6), tranquillity and peace are essential. So that peace is the proximate end of human government; not a merely terrestrial peace, but a peace

---

[1] Gierke, *Political Theories*, etc., note 16.
[2] *De Monarch.* I. iii. 45 sqq. (Witte); cf. Gierke, p. 9 and note 3.

which comprises the blessings of the heaven above and the earth beneath.[1] "Whence it is manifest that universal peace is the best of those things which are ordered to our happiness. Hence it is that the shepherds heard from on high not of wealth, nor of pleasures, nor of honours, nor long life, nor health, nor strength, nor beauty, but of Peace. For the heavenly host proclaims, 'Glory to God in the highest, and on earth peace to men of goodwill.'" Hence, too, the Saviour of men gave as his greeting, "Peace be with you." Accordingly the authority of the monarch, which is necessary to the peace of human society, depends not upon any other man, or vicar of Christ, but directly upon God Himself. In spiritual things, he will recognise the Pope as his Father; to the Pope "we owe, not whatever we owe to Christ, but whatever we owe to Peter." Christ refused, as the exemplar of his Church, the charge of earthly monarchy; and if the Church undertakes it or claims it, she contravenes her essential nature. "So, then, it is clear that the authority of temporal monarchy comes down to it immediately from the fountain-head of universal authority. This fountain-head, united in the citadel of its oneness, flows out into many channels from the overflowing of goodness." "By this conception, human society is reconsecrated, as that which is willed by GOD, and necessary for spiritual life. Without the *civitas terrena,* the heavenly *civitas* becomes unattainable, since only in the brotherhood of mankind can

---

[1] Dante has in mind Aristotle's famous conception of the State as γινομένη μὲν τοῦ ζῆν ἕνεκα, οὖσα δὲ τοῦ εὖ ζῆν (*Polit.* I. ii. 8, cf. *de Mon.* I. v. 33); cf. Gierke, notes 310, 311, 313, and p. 91.

man develop all the capacities of the soul necessary for his entrance into the kingdom of heaven."[1]

"What is essential here is the vindication for secular life and secular authority of its own proper dignity and height, as independent of all else on earth. Civil society and human law hold their commission, as it were, direct from GOD, and not through the papacy or through any other medium claiming to be nearest to him and to act on his behalf. Within its proper sphere and for the rendering of its proper service to mankind, human law is in truth GOD'S will, and He fulfils himself through the State as directly as through the Church."[2]

The Gregorian interpretation of the Kingdom of GOD had, when the *de Monarchia* was written, achieved its final and decisive victory over the Imperialist ideal by which Dante is inspired. But Dante, the spokesman of the lay conscience of medieval Christendom, records its moral failure. He has no shade of suspicion of the Pope's spiritual authority, but he reaffirms the demand of Arnold of Brescia that the Pope should be the purely spiritual head of a purely spiritual Church. His appeal rests, as its intellectual basis, on the political philosophy of Aristotle; but theologically he goes back to Scripture, the early Councils, the Fathers, and to St. Augustine. He heaps grave scorn upon the stock papal arguments of the two swords, the two great lights, and the donation of Constantine which he says the Church, from its

---

[1] Villani, as quoted by Antonelli, *l'Idea Guelfa*, etc., *sub fin*. Dante is not afraid to quote Averroes (on Arist. *de An.* iii.) in support of his doctrine (cf. *Inf.* iv. 144).

[2] Paget (as above, p. 288, note).

essential nature, was as incapable of receiving as the emperor of conferring.

Dante is wholly unconscious, apparently, of the contrast between his position and that taken up in the *de Civitate Dei*; but the contrast is unmistakable and significant. Augustine had, in an ideal and unpractical form, suggested a relation between Catholic Church and Christian State, which the development of a papacy had rendered capable of practical trial. The trial had been made on a magnificent scale, and Dante leaves on record what the trial had brought to light, namely, that the Church cannot assume the government of human affairs except at the cost of her spiritual character. The *de Monarchia*, then, is the reversal of the principles of the *de Civitate Dei*, in so far as those principles had laid the foundation for the conception of the Kingdom of GOD as an omnipotent Church. But it does not directly touch the further question which is really involved, that, namely, of the constitution of the Church itself. And yet, without something of that temporal power of which Dante pronounces the Church inherently incapable, the concentration of spiritual authority in the papacy lacks its indispensable means. So Gregory VII. had held, and so the most consistent upholders of the papacy maintain to this day.[1] But Dante, who uncom-

[1] The "temporal power" includes the two distinct ideas of (*a*) universal jurisdiction (whether direct or indirect) even *in temporalibus*, and (*b*) exclusive sovereignty over the pope's own territory. As to (*a*) the whole world is the Church's territory; Tarquini (*Inst.* I. i. 2, *ad. obj.* 2) quotes a Bull of Clement XI. (*Accepimus*), which condemns the idea that any papal Bull can arrive *in territorio alieno*. The limits of this power must be determined by the authority in which that power resides. The *Christian* Prince as such has no power in Church affairs. He will show himself

promisingly condemns the temporal power in every shape and form, looks for its abolition only to purify and strengthen the spiritual. Yet, perhaps, we may see an inkling of further insight in his complaints of the exclusive study by Churchmen of the papal decretals to the neglect of the Fathers and Holy Scripture.[1] The decretals, and not the Theology and Philosophy of which the Decretalists were, as he says, *inscii et expertes*, had as a matter of fact been the basis on which the entire papal system was reared.[2] Dante is protesting against the substitution of the decretals for Scripture, not against the decretals in themselves, "quas profecto venerandas existimo." What would he have said had he known their true history!

such by submitting himself "tanquam agnum" (Palmieri, *de Rom. Pont.* ed. 2, § 18. iv.). As to (*b*) the principle follows from the fact that *iure divino naturali* the head of the Church (which is a *societas perfecta*, not a mere *collegium* or association) cannot be the subject of any civil ruler. *De facto* independence is indeed not *absolutely* necessary; for it did not exist under the Roman Empire. But even then (see also Gierke, note 55), as Leo XIII. pointed out when bishop of Perugia, "pontifices subditi erant *quoad factum*, non *quoad ius*" (in 1860 quoted by Lehmkuhl, *Theol. Mor.* vol. i. § 139). Temperate defenders of the temporal power, in sense (*b*), maintain that it is indispensable in order that the pope may effectively fulfil his universal charge, "negotiate with Christian princes on questions of Faith and Morals as a superior, on purely political questions as an equal" (A. Weber in *Kirch.-Lex. s.v.* "Kirchenstaat"). This at the least is involved in the conception of the *societas perfecta* to be referred to below (p. 344).

[1] See *de Mon.* III. iii., and *Par.* IX. 132 sqq.: gold, he says:—

"fatto ha lupo del Pastore.
Per questo, l'evangelio e i Dottor magni
Son derelitti, e *solo ai Decretali*
Si studia sì che pare a'lor vivagni."

[2] See above, p. 229. On the development of Canon Law see Rashdall, *Universities of Europe*, i. 128 sqq. and reff. By Dante's time it consisted of Gratian's *Decretum*, the Five Books of Decretals collected by Gregory IX., and the "Sextus" lately issued by Boniface VIII.

In any case Dante recognises no divine law outside the Scriptures. They alone are above the Church.[1] The Councils and the Fathers are on a level with the Church; traditions, including Church law, are *post ecclesiam*, of ecclesiastical origin, although to be respected on the ground of their "apostolic" (*i.e.* papal) authority.

(*b*) Dante writes in the middle of a period of over forty years, during which the history of the empire is, so far as Italy is concerned, a blank. The popes had waged a war of extermination against the last scions of the House of Hohenstaufen; they had succeeded by the aid of Charles of Anjou, to whom they had given the kingdom of the Two Sicilies. But they had purchased an ally to find a master. The popes become from henceforth more and more the dependents of the French Crown, and in a few years were to begin the seventy years' exile at Avignon. The cities of the North of Italy were fast exchanging their republican freedom for the reign of despots, and the old parties were degenerating into petty factions without principles or ideals. Italy was drifting into moral anarchy, the prelude to political servitude. What wonder if the higher minds sought refuge from the gloomy present in the past glories of the empire, —idealised as it was in a generation that was already forgetting the sad vicissitudes of its struggles with the papacy and with the popular liberties of the towns? In the very year of the transfer of the papacy to Avignon, Dante's ideal of the emperor

---

[1] *De Mon.* III. xiv., "*omnis* . . . divina lex duorum Testamentorum gremio continetur."

found a brief promise of realisation in the person of Henry of Luxemburg, who came to Italy with the blessing of Clement V.[1] and the acclamation of patriots, and obtained the crown at the cost of papal disfavour, factious opposition, and a mysterious death. Dante's *de Monarchia* was in a true sense the epitaph of a dead ideal; but in a truer sense still the prophecy of a more glorious future.

That future was not to come so quickly as Dante hoped, nor by the means that he foresaw.[2] His actual anticipations were coloured by a train of thought which links him to another of those movements of the time which mark a reaction from the secular lordship of the papacy, I mean the aspirations of the spiritual Franciscans.

The great movement of the Friars, now a century old, is typical of the twofold genius of the medieval Church; in the persons of Francis and Dominic she puts forth the two great powers which secured her hold upon the world, the power of repressive force, and the power of pure self-sacrificing love. Not of course that either is thus exhaustively, or adequately, summed up. Dominic and his order certainly stand for much more than mere force and persecution. If

[1] *Par.* xvii. 82: "il Guasco l'alto Arrigo inganni" (cf. xxx. 137). That the prophecy in *Purg.* xxxiii. 37-45 refers to Henry has been convincingly argued by Dr. Moore in his recent lecture, *The DXV Prophecy*, etc. (Oxford, 1901. Briefly, it is a Hebrew "Gematria." As 666 to "Nero Caesar," so DXV to "Arrico").

[2] Of the mass of interpretations of the great historical allegory, *Purg.* xxix.-xxxiii., Mr. Butler's notes and Döllinger's deeply interesting essay, "Dante als Prophet" (*Akadem. Vorträge*, i. 78 sqq.), and the notes in Costa's ed. represent the extent of my knowledge. Dr. Moore's Lecture (above quoted) sums up the result of his unsurpassed command of Dante lore.

their spiritual ideal was less tender and exalted than that of the saint of Assisi, the order in its after-history has on the whole maintained a higher level of intellect and work. The Friars Preachers are to be judged not so much by the Inquisition as by Albert the Great and Thomas Aquinas, by Fra Angelico and Savonarola, by the long roll of austere and truth-loving students, second only to the Benedictines of St. Maur, who adorned the order in the "great century" of France. But the person of Francis and the Franciscan ideal are more universal in their appeal to Christian sympathy, more directly expressive of what is characteristically noble in the spirit of medieval religion. "In religion a leader of leaders. Allowing himself neither food nor clothing beyond what strictest necessity compelled, he went about preaching; seeking nothing for himself but all for God. And he became loved and admired by all." These words, taken from a contemporary description [1] of Arnold of Brescia, are a not unworthy description of Francis. In him, Arnold's aim of reviving the example of evangelical poverty lived again, but with a winning poetical graciousness in the place of Arnold's stern implacability, and wedded to absolute submission to that Church which alone represented God upon earth. But the fundamental idea of Francis is that of Arnold, and of Dante also, that the example of Christ and the Apostles, who had no property individually or in common, is the true standard of Christian life. We know how rigorously Francis himself kept and enforced this principle; he would neither have, nor

[1] Map, *de Nugis curial.*, Dist. i. 24; see above, p. 261, note 1.

permit his brethren to have, where to lay their head; no church for the order, not even a breviary was to be possessed by its members.[1] They were to live upon work and alms, not of money but in kind, and every particle that they received beyond the strict necessaries of life was the property of the poor. But before long the very success of the order made the strict observance of its rule impossible.[2] The Franciscans had made their way into the university of Paris before the short life of their founder was ended;[3] and while some of the brethren were carrying Catholic missions into the furthest East, in Europe the order was leading the way in the new scholasticism, and acquiring monasteries and corporate property.[4]

The unworldly enthusiasm to which the order owed its existence began to chafe against the requirements of an establishment organised on a permanent basis.[5] Within some twenty years of St. Francis' death, the Friars Minors had absorbed, and were developing further, the ideas of Abbot Joachim the prophet of

[1] Francis rebukes a novice who wishes to possess a psalter: "Postquam habueris psalterium concupisces et volueris habere breviarium. Et postquam habueris breviarium sedebis in cathedra tanquam magnus praelatus et dices fratri tuo: apporta mihi breviarium," *Speculum Perfectionis*, ii. 4 (Sabatier's editio princeps, 1898).

[2] Lempp, *Frère Élie de Cortone*, 1901.

[3] *Supra*, p. 279, note 2. Francis died Oct. 4, 1226, aged 44. Alexander of Hales ("Doctor irrefragabilis," "Theologorum Monarcha") at Paris 1222; joins Franciscans (who had had a college there since 1217) in 1229. (Rashdall, i. 345-371.)

[4] Lempp, *Frère Élie*.

[5] This is bound up with the story of Cardinal Ugolino (afterwards Gregory IX.), and his relations with the Brethren, whom he was instrumental in transforming into an Order, in spite of the reluctance of St. Francis himself (see Lempp's work, cited above).

Fiore in Calabria. This visionary recluse, elevated by Dante to the heaven of the sun, in company with SS. Anselm, Thomas Aquinas, Bonaventura, and the other heroes of Christian philosophy, was, like the "Seraphic Doctor," a student of the Apocalypse. In him there reappears the same eschatological reaction against the hierarchical embodiment of the Kingdom of GOD which had inspired Montanus in the second century.[1] Joachim can hardly have known of the Phrygian prophets, or have borrowed directly from them; but the essential kinship of ideas is unmistakable. The three dispensations of the Father, the Son, and the Spirit, the millennial Kingdom in which the latter is to find its fruit-bearing period, are common to the two, though the crude realism of the second century, and its abrupt breach with the organised Church, give place in Joachim to the idea of a regeneration which will transfigure and spiritualise rather than supersede the existing forms. The Old Testament was the dispensation of bondage, of the law, the time of the married and of the laity;[2] the New that of the gospel of Christ, of freedom mixed with bondage, of letter and spirit, of the clergy.[3] The third dispensation is that of the Spirit, the eternal gospel,[4] the period of the monks. Its beginning was with Benedict, to whose order

[1] See Lect. IV. pp. 136–143. On Joachim, see Döllinger, *Prophecies and the Prophetic Spirit*, chap. vii.; Dante, *Par.* xii. 140.
[2] Answering to the Apostle St. Peter (see Matt. viii. 14, etc.; 1 Cor. ix. 5, R.V.).
[3] Corresponding to St. Paul (1 Cor. vii. 8).
[4] The dispensation of St. John (see John xiv. etc., Rev. xiv. 6, and Lect. IV. p. 123, note 1). The scheme of seven stages (*status*) for the world's history is also a revival of primitive Millenniarism (see above, p. 129).

Joachim had first belonged, its fructification was to be brought about by a new order of spiritual men, who would preach the Everlasting Gospel, unite divided Christendom, convert the Jews and the elect of all nations, and complete the Kingdom of Christ.

To enthusiastic Franciscans, Joachim seemed the divinely-inspired herald of their order and its mission. In 1254 Fra Gerardino published at Paris his "Introduction to the Everlasting Gospel,"[1] *i.e.* to the writings of Joachim, which now take rank as a third Testament, the bible of the new dispensation, of which St. Francis and his order were the accredited ministers, and which was actually to begin in the year 1260. The ideas of Joachim were fermenting throughout the order, and were to no small degree responsible for the schism between the "spirituals," who insisted on the literal maintenance of the example of their founder, and the conventuals, the regular and official portion who acquiesced in the requirements of established life. The question at issue was twofold. All alike were agreed that the possession of individual property was inconsistent with the example of Christ and the Apostles. But firstly, does the condemnation of "possession" (*dominium*) carry with it the condemnation of mere "use"? and secondly, does the condemnation of *personal* possession involve the condemnation of *common* property? The spirituals answered the latter question wholly in the affirmative. Christ and his apostles *possessed* nothing, even in common; and even their common "use" was restricted to the most elementary necessities.

[1] See Döllinger, *Prophecies*, etc., p. 124 sq.; A. S. Farrar, *Bampton Lectures*, p. 120; Rashdall, *Universities*, i. 382, ii. 738 (and reff.)

This principle cut straight at the root of the idea of the Church as a body capable of holding temporal *dominium*,[1] and we have seen that Dante so employs it; but this point was not at first in the foreground of controversy. The question was treated, as involving not the general life of the Church, but the specific observance of the mendicant friars. The order had common property; but its "possession" was vested in the Pope as trustee for the Society, while the *usus* was for the order itself. But even so, the order possessed an income in money and in kind far beyond the needs of its individual members. The conventuals justified this by branding as heretical the axiom of the spirituals, that Christ and the Apostles possessed nothing in common. This was the issue brought before Pope Nicolas III. in 1278. In his Bull "Exiit qui seminat," he decided, on the basis of a strict distinction between possession and use, that the renunciation of all property, corporate as well as personal, was holy and meritorious, and commended to us by the example of Christ and of his Apostles. This decision was to be taken as the official explanation of the rule of St.

---

[1] Dante, *de Mon.* III. x., xv. The term "*dominium*," in medieval thought, comprises without very clear distinction the to us quite separate conceptions of *personal property* and *political jurisdiction*. The Franciscan ideal, at first held up as a standard for the Christian life generally, soon became reduced to the distinctive rule of an Order; but its practice constituted the Minorites as "Perfecti" in comparison with other Christians (*e.g.* "perfectus" in Marsil. *Def. Pacis*, II. xiv.: "posset piscem capere perfectus atq. comedere, *cum expresso tamen prius uoto* nunquam praedictum piscem *aut rem aliquam* temporalem vendicandi contentiose coram iudice coactiuo"). See also the strong utterances of the Minorite Abp. Peckham in Little's *Grey Friars in Oxford*, p. 76. The original idea revived in the controversy under John XXII. On the whole subject, Mr. Little's book contains much interesting material.

Francis, and to be taught literally without explanatory glosses, on pain of excommunication.[1] The schism in the order continued. The conventuals claimed a *usus moderatus*, while the rigorists would allow only a *usus tenuis vel pauper*. Clement V. in the Council of Vienne,[2] by the Bull " Exivi de paradiso," renewing the decision of his predecessor, decided in favour of the latter section, and bade all spirituals return to the order on pain of excommunication. But some still stood out. The convents had larders and cellars, and this was an offence to the uncompromising defenders of the *pauper usus*; the latter also affected a more meagre habit than their brethren. When John XXII. became pope (1316), he at once issued a Bull[3] against them, and seconded the efforts of the general, Michael di Cesena, to put them down.[4] Meanwhile another section of the order, the Fraticelli, had gone further still. In their zeal for Holy Poverty they outdid even the spirituals; they denied the validity of the sacraments ministered by a worldly priesthood, the primacy

[1] The definitive words are quoted by Riezler, p. 63, n.: "Dicimus quod abdicatio proprietatis huiusmodi omnium rerum tam in speciali quam etiam in communi propter Deum meritoria est et sancta, quam et Christus uiam perfectionis ostendens uerbo docuit et *exemplo firmauit*."

[2] A.D. 1311-12. The ownership of all the property of the order was regarded (since 1245, Innoc. IV.) as vested in the pope (Little, p. 77). But see the curious controversy between the Minorites and Friars Preachers (A.D. 1269), published in Little, p. 320 sqq., where this solution does not occur (pp. 322, 325, 331).

[3] "Quorumdam exigit," A.D. 1317. Cf. Döllinger, *Akad. Vorträge*, i. 127 sq.

[4] In 1318 four brethren were burned at Marseilles for disobedience. They refused to alter the shape of their cowls, or to acquiesce in larders and cellars. The "spirituals" were regarded as "heretics" on the question of poverty only, the Fraticelli were charged with various other errors as well. See Denzinger, *Enchir.* lxii., and for references, Riezler, *Lit. Widersächer*, 61, n., and Rashdall, i. 529, n.

of the Pope, and the lawfulness of oaths. They rejected the rich and secularised Church, and claimed that the true Church is to be realised only by poverty, purity, and simplicity. The Fraticelli, who are not to be confused with the spirituals, were widely spread in the South of France and in Sicily. Within a few years one hundred and fourteen of them were burned as heretics in Catalonia and Narbonne.

Dante was in profound sympathy with the spirituals; he looked to the principle of Holy Poverty for the expulsion of greed and simony from the Church; for the purification, not the destruction, of the papacy; for the destruction of the temporal power and the restoration of the spiritual. For the victory of Holy Poverty in the Church, for the regeneration of Italy and the end of the woes of the nations, he is by some thought to point expressly to a felt-clad friar.[1] But

[1] Thus Döllinger (*Akad. Vortr.* i. 93 sqq.) understands *Inf.* i. 101 sqq. :—

> . . . infin che il veltro
> Verrà, che la ferà morir di doglia.
> Questi non ciberà terra ni peltro,
> Ma sapienza e amore e virtute,
> E sua nazion sarà tra feltro e feltro.

To pronounce between Döllinger and the great mass of modern interpreters is a task which I do not presume to attempt. Döllinger insists that "feltro" is not a place-name (for this he appeals to the express statement of the poet's son), but means literally *felt* (for this he appeals to "all interpreters before the 16th cent."). The Veltro (cf. the Dominican badge of a dog, *domini canis*, with a burning torch) is either the personal bringer-in of Joachim's "sextus status," or the Spiritual Order generally (*Par.* xi. 131). The latter alternative can hardly be entertained ; the Veltro must be intended for a person, not a corporate body or abstraction. On the other hand, whether Dante actually joined the Franciscan order or not, his sympathy for its ideas, and for the "spirituals" especially, and his belief in Joachim as a prophet, would hardly be likely to leave no traces upon his prediction of the downfall of the reign of avarice.

FRANCISCANS AND JOHN XXII 303

the logic of events was soon to show the impossibility of attacking the temporal without examining the foundations of the spiritual power; and the friars had to choose between an open rebellion, doomed, however lasting in its consequences, to fail in its immediate purpose, and the position of an endowed and established institution in the service of a wealthy Church.

John XXII. is one of the least lovable figures in papal history. He had the respectable virtues of industry and frugality, and the respectable failing of avarice. Like Clement V. he was a son of Cahors, then the centre of usury in Christendom.[1] In his pontificate of eighteen years (1316–1334) he spent largely, on wars of his own, money collected for a new crusade, and yet at his death he left a treasure equivalent to ten millions sterling.[2] He apparently introduced the universal levy of annates, which by systematic translations yielded the revenue of two, three, or four benefices upon every important vacancy. The question whether Christ and his Apostles possessed property singly or in common came before John in 1321. The inquisitor of Narbonne, in the course of proceedings against the Fraticelli, had pronounced the negative opinion heretical. A conventual Franciscan

[1] *Inf.* xi. 50:—
    . . . e Sodoma *e Caorsa*
    E chi, spregiando Dio, col cor favella.
And cf. Matth. Par. *ad ann.* 1235.

[2] Twenty-five million "florins" (seven millions in jewels, etc., the rest in gold coin). The collections were for a crusade, for which the pope also prepared by a geographical commission. But meanwhile the fleet was lent to Robert of Naples (1319) for his campaign against Genoa, the money levied from the rich bishopric of Salzburg was allocated to Leopold of Austria for prosecuting the war against Lewis; Clement VI. followed this example a few years later (Riezler, *Lit. Widers.* p. 6).

protested, and the rival orders brought the matter to the Pope, who was still informing himself on the subject when the general chapter of the Minorite order at Perugia, under Cesena, published as their mature conclusion that the impugned doctrine was not heretical. As this doctrine had been expressly laid down in the Bull of Nicholas III., the assertion of it by the chapter can hardly be called a rash one. The Pope, however, was roused to indignation. His sympathy with the fantastic heroism of the spirituals was hardly greater than that of Alexander VI. for Savonarola. He called upon the order to assume formal responsibility for its corporate ownership, rejected, at any rate as regards perishable things, the distinction of "*usus*" and "*dominium*," and declared *heretical* the doctrine that Christ and His Apostles possessed nothing even in common.[1] The Minorites' appeal to the previous and contrary papal decisions of Nicolas and Clement was summarily disposed of by a new decretal,[2] to the effect that a pope might at any time reverse decisions given by his predecessors (*per clavem scientiae*) upon matters

[1] See above, p. 301, note 1. The Bulls in question are "Cum inter nonnullos" (1323, Denzinger, lxiii.) and the constitution "Quia uir reprobus" (1329).

[2] "Quia quorundam" (1324). Defenders of papal infallibility argue that this was no question of faith or morals. But why then did John pronounce it a matter of *heresy*? An infallible authority can apparently make mistakes as to its proper sphere of exercise. See Bellarmine's admission (quoted by Döllinger, *Papstthum*, p. 493) : "uidetur facere quaestionem de fide, utrum usus, etc. . . . nam semper uocat haereticum eum qui contrarium sentit . . . Itaque exurget aliud 'bellum Papale,' *si haeretici haec aduertant.*" (For the defence, Denzinger refers the reader to Natal. Alex. *H. E.* Saec. 13 et 14, diss. xi. art. 1 ; the point to be met is that Nicolas lays it down that Christ set the example of abdicating all property, individual or common, while John pronounces this tenet erroneous and *heretical.*)

of faith and morals.[1] Horrified at this pronouncement, Cesena, general of the order, betook himself to the protection of the new emperor Lewis of Bavaria (1327). Recalled to Avignon, he appears only to be overwhelmed with reproaches by the pope, who refers his cause to a hostile committee. In fear for his person, he escapes from Avignon (1328) in company with two prominent brethren of the order, Fra Bonagrazia of Bergamo and Friar William of Ockham, the " Invincible Doctor " of the University of Paris.

(c) Lewis, chosen emperor by the majority of the seven electors in 1314, had in 1322 signally defeated Frederick of Austria, the candidate of the minority, at the battle of Mühldorf. But the Pope would not recognise his imperial right. Italy was the apple of discord. The Pope, who, while the fortune of war seemed doubtful, had played a waiting game, now made it clear to Lewis that he would not recognise him as emperor, nor even as king of the Romans, unless he practically surrendered all Italian pretensions. He replied by taking practical steps to assert his imperial rights in the peninsula. John replied with an imperious summons to submit to the papal right to administer the empire "during a vacancy" (*i.e.* until the Pope should please to recognise a new emperor). Lewis made a formal protest (December 1323). After further wrangles the Pope, on March 23, 1324, launched an excommunication against Lewis and an interdict against his territories.

[1] John also condemned the writings of d'Oliva of Beziers († 1297) the leader of the spirituals. They were afterwards re-examined by order of Sixtus IV. and pronounced orthodox (Döllinger, *Prophecies*, p. 126, cf. *Papstthum*, 493, note 66).

Cesena and Ockham found Lewis in Italy, whither, after some vacillation, he had gone in the beginning of 1327. By the beginning of 1328 he had victoriously entered Rome, and a decisive blow might have crushed Robert of Naples, secured the allegiance of Italy, and opened a prospect of success to his claim to treat John XXII. as a heretic, *ipso facto* deposed from the papal throne. But Lewis had missed his opportunity. He wasted his time in the parade of a Roman coronation, in the election of an antipope by the Roman people, and his popularity in a series of violent measures, which finally lost him all hold upon his Italian supporters. Slowly and reluctantly he retreated from Italy; in 1330 he had retired to Bavaria. Italy drops out of the imperial horizon; for the remaining seventeen years of his life Lewis fights simply for his position as German emperor, and is only prevented by French influence at Avignon from becoming reconciled to the pope.[1] The struggle of Lewis was of importance solely because of the new intellectual forces which it arrayed against the papacy. Lewis, the "brave, gentle, good-natured, but all too weak and irresolute Lewis," failed, the great protagonists in the struggle surrendered almost without exception before it was

[1] Lewis crowned at Aachen, 1314; defeats Frederick at Mühldorf, 1322; John XXII. summons Lewis to resign, 1323; Lewis protests, 1323-24; John "deposes" Lewis, 1324; Marsilius at Nürnberg, *Defensor Pacis*, 1325; Ockham in Bavaria, 1328; Lewis crowned at Rome, January 1328; Nicholas V. antipope, May 1328; captivity and recantation of Nicolas, 1330; Benedict XII. pope, 1334; Lewis prepared to seek Benedict's pardon, 1336-38; Electoral Declaration at Rense, 1338; Ockham's *Dialogus*, 1335-38; Clement VI. pope, 1342; fruitless overtures of Lewis to Clement, 1343-46; Clement excommunicates Lewis, 1346; Charles of Moravia rival emperor, 1346; death of Lewis, 1347. On Lewis and his "Sisyphus-task" see Döllinger, *Akad. Vortr.* i. 29-31, 120 sqq.

over. But new ideas emerged, never again to disappear, new questions were raised which no ephemeral victories could evade. The break-up of the theocratic idea of the Middle Ages, the slow growth of the modern theory of the State, was, for better or for worse, inexorably making its way.

The idea of the *de Monarchia* was carried forward by two remarkable men, William of Ockham and Marsilius of Padua. Ockham had made his fame as a doctor at Paris, and Pope Clement VI. ascribes to his influence the doctrines formulated by Marsilius. This may be true, but Ockham's political writings belong to a much later date than that of the *Defensor Pacis*. Ockham accompanied Lewis to Munich, and it was there, in the years following 1330, that he wrote his epoch-making criticisms of the fundamental ideas of the medieval papacy. His method is strictly dialectical, the method of *Sic et Non*. He writes with great caution and reserve, giving both sides of every question, and rarely if ever expressing a verdict of his own. His voluminous works may easily be made, by judicious extracts, to support quite opposite views of the questions in debate. He is entirely orthodox and indeed ascetic in his interests. The Beatific Vision, the Sacrament of the altar, apostolic Poverty are the subjects that engross an almost preponderating proportion of his zeal. On two of these points, indeed, he is convinced of the heresy of Pope John,[1] and this conviction no doubt went far to determine him in his attitude toward the papacy in relation to Church and empire. This last is the subject of his first political

[1] In the *Opus xc dierum*.

tract: "Super potestate summi pontificis octo quaestionum decisiones." It was written shortly after the Diet at Rense in which the electors vindicated their right to an absolute choice of the emperor without any papal veto.[1]

Ockham bases his work on Scripture, Aristotle's Politics, the Civil and Canon Law, the Fathers, including St. Bernard *de Consideratione*, the Sentences, and the historians, including Otto of Freisingen the historian of Frederick Barbarossa. He deals with the donation of Constantine, which he uses to prove that the pope received the *plenitudo potestatis* from the emperor; with the election of Charles the Great, as to which he observes that only a knowledge of more details than were on record would warrant any definite conclusion. As to the difference between the Kingly Power, conferred by the electors, and the imperial coronation and unction by the pope, he apparently holds that the former comprises all the substantial right of an emperor. The coronation confers not a temporal but a spiritual gift; for this he quaintly appeals to the case of the French and English kings, who by anointing and coronation receive, "as it is said," the supernatural power of touching for the King's Evil. All this is somewhat technical and relative to the claims of the pope against the medieval emperors. It is otherwise with the Dialogue between a master and his disciple, which was called forth by the new excommunication and interdict pronounced against Lewis by Clement VI. in 1343. This Dialogue, which the

[1] On the "Weisung" of 1338 see Bryce, *HRE.* pp. 220, 236, note (ed. 4).

contemporary chronicler Abbot John of Viktring [1] praises for its moderation, discusses the origin of the papacy. The master holds that Christ gave Peter no principality over the Apostles, that Peter was never bishop of Rome, and that the primacy of the pope is of human origin. He goes on to the indefectibility of the Church, which he maintains as guaranteed for all time, in contrast to its infallibility at any given time. Neither pope, nor council, nor clergy, nor the majority of the faithful are exempt from the possibility of error. In the latter part of the book, he discusses monarchy both in Church and State, and decides that it is essential in neither. Aristotle's qualified preference for monarchy applies to particular States, not to the world as a whole. The world as a rule, though there may be exceptions, is better without a universal monarchy.

Passing to the question what books contain all doctrine necessary to salvation, Ockham decides, with Dante, that this can be claimed for the canonical Scriptures alone, as interpreted by the ecumenical councils, and on the points necessary for eternal salvation, as they are to be found in the creeds. This at least appears to be his view, though he hesitates on the one hand as to the inclusion of other writings by apostolic men, on the other hand as to the authority of *all* conciliar decisions, which often are based upon mere human wisdom. Toward the end of the book he comes back to the office of St. Peter and the infallibility of the whole Church at any given time, and appears disposed to assert, at least in part, what in the first part of the book he had called in question.

[1] As quoted by Riezler, *Lit. Widersächer*, etc., p. 257.

But on two points he is quite clear throughout, namely, that the pope has no power over the world in temporal matters, and that he is not infallible. These are the two cardinal points of the Gregorian system, and in Ockham we see the scholastic mind shaking itself loose from the presuppositions which had governed the medieval conception of the Kingdom of Christ on earth.

Repeatedly he gives utterance to the conviction, distinctive of modern as against medieval thought, that the forms of government both in Church and State must change with the changing needs of the times.[1] The great nominalist comes, in fact, very near to the ideas of relativity and of development which lie at the root of the modern and scientific conception of history.

Of Ockham's philosophy, and of its profound influence in the last centuries of the Middle Ages, I cannot speak here. But it is worth noticing, to his honour,

---

[1] The monarchy of the bishop, he argues, may be expedient for the diocese, while a monarchy may yet be undesirable for the Church as a whole (*Dial.* II. xxx.). For more details of Ockham's views than I can give in the text, and for interesting extracts from his contemporary, Lupold of Bebenburg, the reader must refer to the notes in Gierke, *Political Theories of the Middle Age* (Camb. 1900). One striking passage on the papal *plenitudo potestatis* must be quoted (*Dial.* III. v., in Goldast, *Mon.* ii. 776 sq.). "Lex Christiana," argues the *Magister*, "est lex libertatis respectu ueteris legis, quae respectu nouae legis fuit lex seruitutis. Sed si Papa habet a Christo talem plenitudinem potestatis ut omnia possit quae non sunt contra legem diuinam nec contra legem naturae, lex Christiana ex institutione Christi esset lex intolerabilis seruitutis . . . Lex Christiana est lex libertatis per quam Christiani a seruitute sunt erepti, ultra in seruitutem minime reducendi," etc. The *Discipulus* objects that this applies only to freedom from *sin*, and from the old law, otherwise a "religious" Rule, and even civil obedience, would be unlawful. The *Magister* replies that the principle does apply quantitatively; we are emancipated by Christ from any servitude equal to, or greater than, that of the Jews, as the Apostle says "ubi Spiritus Domini ibi libertas."

how absolutely free he is from servile accommodation to the imperial cause in which he writes. He is not the hireling scribe of a royal master, but the resolutely analytical mind, weighing argument against argument in a balance sensitive almost to instability, but ever in search not of the opportune but of the true. His indecision is characteristic of the sceptical element in his philosophy, a scepticism which finds the highest exercise of the intellect rather in the pursuit of truth than in its apprehension, a scepticism which distrusts all proofs and throws the soul back upon the intuition of Faith, a scepticism which will end by taking refuge in external authority.[1]

Ockham's influence on subsequent Christian thought has been twofold. If his example and direct teaching have favoured Christian liberty, his more lasting intellectual heritage has been the distrust not only of individual but of common reason and the strengthening of the tendency to rest belief simply upon the authority of the Church.

(*d*) Marsilius of Padua[2] resembled Ockham in his

---

[1] On the general tendency of Ockham's thought, cf. Prantl, *Geschichte der Logik im Abendlande*, iii. 328. In theology, his nominalistic scepticism encouraged the tendency to despair of rational proof of the articles of faith, and to rest in the *fides carbonarii*, the old antithesis of νόμοσ against φύσισ. Ockham, before he died, sent the Seal of the Franciscan order, which had been in his custody since Cesena's death in 1342, to the General, intimating his desire to make his peace with the Church. (Clement VI. had in 1343 called God to witness that he desired Ockham's salvation only next to his own.) He died probably April 9, 1347; a later tombstone existed in the old Franciscan church at Munich which was cleared away before the present Hof-Theater was built on the site (Riezler, pp. 126-128).

[2] Not to be confused with the less famous "Marsilius ab Inghen." The name Raimundinus (al. Mainardinus, Menandrinus) is attested by his fellow-townsman Mussato. He was a Paduan, versed in medicine, philosophy, and theology. In 1312 he was Rector of the University of Paris, a

learning, in his genius, in his fearless sincerity. But no two minds could be more differently constituted. Of Ockham's nominalism,—in fact of metaphysical interests as such,—the *Defensor Pacis* has not a trace.[1] The Italian is positive, systematic, practical. Much again as he has in common with Dante, we miss in him the soaring poetry, the religious fire, at once transcendental and deeply personal, of the great Florentine. The physician-cleric of Padua is prosaic, impersonal. But the moral dignity and right-mindedness, the sincere sober zeal for religion, enlist the personal respect of the candid reader for the writer's character, as well as wonder at his genius. For inferior as Marsilius is in many respects, especially in human interest, to Ockham and still more to Dante; as a political thinker this obscure student ranks high above them both. Others have, like him, amid institutions wholly different from their ideal, and with little help or suggestion from any living or past example, thought out the constitution to be desired for State or Church. But these have been

quarterly office, filled from among the Masters of Arts. At Paris he was a hearer of Ockham. Marsilius is a man to be judged by his book. The little that is known of his personality from other sources is very thoroughly sifted by Riezler, pp. 30-38. It goes without saying that all that could be attempted by way of belittling his fame has been done, even down to a rigorous examination of his valet by the Inquisition in 1328. The result is naturally trifling. The most serious faults to be found with him concern his Roman administration in 1328,—Riezler's rubric "der Theoretiker als Praktiker" conveys the most just impression.

[1] John of Jandun, who is said to have assisted Marsilius in the preparation of the *Defensor Pacis*, was (like Dante) a student of Averroes. But he is wholly orthodox on the origin of the soul, and rejects the doctrine of an "intellectus communis" holding "quot corpora humana tot intellectus." John says he received the Commentary of Peter d'Abano on Arist. *Probl.* "per dilectissimum meum magistrum Marsilium de Padua." (On John, who also combined philosophy with medicine, see Renan, *Averroes* (ed. 3), p. 339 sqq.; also Riezler, pp. 55-58.)

the Utopians, the dreamers. Marsilius alone has divined the secret of an age unborn, and laid down, in all essentials, the principles which were to mould the political institutions of the distant future.

Marsilius fled from the University of Paris to join Lewis of Bavaria at Nürnberg in 1325 during the two years' pause between the emperor's first excommunication by the pope and his descent into Italy. Till the end of his life he was in the confidence of the king, and as a practical statesman he cannot be said to have attained success.[1] His title to greatness rests upon his book, which he brought with him finished from Paris, and issued in Bavaria. The result of a few weeks of rapid writing, it evidently condenses the study and thought of many years.

The title, *Defensor Pacis*,[2] was probably due to the

[1] See above, note 2, and Riezler, pp. 42-55; Creighton, *Papacy*, vol. i. p. 47 (ed. 1897). Marsilius' failure in Italy is the natural failure of the attempt to apply modern liberalism to medieval conditions; but further, "It was Marsiglio's misfortune that he was allied to a cause which had not a leader strong enough to give adequate expression to the principles which the genius of Marsiglio supplied" (Creighton). The appointment of an antipope was a blunder only too characteristic of the Middle Ages.

Marsilius died between 1336 and 1343, probably nearer the earlier than the later date. A tract ascribed to him, dealing with the nullity of the marriage of Margaret of Tirol to John of Luxemburg, and her marriage to Lewis' son (1342) is pronounced spurious by Riezler (p. 234 sq.).

[2] Printed in Goldast, *Monarchia*, ii. 154 sqq. I have used the Frankfurt edition (Wechelius, 1592, small 8vo). His recapitulation may be read in Mirbt, *Quellen*, No. 100. The English edition of 1535 ("The Defence of Peace; lately translated out of laten into englysshe; with the kynges most gracyous privilege.—The Preface of Licentius Euangelus unto the Apologye or antswere made by Marsilius of Padway, for the defence of Lodowyke (which descended of the most noble lynage of the Dukes of Bavary), Emperour of the Romaynes," etc. etc.) carefully suppresses the most fundamental points of Marsilius' political system, which were no doubt likely to collide dangerously with Tudor principles. In view of Marsilius' unflinching assertion of the sovereignty of the people, it would be difficult to imagine a more unjust or superficial characterisation of his spirit than that of Tarquini: "Ludovico Bavaro adblanditus."

direct suggestion of Dante, *de Monarchia*. In any case, it is well chosen. That the peace of the world had been disturbed by the attempts of popes to enforce their authority in temporal things was painfully manifest. Like Dante and Augustine, Marsilius ranks peace as the highest earthly good. Adopting Aristotle's famous axiom that the State is a self-sufficing whole, originating in the need to live, but existing in order to a good life (*Pol.* I. ii. 8), he defines peace as that "good disposition" of the State which allows every part of it to discharge perfectly its reasonable and normal functions. He seeks a principle which will relieve the nations of the strife and confusion which is inevitable when two authorities claim the sovereign power. In order to find it, he examines the fundamental principles of government in Church and State. And first as to the State: with an insight which marks a signal advance upon Dante, he distinguishes with perfect firmness of touch between the "prince" and the "legislator." The latter is sovereign in the ultimate sense; the prince is the supreme organ of the law, the head of the judiciary and of the executive. The legislator then is the "civium universitas, aut eius valentior pars":[1] the first assertion in European

[1] See Gierke, *Polit. Theories*, p. 43, and cf. Thom. Aq. *Summa Th.* 1ma. 11^{ae}. xc. 3 (3): Princeps ciuitatis potest in ciuitate legem facere.... Respondeo dicendum quod... condere legem uel pertinet ad totam multitudinem, uel pertinet ad personam publicam quae totius multitudinem curam habet. (See above, Lect. VI. p. 272, note 5.) The advance of Marsilius on Thomas, namely, the clear separation between the *legislative* power vested in the *universitas*, and the *executive* power of the princeps, is due to his more consistent grasp of Aristotle's elementary conceptions. Thomas, who held that the Church is a *ciuitas* (Gierke, note 49, cf. 217), could never (consistently with 11^{a}. 11^{ae}. i. 10) have allowed that its princeps, the pope, was "gerens uicem totius multitudinis" (Gierke, notes 165, 201).

politics of the sovereignty of the people. The legislator alone (or the person or persons entrusted by him with this power) has the right to suspend or dispense from laws. The duties of the prince are as far as possible to be settled by law, and he is responsible to the legislative authority for his conduct in administering it. He may be either a hereditary or elective prince; as a rule the latter is preferable.[1] There is room for one and one only supreme authority in the *civitas* or kingdom. Coercive jurisdiction is lodged with the prince alone. He derives it solely from the legislator. No decretal, nor any ecclesiastical officer, can have coercive power except it be given by the human legislator. All questions of property, all educational appointments and professional licences, all dispensations for marriages against human law (against divine law no such dispensations are possible), the control, after the service of the Church has been provided for, of all surplus religious endowments, the administration of charitable bequests, the punishment of heretics or other delinquents, the determination of the conditions under which oaths may justly be dispensed from, appeals from any judgment, in whatever cause, involving coercive punishment,—all depend ultimately on the legislator alone. In fact, with the natural exception of the machinery of representative institutions,[2] the

[1] Here Thomas Aq. would agree; for the papal constitution of the Church (to Thomas the standard type of government) is that of an elective monarchy. (See Gierke, notes 131, 153.)

[2] The principle of course is there. In their essential principles, the "Order in Council," "Charity Commission," "Ecclesiastical Commission," in a word the whole relation of the Crown and its executive to Parliament, are anticipated with extraordinary accuracy.

essential conditions of modern constitutional government are here for the first time clearly thought out.

Turning to the Church, Marsilius anticipates the most accurate modern scholarship in defining his terms. "Ecclesia," in its original sense, denotes the assembly of the whole body. This, he points out, is its original meaning in Greek politics. In modern times it has come to mean either a building, or else the clergy and specially the pope and his cardinals. But its true Christian meaning, as we see from St. Paul's speech at Miletus, is the "universitas credentium fidelium."[1] The term "spiritual" is properly applied to religious acts and religious persons; but he rejects its application to property, or to persons in respect of actions relating to temporal matters. He then proceeds to discuss the fundamental question whether Christ conferred upon the Church, and especially on the popes, any power over temporal things. The question, he insists, is not what Christ *could* confer (for he is Lord of all), but what he *intended* to confer and actually *did* confer.[2] Here his arguments are like those of Dante, but fuller; he comes to the same conclusion as Dante, but on principles which he derives from St. Augustine's conception of Christ's Kingdom.[3] He strongly and elabor-

---

[1] The most modern scholarship entirely confirms this, but would add what was beyond the knowledge of the fourteenth century, namely, a reference to the LXX and its original.

[2] The constitution of Oct. 29, 1327, by which John XXII. condemned the errors of Marsilius, directly misstates his posistion, ascribing to him the view that in paying tribute our Lord "hoc fecit *non* condesencsiue e liberalitate siue pietate sed necessitate coactus" (Denzinger, lxv. 423)! Mars. expressly insists that had Christ willed to do so he might have conferred *any* degree of power over *temporalia* (*Dic.* II. iv.).

[3] He supports the axiom that Christ came to set up a kingdom not of this world by Augustine's definition of that kingdom: "quod fideles

ately works out the subject of evangelical poverty, as to which his convictions are very warmly on the Franciscan side. The Church as a spiritual body, he argues (once more coinciding with Dante), cannot possess property. Its material requirements must be supplied by the faithful (upon this duty he strongly insists), but the regulation of all that remains over is for the State, which also must insist upon the clergy performing their allotted functions (*i.e.* in spite of interdicts, etc.). He then brings into relation his two axioms (1) that the clergy owe their institution to Christ alone, and (2) that the legislator alone appoints all officers in the body politic. They are harmonised by aid of the distinction between (1) the right to minister in any given place, and (2) the priesthood in itself, which comes from GOD by human transmission, that is, from Christ as at once GOD and man. In their most essential functions, *i.e.* that of eucharistic consecration and the power of the keys, all priests from the pope downwards are alike. He here strongly presses the well-known view of Jerome, taking care to point out that in the New Testament "presbyter" and "bishop" are synonymous terms (he quotes Acts xx., Phil. i. 1, and the Pastoral Epistles). He is not

Christi sunt regnum eius quod *modo* colitur, *modo* emitur per sanguinem Christi; erit autem *aliquando* regnum manifestum," etc. (I have not succeeded in identifying this reference, but it closely resembles some passages cited above, Lect. V. sub init.) Marsilius' thought is also expressed by Cesena in his *Litterae ad omnes Fratres ord. min.* (Goldast, *Mon.* ii. 1137, *after* p. 1342 !); he accuses John XXII. of following the Jews: "Quia sicut iam in saepedicto libello qui incipit *Quia vir reprobus*" (*sup.* p. 304, note 1), "ipse dicta Danielis prophetae et aliorum prophetarum loquentia *de regno Christi spirituali et aeterno* exponit et intelligit *de temporali et mundano* regno," etc. etc.

quite clear on the differentia of the episcopal order; from the equality of all priests he glides on to the equality of all bishops, quoting Jerome again for the principle that all bishops are successors of the Apostles, which, he argues, implies that Jerome thought all the Apostles equal.[1]

After the death of the Apostles, then, priests derive their priestly character from their ordination, but their *local appointment* from the *fidelium multitudo*, and so ultimately from the *fidelis legislator humanus*. For example, the Apostles lay hands on the Seven; but they leave the choice of the actual persons in the hands of the brethren.

Marsilius here concentrates his argument on the origin and powers of the papacy. He quotes the most relevant New Testament passages which show that St. Peter exercised no jurisdiction over other Apostles, and justly argues that the Apostle whom scriptural evidence connects with Rome is St. Paul rather than St. Peter. He denies any connexion of St. Peter with Rome in the New Testament.[2] He is on firmer ground when, in face of the negative evidence of the Acts (xxviii.) and Epistle to the Romans, he dismisses as fabulous the "legenda" that represents St. Peter's arrival at Rome as prior to that of St. Paul. The true origin of the papacy is by ecclesiastical custom. Other Churches went to Rome for advice and precedents, just as the writer has known other universities apply to that of

---

[1] Jerome's views are stated and discussed by Lightfoot, *Philippians*, 98 sq., 229 sqq.; Gore, *The Church and the Ministry*, 173 sq., 274, etc.

[2] Apparently overlooking the Babylon of 1 Pet. v. 13. The inferential connexion, deduced from Acts xii. 17 (see Harnack, *Chronol.* i. 244, note), was hardly likely to occur to him.

Paris, without any idea of jurisdiction being implied. But hence arose the custom of decretals,[1] which he supposes to be practically coeval with the Church. Like Dante he does not divine the truth about the decretals of the first four centuries. Marsilius, for the convenience of the Church, desires a papacy, but a papacy of ecclesiastical appointment.[2] Such a pope would stand to the whole Church much as does the "prince" to the State; but having no pretence to divine right, he would lack the boasted *plenitudo potestatis*,[3] the fruitful source of strife, bloodshed, and civil anarchy. The *plenitudo potestatis* has shown its untrustworthiness in the settlement of controversies of faith. For the pope may fall into heresy like Liberius, or give a wrong decision as "a certain pope" has done on the poverty of Christ and his Apostles.[4]

Marsilius, in agreement with Dante, lays it down that nothing is to be propounded for belief as necessary to salvation, save what is contained in canonical Scripture, or is to be proved thereby. The question of proof and interpretation is to be decided by general councils only. They alone also can excommunicate,[5] canonise, order fasts and feasts and the like. But if their decisions are

[1] This is strictly accurate (*supra*, Lect. VI. p. 236, note 1).
[2] This was what the Greek Church was prepared to allow in the fifth century; see *Concil. Chalced.* Can. xxviii., and Bright's note.
[3] *Supra*, p. 310, note 1; Gierke, notes 131 and 18.
[4] John XXII. (see above, p. 304, note 2). He urges the risk to faith of such a pope as Boniface VIII. had claimed to be. The claim of the latter in the Bull *Unam Sanctam*, which, with one of his rare outbursts of feeling, Marsilius characterises as "most mischievous of falsehoods," had subsequently been declared (by Clement V. in the Brief *Meruit carissimi*) *not to apply to France*. Marsilius mercilessly presses the contradiction involved.
[5] Individual bishops may do so, but only if allowed by the legislator (*supra*, Lect. VI. p. 271, note 2).

to be enforced, the *legislator humanus*, who alone has the *potestas coactiva*, must be a party to them. Accordingly they can only be summoned by the will of princes. The emperors, for example, summoned, and were present at, the four general councils which once for all settled the great controversies of faith. Those councils were composed of bishops and clergy alone; but the council of the future must answer to the changed conditions of the times. The different provinces and "notable communities" must be proportionably represented, and there must be a lay element, like the elders of Acts xv.[1] In the primitive Church the clergy and the learned were nearly coextensive. But in these days, he has known bishops and abbots too ignorant to express themselves grammatically, and a wholly ignorant youth under twenty, not even in minor orders, made by papal favour bishop of a famous and populous town. Such men are no fit judges in controversies of faith. The large number of ignorant bishops and clergy makes the need for a lay element in councils far greater in these times. The legislator then should depute fit priests and laymen, who should be present and judge as experts.[2] In any case, in matters of conscience men must not be coerced by civil penalties. If a heretic breaks the law, he must be punished for breaking it; but not as a heretic. The New Testament does not authorise this; and only the precepts of the New Testament,—by no means all those of the

[1] "Elder brethren" is the correct reading (Acts xv. 23, R.V. and Vulg.). On the lay element in councils in the *fifteenth* century, see Gierke, note 205.
[2] He quaintly quotes St. James to prove that this is the *duty* of the learned laity, for, "Scienti bonum facere et non facienti, peccatum est illi."

Old Testament,—are to be observed as necessary to salvation.

The *Defensor Pacis*, of which the above is a very imperfect sketch, is a marvel not only of political and scriptural insight, but of sustained and luminous argument. No term is employed without careful definition, and every step is made by strict method, carefully prepared for, and tested by every objection the writer can bring to bear upon it.

His great and lasting achievements are the constructive theory of the modern State, in which his noble conception of the "prince" and his office stands in eloquent contrast with the "Prince" of Macchiavelli; and again the negative criticism of the papacy. His conception of the Church, moreover, is sound, philosophic, and spiritual. His theory of the relation between Church and State is open to more objection. Accepting without question the whole body of medieval dogma, he does not foresee the difficulties which liberty of conscience, and the inclusion in the State of men of different creeds, will import into these relations. He assumes the "*fidelis* legislator humanus" as a constant and fundamental factor in the system. Accordingly starting out from the substitution of one Augustinian conception of the Kingdom of GOD for another,—discarding the conception of that Kingdom as an omnipotent Church in favour of the deeper, and more characteristically Augustinian interpretation of Christ's Kingdom as his reign *per fidem credentium*, Marsilius proceeds to assume that the citizens of the State will correspond to the latter idea; and so, by aid of the assumption of the *fidelis* legislator, meets the claims of the omnipotent Church with the counter-principle of an omnipotent Christian State; omnipotent even, since the legislator lies behind the general council, in matters of faith. He is not "Erastian," for the Church is to him a purely spiritual society, whose origin and mission is solely from Christ. But in the last resort, power in the Church lies with the laity who constitute the "fidelis legislator." If then the citizens are not at one in faith, if the legislator is no longer "fidelis," the Marsilian theory of Church and State becomes impossible. In these conditions, the tendency of the *Defensor Pacis* is toward the separation of Church and State, the State remaining the arbiter of personal and property rights, while the Church exists, in the eye of the law, as a voluntary contractual society, free to pursue its own ends subject to the general law of the land.

(*e*) But we are not now concerned with the application of the Marsilian principles to the modern relations of religion to the State. What is important to observe is that the hierarchical system of the Middle Ages has lost its hold upon the greatest thinkers of the opening century. That Marsilius in his criticism of the papacy represents the deepening feeling of thoughtful men, it it is impossible to doubt. In common with Ockham, he went beyond its temporal claims, at which Dante's criticism stopped short, and examined its credentials as a spiritual office. This was inevitable; for with the one, the other stood or fell. The *plenitudo potestatis* cannot be partly denied and partly affirmed.[1]

---

[1] Alvarus Pelagius: "potestas sine pondere numero et mensura" (Gierke, note 131); also the quotations in Gierke, notes 13, 17–25. This is of course involved in the modern doctrine of the "Societas Perfecta" (*supra*, p. 292, note 1, and *infra*, p. 344, note 2).

If so, Marsilius was right in his theory of the State; for the temporal power of the popes was the direct antithesis of the sovereignty of the people. Adrian IV. and Alexander III. might, in their campaign against the emperor, encourage popular government in the Guelf cities of Northern Italy, but they could have permitted it in Rome only at the cost of renouncing their own divine right. Dante, Ockham, Marsilius, mark the irresistible and irrevocable movement of Christian thought. The Church, from Gregory VII. onwards, has attempted a mighty task, and the result is destructive of the highest ideal of human society; the attempt has failed. The Church has not failed, but the attempt to invest her with a certain function and character has done so. The conclusion is that this function and character are no part of her divine commission, that if the Church is to realise her character as the Kingdom of Christ upon earth,—and that this is her character these men rightly believe,—it must be in some other way.

The growing perception of the contrast between the secular wealth and dominion of the Church and the example of Christ and the Apostles is characteristic of the century and a half which lies between Arnold of Brescia and the Pontificate of John XXII. It would be a mistake to derive all, perhaps any, of the later movements which give utterance and shape to this perception from the direct influence of Arnold. He died, and in a sense, as a contemporary boasts, his doctrine died with him:—

"Ecce tuum, pro quo penam, dampnate, tulisti
Dogma perit, nec erit tua mox doctrina superstes."[1]

---

[1] From the Bergamo poet quoted *supra*, Lect. VI. p. 260 sqq., notes.

But the principles to which Arnold had devoted his life were in the air, and were certain to inspire others also. Within a few years of his death, Waldes sold his goods and gave all he had to the poor, and began his great movement of lay-preaching. After a partial approval by one pope, the movement was condemned by another,[1] and developed an anti-ecclesiastical puritanism. In spite of stern suppression, and some of the extravagances which repression encourages, the sect of the poor men of Lyons, with its branch-movements in Piedmont and in the Rhine-country, lived on, and coalesced in turn with the Hussite and Protestant reactions,[2] and it lives to this day. In some of its ramifications, it was brought back into the Church as a recognised order. The *béguinages* of Ghent and Bruges are the catholicised survivals of a society of Waldensian origin which was stamped out in the Low Counties by the Inquisition.[3]

[1] Their poverty, but not their preaching, was approved by Alexander III. at the council of 1179 (*supra*, p. 264, note). In 1184 they were condemned by Lucius III. Waldes was wholly unconnected with the Albigenses, a sect of Eastern origin, whose tenets were in part Manichean. The persecutions of the thirteenth and fourteenth century tended to confuse the two bodies, but they were never really identified. There is no reason whatever to regard the Waldensian movement as of greater antiquity than Waldes himself. The Waldensian errors, Denzinger, lxiii. ; see an excellent sketch in Möller, *Kirchengeschichte*, ii. 383-391 ; also Trench, *Medieval Church Hist.*, Lect. xvii.

[2] For this subject, consult Dieckhoff, *die Waldenser in MA.* (Gött. 1851); Gindély, *Gesch. d. böhm. Bruder* (Prag. 1858); Preger on Taborites and Waldensians in fourteenth century in *Bavarian Academy*, 3 cl. XVIII. i. pp. 1-111 (Taborites a fusion of extremer Hussites with Italo-Bohemian Waldensians) ; Palacky's *Geschichte Böhmen's* (Prag. 1867).

[3] The Beguines seem to have originated at Liège, *c.* 1180; about a century later we hear of a society of men (Beghards) at Louvain. Möller (*ut supra*, 456-469) sketches the history of the movement, every detail of which, including the name, is the subject of much debate.

DIVERGENCE OF IDEALS 325

Before Waldes was dead, Francis of Assisi had founded his brotherhood, with a closely similar aim but in perfect submission to the Church. Only, as we have seen, after his death the more uncompromising spirits of the order carry into effect the essential antagonism between their ideal and the wealth and power of the popes and cardinals.[1] Of all these movements, so far as the essential principle of absolute poverty is concerned, Arnold of Brescia is the type. But he also represents, unlike either the Waldensians or the Franciscans, the spirit of municipal self-government, stimulated by the growing importance of the middle-classes in the Lombard towns, and associated in Rome with the lingering reminiscence of the lost republican idea. This side of Arnold's spirit reappears in Marsilius, whose early life in Padua probably prepared him to appreciate the political ideas, the outcome of the city life of ancient Greece, which he found in the Politics of Aristotle. These ideas, once more, had already, in Dante, fertilised the expiring idea of the Medieval Empire, and laid the foundation of a new conception of government which was to supersede the old barren strife of Guelf and Ghibelline. The Guelf conception of Divine Right, embodied in the papacy, the Ghibelline idea of Historical Right, embodied in the empire, were to give way to the higher principle of law rooted in freedom, and of the essential moral end of human society.

[1] The Fraticelli seem to have been in close connexion with the Beghards and Beguines; the errors of the latter, condemned by Clement v. (Denzinger, lxi. A), approach to "quietism," while those of the Fraticelli (*ibid.* lii.) are not unlike the tenets of the Plymouth Brethren.

II

None of the movements which meet in Dante, Marsilius, and Ockham represent any revolt against the established doctrines of the Church. The *de Monarchia* is certainly a contradiction of the Gregorian claim to temporal power, and the *Dialogus* and *Defensor Pacis* follow this contradiction to its logical result in respect of the external constitution of the Church; but no creed nor council had as yet committed the Church to any doctrine on the subject; the revolt we have been considering is not against the medieval system of doctrine, but against the medieval system of Church law. That both the system in question and the revolt against it go back to principles formulated by Augustine, is in part due to the logic of history, only in part due to conscious dependence upon Augustine's writings.

It is otherwise with the movements of Wycliffe and Hus, which can be touched upon here only in so far as they affect the conception of the Church and of its relation to the civil power.

Wycliffe, in his reaction against the power of the pope and hierarchy, rests upon the Augustinian idea of the Church in its transcendental aspect as the *numerus praedestinatorum*. With him begins the strictly theological opposition to the medieval system. It is true that he was at first in sympathy with the Franciscan and political movement considered in the early part of this Lecture. The pope complains of him as teaching the condemned errors of Marsilius,

THE EVE OF THE REFORMATION

and the affinity of some of his leading political and ecclesiastical tenets with those of Marsilius and of Ockham is conspicuous. But Wycliffe was first and foremost a theologian and a schoolman, and his distinctive doctrine of the Church is directly due to the revival of Augustinianism in Oxford, exemplified in the person of Thomas Bradwardine the "Doctor Profundus" of Merton. In fact as compared with that of Bradwardine, Wycliffe's Augustinianism is very moderate. He does not, like Bradwardine, object to merit *de congruo*, and he abandons the Augustinian condemnation of "natural" morality.[1] Wycliffe and Hus both set out from the predestinarian idea as the exclusive basis of their conception of the Church, but practically fall back on the existing Church organisation, only demanding reform of abuses, with a view to bring the Church back into correspondence with their ideal of a Holy Society, marked out by the prevalence of Christ's law of Love, Humility, and Poverty. With the exception of Wycliffe's rejection of transubstantiation, both he and Hus are concerned for the reform of the life rather than of the dogmas of the Church. The authority of the pope, the validity of the ministry of unholy priests, the validity of ecclesiastical censures and absolutions if unjustly administered, and of indulgences for which money was paid, the spuriousness of the decretals, all these were questions involving far-reaching principles, but in view of the fact that the definition and constitution of the Church had not

[1] See Rashdall's article on Wycliffe in *Dict. Nat. Biogr.*, and his *Universities*, ii. 540.

as yet been laid down by any general council, they rank as questions of discipline rather than of doctrine properly so called. Wycliffe was, or became in the later part of his life, an extremist. But except in his exaggerated opposition to clerical endowments [1] he was a sober thinker, and Oxford supported him throughout until "Archbishop Arundel's triumph over the University in 1411 sounded the death-knell of Oxford Scholasticism." [2]

Meanwhile the Avignon papacy and the great schism were undermining the moral authority of the papacy, and strengthening the movement for constitutional reform of the Church "in its Head and in its Members." The conciliar movement in the early fourteenth century was inspired by the idea that the Church had drifted from its primitive episcopal constitution; men looked for regeneration to a restored conciliar government, which by practically reasserting the council of bishops as the supreme authority would bring back the Church to the purity of early times. The idea was theoretical,—"a professorial Utopia,[3]—and the attempt to carry it to effect was half-hearted. It was found easier at Constance to depose the rival popes and elect a new one, than to restore to working order the constitution of the early Church; easier to burn Hus, his safe-

---

[1] This "was the peculiar doctrine of the friars, exploited and brought into practical politics by Wycliffe. . . . It was characteristic of those times for partisans to ask far more than they expected to get; to lay claim, on the ground of some theory, to infinite space when a nutshell was the end in view" (Trevelyan, *England in the Age of Wycliffe*, p. 151; cf. p. 198 sqq. etc.)

[2] Rashdall, *Universities*, ii. 436, 542.

[3] Harnack.

THE EVE OF THE REFORMATION

conduct notwithstanding, than to touch the profound evils complained of by the German nation.[1]

The Council of Basel was foredoomed to failure before it met. Its convocation, the unwilling fulfilment by the pope of an unwilling promise, was soon followed by discord between pope and council, which finally degenerated into open war. Victory was eventually on the side of Eugenius IV., who was able to draw away the more moderate members to his own council at Florence, where a hollow peace with the Eastern Church invested the papal cause with the transient glamour of a sensational triumph. With the failure of Basel, the conciliar movement failed hopelessly. The councils had asserted their superiority to the pope, but had not succeeded in giving effect to it. All attempts at reform were checkmated, and in the two generations which constitute the eve of the Reformation the prestige of the papacy stood higher than it had stood since the fall of the Hohenstaufen. The authority of the popes over kings and emperors, as it had been claimed by Gregory VII. and Innocent III., was indeed gone for ever; but it remained as a theoretical claim,[2] and every attempt

---

[1] See Mirbt, *Quellen*, 101, 102. The Germans pressed urgently for reform *before* the election of a new pope, but were unable to carry their point. On the general state of the Church, see Möller (*ut supra*), 477-480 and references.

[2] *E.g.*, see the Bull of Alexander VI. bestowing all "insulas et terras firmas *inventas et inveniendas detectas et detigendas*," west of a line 100 leagues west of Cape Verde and the Azores, upon Ferdinand and Isabella; the Bull is issued "motu proprio . . . *de nostra mera liberalitate* . . . *auctoritate omnipotentis Dei* nobis in b. Petro concessa ac uicarius Jesu Christi qua fungimur in terris' (Mirbt, *Quellen*, 108). To enumerate instances of deposition of kings (*e.g.* that of Henry VIII. by Paul III., *ibid*. 113; 1535) is needless. But it is curious to recall that as lately as 1701

to cut at its roots by challenging their spiritual supremacy had ended in failure. The long series of protests, founded upon the principle of Holy Poverty, begun by Arnold of Brescia, continued by the Waldenses, the Franciscans, by Dante and Marsilius, by Wycliffe and Hus, found their answer in the undisturbed splendour of the papal court of the age of the Renaissance. They had proved as unpractical as the apocalyptic dreams of Abbot Joachim. The imperialist movement was dead, the conciliar movement defeated and discredited. The reassertion by Wycliffe and Hus of the Augustinian transcendentalism of an invisible Church had filled Bohemia with war and confusion, and had already spent its force; in England it had been stamped out by authority. All these movements for building up the Church from below upon the holiness of its members, forgetful of the danger of rooting up the wheat with the tares, had failed to appreciate the need of human nature for a visible embodiment of the reign of Christ over sinful men. They were violent and sweeping, partly because they lacked a secure positive footing of constructive principle. That the government of the Roman Curia was corrupt and tyrannous, and that the constitution of the ancient Church had become altered, were convictions shared by all the medieval parties of opposition, and by many orthodox Churchmen besides. But these convictions, true as they were, were too purely negative, too tentative in the then state of critical knowledge, to lead to anything

Clement XI. denounces the erection of Prussia into a kingdom without his authority as an "audax et irreligiosum facinus" (*ibid.* No. 136–138).

but failure in practice. The general result was despair of reformation either in head or in members. The evils which Gregory VII. had thought to remedy by an omnipotent papacy were still unhealed.[1] But while the evils were felt, there was no longer any strong impulse toward reform. The pontificate of an Innocent VIII. or an Alexander VI. might insult the conscience of Christendom, but without challenging any attack upon the principles which had triumphed over the reforming movements of the age of the Captivity and of the schism.

It is difficult to generalise as to the religious state of Europe on the eve of the Reformation. It was an age of contradictions, "the age of Savonarola and of Macchiavelli"; an age of declining interest in theology coupled with increased interest in both the higher and the lower forms of practical religion; an age of Gothic decay and Classical revival in architecture,—of the revival alike of learning, and of grovelling belief in witchcraft,—an age of Christian conquest in Spain, of new worlds opening new fields of wealth and adventure,—of the first beginnings of the great Catholic missions, while classical paganism and scepticism

[1] As to simony, it is said of a pope in a contemporary epigram:—

"Vendit Alexander claves, altaria, Christum;
Emerat ista prius, vendere iure potest."

On the whole subject, see Möller (*ut supra*, note 1). That profound corruption reigned in the monasteries and among the clergy of the fifteenth century is not seriously denied. In Italy, to take one example, the order of Camaldoli, which had sent forth Peter Damiani to purify the Church of the eleventh century, was found by its general, the learned Ambrogio Traversari, to be festering "from head to foot" with the very worst of evils against which Damiani had contended. See the appalling facts disclosed in his *Hodoeporicon* (a description of his visitation A.D. 1431).

flourished in the high places of the Church. It is possible, by judicious insistence upon different classes of facts, to represent the age on the one hand as one of deep intellectual unsettlement, moral depravation, and religious bankruptcy,[1] or on the other, as a time of sincere popular religion, coupled with serious thoughtfulness and enlightenment, all too rudely disturbed by the wanton self-will of the inexplicable Luther.[2]

Perhaps we shall not be far from the mark if we recognise that an age when the boundaries of knowledge were suddenly widened, and the resources of life rapidly enriched, was marked by progress in religious seriousness also, coupled with the moral disorder which is the penalty civilisation too frequently pays for a loosening of old moorings before it has found the new; that the authority of the Church, which under the intellectual limitations of the Middle Age had scarcely succeeded in holding the best thought of the times in allegiance, was still less able to command

---

[1] See last note. This estimate is too familiar to need much illustration. A very impartial sketch is given by Harnack, *Dogmengesch.* iii. 570-577; more facts in Möller, ii. 532-539. See also Dr. C. Creighton's *History of Epidemics* on one painful side of the case. On the need for reform, Lord Acton (*EHR.* Oct. 1890) quotes an interesting letter of Möhler to Döllinger: "At that time [about 1500] the existing form of the Church was really blameworthy in the highest degree, and needed purification. The popes had become despots,—arbitrary rulers. Practices in the highest degree opposed to Faith and Christian piety had grown to a height. On many points Luther was certainly right when he says, of abuses of the Roman power, that there everything was purchasable. Tetzel, moreover," etc. etc. On witchcraft, see the extraordinary Bull of Innocent VIII. in Mirbt, *Quellen*, No. 107.

[2] This is the side ably put forward by Father Gasquet in his temperate and interesting *Eve of the Reformation*. He hardly appears to contemplate the possibility of religious motives in Luther or any other Reformer; on the other hand he appears somewhat detached from strictly curialist principles.

the rising intellectual activity of the fifteenth century with its command of a larger range of interest and knowledge; and that the ideas which had persistently asserted themselves through the Middle Ages, and had been suppressed by authority rather than answered by reason, were certain by the logic of history to demand their revenge. The one-sidedness of the Reformation was the unavoidable reaction from the one-sidedness of the system which embodied itself in the medieval papacy.

Not by the arbitrary wilfulness of one man or of many, but by the sure process of development, the interpretation of the Kingdom of Christ on earth in the form of an omipotent Church had broken down; the Reformation only gave violent expression to a fact which stands revealed already in the age of John XXII., that the Gregorian ideal is henceforth not the ideal of a united Christendom, but the ideal of a party.

III

The three questions[1] left open by Augustine, questions upon the answer to which depended the realisation of his thought of the *Imperium in Ecclesia*, had been answered by the medieval Church, but the answer was no longer adequate to the moral needs of mankind. The constitution of the Church as a papal monarchy had proved a source of disunion, it had involved consequences against which the enlightened conscience had revolted, and which no healthy government could allow. The absolute validity of Church

[1] See above, Lect. V. sub fin.

censures had been asserted until excommunication fell into contempt, and even saintly princes refused to enforce it.[1] The relation between the Augustinian doctrine of grace and the purely hierarchical idea of the Church had not been faced,—the two came out in hopeless conflict, first in the movements of Wycliffe and Hus, afterwards in the incurable schism of the sixteenth century.

(*a*) The storm of the Reformation withdrew more than half Europe from the allegiance of Rome; but the loss was not permanent. The medieval system was too deeply rooted to lack recuperative power, and the questions in dispute were not so simple as to admit of a one-sided solution. Europe was henceforth divided into two religious parties,[2] corresponding to two aspects of a question on which seriously religious minds were inevitably divided. The Counter-Reformation was as inevitable a reaction as the Reformation itself. On one side of it—regarded as a reformation of the Church—by the tardy reform of many of the practical evils which had given right and reason to the Reformers, it drew forth the best moral energies of those who sided with the old system. The Council of Trent, from their point of view, marks a beneficent epoch in the ecclesiastical life of Europe. On its other side, the

---

[1] *Supra*, p. 271, note 2.

[2] That, quite apart from the details of doctrine or worship, the peoples of Europe were henceforth divided into two broad parties, is as obvious as is the side on which England ranged itself. On which side justice, liberty, and enlightenment found their principal support, or whether these may not be balanced by assets on the other side, are questions on which the representatives of either may not agree. But that either side has the monopoly of practical religion, or of moral ideas, is a supposition now happily confined to the blindest partisans in both camps.

Counter-Reformation was a great party campaign to reconquer from Protestantism the ground lost by the Latin Church. This movement, again, drew forth boundless energy, devotion, and organising power, seconded, in the Protestant camp, by the inward decline of religious enthusiasm, and the many dissensions which appeared as the first energy of the Reformation had spent itself. For a time the return current set strongly; after a while it in its turn had spent its force, and for some two centuries the ecclesiastical geography of Europe has been substantially unchanged.

Both as a movement of reform and of aggression the Counter-Reformation has moulded the character of the Roman Catholic Church of modern times. The naïve picturesque abuses, the naïve piety of the Middle Age, are exchanged for an organised regularity and a devotion coloured by the sense of a controverted position. The *sancta simplicitas* of the medieval repression of heresy has given place to a persistent policy which, while asserting in theory the right to persecute,[1] rarely puts it in practice, but carries on the campaign in literature, education, and social work.[2]

[1] This is true, if we except the signal atrocities of the sixteenth century, especially in the Latin countries, the dragonnades, and the banishment of whole populations, to which Salzburg, Tirol, etc., owe their religious homogeneity of to-day. As to theory, see the *Syllabus* of Pius IX., No. 24, and his Encyclical *Quanta Cura*, which have behind them the influence of the Roman Jesuits, who argue that the Church, comprising men with bodies, must be able to apply bodily means, as St. Paul threatens to do (1 Cor. iv. 21, which they appear to take literally; Tarquini *Inst. Iur. Eccl.* p. 41).

[2] The subtle, but always perceptible difference between the characteristic products of post-Tridentine and of medieval religious life is analogous to that which distinguishes "rococo" from medieval architecture. The "rococo" style is often most effective, and personally I admire many examples of it; but it does not, like the "Gothic," adequately express the highest spirit of the age to which it belongs.

The Counter-Reformation starts from the Council of Trent, in which the Church, by crystallising into dogma almost all the disputed points of medieval doctrine, irrevocably closed the door to any synthesis of the opposing half-truths which divided the best minds of the sixteenth century. But there were three questions, all-important in their bearing upon the question with which we are concerned, which the Council left open to debate.

(*a*) First there was the old insoluble question of the relation between the theory of the Church and the Augustinian doctrine of grace. What was to be the authority of Augustine in the reformed Roman Communion? The council left this an open question, the *Catechismus Romanus* drawn up after the council represents a moderate but decided Augustinianism.[1] But from the end of the sixteenth century onwards the cause of Augustinianism has been a losing one. Baius of Louvain and Jansen of Ypres taught what Augustine had taught them, but only to incur condemnation, and light a flame of controversy which it took three centuries to bring under control. The subtle semi-Pelagianism favoured by the Jesuits gradually prevailed, the dogma of 1854[2] symbolises its triumph, and it

[1] Substantially that of Thomas Aquinas, on whose doctrine as compared with Augustine's see Mozley, *Augustinian Doctrine of Predestination*.

[2] Mozley, comparing the Thomist and the post-Tridentine doctrine of grace, puts the case in strong, but not exaggerated words: "Having excluded Augustinianism from the pale of tolerated opinion, the Church of Rome is obliged to prove that S. Augustine was not Augustinian" (p. 226, note; cf. 234). The Thomist doctrine is so far decidedly Augustinian as to involve the direct negative of the dogma of 1854. Thomas maintains (*Summa*, III. xxvii. 2 ad 2), "dicendum quod si nunquam anima Virginis fuisset *contagio originalis peccati inquinata*, hoc *derogaret*

may be doubted whether the repristination by Leo XIII. of the authority of St. Thomas Aquinas will extend to bringing back his modified Augustinian doctrine of Grace to theological supremacy.

(β) A second question was that of the constitution of the Church. The centuries between Augustine and the Council of Trent had settled this as far as the divine right of the papacy was concerned. But there still remained the leaven of the conciliar movement which had closed the great Schism. Have bishops a divine right independently of the popes, or do they rule as their delegates " by grace of the Apostolic See "?[1] And is the Pope above the Council or the Council above the Pope? These questions, really involved in the practical reforms of the third period of the council,[2] were not brought to an issue there, but were

dignitati Christi secundum quam est universalis omnium Salvator," and further on, art. 6, he explains that her purification before *birth* is simply on a level with that recorded (as was inferred from Jer. i. 5; Luke i. 15) of Jeremiah and John Baptist, her pre-eminent privilege consisting in her exemption from all, even venial, *actual* sin, whereas they were protected from mortal sin only. Pius IX., in 1854, defines, as a doctrine revealed by God, that the blessed Virgin "*in primo instanti* suae conceptionis fuisse, *singulari* omnipotentis Dei gratia et privilegio, intuitu meritorum Christi Jesu Salvatoris humani generis, *ab omni originalis culpae labe praeservatam immunem.*"

[1] A modern formula in the "style" of a diocesan bishop. I have not observed it in any pre-Reformation document, though it is claimed (*Kirchenlexicon, s.v.* Bischof) that it can be traced back to the eleventh century. If so, the traces are very faint. The Vatican Council of 1870 (*Const. de Eccles.* I. iii.), while recognising the direct divine source of episcopal jurisdiction, claims for the pope an ordinary *and immediate* jurisdiction *quae est vere episcopalis* in all matters and over every member of the Church. Those who assert that it is not ordinary and direct as regards *omnes et singulos,* or who deny the *plenitudo potestatis,* are anathematised.

[2] Ranke, *Popes,* i. 336 sqq.; Mendham, *Council of Trent,* for a *précis* of the debates.

evaded. The answer was first settled in 1870. Once again, as to tradition. The council decided that tradition is of equal authority with Scripture. But is tradition to be understood in the old Vincentian sense, admitting the appeal from the *quod ubique* to the *quod semper*, or is the *quod ubique* enough by itself? And if so, the bishops being under the episcopal rule[1] of the Pope, is the Pope himself the ultimate and decisive vehicle of tradition? Here again the council decided nothing; the question was closed only in 1870.[2] Accordingly, internal as well as external pressure compelled the Church of the Counter-Reformation to devote its attention to the completion of the theory of the Church, which now otherwise than in the Middle Ages occupies a place of its own in the topics of dogmatic theology.

(γ) Thirdly, there has been the question of the administration of the moral law. The enforcement in the Middle Ages of the universal obligation of confession was founded upon the assumption that grave sin after baptism can be forgiven by sacramental absolution only.[3] Confession must be universal because

---

[1] *Supra*, note 1. The *plenitudo potestatis* in theory, the imperative necessity to a bishop of powers granted by the pope for short periods only, and renewed or suspended at the pope's discretion, in practice, make any conflict of powers impossible.

[2] *Const. de Eccl.* 1. iv. end: The pope's definitions *ex cathedra* are " ex sese, non autem ex consensu ecclesiae, irreformabiles."

[3] Thom. Aq. *Summa*, Suppl. vi. 1 and 6, viii. 1 (from the commentary on the fourth book of the Sentences). Practically the same view in Pet. Lomb. *Sent.* iv. But Peter Damian, in his sermon (69) on the twelve Sacraments, while including *sacram. confessionis*, has no word as to absolution (but he also omits the Eucharist from his list!); he adds, "in hac uirtute caligant oculi *plurimorum*." Arnold at his execution is urged to confess to a priest "more *prudentum*" (*ut supra*, p. 262, note 2).

absolution is necessary for all. But the universality of confession had the effect of giving a new prominence to the direction of consciences as the function of the priesthood. Morality became a thing not only to be inculcated and enforced by the *correptio* of the Christian Society, but to be actually administered by the clergy, in whose hands the decision of the details of moral conduct, the decision in detail of the daily problems of moral action for every faithful Churchman, must henceforth be lodged. In the Middle Ages, when the rule of the Church had no serious rival, this raised no very difficult problem. The departments of conduct were mapped out, and the acknowledged principles of Christian ethics were applied to them. But when Europe became divided into two rival camps, and the problem arose of preventing the spread of Protestantism, and of reclaiming the ground lost to it in its first period of vigour, the question had to be faced of the extent to which moral strictness was to be insisted upon, or on the other hand relaxed in order to retain as many as possible in their allegiance to the authority of the Church.[1]

Briefly, the system known as probabilism, *i.e.* the doctrine that, in order to be justified in acting on the less safe side in a moral alternative, it is not necessary to be supported by a preponderance of reasons, but

[1] This was specially necessary in dealing with persons of influence. Even Loyola, who at first wished his Fathers to accept no court appointments, afterwards gave way, and remonstrated with Father Polanco, confessor to Duke Cosimo de Medici, for disturbing the duke and duchess with inconsiderate counsel, instead of accommodating himself to their wishes. Cardinal Casini (1713) accuses confessors of dealing strictly with the common sort, mildly with the great. See Döllinger-Reusch, *Moralstreitigkeiten in d. römisch-katholischen Kirche*, i. pp. 101, 116.

sufficient to have *some* reason for doubting the obligation to act on the safer side,[1] has been the means of establishing an accommodating scheme of practical ethics in the accepted moral theory of the Roman Church. The principle "Licet sequi opinionem probabilem" is the reversal, in the sphere of moral practice, of Butler's axiom that "probability is the guide of life." The system was introduced late in the sixteenth century, and in two generations, in spite of grave and strongly expressed objections,[2] it had gained

[1] In a case of doubt as to the lawfulness or obligation of some action, the course which is "legi favens" is recommended by the *opinio tutior*, the course *libertati favens*, by the *minus tuta* (*e.g.* 1 Cor. viii. 8). Again, in such cases, where neither "opinion" is *certa*, each of the two alternatives is in some degree *probabilis*. The two may be *aeque probabiles*, or one may be *probabilior*. Now to (1) insist that the *tutior* must always be acted on, even if the *minus tuta* be the *probabilior*, is "extreme rigorism," and in fact opposed to common sense. The contrary principle (2) that the *minus tuta* may be followed if *probabilior*, agrees in substance with the principle of Butler referred to in the text. If the two "opinions" are *aeque probabiles*, on the same principle the *tutior* must be acted upon. This is what is known as *probabiliorism*. Probabilists call it rigorism. But others hold (following the Tirolese Eusebius Am Ort) that (3) when "probability" is *equal* on either side, the *minus tuta* may be followed : *aequiprobabilism*; while (4) *probabilism* maintains that the *minus tuta* may be followed even when *minus probabilis*. If it is required that the *minus tuta* shall be *nearly equal* in probability, we have an approach to (3); if merely that it be *vere ac solide probabilis*, probabilism proper; if we are to be satisfied with an opinion *tenuiter* or *dubie* probabilis, the result is *lax probabilism*. Lastly, the "probability" may be based on the merits of the case: *probabilitas intrinseca*, or upon the authorities adducible on either side: *probabilitus extrinseca* (Döllinger-Reusch, i. pp. 5-7).

[2] Many of these are quoted in Döllinger-Reusch; *e.g.* Mabillon says of its representatives: "Quorum moralis theologia bonos mores pessimo veneno iam diu corrupit." De Rancé, the founder of La Trappe: "The moral teaching of most of them is so corrupt, their principles so contrary to the holiness of the gospel . . . that nothing pains me more than to see my name used to sanction views which I abominate with all my heart." Contenson, a brilliant Dominican who died in 1674 only 33 years old: "Nothing could be devised more convenient or welcome to the morals of this age, *the most corrupt in the memory of man*." Another Dominican

THE COUNTER-REFORMATION 341

almost universal acceptance, especially in the Jesuit order. By aid of the principle of "extrinsic probability," *i.e.* the decision of doubts, not by weighing the moral principles involved but the number and repute of authorities quoted on one side or the other, the system of Probabilism undoubtedly worked great havoc in the moral life of Christendom. Its fundamental axiom, " Lex dubia non obligat," interpreted by the aid of extrinsic probability, made the evasion of almost every moral and ecclesiastical precept possible.[1] The shock of the Provincial Letters, although the Letters themselves were condemned, told in the highest quarters of the Church. Alexander VII. and especially Innocent XI. set themselves to stem the rising tide of laxity. Innocent condemned a large number of lax principles,[2] and his policy produced one permanent result. Probabilism was banished for ever from the sphere of ecclesiastical duty. The precepts of the Church are to be enforced in their strict sense, and can no longer be explained away. But it was not so easy to achieve the same result with regard to merely moral obligations. Innocent attempted indeed a drastic

describes Probabilism as "ars cum Deo cavillandi" (Döllinger-Reusch, i. pp. 43, 79, note, 113, 112; see also pp. 36, 95 sq., 105 sq., 263 sq., etc.).

[1] It became, as one of the school boasted, more easy to confess sins than to commit them. Bishop Caramuel, whom even Liguori calls "the laxest of the lax," profanely pointed to the Theatine probabilist Diana with the words, "Ecce Agnus Dei qui *tollit peccata mundi*" (*Kirchenlexicon, s.v.*). Of Caramuel's seventy-seven folios, only one tract is on the index, and that because he accused Fagnanus of Jansenism (Döllinger-Reusch, i. 123, note).

[2] The common editions of the Decrees of Trent contain in the Appendix the condemned propositions of Baius, Jansen, Quesnel, etc. ; but for the condemned theses of the lax school it is necessary to go to Denzinger, *Enchiridion*, or to the larger works on Moral Theology, *e.g.* Lehmkuhl.

remedy, namely, the extirpation of Probabilism in the Jesuit order itself. He brought to Rome the learned Spanish Jesuit Thyrsus Gonzalez, whom his experience as a mission preacher had converted from Probabilism by forcing him to realise its deplorable effect upon lay morality. Innocent succeeded in securing the election of Gonzalez as General of the Order, and impressed upon him his mission to save the order from the precipice down which it was rushing.[1] But Gonzalez was unequal to the task. The steady opposition of the assistants and of the whole spirit of the Order made it impossible for him even to publish his book against the objectionable doctrine. At last it saw the light in a remote corner of Bavaria, but every copy of it has apparently disappeared.[2] After years of fruitless struggle, Gonzalez lost his mental faculties, and died a broken man. But meanwhile the general judgment of the Church was increasingly strong on the side of the stricter morality. Till late in the eighteenth century this wholesome tendency gained the upper hand. But the French Revolution frightened the Catholic powers and the princes of the Church back into the camp of the Jesuits, and the influence of St.

---

[1] Gonzalez says: "Cum Innocentius XI. mihi dixisset, me factum fuisse Generalem in illum finem, ut Societatem averterem a praecipitio in quod ruere videbatur" . . . (Döllinger-Reusch, 113, note). It may be necessary to warn the English reader that the position of Gonzalez is quite wrongly stated by Sohm in his very able and suggestive *Outlines of Church History* (Eng. trans.).

[2] *Tractatus succinctus de recto usu opinionum probabilium*, Dillingen, 1690. Four years later, he published at Dillingen his *Fundamentum Theologiae moralis*, in which he slightly modified the statement of his case. The history of Gonzalez is told at immense length by Döllinger-Reusch, i. 120-273, with documents in support in vol. ii. The story is full of interest in its details for those who desire to follow up the subject of Probabilism.

THE COUNTER-REFORMATION 343

Alfonso Liguori[1] regained for Probabilism more than all the ground it had lost. Here if ever is a case of the better judgment of the Church being overborne by the force of irresistible tendencies. Discredited and fairly argued down, the cause of the laxer morality yet triumphed in the end. Popes and saints strove to suppress it, the lay mind rejected it, it seemed driven finally beneath the ground. But in spite of all, the turbid waters of Probabilism surged up again, and the elevation of St. Alfonso to the rank of a Doctor of the Church makes any prospect of a change in the tide almost hopeless.

(*b*) The result is in reality due to the logic of facts, the inward coherence of ideas which has triumphed over all endeavours to sever them. Extreme curialists, like Bellarmine, may have objected to Probabilism, Augustinians as sincere as Christian Lupus of Ypres[2] may have extolled the ultramontane theory of Church government and tradition, the first probabilist may have been a member of the order[3] specially pledged to the Thomist and Augustinian doctrine of grace. But such facts do not modify the broad general truth that the three controversies we have referred to have

[1] The work and character of this extraordinary man (1696-1787) are described by Döllinger-Reusch, i. 356-476. Well-worn as the subject is, the English reader will find much that is new and instructive in their discussion, based on a thorough mastery of the sources. Liguori, tortured all his life by scruples as to his exact position as a moralist, professed, on the whole, aequi-probabilism, but was at heart a thorough probabilist, and is claimed as such by the modern probabilists, Marc, Lehmkuhl, etc. His enormous, but hopelessly uncritical, industry has done more than any other one cause to give to the characteristically modern elements in Roman Catholicism a secure hold in the current teaching of the Church. In 1871 Pius IX. proclaimed him a Doctor of the Church.

[2] His self-chosen epitaph, " Natura filius irae," etc., in Hurter, *Nomenclator, s.v.*

[3] The Dominican Barth. de Medina in 1577 (Döllinger-Reusch, i. 29).

ranged on either side substantially the same influences and the same combatants. The cause of constitutionalism in Church government and of the appeal to history [1] as the authentic criterion of tradition has also been the cause of the Augustinian doctrine of Grace and of the stricter moral principles, while on the other side the cause of papal absolutism, of the less rigid doctrine of grace, and of the laxer morality, is one and the same. This cause is the cause of the great Jesuit order, which under Pius IX., by the dogmas of 1854 and of 1870, and by the elevation of St. Alfonso to the rank of a Doctor of the Church, triumphed all along the line. The cause is one and the same, because in all three questions alike there is involved the simple issue of the two alternative conceptions of the Kingdom of Christ on earth as embodied in the Christian Society. The Jesuit conception of the Church as a *Societas Perfecta*,[2]—a Society, that is, which has at its disposal, by

---

[1] Looking over the enumeration of the Church historians of modern times, say as given by Card. Hergenröther in the *Einleitung* to his Church History, the impression is irresistible that in the Roman communion, apart from the collectors of material such as Baronius, Raynaud, Petavius, etc., the greatest names are with hardly an exception on the side which lost the day in 1870. Natalis Alexander, Fleury, Tillemont (perhaps the greatest of all), and in the nineteenth century Hefele and Döllinger. Hergenröther remarks justly in his conclusion, "Wie der Historiker Theologe, so musz auch der Theologe Historiker sein"; this is suggestively illustrated by Lord Acton's closing verdict on Döllinger, that probably no historian has ever owed more to Theology, nor any theologian owed more to History (*Eng. Hist. Rev.*, Oct. 1890).

[2] This doctrine (referred to *supra*, pp. 214, 257, 292, note 1, 322, note 1, etc.) is the characteristic and keystone of the modern Jesuit conception of the Church. (I have not met with it in any treatise earlier than the nineteenth century, nor in any non-Jesuit work, except in the *Syllabus* of Pius IX. No. 19: "Ecclesia non est uera *Perfectaque* Societas," etc.). The principle, however, is simply that of the Church as a world-State in the Gregorian sense (cf. Gierke, *Political Theories of the Middle Age*, p. 19,

divine right, all resources of government, and depends for their unrestricted employment upon no other power, —a Society absolutely complete in itself, resembling earthly kingdoms in this, but differing from them in its freedom from their limitations by virtue of its distinctive and paramount aim,—this conception of the Church exalts submission to external authority as the supreme and all-important demand of Christian ethics,[1] sacrifices everything to this, and looks with disfavour upon the distinctively Pauline doctrines which make the faith of the individual Christian the spring of moral initiative and the root of responsibility to GOD. A new legalism[2] is the result of a new appreciation of obedience to

and notes 20, 49, 51, 332, 311). It is the product of juristic or political, not of theological thought. Its ultimate source is Aristotle's definition of the State as κοινωνία τέλειοσ . . . πάσησ ἔχουσα πέρασ τῆσ αὐταρκείασ (*Pol.* I. ii. 8), which is reproduced by Thomas Aquinas (*Summa,* 1ma. 11ae. xc. 3 ad 3) without any reference to the Church. The latter application (contrast *supra*, p. 226, note 1) is worked out into its most extreme consequences by the authoritative school of Roman Jesuits represented by Tarquini (*Juris Ecclesiastici publici institt.*, ed. 4, Rome, 1875) and Palmieri (*Tract. de Romano Pontifice*, ed. 2, Prato, 1891). By a *Societas Perfecta* is meant one "quae est in semetipsa completa, adeoque media ad suum finem obtinendum sufficientia in semetipsa habet"; moreover it follows *ius esse societati iudicandi* de mediorum necessitate," except "where the error is manifest and incontrovertible" [who is to judge as to this?]. If this leads to conflicts with civil authority, so much the worse for the latter. But if men were good, no conflict would arise, for the civil society would recognise its proper subordination to the Church (Tarquini). In fact the principle of *Imperium in gremio ecclesiae* (*supra*, p. 214) is pushed so far as to leave the Church the only *Societas Perfecta* on earth.

[1] This is a very real legacy of nominalism to the Counter-Reformation (*supra*, p. 311, note 1).

[2] The essence of legalism appears to underlie the very categories of the moral theology developed under this system. The ever-recurring antithesis of opinion *legi* favens and *libertati* favens carries us back to a conception of "law" as a factor in the moral life (ὑπὸ νόμον, Rom. vi. 14, vii. 6), and above all to a conception of "liberty" (Rom. vi. 22, viii. 15; Gal. v. 1; 1 Cor. iii. 17, etc.), wide as the poles from the factors of the Christian life as conceived by St. Paul.

spiritual rulers as the essence of Christian morality, and legalism, in this case as in all others, by resting all duties on an external motive, shifts the incidence of the law from the moral to the positive.[1] The principle *Lex dubia non obligat*, inapplicable now to the precepts of the Church, finds wide application to duties purely moral, and the principle of *probabilitas extrinseca* completes the process. Objectionable, and tainted with moral scepticism,[2] as the whole system taught by the Liguorian handbooks of morals must ever appear to those who compare it with the ethics of St. Augustine and St. Paul, it is none the less inexorably consequent upon the conception of the Kingdom of Christ upon earth which is involved in the modern theory of the Church as a *Societas Perfecta*. That this conception has its roots in the Middle Ages, in the principles of Gregory VII. for which his successors fought so consistently and with so much success, is of course true.[3] But the history of the Middle Age itself shows how subversive it is of the divinely-appointed functions of States and rulers, how inadequate it is to the moral and social ideals which no less than itself owe their origin to Christian instinct and reflexion.

To have learned nothing from Christian experience,

[1] Compare the very interesting section of Schürer, *Gesch. d. Jüdischen Volkes* (ed. 2, § 28), "das Leben unter dem Gesetze."

[2] Because the interest is centred not on character, nor indeed on moral conduct *per se*, but upon the formal principle of compliance with law (*supra*, p. 311, note 1). Contenson (in his *Theologia mentis et cordis, ut supra*, p. 340, note 1) speaks of the probabilists as substituting "pro Christi disciplina Pyrrhonis schola." A demonstration of the truth of Probabilism appears to be nowadays an indispensable chapter of the prolegomena to any Roman Catholic treatise on Moral Theology.

[3] See above, p. 252, note 1, and 273, note 1.

CHRISTIAN UNITY 347

to have elaborated into a consistent theory a system which involves the condemnation as abnormal and monstrous[1] of all the dearly-bought liberties upon which what is best in modern civilisation has been built,—rights of conscience, rights of self-government, the freedom of learning and science,[2] the enlarged moral aim of Society and the State,—cannot, one would hope, be a final result. We must believe that the Church can and ought to effect a reconciliation—understanding those terms in their best sense—with progress, liberalism, and modern civilisation,[3] and our sympathy should be generously extended to those numerous and loyal sons of the Roman Communion who cherish that belief and work patiently toward its realisation in the distant future.

IV

The Reformation has been accused, with some show of reason, of sacrificing the unity of the moral and religious life of Europe in its impatience of abuses which the Church might have reformed from within.

---

[1] Tarquini's view of modern history is that Christ has punished the sovereigns of Europe (for imposing constitutions upon the Church) by allowing their subjects to impose constitutions upon *them*. "Non penitus tamen," for the Church has "eorum [*sc.* Principum] caussam ultro suscepit," etc. etc. (p. 160 sq.).

[2] The *Syllabus* condemns (No. 12) the proposition that "the decrees of the Apostolic See and of the Roman congregations *impede* the free progress of science"; but had the lesson of Galileo been completely learned by 1864?

[3] *Syllabus*, No. 80. The ardent desire of many evidently sincere Roman Catholics for this reconciliation is finding manifold utterance at the present day; the volume of opinion will probably not diminish, and no generous mind will wish it anything but increasing influence.

But the history of the Middle Ages, with the slow but sure divergence of the highest ideals which that history reveals, shifts the accusation further back. It falls upon no one man, on no one group of men, hardly even upon the papacy as an institution; but rather on the causes which made the growth of that institution, and of reaction against it, equally inevitable. So far as the diverging streams can be traced back to a definite point of parting, it is in the person of St. Augustine. But this fact again is due to his many-sided idiosyncrasy, which enabled more of the richly diverse elements of Christian thought and feeling to find expression in him than can coexist in the generality of men. The Christian religion, and the Christian character, is many-sided and capable of development in endless varieties of harmonious type. That their harmony is to be maintained by external authority was the presupposition—a natural one—of the medieval system, a presupposition upon which was founded an attempt that failed. As a result, Christendom has become divided into parties whose separation has all the appearance of being permanent and incurable. But, hurtful as is such a state of things to the external influence of the Church, we must look below the surface to measure justly its effect upon the true Reign of Christ on earth. As Dante has said, "Forma ecclesia vita Christi." And history warns us that where any uniform system reigns undisturbed and uncriticised, the flame of the Christian life is apt to burn low. Diversity, as well as unity, has its benefits and blessings. The Reformation, let us allow, got rid of the evils of a false unity only to exchange them for those of an irreconcilable diversity. We cannot hope for any lasting good from a mere reversal of this exchange. But in the far future it may be given to our children's children to see the dawn of a unity which shall include all that is lasting and healthy in the diversities of to-day, and without loss or injury to truth, uphold to mankind the example of the whole body of Christ's faithful people bound together in His common Love.

LECTURE VIII

THE KINGDOM OF GOD IN MODERN THOUGHT, LIFE, AND WORK

Forma ecclesiae Vita Christi.
                                              DANTE.

   What we have to choose then in the days of choice is nothing less than the character of the bond which is to make our actions coherent. . . . Much may remain dark to us ; but the purposes of life receive a clear and powerful direction the moment we believe that the one supreme way of life is that Jesus Christ, GOD's Son, our Lord, who has been made known to us from the first in the Creed. No other single way, capable of uniting the whole nature and life of man, has yet been discovered which does not tend to draw us down rather than lift us up.
                                              HORT.

LECTURE VIII

THE KINGDOM OF GOD IN MODERN THOUGHT, LIFE, AND WORK

> Behold the days come, saith the LORD, that I will make a new covenant with the house of Israel, and with the house of Judah : . . . [and] this shall be the covenant that I will make with the house of Israel : After those days, saith the LORD, I will put my law in their inward parts, and write it in their hearts ; and will be their GOD, and they shall be my people. And they shall teach no more every man his neighbour, and every man his brother, saying, Know the LORD : for they shall all know me, from the least of them unto the greatest of them, saith the LORD : for I will forgive their iniquity and remember their sins no more.—JER. xxxi. 31, 33, 34.

IT was part of the strength as well as of the weakness of the Reformation that it did not set up a system of thought as complete as that which it displaced. In an age of vehement reaction it was easier to see what was wrong than what was wholly right. The Reformation broke up—or rather registered the break-up of—a grand and comprehensive concrete interpretation of the earthly Reign of Christ; but it put no structure in its place that could compare with it in concreteness, or in grandeur of scale. Had it done so, the result must have been premature and therefore precarious,—as precarious a substitute for the medieval system as was the Protestant Scholasticism of the seventeenth century for the handiwork of the medieval School. The very failure of the Reformation in this respect left open the road to constructive thought in future and more favourable times, when the exigencies of theological warfare should give place to a serener outlook upon life, aided by a knowledge of the universe, a historical sense, and a command of method and material for the study of Scripture and of history far beyond the resources of the sixteenth century.

We look in vain, accordingly, to the Reformation period for any fruitful or epoch-marking conception of the Kingdom of GOD. Such as they are, the utterances on the subject are of interest mainly in their bearing upon what were then really urgent and practical questions, those namely of the constitution and nature of the Church of Christ.

It is a commonplace of controversy that the Reformers, pressed with their separation from the visible Church, originated (whether for better or for worse) the idea of a true and invisible Church, in comparison with which the visible Church was treated as of little account. But this, like some other commonplaces, is true only to a very limited extent. Firstly, the idea of an invisible Church, in so far as it has really been held, is, as we have already seen, nothing but the Augustinian idea of the *Communio Sanctorum*, sharpened by an exclusive insistence upon the predestinarian doctrine which Augustine certainly held, though not in the isolation in which it appears in more modern thinkers. This applies, as we saw, to Wycliffe,[1] and in some degree to Hus also. Of the Reformers, it applies fully to Zwingli alone.[2] In opposition to Luther, Zwingli held that State and Church having but one aim, the

---

[1] *Supra*, p. 326 sq.
[2] See the useful study of this subject in Ritschl, *Gesammelte Aufsätze*, p. 68 sqq., and *Lehre d. Rechtfertigung u. Versöhnung* (ed. 2), iii. 267 sqq.

THE REFORMATION

visible Church merges in the Christian State,[1] which represents the Kingdom of GOD on earth, *Regnum Christi est externum*. The Church, as distinct from the State, was to Zwingli simply the invisible *numerus praedestinatorum*. Zwingli's conception of a purely invisible Church influenced some of the later Lutheran scholastics, but among the leading Reformers he maintains it alone. Luther and Calvin, while asserting with lesser or greater emphasis the doctrine of predestination, treat the invisible number of the elect or communion of saints simply as the core of the visible Society which is concentric with it. The Church to them is one only, not two. It is at once invisible and visible; invisible in respect of the bond which unites its true members to Christ, visible in the external notes of the Word and Sacraments, the presence of which denote the body in which they are found as a true portion of the Church of Christ. Luther's insistence on the invisibility of the Church is an assertion, against the contention that an earthly society must have a visible head, of the invisibility of the vital unity of the Church: *Regnum Christi internum*.[2] He founds his idea of the Church not upon predestination but upon the Communion of Saints, visible to faith, recognisable by the external signs of "Word and Sacraments."[3]

[1] Which as such is charged with the duty of enforcing virtue and godliness by law.

[2] Ritschl (as above, note 2).

[3] This is from Augustine: *e.g. Ep.* 21. 3, "Sacramentum et uerbum populo ministrare"; *c. Petil.* iii. 67, "minister uerbi et sacramenti euangelici, si bonus ... si autem malus est non ideo dispensator non est euangelii"; *c. Faust.* XIII. xvi., "cum paucis haereditatem Dei, cum multis autem *signacula* eius participanda" (where the context explains the *signacula* as *sacramenta*). More passages might be quoted.

Calvin's idea of the Church is more closely bound up with the predestinarian idea, and so far approximates to that of Zwingli; but he, also, recognises in the visible society the indispensable vehicle of grace, the divine provision for the infirmity of man, the instrument of God's grace for His elect.[1] Practically his system issued in a subjection of the civil to the ecclesiastical organisation as complete as that of the Middle Ages, but differing from it in aim and spirit. Political freedom and self-government were enlisted in the enforcement of personal morality and of the realisation of the Church as the visibly holy Society united by the express aim of religious regeneration.[2]

Neither Luther nor Calvin can be said, therefore, to have maintained the dogma of an invisible Church; but while Roman Catholicism makes the visible hierarchy an object of faith as a divinely-instituted system of government, Luther and Calvin point to the visible Society as the casket which enshrines the reality, visible to faith, of the true body of Christ. Both agree that the preaching of the Word and the due ministration of the Sacraments[3] are the external notes of the Church; and this definition has passed into our own formularies. The definition is, as a definition, hardly satisfactory. It is rather a description of the local and particular Church than a definition of the Church as a

---

[1] By the principle of "obsignation": "obsignant uero, quatenus diuina testimonia sunt, ad idipsum testandum adhibita quod ipsa Promissio testatur; nempe sacrificio Christi partam esse credentibus remissionem peccatorum, gratiam Spiritus sancti et uitam aeternam" (Pisc. *Loci Comm.* xxiii. 3).

[2] See Mark Pattison, *Essays*, vol. ii. (xii.), *Calvin at Geneva*.

[3] Ritschl, *Aufsätze*, pp. 76, 80, 112 sq.

whole,[1] and it leaves open great variety of opinion as to what constitutes the pure Word of GOD, and what conditions are involved in the due ministration of the Sacraments. But these questions, and the answers to them which our own Church has adopted, lie outside the purpose of this Lecture. It may suffice to say that the English Church, practically alone among the reformed Churches of Europe, embodies the attempt to give effect to the episcopal theory of the constitution of the Church which animated the unsuccessful efforts of the conciliar party at the beginning of the fifteenth century.[2] That this attempt has so far failed to solve the difficulty involved in the relations between the civil and the ecclesiastical power is in part due to the legacy of unsolved problems bequeathed by the break-up of the medieval system. The difficulty is the legacy of many centuries; its solution can only come with time, and must be attempted with infinite patience, and with acceptance of historical conditions.

II

The present age has been marked by the attempt to go back to the fountain-head with the aim of reinterpreting the fundamental Biblical idea of the Kingdom of GOD. The recognition of Biblical Theo-

---

[1] This defect is in part due to the tendency to identify the visible Church with the local "Gemeinde," while the Universal Church *as such* is held to be "invisible." If we hold the principle of unity to be not a visible head, but a hidden and sacramental union with the living Christ, it is impossible wholly to reject this distinction. The Holy Catholic Church is in part an object of *sight*, but *qua* object of *faith* it is not seen.

[2] *Supra*, p. 328.

logy,[1] built up in the light of historical criticism and exegesis, as the necessary preliminary to the systematic treatment of theology, is favourable to such an attempt. As a result, we may hope for a fertilisation of the conception of the Church and of its relation to the problems of human life in the light of the master-idea of the Kingdom of Christ on earth.

Among the most suggestive of modern endeavours to do justice to this task is that of Albert Ritschl.[2] Much as there is in his method and conclusions which is uncongenial to English habits of thought, he has the merit of doing justice to a side of Christian teaching from which Protestant theology had too much drifted away, namely the theological significance of the Church in relation to the Kingdom of GOD. Minimising somewhat unduly the eschatological character of the latter doctrine, he finds its essence in the conception of a society, which embodies the Divine Purpose for humanity and the chief good of man. This is the ideal moral brotherhood, bound together by Divine Love in the realisation of the sum of supernatural ends. This Kingdom is not to be identified with the Church *in respect of the Church's organisation* and hierarchy; this identification he regards as the fundamental mis-

---

[1] That division of the general Biblical section of Historical Theology which, building on the results of critical and exegetical study of the text, arranges in order of historical development the religious ideas embodied in the various books or group of books. It thus *prepares the ground* for "Systematic," Constructive, or Dogmatic Theology.

[2] Lived 1822-1887. At first under the influence of the Tübingen School, whose conclusions he afterwards abandoned (Lightfoot, *Galatians*, p. 285, note (ed. 3)). Ritschl's principal works bearing on this subject are: *Lehre d. Rechtfertigung*, etc. (*supra*, p. 354, note 2); *Unterricht in der Christlichen Religion* (ed. 2, 1881); and the *Aufsätze*, also quoted *supra*.

take of St. Augustine;[1] but he sees in the Augustinian thought of the *civitas Dei* on earth a great advance upon earlier Christian conceptions in which the biblical idea of the Kingdom of GOD had, as he holds, been obscured.

The Church is the Kingdom of GOD in the making, in so far as she is, by her priesthood, faith, and life, progressively realising the character of the ideal moral unity described above. These activities belong to the ethical[2] idea of the Church, which must always be viewed in subordination to her primary character as embodying the Grace of Christ. This she does in the Word and Sacraments which are given her by GOD, not produced by her in response to divine grace. Whatever is so produced belongs not to the theological and primary, but to the ethical side of the Church. But the latter depends upon the former, and it is through the sum total of her "ethical" activities, the priesthood of Christians as such, their creed, prayers, worship, and diversities of administrations, that the Church is realising, is coming to be, the Kingdom of GOD. This distinction between the primary and the practical idea of the Church corresponds to that between divine grace and human responsibility, between the Church in itself and the Church in history, the one universal and the particular and national Churches. The *Gratia Christi* is the efficient cause, the Kingdom of GOD the end and

---

[1] A historical error in which Ritschl has been followed by others (see above, Lect. V. p. 173, note 1).

[2] *Aufsätze*, p. 118; *Rechtfertigung*, iii. 29-33, etc. By "ethical" he means those manifestations of the life of the Church which summon *will* into activity, in response to the Grace of GOD (see also *Unterricht*, §§ 7-9).

goal;—the process from the one to the other, in which the several members of Christ are being trained up "to a perfect man," is embodied in the historical Church, which may be divided to the eye of flesh, but which faith, looking to the beginning and the end, embraces as one.[1]

The Church, then, to Ritschl is invisible in so far as Faith in the Church is directed to her invisible life. To demand that this should be visible, that her holiness should be visible without spot or wrinkles, is the demand of puritanism, exemplified in the Novatians and Donatists of old, and to some extent in the discipline of Calvin at Geneva. The demand must fail, because it seeks to hasten a process the completion of which is in the hands of GOD. But although, to borrow terms from the Theology of the Sacraments, the *Res* Ecclesiae is invisible, the Ecclesia is visible; an invisible Church would be no society at all, for a society must be united by the conscious pursuit of an aim in common. Even in respect of its primary character, the Church has visible notes, and in its practical self-realisation it is either visible or non-existent.

The system of Ritschl, of which the above is a meagre but I think a fairly correct sketch, has no finality. He does inadequate justice to the eschatological side of the Kingdom of GOD in our Lord's teaching and in the mind of the Church of all ages; he fails to do justice to St. Augustine's contribution to

---

[1] See the important passage *Aufsätze*, p. 133; he concludes: "Theological theory is of value only so far as it answers to Faith. But Faith knows the Church only in her Unity."

the subject; his conception of the "supernatural"[1] requires careful scrutiny; and the whole is coloured by an attitude toward metaphysics which is at least paradoxical.[2] The system has no finality, but it is certainly rich in suggestion, and future investigation cannot pass it by without doing justice to its root-ideas. In particular, Ritschl's agreement with St. Augustine is more important than he himself realised. In so far as we can detach the fundamental and spiritual doctrine of the Kingdom of GOD in Augustine's theory of the Church from his rigid predestinarianism, we have as the result a conception of the Church as the Kingdom of GOD in the making, not indeed the same as that of the modern thinker, but yet in essential harmony with it.

The resemblance and difference between the two may perhaps be seen if we consider their bearing upon the most permanent and fundamental problems involved in the conception of an earthly kingdom of Christ,—

[1] He very seriously underrates the eschatological aspect of the Kingdom of GOD, in which, as we have seen (Lects. I., II.), lies its original and most persistent significance. He holds that, our Lord's teaching on the subject being above the receptivity of His hearers, the Jewish Christians understood it of a millennium, the Gentiles merely of a future life.

By "supernatural" Ritschl appears to mean (*Unterricht*, § 8; cf. *Rechtf.* iii. 464, 564, etc.) that which transcends the ethical and social obligations which are based upon man's natural endowments. These, left to themselves, offer occasion for self-seeking. The Kingdom of GOD is "supernatural" *because based on love*: in realising it man overcomes "the world" of which he is by nature a part, and, assured in Christ of eternal life, knows that he is united to GOD by a bond which death itself cannot sever (so *Unterricht*, §§ 45, 76).

[2] The demand to keep metaphysics out of theology colours all Ritschl's system. He devoted to it a special work, the small but interesting tract *Theologie und Metaphysik* (1881). But the demand is one that defeats itself, for theology, like man himself, is metaphysical *nolens volens*. Ritschl's whole theory is based on metaphysics in so far as it depends (as every system of theology ultimately must) upon a very definite theory of knowledge.

I mean the Christian attitude toward common life and its interests, civil, political, intellectual and social. It is possible either to condemn all such interests and concerns as worldly, the attitude of Millenniarists and sectaries, or to regard them as sanctified only if brought under ecclesiastical direction,—the medieval view, anticipated by Augustine in one side, not as I think the most fundamental side, of his philosophy of history. Or it is possible to invest them with exclusive value *per se*,—the secularist view, tending to practical materialism, and as abhorrent to Ritschl as to Augustine himself. Or lastly it is possible to view these things as the proper field for the exercise, the trial and the display, of Christian character;[1] a view which goes back to St. Paul, and is consecrated by the example of our Saviour's free intercourse with men and interest in human joys and sorrows.[2] That the Church trains her members not to fly from active life, but to live it in the love and fear of GOD, is a truth easier perhaps to realise in our time than in that of St. Augustine, but there is much in his conception of the kingdom of Christ, much in the *de Civitate* itself, that supports the conviction that human government and society itself finds no bond so enduring as the Christian character, and that the Christian life must be a useful life.[3] It is in emphasising this as the true Christian outlook upon life that Ritschl's conception of the Kingdom of GOD is most important in its suggestiveness for the future.

---

[1] Phil. iv. 8; 1 Tim. v. 8; Eph. v. 22–vi. 9, etc.

[2] This is the strong side of the remarkable book, full of real insight, but one-sided and in some respects a psychological enigma : *Pro Christo et Ecclesia.*

[3] This is very strikingly enforced by St. Augustine, *de opere Monachorum.*

He does not in the least share the instinct of Rothe in Germany or of some distinguished Churchman of our own country, to disparge the ecclesiastical organisation as practically obsolete, and destined to merge in the forms of civil life. Such idealised secularism ignores, as Ritschl saw, the plain facts of life and the equally plain purpose of Christ. On the one hand our Lord committed his purpose for man's salvation to a Society which he commissioned to teach what he had taught, to live as he had lived, and to seek before all things the Kingdom of GOD and his Righteousness: he gave no hint that this society would ever have so far discharged its distinctive message that it could merge its corporate existence in the society around it. On the contrary he warned his followers against dangers which would always threaten them from "the world," and assured them of his perpetual presence so long as that world should last. And on the other hand experience tells us that human society is ever drifting from its highest ideals, ever needs to be led back to them, that men who are weak as individuals are strong in combination, and that no influence can be permanent which has no body of men specially devoted to its cause. Moreover we have come to see that the State can realise its moral aim not so much by laws or official action as by the character of its citizens, and that for the maintenance and elevation of that character it must rely upon resources which it cannot itself command.

It is for the Church, not for the State, to bring about the day when the kingdom over this world is to pass to our GOD and to his Christ.

How then does this affect our ultimate question?

III

The Christian Church has at all times and with one consent sought the Kingdom of GOD in the eternal reign of the Father, to be inaugurated by the Second Advent and the last Judgment. Nothing short of an eternity is a worthy sphere for the perfect moral government of GOD. Nor again has there ever been a time when the Christian consciousness has not responded to our Lord's assurance that the Kingdom of GOD is within, that the heart and conscience are its seat and home, the new birth of will and character the measure and sign of its coming. When we have made sure of these two interpretations, we have satisfied very much of the language of our Lord; but not quite all. It is natural, in the highest sense, to man,[1] to direct his energies upon the society around him, to live not for himself alone; and this, we may be sure, is an instinct of our nature to which the Son of Man will do justice. "The Kingdom of GOD is within you," but is isolated self-culture, therefore, the path towards its realisation? It is within, but may none the less have to be sought without. Its home is the conscience and the heart, but where do these find their scope for action? Its coming is seen in the new birth of character and will; but does this come direct from GOD unaided by secondary causes? or again does it issue in atomistic individualism?

The irrepressible Christian instinct has always been to seek the Kingdom of GOD in this world, not in the next only; and not within only, but also without.

[1] Arist. *Eth. Nic.* I. vii. 6, ἐπειδὴ φύσει πολιτικὸσ ἄνθρωποσ.

SUMMARY OF IDEALS

Revealed religion has never appealed to the individual merely as such, but to individuals federated in a brotherhood, first of blood, then of faith.[1] And so, from the Gospels onward, the eternal and perfect Kingdom of GOD demands its earthly counterpart in the society of Christ's people on earth. But the relation between the two has been conceived in two alternative ways. The Church has been held to correspond with the divine kingdom either in respect of her internal holiness, that is in so far as her members are, to use Augustine's expression, even now, though in a far inferior degree, as truly reigning with Christ, as they will reign with him hereafter; or, on the other hand,[2] in respect of her governing power, firstly and essentially over all her members, but secondly, over all the kingdoms and societies which exist among mankind. These two last-named conceptions of the earthly kingdom of Christ, firstly as embodied in the Church as a government within her own limits, secondly in an ideal state of the world in which the Church is the supreme authority, ruling absolutely within limits which she alone is competent to define, are in reality one and the same. The second is the necessary complement of the first, and, if we assume the first, to realise the second becomes the necessary aim of the Church and of all her loyal members. Its only complete form is the papal system, for

---

[1] Ritschl, *Unterricht*, § 7 (and *supra*, Lects. I., II.).

[2] It might appear at first sight that the alternative has been between identifying the kingdom of Christ on earth on the one hand with the Church as such, or, on the other hand, with a state or position which the Church is to acquire, whether of internal perfection or of external power. But the true alternative embraces those just mentioned on each of its sides as subordinate branches.

in that system alone has the problem been solved of a constitution capable of carrying on the legislative and executive machinery adequate to enforce a common system of law for the whole body. The first assertion of this idea of the Church was indeed very different in form and spirit. The millennial reign of Christ was the hope of the persecuted Church which looked for a visible reign on earth of Christ and his saints, to whom the kingdom of the world would belong at his coming. Compared with this hope, the ideal of the visible reign of Christ in the person of the Pope his Vicar was rational and practical. But both Millenniarism and the papal system have in common the idea of the earthly reign conceived of as an external government.[1] Both alike, though with very unequal influence, retain a strong hold upon men's minds to the present day. But just as Millenniarism could not, as a dominant belief, survive the long delay of its hopes, coupled with the development of the speculative activity of the Church, so the papal system has long since lost all power to direct either the political or the intellectual life of Christendom. Practically, it has been obliged to recede from its medieval ideal of universal rule; its authority has become confined to the exercise of ecclesiastical government, and to technical control of doctrine as distinct from matters of science or general thought and culture. The idea of universal rule is indeed maintained in theory, but its assertion is ineffectual and

[1] See above, p. 316, note 3 (Cesena). Theologians are apt to underrate, or overlook entirely, the strong hold which Millenniarism, even at the present day, retains over minds disposed to simple realism, and often as the nucleus of still more strange systems of literalism. Such simplicity deserves no less respectful treatment than that of Justin or Irenaeus.

academic. Political and scientific activity takes, and will continue to take, its own course, untroubled by the thought of ecclesiastical control. The power of the Church over the moral life of her members is exerted by spiritual means only, without the aid of the law. In a word, the civil sword no longer even sharpens [1] the ecclesiastical.

Now this result is so far purely negative. The verdict of history has condemned the attempt to realise the earthly kingdom of Christ in the form of a Church whose organisation is omnipotent in the affairs of the world. The verdict of history has condemned it, not merely in the sense that it is no longer in force,—for what time brings forth may, after a while, disappear, and what is now out of fashion may return again,—but in the sense that history has shown that the system inevitably collides with indispensable moral ideals, and that it falls short of the full grandeur and height of the Christianity of the New Testament.

But all this leaves untouched the more spiritual identification of the Church with the kingdom of Christ on earth, as Augustine conceived it, in which the point of contact is not the external organisation but the inward holiness of the Church; an identification already accomplished in so far as the Church is the seat of Christ's reign in the will and character of his members, and to be fully accomplished when " the earth is filled with the knowledge of GOD as the waters cover the sea." Hildebrand was right, a thousand times right,

[1] Peter Damiani, stopping short of the claim of Hildebrand, says: "Felix autem si gladium regni cum gladio *iungat* sacerdotii, ut gladius sacerdotis *mitiget* gladium regis, et gladius regis gladium *acuat* sacerdotis" (*Serm.* 69).

in his conviction that for the good of man, for the realisation of the Kingdom of GOD, Christian ideas must rule mankind. He sought this lofty end by means, obviously commended to religious zeal in the then stage of historical development, but which experience eventually showed to be mistaken. If it is given to us in these latter days to perceive his mistake, we must none the less see to it that we reverence and emulate his zeal for GOD'S Kingdom. His mistake was the natural one of seeking to drive rather than to lead, of substituting the Jewish ideal of righteousness by means of government for the Christian ideal of government by means of righteousness.

Bishop Butler, in his famous chapter on the moral government of GOD, gives noble utterance to this latter ideal.[1] He asks us to imagine "a kingdom or society of men perfectly virtuous for a succession of many ages," in which "public determinations would really be the result of the united wisdom of the community; and they would be faithfully executed by the united strength of it." "Add," he says, "the general influence which such a kingdom would have over the face of the earth, by way of example particularly, and of the reverence which would be paid it. It would plainly be superior to all others, and the world must gradually come under its empire." "The head of it would be an universal monarch, in another sense than any mortal has yet been; and the Eastern style would be literally applicable to him, 'that all people, nations, and languages should serve him.'" Such a Society would fufil what Butler elsewhere claims for conscience, that

[1] See above, p. 281; Butler, *Analogy*, I. iii. § 29.

SUMMARY OF IDEALS

"Had it strength, as it had right; had it power, as it had manifest authority, it would absolutely govern the world."[1] Butler is unconsciously reaffirming the ideal of monarchy embodied four centuries previously by Dante, but his universal monarch is more clearly than by Dante conceived as the representative and minister of the citizens upon whose character the power of the Society is built up. The Society is a State not a Church. But its glory is the result not of its institutions, but of the moral regeneration of its members. This regeneration, he adds, can only be looked for as the result of miracle; but it is not extravagant to say that this miracle is the ideal towards which the Christian Church directs her aspirations and aims, and that the Christian Church is the only body of men conscious of a common aim in any way corresponding to Butler's ideal. Institutions may react upon the moral character of those who live under them; but bad institutions are more potent to depress the moral life than good ones are to raise it, while if the moral life of the community is pure and strong any institutions controlled by it will produce the best of which they are capable. It is, as Butler saw, to the moral sense of the common people that we must ultimately look, and experience has taught us that institutions, though they may coerce wrong-doing and enforce external justice, can neither produce morality nor dispense with its support. On the other hand the possibility of a society such as Butler imagines does not depend, quite so simply as Butler appears to assume, upon the aggregate morality of so many righteous individuals. The leaven of Stoic

[1] Sermon 2 (p. 406 in Bohn's ed.). See Lect. VII. sub init.

individualism, which hampers the Arminian morality of Butler not less than the religious side of the philosophy of Kant,[1] has been sufficiently unlearned by religious thinkers since Kant's time. That we cannot live upon mere individualism, whether moral or religious, *extra ecclesiam nulla salus*, is now a truism, misleading only when dependence upon institutions, as if they could regenerate our nature, is suggested as the only alternative. To a false individualism, not government but brotherhood is the true antithesis. And if the Church is to display all her latent power to regenerate human character, and is to gather into her bosom all that in the life and thought and work of mankind belongs to the proper heritage of the Kingdom of GOD, it must be by the recovery of her original sense of brotherhood.[2]

Organisation and system are good in themselves, and those responsible for them will always, so far as they are zealous in their duty, endeavour to make them complete and perfect. But perfection of system, however desirable for the Church as a visible society, is not the special note of the Kingdom of GOD; in organising herself, in legislating, in governing as every

---

[1] Kant founds the conception of a Kingdom of GOD not upon historical revelation but upon pure *a priori* principles of practical reason: it is my duty to work for the moral society of all rational beings; as man cannot possibly produce such a society, GOD is demanded by the elementary presuppositions of morality,—in order to synthesise "can" and "ought." But the evil in man's nature remains undealt with; Atonement reduces itself to the duty of suffering the consequences of past sin. But Kant has other thoughts which modify this and open the way to historic faith. (See Ritschl, *Rechtf.* i. 456–459.)

[2] The above had been written as it stands before the writer had seen Mr. Gore's book on the *Body of Christ*. It is a special pleasure to refer in confirmation of what is here urged to the striking close of that very striking book (pp. 320–330).

society of men must, the Church is doing what is absolutely necessary, as necessary as eating and clothing to the individual; but she is acting below the height of her commission; she is enacting necessary rules for the time, not divine laws; acting as a society of men, not as the Kingdom of GOD.[1] It is not as a governing body, as a "Societas Perfecta," that the Church will regenerate human nature, but as a brotherhood. She will possess and exercise the authority inherent in her divine mission, the authority to deliver the message of Christ and to insist with charity and wisdom upon the holiness of his Body in its members. But she will use the authority in order to educate her members into the capacity for and the exercise of perfect freedom, nor will she erect dependence upon a human guide into the ideal of Christian perfection. Such dependence is the necessary incident of the Church's imperfection. Her horizon must never be bounded by it; her effort must ever be directed toward the goal of Jeremiah, the day when "they shall no longer teach every man his neighbour and every man his brother, saying, Know the Lord: for all shall know me from the least of them unto the greatest of them, saith the Lord." The goal of Jeremiah's vision was

[1] How far the power of "binding and loosing" (*supra*, Lect. II. p. 66, note 1) refers to legislation, how far to the treatment of moral duties and the dealing with sinners, is a point deserving more extended consideration than can be given here. I am disposed to refer it less to the legislative or governmental action of the Church than to the judgment of the Christian consciousness, progressively enlightened by the Holy Spirit. In any case Dante was right in his contention that it cannot be understood "*absolute*," *sed respective ad aliquid* . . . posset [enim] soluere me non poenitentem, quod etiam facere ipse Deus non posset" (*de Mon.* III. viii. 34). Tarquini, on the other hand, deduces from Matt. xvi. 19 that St. Peter is invested with "potestas absoluta et monarchica" (*Juris. eccl. Inst.* p. 98).

also that of St. Paul's apostolic work—to "present every man perfect in Christ"—to bring to maturity the "spiritual man, judging all things, but himself judged of none," like the wind which "bloweth where it listeth, and thou hearest the sound thereof, but canst not tell whence it cometh and whither it goeth." The ideal is no doubt unpractical, in the sense that after two thousand years of Christianity we might seem to be further from it than we were at the beginning. Individualist licence which drives men apart is fatally easy to realise; hardly less easy is the unity of mere conformity where the energy of individual conscience and conviction is replaced by acquiescence in a central authority; no sacrifice comes easier to weak humanity than "the sacrifice of the intellect." But to idealise the practicable is the note of inferior religions, not of the kingdom of Christ. Mahomet sounded shrewdly the probable capacities of the average man, and made it the measure of his moral demand;[1] our Saviour viewed men as the sons of His own Father, and founds his Society on the rock of a faith which will raise man above his native self, and bring all together in one Body and one Spirit as children of GOD and brethren by a common adoption.

The weakness of the false individualism has its remedy, neither in the neglect of the individual soul nor

---

[1] Mozley (*Bampton Lectures* on Miracles, p. 178 sq. ed. 2): "Man is weak," says Mahomet. And upon that maxim he legislates. "There were two things which he thought man could do and would do for the glory of God—Transact religious forms, and fight; and upon those two points he was severe; but within the sphere of common practical life, where man's great trial lies," etc. etc. (The whole passage ought to be read.)

in the suppression of the individual conscience and intelligence, but in the recovery of the true idea of Christian freedom hand in hand with the reality of Christian brotherhood. Individual licence is destructive of brotherhood, because it destroys mutual trust. True liberty, emancipation from self and the world, realised where the individual responsibility is fullest, is coextensive with the Spirit which "maketh men to be of one mind in an house."[1]

IV

The New Testament ideal of the regeneration of individual character by free fellowship in the body of Christ has an unpractical look, but the same may be said of the brotherhood of man and of moral progress in human society. This much may safely be said, that from the Christian ideal the humanitarian ideal derives at the present day, and has always derived, almost all the practical power it has exercised in the world.[2]

(*a*) To ignore this fact,—to seek what may vaguely be called the Kingdom of GOD in the form of schemes of social amelioration coloured by the language of a hazy and otiose theism and supported by a scheme of ethics from which religion is sedulously excluded, is an attempt which commends itself to some earnest minds at the present day, mainly as an escape from the intellectual difficulties of religious belief and from the embarrassments brought into philanthropic and educational work by the deep divisions which

---

[1] Ps. lxviii. 6 (Prayer-Book); 2 Cor. iii. 17.
[2] Brace, *Gesta Christi*.

exist in the Christian world. But if regeneration of character, the essential foundation of all social progress, is attempted in vain by anything short of an appeal to our higher nature as a whole, and if religion is as certain, as permanent, and as legitimate a constituent of that nature as reason and morality themselves (and to dispute either of these suppositions would be philosophically very rash), the substitution, under whatever form, of the humanitarian for the Christian ideal will succeed in evading the difficulties of religious belief only at the cost of foregoing all power to deal with human nature as it is and always will be; it will end either in abortive attempts at legislation, or in the merely material improvement of things as they are.

But still the fact that such ideals attract men and women of unquestionable goodness is itself a warning of the imperfect correspondence of the actual Church to the truth of the Kingdom of GOD.

That sin and self-seeking, ignorance and folly and lawless power of all kinds should lie outside the Church and hinder its work, is what the New Testament prepares us for and what no doubt we often see. But that there should be in the world unimpeachable moral virtue and self-denial, fearless love of truth, high-souled devotion to causes fraught with benefit to mankind, a whole world of good which the Church has failed to assimilate and for much of which it can find no room, is a fact as indisputable as it is significant. The Kingdom of GOD is promoted only by what is good, and by all that is good, it is hindered only by what is really evil. And yet there have been cases[1] in which in seeking the

[1] Cf. Lect. VI. (on Arnold), Lect. VII., and too many other examples.

Kingdom of GOD men have been brought into collision with the Church, and more cases still in which men have given their best for the good of humanity, for the advancement of truth or the raising of human life, while the Church has turned aside in jealousy or at best looked coldly on.[1] As a rule in these cases individuals are not greatly to blame; the one-sidedness of human nature is at fault, a one-sidedness which seems too often the necessary price paid for enthusiasm and practical effectiveness. But we must look back upon the history of all this friction and lack of sympathy with continual regret, with much tolerance for all sides, and not least for Churchmen who have failed fully to answer to their birthright; as to the future, our faith demands of us the conviction that in proportion as the Christian society becomes the worthy vehicle and embodiment of Christ's reign upon earth, it will become more and more completely the home of all high moral ideals and all good causes, and of all who pursue them in simplicity and singleness of heart. It is an idle dream to think of the Church, or the Kingdom of GOD, simply as a moralised or idealised civil society, as if that completer union of religion with common life which we all desire were to be effected by reducing religion to civilisation and not rather by raising civilisation, as it so sorely needs to be raised, by the leaven of personal religion.[2] But idle as the dream is, it contains this grain of truth, that the

[1] Without overrating Bentham as a philosopher, it is possible to lament the scant sympathy he received from the Church in his noble and successful labours for the reform of the cruel criminal law. To multiply examples would be possible but most distasteful to a Churchman.

[2] See above, p. 362 sq.

prevalence of right and truth among mankind, even outside as well as within the Church's nominal limits, cannot but be a matter of the deepest moment to the citizen of the Kingdom of GOD. That "we are members one of another" is a truth that concerns us primarily as Christians, but it concerns us not less really as men.

It might seem at first sight—it does seem to some—that we are as Christians to look for the salvation of souls and not for the improvement of the world,—not for the regeneration of society, but for the detachment of individuals from a corrupt society by their incorporation in a Holy Society,—and that consequently we may dismiss from our mind the fortunes of morality, justice, and truth in "the world," except in so far as the peace and power of the Church is concerned.[1] We are reminded of the hints given by Christ and his Apostles of a great Apostasy, of Antichrist, and of the fewness of the chosen. But these hints, sufficient to warn the over-sanguine, are yet fragmentary and dark, and are balanced by other sayings which point in a more hopeful direction. Nor can we overlook the whole tenor of the revelation of GOD'S character in Old and New Testament alike, as a GOD who loves right and truth, and hates the false and evil, for their own sake, and blesses all that makes for the cause of righteousness in human society. And once more, as surely as mountains whose base is on the highest ground reach the nearer

---

[1] See Lect. IV. sub fin. This conventual idea of the Church and the world appears to underlie the idealism of Hildebrand (Lect. VI. p. 249 sq.).

to heaven with their summits, so surely does all that weakens evil and aids the good among the mass of mankind, tend to the greater strength and wholesomeness and the wider influence of the Christian character.

It is possible to adhere to the spirituality of St. Augustine's conception of the kingdom of Christ on earth, without following him either into conclusions in which he transgressed the limits of what God has revealed, or in his almost wholesale condemnation of secular morality. That real goodness exists outside the Christian name, that real goodness, wherever it exists, is the natural ally of the Christian life, and cannot but be pleasing to God,—these are truths now so evident to all honest observers of human nature that they are recognised by those whom no one will suspect of Pelagianism. Rather we hold all the closer to our conviction that all good in man is inspired by GOD alone, and recognise the traces of His Spirit even in those who are serving Him unconsciously. To recognise this is no derogation to our belief that GOD "wills all men," not only "to be saved," but "to come to the knowledge of the truth," and to our duty to aid them thither. Nor does it impair the general truth, imposed upon us by experience, that the normal tendency of all that is best in men is toward Christ, and that it is in Him alone that, as a matter of experience and fact, men have found, not only wisdom and righteousness, but sanctification and redemption.

(*b*) It is the perception of this truth, namely, that the mission of the Christian Society is not exhausted either by the salvation of the individual or by work of a purely ecclesiastical kind, that has given birth to the assemblage of aspirations and endeavours which are grouped under the head of Christian Socialism. So far as this is founded upon the distinctively socialist assumption [1] that good institutions can make good men, that to reorganise society is to regenerate it, it is exposed, I venture to think, to all the objections which lie against any system which seeks to realise righteousness by means of government. No government, no institutions, can regenerate character unless the beginning is made with the individual, righteousness works outward from within, not inward from without. To work well, institutions, however good, presuppose the character of those who share them. What the Church has proved unable to do, the civil society will *a fortiori* be powerless to accomplish. Christian Socialism must be Christian first, and the social effects will, with GOD'S help, follow. But if by Christian Socialism we understand the resolve to bring Christian principles of justice, humanity, and self-denial into common life, and to administer in a Christian spirit, with thoughtful and patient study of all the complex conditions of modern life, all the responsibilities, public as well as private, which fall to the lot of the modern citizen, to maintain—in the face of the reckless race

---

[1] (*Supra*, p. 369.) That bad institutions can make bad men, or at least can intensify the action of the lower motives which sway human action, is too true. And to work for the amelioration of such laws and institutions will therefore tend to liberate the better motives, and so to increase the number of good men. This is the truth urged in a remarkable little book, *Commerce and Christianity* (Sonnenschein, 1900); a book to be read with profit, whether or no we can follow all the author's contentions.

for wealth, the unscrupulous assertion of the right of the stronger, and the inordinate value set upon worldly enjoyment — the standard of Christian duty and Christian love,[1] then Christian Socialism is but another name for recognition of the duty of the Christian to human society, of the plain truth that it is only by bearing one another's burdens that we can hope to fulfil the law of Christ.

That the Kingdom of GOD cannot find its approximate realisation on earth while unrighteous relations prevail among men, that it demands social regeneration, the purification of trade and commerce, the moralisation of the relations of employer and employed, the treatment of wealth as an opportunity[2] for good work, not as a means of luxury and ostentation, that so far as Christianity fails to effect this the fault is largely with Christians themselves; that men who are, as Augustine expresses it, themselves the Kingdom of GOD, will inevitably assert the life that is in them by raising and purifying the life around them, this is one great truth to which Christian Socialism bears witness. And another is this: that not only as a man influencing his neighbour by "conversation" and personal example, but as a citizen, as a professional man, as an employer of labour, as a trader and a landlord and

---

[1] The debt of English Christianity to the social teaching of Maurice and Kingsley, and, I would add, of Bishop Westcott, will not be exhausted for many an age. (Written a few hours before the tidings of the bishop's holy death.)

[2] Arist. *Pol.* I. iv. 1, ἄνευ γὰρ τῶν ἀναγκαίων ἀδύνατον καὶ ζῆν καὶ εὖ ζῆν: 2, τὸ κτῆμα ὄργανον πρὸς ζωήν ἐστι, καὶ ἡ κτῆσισ πλῆθοσ ὀργάνων: viii. 15, ὁ δὲ πλοῦτος ὀργάνων πλῆθόσ ἐστιν οἰκονομικῶν καὶ πολιτικῶν: and 14, ἡ γὰρ τῆσ τοιαύτησ κτήσεωσ αὐτάρκεια πρὸς ἀγαθὴν ζωὴν οὐκ ἄπειρόσ ἐστιν.

a shareholder and a voter,[1] every Christian is administering a trust committed to him by CHRIST, and is charged to give effect in whatever way he can to the Christian law of justice and charity, of seeking the good of the many, and respecting the rights of even the weakest of his fellow-men. In these respects we must all be agreed that Christian Socialism is a witness to duties which Christians have inadequately realised, and to Christian responsibility for evils which we are too apt to accept as part of the order of nature. But to look for the Kingdom of GOD on earth only or primarily in the shape of social reform, is to invert the inexorable order of cause and effect in human life, and to depart from the interpretation of the Kingdom of GOD which is stamped upon Christian thought and experience as it has unfolded itself in the course of history. It has been the constant experience of mankind that ideals most readily succeed in engaging the enthusiastic service of masses of men in proportion as they offer a concrete and tangible object of pursuit; and at the present day this is offered to some by social work,—as it is offered to others by ecclesiastical or political partisanship,—to others again by some still more limited interest. But effectiveness is not the only standard of real value and truth; and the concrete and tangible is apt to be pursued at the cost of one-sidedness, with the

---

[1] St. Augustine, *Ep.* 138. ii. 15: "Proinde qui doctrinam Christi aduersam dicunt esse reipublicae, dent *exercitum* talem quales doctrina Christiana esse milites iussit; dent tales prouinciales, tales maritos, tales coniuges, tales parentes, tales filios, tales *dominos*, tales seruos, tales reges, tales *iudices*, tales denique *debitorum ipsius fisci redditores* et exactores," etc.

risk of reaction, when the first force of a movement is spent, in some opposite but equally one-sided direction.

V

But it remains true that the chief good of man, although he must seek it as an individual and in constant truth to his highest and best self, cannot be realised by him merely as an individual in and for himself. For an adequate conception of the Chief Good, for an aim so lofty, so comprehensive, as to satisfy the ultimate desire of man, two things are necessary. It must be something we can gain, can in some degree produce,—an object of work; and yet it must be something independent of our failures, above the contingencies of life and history, something we can believe in as Real, and love as transcendently Good. Such an object is placed before us by our Saviour in the Kingdom of GOD: "Seek ye first the Kingdom of GOD and His Righteousness." The Kingdom of GOD is *above* the world and destined to outlive it, while yet it is in a true sense *in* the world as the goal of all moral and spiritual endeavour.

The Apostle St. Paul has been criticised for his saying [1] that "if in this life only we have hope in Christ we are of all men most miserable." If he meant that but for the prospect of compensation in the next world, Christian self-sacrifice and suffering would be so much dead loss, there would I think be justice in the objection. The Christian religion is not worthily presented as a religion simply of prudence; as if,

[1] 1 Cor. xv. 19.

personal enjoyment being assumed to be the goal of legitimate desire, we were bidden to surrender it wholly or in part for the present in order to secure it in a greater degree hereafter. "Otherworldliness" is morally superior to ordinary worldliness in the sense that farsighted calculation, subordinating the pleasure of the moment to the pleasure of the future, involves the exercise of prudent self-denial. But the one as little as the other touches the higher atmosphere in which morality and religion meet together. No reader of St. Paul who is possessed of his general outlook upon life can for a moment tolerate the supposition that this is the assumption upon which he founds the dictum to which I have referred. It is, on the contrary, just because the Christian has already found, in this life, something infinitely more precious than all those pleasures of men [1] which he has in his heart renounced, because the Kingdom of GOD is displayed to him in all its richness and ennobling power, because he knows how great, how terrible, would be the loss of it, that the thought that his hope is a hope bounded by the brevity and incertitude of human life draws from the Apostle his horrorstruck disclaimer. Those who have learned merely what this world can teach, namely the superficiality even of its most engrossing desires, the impossibility of satisfying them in most cases, their unsatisfying character in the few cases where they are gained, will in the end find it possible to reconcile themselves to the surrender of a life which brings disappointment to nearly all. But once to have risen above this disillusionment, to have discovered the true riches,

[1] Phil. iv. 12, μεμύημαι.

to have found the pearl of great price, and then to discover that it is as transitory, as fleeting, as our uncertain human life,—*that* is to have hope in Christ in this life alone, and to be of all men most miserable. The loss of the highest is bitterer than the loss of things of no account. The Kingdom of GOD is righteousness and peace and joy in the Holy Ghost. It is realisable in the highest life, and the highest life is directed not towards the mere perfecting of self, but to the love and service of GOD and of man for GOD'S sake. Yet what I am to serve with my whole soul must be not transitory but eternal. The life of mankind began ages before the individual life, and will doubtless survive it by many ages after. But whether it is to be closed by some sudden catastrophe of the visible universe or of our little sun and system, or by the slow loss of the heat and energy which, while they are still unspent, make life possible on our planet, nothing is more certain than that the existence of man on earth has had a beginning and will have an end. And with it will end not only the works of man's hands, but, so far as this world is concerned, all the works of man's spirit as well. Not only flesh and blood, not only pleasure and pain, love and hate, emotion thought and action, but all that man has made his own in the slow conquests of thought and morality and civilisation,—the Good, the Beautiful, and the True. The death of our world will destroy both it and them. And immense as seems the span of history, known and unknown, upon which we look back, immense as may be the ages still remaining for the life of our planet, the whole is finite, numbered and measured, not to our present knowledge, but none the less measured and numbered by laws in actual full operation. And if finite, how minute,—when compared with the stupefying vastness of the time-scale suggested to us by astronomical facts, and when this in turn is compared with the unimaginable void before and after,—how minute and insignificant is the time of the habitable earth itself, a mere twinkling of an eye in the march-past of the universe, of which our race sees but a moment, and a part! The thought, to a non-religious mind, is depressing just in proportion as the interest is centred upon the highest ideals of life. Right, and truth, and human affection, enlist the higher minds by their intrinsic value, but if they are after all mere products of planetary conditions to which they owe their origin and with the disappearance of which their very ground and meaning will be gone, they will enlist, after all, only such devotion—sincere but without rational hopefulness—as is proper to transitory though desirable objects. But the true suggestion of the facts has been perceived long ago—

> When I consider thy heavens, the work of thy fingers,
> The Moon and the stars which thou hast ordained;
> What is man, that thou art mindful of him?
> And the son of man, that thou visitest him?
> For thou hast made him but little lower than GOD
> And crownest him with glory and honour.

The insignificance of man disappears in the conscious service of his Creator, the hope of the eternal Kingdom of GOD gives meaning to the vanity of life.

That purpose of some kind underlies the superabundant evidence of method in the processes of Nature ought not to be hard to believe. That this method is the work of unconscious reason appears to be an unphilosophical explanation, for we can only imagine such an agent by reference to a reason which is conscious. Otherwise, the phrase has no more meaning than " unreasoning reason " or " unconscious consciousness." But, although where there is reason there is purpose, the evidence of reason in nature is in itself merely evidence of purpose, not evidence as to what that purpose is, still less does it furnish a basis for an adequate interpretation of life. From the idea of impersonal reason it may be possible to deduce the thought of inexorable moral law, of the indefeasible sovereignty of truth and right. But no impersonal ideal is adequate to the highest capacities of human nature, or able to draw out from it its very best. The highest morality is not impersonal, but personal in the intensest degree. It is set free to act, by the conviction not merely that GOD is around us as reason, immanent in the processes of nature and the laws and conscience of mankind, but that he has by one great act taken His place in the outward history and inward experience of mankind as Love. The highest morality, reason, and religion meet together and are satisfied in the Kingdom of the Eternal God, in whom Reason and Love are one.

In whatever way, therefore, and to whatever extent, the Kingdom of GOD finds its present realisation now on earth,—and we are here as Christians to realise it in as many ways and as fully as it is given us to do,— Christian faith and hope, moral faith in GOD, can never dispense with the promise of GOD'S eternal

Kingdom, can never cease to enthrone it as Christian faith and hope have continuously and in all ages enthroned it, high above all temporal embodiments of the reign of Christ on earth, as the supreme goal of endeavour, as the ultimate object of desire and prayer.

We are to work for the Kingdom of GOD in the Church and in the world; we may hope that in both it is to be realised far more conspicuously, far more in correspondence with its reality, than it has ever been in the past; but we have no certain knowledge of the issue to which GOD'S providence is leading human history, or whether the moral government of GOD among men is destined some day to be more perfect than it is now. We are to seek the Kingdom of God within us; but even should GOD give us grace to realise it more than we have yet done in our personal character, we shall be all the more conscious how miserably imperfect it will be even then. Within and without, the higher we set our aim, the more earnestly we seek the Kingdom of GOD, the more certainly will failure mock and humble us; the more certainly must we be prepared to witness the frustration of the highest hopes we have cherished, the apparent downfall of causes with which our most sacred convictions are intimately concerned, and to bear the galling shame of personal self-reproach. The Passion and the Cross, the Dereliction and the cry of death, must enter into our individual experience before we can endure with cheerful courage, confident in the joy that is set before us. In those great facts of redemption Love challenges love, and assures us that love is never failure, and that to the

THE KINGDOM OF GOD ETERNAL

great treasure-house of GOD'S Love no sacrifice is entrusted in vain. *There* is the link, the underlying unity, between the Kingdom for which we are to strive on earth and the Kingdom that lies, above and independent of our efforts or failures, eternal in the heavens.

INDEX

A

Abano, Peter de, 312.
Abelard, 260.
Acacius. See *Achatius*.
Achatius, confessor, 143.
Acton, 270 n., 332, 344.
Acts of the Apostles, 47; objections to history of, 48 sq.
Adrian II., 240.
Adrian IV., 264, 277, 323.
Advent, twofold, 47, 48, 49 sq., 52, 54, 66. See *Christ, Kingdom*.
Aeneas Silvius. See *Pius II*.
Agatho (quoted), 232.
Agilulf, 230.
Agnes of Tirol, 265.
Alaric, 206.
Alberic, Marquess, 241.
Alberic of Tusculum, 241, 249.
Albertus Magnus, 279, 296.
Albigenses, 277, 324.
Alcuin, 231, 234.
Alexander of Hales, 279.
Alexander II., 248.
Alexander III., 252, 259, 264, 266, 277, 323, 324.
Alexander VI., 304, 329, 331.
Alexander VII., 341.
Alexandrian theology, 152 sqq., 199.
Allegorism, 155 sq.
Alogi, 123, 139 n.
Alvaro Pelayo, 322.
Ambrose, 154, 212, 254.
Ammia, 142 n.
Amort, 340.
Amphilochius, 123.
Annates, 303.
Anrich, 151 n.
Anselm. See *Alexander II*.
Anselm, St., 298.
Antichrist. See *Enemies*.
Antioch (exegesis), 156.

Antonelli, R., 265, 291.
Antony, 163.
Aphraates, 163 n.
Apocalypse, 156, 170 sqq.; date of, 107 n.; structure of, 108; interpretation, 109 sq.
Apocalyptic writings, 27 sq., 105; Apocalyptic, Jewish and Christian, 121; Apocalyptic spirit, 134.
Apollinarius, 153 n., 158.
Apologists, 106, 130 sq., 152, 154, 199, 213.
Apostolic Poverty, 319. See *Poverty*.
Appeals, 318 sq.; St. Bernard on, 267.
Aquinas. See *Thomas*.
Ariald, 248.
Aristotle, 212 n., 364 n.; on wealth, 379; political theory of, 101; Politics of, 263, 272, 272 sq., 288, 290, 291, 308, 309, 314, 325.
Arnold, 212 n., 255, 260-262, 279, 291, 323 sq., 330; Arnold and Francis, 296.
Arnulf (King), 242.
Arnulf (of Reims), 244.
Arundel, 328.
Athanasius, 123, 158.
Atys, 136 n.
Augustine, 114, 124, 132, 140, 154, 161 n., 165, 169-225, 228 n., 280 sq., 291; (chiliasm), 169 sq.; metaphysics, 196.
Augustine, theory of property, 254; on social life, 207, 362, 380; theism, 182 sqq.; doctrine of grace, 187-194; "Gratia Christi," 189; Catholicism and predestinarianism irreconcilable, 193, 202.
Augustine, change of mind (chiliasm), 171; change of mind (grace), 188; change of mind (persecution), 215; his doctrine of grace, unwelcome, 193.

INDEX

Augustine, influence, 326 sq., 336 sq., 348; medieval influence, 252 n.; and medieval theocracy, 216, 222; Augustine and Gregory VII., 251; Aug. *de Civ.* and Dante, 286 sqq., 292; Augustine and St. Paul, 205; Aug. and Marsilius, 316; Aug. and Ritschl, 361 sqq. See *Church, Kingdom.*
Authority and faith, 311; authority (Augustine), 217; authority, Episcopal, 176; authority for faith, 175, 185; authority and reason, 218; authority and freedom, 282.
Averroes, 291.
Avignon, papacy at, 274, 294, 306, 328.

B

Bacon, R., 279.
Baius, 336, 341.
Baptism, 205.
Barbarossa. See *Frederick I.*
Barmby, 230 n.
Barnabas, 122 n., 125.
Baronius, 344.
Basil, 123, 157.
Basil (Emperor), 240.
Basilides, 150.
Beatitudes, 89.
Becket, 252 n.
Bede, 231 n.
Beghards and Béguines, 324.
Bellarmine, 304, 343.
Benedict, 298.
Benedict IX., 244 sq.
Benedict XII., 306.
Benedictines (French), 296.
Benedictus, 10, 30.
Beneficia gratiae, 192 n., 201 n. See *Augustine.*
Benson, 141 n., 176 n.
Bentham, 375.
Berengar, King, 241 sq.
Bergamo, poet of, 260 sq. nn., 323.
Bernard, 259 n., 260 nn., 308.
Bigg, 153 n.
Binding and loosing, 66, 76 sq., 221, 371.
Bologna, 263.
Bonagrazia, 305.
Bonaventura, 278 n., 279 n., 298.
Boniface, 231, 239.

Boniface VIII., 252, 274, 286 n., 293.
Bonifatius, Count, 165.
Bonwetsch, 136 n.
Brace, 373.
Bradwardine, 327.
Briggs, 23 n.
Bright, 319.
Brotherhood, Christian, 100, 370–373.
Bruno of Cluny, 249.
Bryce, (referred to), 234, 242, 262, 263, 268, 276, 308.
Buddhist element in Gnostics, 150.
Burchard of Würzburg, 232 n.
Butler, 204, 340, 368 sq.
Butler, A. J., 287, 295.
Byzantinism, 226.

C

Cadalous, 248.
Cahors, 303.
Caius. See *Gaius.*
Calixtus II., 258 n.
Callistus, 136 n.
Calvin, 355.
Camaldoli, order of, 249, 331.
Canon of Scripture, 40; of New Testament, 122.
Canon law, early collections, 235 n.; Canon law, earlier and later, 237; Canon law, codified, 293.
Canossa, 256, 257, 258 sq.
Caramuel, 341.
Cardinals, origin of, 247.
Casini, 339.
Cassian, 162, 164 n., 165, 203.
Casulanus, 174 n.
Cataphrygians, 135 sq.
Catechisms, Roman, 336.
Catholic Epistles, 103 sq.
Catholicism, Liberal, 255, 347.
Catullus, *Atys*, 136 n.
Celestine I., 192.
Celestine V., 270 n.
Centralisation, evils of, 267, 348.
Cerinthus, 126 sq., 129.
Cesena, 301, 304, 305, 311.
Chaeremon, 162 n.
Charles, R. H. (referred to), 17, 20, 21, 23, 24, 25, 26, 28, 29, 43, 45, 47, 52 sq., 54, 65, 66, 71–74, 88, 92 sq., 107, 113, 121, 126, 128, 129.

INDEX 391

Charles the Great, 231, 233-235, 239; break-up of his empire, 235, 239, 242.
Charles of Anjou, 269 sq., 294.
Charles the Bald, 240.
Charles the Fat, 242.
Charles Martel, 231.
Charles IV., 306.
Cheetham, 233 n.
Chiliasm, 119, 124 sqq., 298; tenets, 129; how far general at first, 120 sq.; (Augustine), 169; attitude of Origen, 156 n.; (Montanists), 138; discredited by Montanism, 147; Chiliasm and curialism, 317, 366; Chiliasm hostile to Church order, 134, 141; discredited by theology, 157; latent truth in, 135; vitality, 129-133, 366; vitality in West, 161; why not permanent, 133, 135, 141. See *Realism*.
Chilperic, 232.
Christ, ipsissima verba of, 61 n.; Christ, synoptic and Johannine, 92; Christ, poverty of, 290, 296, 299 sqq., 319 (see *Poverty, Arnold*); Christ, return of, imminent, 48, 129, 137, 138, 143 sq. See *Eschatology, Kingdom, Messiah*.
Christian, citizen, the, 207, 362, 380.
Christian Empire, 158 sqq.; illusion of, 159, 226, 234, 263 sq.
Christian ethics, 345, 362; problem of, 54.
Christian liberty, 310, 371 sqq., 345 n.
Christian religion aboriginal, 198 sq.
Chrysostom, 124.
Church, the, 55, 57, 60, 70, 76, 84 sq., 98-102; meaning of word, 316; Augustine's devotion to, 184; Augustinian idea of, 281, 330, 365, 367, 377; Augustinian idea not hierarchical, 177 sqq.; Augustinian idea spiritual, 254 sq.; *extra eccl. nulla salus*, 186, 192, 221.
Church, the true to assemble at the Advent, 126 n., 138 n.; Roman and Greek compared, 226.
Church, theological conception of, 174 sqq., 203, 216, 217 sq., 222, 227, 239 n., 327 sq., 338, 354 sq., 358; function of, 201, 227, 363; theological conception supplanted by law, 229, 237, 326.
Church, moral discipline of, 138, 145 sq., 198, 339; authority in, 101, 371; Church authority, organ of, 218 sq.; Church, faith in the, 186 sq.; Church, unity of the, 357 n., 360; in what sense Kingdom of GOD, 178-180.
Church, indefectible, 309; predestin. idea, 326, 355 sqq.; "invisible," 187, 302, 330; visible or invisible? 194, 360; visible *and* invisible, 354 sq.
Church, does it include all *electi*? 197 sq.; the only real Civitas, 213; communio sanctorum, 195, 196, 197, 201, 255, 355; communio externa, 195, 197, 201; spiritual society, 255, 260, 281, 290, 291, 317, 323; Law of, human, 294 (cf. 177), 309.
Church, institutions of, 100; general organisation, 159, 219, 330; Episcopal constitution, 357; conciliar government of, 309, 328; conciliar movement, 357; patriarchal theory, 226 n.; Gregorian idea, 251; feudal government of, 235; lay power in, 320, 322.
Church in history, 103, 105; medieval, 276 sq.; wealth of, 255, 260 sq.; Church and society, 101, 105 sq., 362, 374-376; "ecclesia in imperio," 213; "imperium in ecclesia," 214, 333; Church and State, 269, 273, 275, 280, 287 sq., 290 sq., 292, 321 sq., 344 n., 355, 357; party ideals, 333-335; position of Anglican, 357. See *Kingdom, Societas Perfecta, Councils, Notes*.
Church (R. W.), 232.
Cistercians, 260.
Civitas, meaning of the word, 210, 212; *Civitas Dei*, 104, 112, 179, 206-214, 251, 256, 280; dependent on *c. terrena*, 211; consists of the *electi*, 211; Civitas superna, 179, 181, 217, 213; Civitas terrena, 208, 210; dependent on *Civ. Dei*, 212.
Clement (Alexandria), 152.
Clement of Rome, 122 n., 125, 126.

Clement II., 245.
Clement III. See *Wibert*.
Clement IV., 269, 270.
Clement V., 295, 301, 303, 304, 319, 325.
Clement VI., 303, 306–308, 311.
Clement XI., 292, 330.
Clementines (second century), 149, 236 n.
Clergy, morals of, 246–248, 331 sq.
Cluny, order of, 241, 249, 269; ideal of Church reform, 249, 250.
Coercive jurisdiction, 315 sq., 320.
Colonna, family of, 241 n.
"Commerce and Christianity," 378.
Commodian, 157.
Conciliar movement, 328 sq., 357.
Conclave, 270 n.
Concordats, 274.
Confession, compulsory, 267, 338.
Conrad, King, 242.
Conradin, 269.
Conscience, rights of, 320, 347.
Constance of Aragon, 269.
Constance of Sicily, 268.
Constantine, 158–160, 163; Constantine, donation of, 233, 236 n., 238 n., 256, 267 n., 291 sq., 308; edict of, 140 n.
Constantine Pogonatus, 232 n.
Constantine (Pope), 240 n.
Constantinople, Latin Empire, 266, 278.
Constantius, 160.
Constitutional government, 314 sqq.
Contenson, 340, 346.
Coronation, 233 n.; meaning of, 259, 308.
Correptio, 198, 201, 339.
Corruption (St. Paul), 51, 55 n.
Councils, authority of, 309, 319 sq.; Augustine on, 218; fifteenth century, 274; Council of Basel, 329; Clermont, 259; Constance, 328; Constantinople (681), 232 n.; Florence, 329; Frankfurt, 234 n.; Nicea, 159; Sixth Canon of, 238; (Second), 234 ff.; Laodicea, 123; Lateran (1179), 264; Lateran (1215), 267 sq.; Lyons (1245), 278; Lyons, 258, 270; Orange (Second), 193; Quiercy, 194 n.; Sinuessa, 238 n.; Sutri, 245;

Trent, 334, 336 sq.; Valence, 194 n.; Vatican (1870), 230 n., 337 sqq.; Vienne, 301.
Counter-Reformation, 214, 334 sqq.
Creighton, 313.
Creighton, C., 332.
Crescentii, the, 241, 244.
Crusades, 259, 266, 269; abuse of, 277, 303; crusade of Barbarossa, 264.
Curialism, 273; and chiliasm, 316, 366.
Cyprian, 175, 176, 179, 219; (forgeries), 238 n.; on Kingdom of GOD, 141 n.
Cyril of Alexandria, 124; (forgeries), 238 n.
Cyril of Jerusalem, 123.

D

Dalman (referred to), 11, 47, 52, 58, 59, 61, 62, 63, 64, 72, 75.
Damasus II., 245.
Damiani, 246–248, 250, 331, 367.
Daniel, 11, 27–30, 44 sq.
Dante, 234 n., 250, 269, 277, 278, 286–302, 309, 312, 314, 316, 319, 325, 326, 330, 369, 371; Dante and Franciscans, 302.
Dark ages, 165, 228, 231 sqq.
David, 10, 15, 16, 17.
Davidson, 13 n.
Day of the Lord, 19, 42.
Death and sin, 55 n.
Decius, 137 n.
Decretals, 319; Dante on, 293; codified, 268 n.; the forged, 235–238, 256. See *Isidore*, *Canon Law*.
Defensor Pacis, 313 sqq.
Denzinger, 341, etc.
Deposing power of popes, 230 n., 233, 252, 265. See *Plenitudo*, *Temporal*.
Diana, 341.
Διδαχή. See *Teaching*.
Didymus, 124.
Dill, 206.
Diodorus, 153 n.
Dionysius the Areopagite, 124 n.
Dionysius the Great, 123, 156.
Dispensation of the Spirit, 136, 142, 298 sq.

INDEX 393

Döllinger, 221, 234, 236, 278, 295, 298 sq., 301 sq., 304, 305, 332, 339-343; Acton on, 344.
Dominic, 295.
Dominicans, 238 n., 279, 296, 301, 340, 343.
Dominium, 300, 304. See *Usus*.
Donatists, 170, 176, 194, 212, 213, 214 n., 215, 254, 255, 360.
Driver, 28, 29 nn.
Druids, Thomas Aquinas on, 272.
Dualism, 250 sq.; (Augustine), 210, 288.
Duchesne, 234 n.
Durandus, 278 n.

E

Eastern Church, 226. See *Schism*.
Ebionites, 149.
Ecstasy, 144 n.
Edward I., 271.
Egbert, 231 n.
Elect, number of irrevocably fixed, 191, 195. See *Predestination*.
Eleutherus, 139.
Elias, brother, 297.
Empire, Roman, and Christians, 110; Holy Roman, 242; medieval ideal of, 261, 263; weakness of medieval, 275 sq., 258.
Empire and papacy, 294; constitution of Otto I., 242 sq.; early settlements, 243 n.; settlement of Henry III., 254; concordat of Worms, 258; (Lateran Council), 264; (Frederick II.), 268. See *Investiture, Gregory VII., Gregory X., Imperial Elections, Plenitudo*.
Empires, founded on robbery, 210. See *Latrocinium, State*.
Enemies, 26 n., 53 n., 110, 129; (Satanic), 51, 109 sq.
England, learning in, 231.
English complaint to Innocent IV., 278.
Enoch, 107 n.
Epiphanius, 123, 206.
Episcopal authority, 220.
Erastianism, 160, 226 n., 322.
Eschatology (Jesus Christ), 69, 71, 72, 74 n.; earliest Hebrew, 18, 24; (St. Paul's), 51 sq., 59; Psalms of Sol., 43 n.; realistic,

120 sqq.; tenets, 129. See *Seven Days, Chiliasm, World to come*.
Eternal Gospel, 298.
Ethical societies, 373.
Eugenius IV., 249, 329.
Europe, growth of modern, 258, 265, 271, 275.
Eusebius, 123, 157, 159.
Excommunication, 220, 257, 271, 327, 334. See *Binding*.
"Excrescences," 132 sq.
Exile, Jewish, 27.

F

Fabianus, 237.
Fagnanus, 341.
Faith, 94; ages of, 131, 286; blind, 311.
Farrar, 155, 299.
Faustus (of Reii), 203.
Feudalism, 277; in Church, 243 253.
Firmilian, 140.
Fisher, 233, 234, 242, 263, 265.
Fleury, 344.
Folrad, 232 n.
Formosus, 240.
Fra Angelico, 296.
Francis of Assisi, 182, 212 n., 295 sq., 299, 325; and Arnold, 296.
Franciscan ideal, 300.
Franciscans, 269 n., 279 n., 295, 311, 317, 325; "spirituals," 295, 299.
Fraticelli, 301 sq., 303, 325.
Frederick of Austria, 305.
Frederick I., 242 n., 262-265, 279, 285, 308.
Frederick II., 268 sq.
Friars, 279, 295.
Fulgentius, 228.
Fundamental and secondary articles, 154. See *Theology*.
Funk, 268.

G

Gaius, 123, 126, 127.
Gaiseric, 208.
Galerius, 158.
Galileo, 347.
Gallicanism, 271 n.
Gasquet, 332.

INDEX

Gebhardt, 41 n.
Gennadius, 161, 228.
Gerardino, 298.
Gerbert. See *Silvester II.*
Gerhoh, 261, 262 nn.
German crown, 242, 268, 270, 285 n., 305, 306. See *Regnum.*
Ghibelline; name of, 265 n.; idea, 325.
Gierke (referred to), 226, 227, 233, 252, 268, 272, 285, 289, 290, 293, 310, 314, 315, 319, 320, 322.
Gnostics, 130.
Gnosticism, 149-152, 175.
GOD, how known to man, 4; idea of in O.T., 33 sqq.; love of, 209, 358, 361, 385-387; moral government of, 87, 204, 364; vision of, 90, 94. See *Reason, Nature, Kingdom.*
Godet, 52 n.
Godfrey de Bouillon, 259 n.
Golden age of Israel, 12.
Goldwin, Smith, 35.
Gonzalez, 342.
Goodness, non-Christian, 374-376, 377.
Gore, 187, 220, 318, 370.
Gospel, origin of the word, 62.
Gottschalk, 194 n.
Grace, problem of, 204; pre-Augustinian doctrine, 193, 205; Augustinian, 336; Gratia Christi, 359; sacramental, 205. See *Augustine, Perseverance, Predestination, Vocatio.*
Greek Fathers, forged extracts, 238 n.
Gregorovius, 260 n.
Gregory, Nazianzen, 123, 157.
Gregory of Nyssa, 123 sq.
Gregory I., 228 n., 229 sq., 231, 233.
Gregory II., 231.
Gregory V., 244.
Gregory VI., 245, 250.
Gregory VII., 222, 231, 241, .245, 246 n., 248-258, 263-266, 271, 274, 275, 277, 285, 288, 292, 323, 329, 331, 367, 376; Gregory VII., ideal of, 276; his ideal criticised, 255-257; Gregory and Augustine, 251 sq.; Dictatus Papae, 252 n.
Gregory IX., 268, 277, 293, 297.
Gregory X., 258, 270, 277.

Grützmacher, 163 n.
Guelfs, 323, 325; name of, 265 n.; Guelfs and Ghibellines, 277, 287.
Guido of Milan, 248.

H

Hadrian, reign of, 142 n.
Hadrian. See *Adrian.*
Hanno of Cologne, 248.
Harnack, 83, 132 sq., 145, 151, 194, 228, 318, 328, 332.
Hatch, 156 n., 173 n., 254 n.
Hazlitt, 92 n.
Heathen objections, 206 sq.
Hefele, 344.
Hegel, 153.
Henry the Fowler, 242.
Henry III., 245 sq., 254.
Henry IV., 248, 252 n., 253, 265; (feud with Pope), 254 n.
Henry VI., 268.
Henry II. of England, 258.
Henry III. of England, 271.
Henry VIII., 329.
Heracleon, 151 n.
Hergenröther, 239 n., 240 n., 344.
Heribert of Milan, 247.
Herlembald, 248.
Hermas, 122 n., 126.
Hermit ideal, 162 sq.
Herodians, 32.
Hierapolis, 142 n.
Hierarchy, form of, 220. See *Church (general constitution),* etc.
Hilarius, 193 n.
Hilary of Poitiers, 154.
Hilary I., 192.
Hildebrand. See *Gregory VII.*
Himerius, 164 n.
Hinkmar, 77 n., 194 n., 237, 240.
Hinschius, 236 n.
Hippolytus, 127 n., 136 n., 150.
Historians, great Catholic, 344.
History, scientific conception of, 310; falsification of, 236 sqq., 256.
Hohenstaufen, 258, 259-269, 294.
Homage of pope to emperor, 235; of emperor to pope, 259.
Honorius, I., 231.
Honorius II. See *Cadalous.*
Hort, 173 n.
Hugh Capet, 244.

INDEX

Hugh of Cluny, 249.
Hugh of St. Victor, 260 n.
Hungary, 246 n.
Hus, 326 sq., 328, 330, 334;
Hussites, 324.

I

Idealism, 182-184, 196; in theology, 155.
Ideals, conflict of higher, 269, subordination of, 281 sq.
Idea and institution, 82-84, 256.
Ideas the ultimate realities, 84.
Ignatius of Antioch, 94, 125, 130, 149.
Illingworth, 55 n.
Imperial elections, 268, 275, 305, 306, 308.
Imperium, 285, 289; and sacerdotium, 252 n.
Imperium in Ecclesia, 252 n., 280. See *Church, Societas Perfecta.*
Incongruities in religion, 132.
Index, 341.
India (Abyssinia), 152.
Individualism, 164, 365, 370, 372 sq. See *Kingdom.*
Inge, 153 n., 155 n.
Ingeborg, 265.
Innocent I., 192.
Innocent II., 259.
Innocent III., 222, 252, 265-269, 271, 274, 275, 277, 329.
Innocent IV., 268, 277, 278, 301.
Innocent VIII., 280 n., 331, 332 n.
Innocent XI., 341 sq.
Inquisition, 267, 270 n., 296, 303, 312, 324.
Institutions, power of, 369, 378; and ideas, 82-84, 256.
Intellectus Communis, 312; possibilis, 289.
Interdicts, 257, 317.
Investiture, 243, 253 sq., 258. See *Empire and Papacy, Feudalism.*
Irenaeus, 93 sq., 114, 125, 127 sq., 130, 135, 139, 142, 149, 174, 366.
Irvingites, 140 n.
Isidore, pseudo-, 235, 247 n. See *Decretals.*
Italy and the Empire, 239; claim to, 270, 277, 294, 305, 306.
Ivo, 278 n.

J

Jansen, 336, 341.
Jarrow, 231.
Jerome, 141 n., 190, 317 sq.
Jerusalem, seat of Kingdom of GOD, 42, 46; the new, 112.
Jesuits, 335, 336, 341 sq., 344.
Jevons, 151 n.
Jewish Christianity, 48; factor in Apostolic Churches, 121.
Joachim, 126, 137, 269, 297 sq., 302, 330.
John, purpose of Gospel of St., 91; Gospel of Life, 92.
John of England, 266.
John of Jandun, 312.
John of Luxemburg, 313.
John of Viktring, 309.
John I., 233 n.
John VIII., 226 n., 240.
John XII., 241-244.
John XXII., 301, 303 sqq., 316, 319, 323, 333.
Joinville, 271 n.
Julian, 160.
Julius I., 161 n., 218.
Justice, bond of Society, 212 sq.
Justin Martyr, 33 n., 114, 126, 129, 130, 174, 366; (philosopher), 154 n.
Justin (Emperor), 233 n.
Justina, 254.
Justinian, 230, 232; age of, 140 n.

K

Kant, 153, 370.
Khomiakoff, 226 n.
Kingdom of GOD, and Kingdom of Heaven, 62 sq.; the Chief Good, 381; supreme goal of conduct, 69; diverse interpretations, 119, 169, 364 sqq.; perfect, 54, 181, 221; (in what sense), 370.
Kingdom of GOD, not an O.T. expression, 11; rooted in O.T., 34; lofty conception of in Jeremiah, 23; (Jewish), 75, 96; Kingdom of Priests, 12, 111; Prominence in the Gospels, 9, 10; Synoptic and Johannine, 90; Parables of, 87 sqq.; "Sons of," 64 sq.; a privilege, 63; not with

observation, 65; mysteries of, 87; difficulty of entering, 67; "receiving," "entering," 65, 91.

Kingdom of GOD, within, 162, 364; and character, 63, 65-67, 89, 95 sqq., 172 sq., 178, 276; includes good only, 172; includes the bad, in what sense, 173.

Kingdom of GOD and sin, 66; and the "violent," 64, 69, 100; and "Life," 68, 85 sq., 92 sqq., 95; (Augustine), 179 n.; "timeless," 93 sq.

Kingdom of GOD in St. Paul, 49 sqq., 345; in Acts of Apostles, 47; and glory of GOD, 50; and salvation, 51; and Advent, twofold, 97 (see *Christ*); eschatology of, 103 sq., 358, 360, 364; realism, 298 (see *Chiliasm, Realism*); chiliastic interpretation doomed, 147; individualism inadequate, 164 (see *Individualism*); coming with power, 71; present and future, 50 sqq., 66, 75, 93, 98.

Kingdom of GOD and Church, 55 sq., 70, 75 sq., 98-102, 135, 141 n., 161 sq., 169, 171 sq., 173 sq., 175, 176-181, 359, 365, 374; identified with the Church, 147. See *Church, Reign*.

Kingdom of GOD in Augustine, 320, 321, 379; and Church (Augustine), 196 sq.; how identified by Augustine with the Church, 203; Augustine's language classified, 179; Augustinian sense, 172, 173; Augustine and Cyprian, 175, 179; Augustine and Marsilius, 316 sq.; legacy of Augustine, 216, 222.

"Kingdom" not of this world, 91; the Kingdom of GOD and Church government, 101; as government, 251; as omnipotent Church, 214, 333 (see *Societas Perfecta*); medieval embodiment, 275, 280, 348, 354; secularisation of idea, 247: ideal of Gregory VII., 251, 256, 310; government and righteousness, 281, 368; Kingdom of GOD and human life, 6, 60; social, 364; and riches, 67; and the world, 67. See *Society, World*.

Kingdom of GOD, invisible, 75 sq.; statical and dynamical senses, 86; in process of becoming, 86; spiritual, 317; kingdom of Christ, 54 sqq., 70-73; kingdom of Christ and K. of GOD, 73; kingdom of Christ distinct, 114, 173; not temporal, 317; earthly, 129; spiritual on earth, 51, 53; to be realised on earth, 161, 174; how to be realised, 281 sq., 323, 383.

Kingdom of Christ, imperfect, 54, 68; kingdom or reign? 58 sq., 76 sq., 86, 98 sqq., 95, 99; reign of GOD, 23, 34, 44 sq.; reign of saints in Christ, 171. See *Reign*.

Kingdom of GOD, Jesuit ideal, 344; Imperialist ideal, 263; Calvin, 356; ethical ideal, 373; in Greek Church, 226 n.; Kant, 370; modern investigation, 358; monastic, 162-165; reformation, 354 sq.; Ritschl on, 358 sqq., 365; secular ideal, 375§; Zwinglian, 355, 360; city of GOD, 104 (see *Civitas*); universalism, 72. See *Universalism*.

Kingsley, 379.
Knights of St. John, 260.
Krüger, 163 n., 234 n.

L

Lactantius, 157.
Ladeuze, 163 n.
Landulf, 248.
Larmor, 5 n.
Latrocinium, state a, 210, 252 n., 288. See *Empire, State*.
Law, new, 149; legalism (Christian), 145, 146, 345; influence of in Church, 229, 293 sq., 344. See *Church (Law of)*.
Learning, extinction of, 231, 232; revival (Carolingian), 231.
Lechfeld, battle of, 243.
Lecky, 280.
Lectures, plan of treatment, 7, 8.
Legnano, 264.
Lehmkuhl, 293, 341, 343.
Leo I., 77, 192, 220, 229, 231.
Leo II., 231.
Leo III., 234, 235.

INDEX

Leo VIII., 243.
Leo IX., 245–247, 250.
Leo XIII., 293, 337.
Leopold of Austria, 303.
Lewis of Bavaria, 303, 305, 306, 308, 313.
Liberal Catholicism. See *Catholicism*.
Liberius, 319.
Libri Carolini, 234 n.
Life, future, 382 sqq. See *Kingdom*.
Lightfoot, 55, 57, 127, 150, 318, 358.
Liguori, Alfonso, 238, 341, 343.
Little, 279 n., 300.
Lombard League, 264.
Lombards, 228, 230, 233.
Loofs, 188 n.
Lothair II. (Emperor), 259.
Lothair II., 240.
Louis (St.), 257, 270 n., 271, 276.
Loyola, 339.
Lucian (Martyr), 153 n.
Lucius, King, 238 n.
Lucius III., 324.
Luke, canticles in St., 39.
Lupold of Bebenhurg, 310.
Lupus, Christian, 252 n., 343.
Luther, 332, 354 sq.; and Augustine, 182.

M

Mabillon, 340.
Maccabean crisis, 27, 30, 53 n., 90.
Maccabean monarchy, 30–32, 40.
Macchiavelli, 321, 331.
Mahomet, 372.
Mahometans in Europe, 231, 271.
Maiolus of Cluny, 249.
Manfred, 269.
Manicheans, 324.
Map, 261, 264, 296.
Marc, 343.
Marcellinus, 207.
Marcellinus (Pope), 238 n.
Marcellus of Ancyra, 52 n.
Marcion, 149.
Margaret Maultasch, 313.
Marozia, 241 n.
Marriage law, 265 sq.
Marsilius ab Inghen, 311.
Marsilius, 300 n., 306–323, 326, 330; and Wycliffe, 326 sq.
Martin, 271 n.
Martin I., 231.
Martin IV., 270.

Mary, St., immaculate conception, 336.
Matilda, 257, 259 n.
Matter and spirit, 51, 55 n.
Matthew Paris, 268 n.
Maurice, 379.
Maurice (Emperor), 230.
Maximilla, 136, 137.
McGiffert, 123.
Means and ends, 266.
Medici, Duke C. de, 339.
Medieval popes, aim of, 280.
Medina, 343.
Mendham, 337.
Messiah, title of, 29 n., 43 n.
Messianic hope, heathen rumours of, 96.
Metropolitan bishops, 235.
Michael, Brother. See *Cesena*.
Middle Ages, 275 sq.; earlier, 228.
Millennium. See *Chiliasm*, *Eschatology*.
Montanists, 123, 125, 126; doctrines, 136; in persecution, 137 n., 143 n.
Montanus, 129, 136 sqq., 144 n., 147, 298.
Moore, 287, 295.
Morality, double standard, 164. See *Church*.
Mozley, 91 n., 336, 372.
Mühldorf, 305.
Munich, 307, 311.
Mussato, 311.
Mysteries (Greek), 151.

N

Natalis, Alexander, 304, 344.
Nature, interpretation of, 84, 85.
Naturalism, 204.
Nepos, 156.
Newman, 82, 252 n.
Nicolas I., 237–239, 240.
Nicolas II., 247, 248, 250 n.
Nicolas III., 300, 304.
Nicolas V. See *Rainalucci*.
Nirvana, 150 n.
Normans in S. Italy, 246 sq., 266.
Notes of Church, 175; catholicity, 176; holiness, 138, 141, 143, 145 sq., 164, 330, 356, 360; unity, 176, 357 n., 360; Word and Sacraments, 355 sq.
Novatian, schism of, 175, 194, 360.

INDEX

O

Ockham, 305–312; asceticism, 307; *Dialogus*, 308 sqq.; philosophy, 311; and Wycliffe, 327.
Octavian. See *John XII*.
Odilo of Cluny, 249.
Odo of Cluny, 249.
Old Testament idea of God, 33 sqq.
Oliva, 305.
Oman, 232 n.
Ophites, 150.
Opinion, public, 267.
Optatus, 176, 213.
Origen, 123, 125, 130, 131, 152, 156–158, 226; and Augustine, 181.
Orosius, 208.
Otherworldliness, 67, 69, 381 sq.
Otto of Freisingen, 308.
Otto I., 239, 249, 242.
Otto II., 249.
Otto III., 239, 244.
Otto IV., 266, 270.
Oxford, provisions of, 271.

P

Pachomius, 144 n., 163.
Paget, 288, 291.
Pagi, 252 n.
Palmieri, 293, 345.
Pantaenus, 152.
Papacy: papal system, 160 sq.; (Augustine), 219, 227; early Middle Ages, 239; post-Carolingian, 240; deterioration of aim, 257, 266, 269; use of forgery, 238; taxation, 271, 278, 303; territorial lust, 257; avarice, 277 sq., 303; usury, 278; simony, 245, 331 (see *Simony*); degradation of, 240 sqq.; revival of, 245; Gregory VII., 250; revival in fifteenth century, 274.
Papacy, Dante's reverence for, 287; medieval criticisms of, 318 sq. (see *Dante, Ockham, Marsilius*); need of, 227, 244, 276 sq., 282; estimate of medieval, 256, 276, 280, 282, 348, 368; disintegrating influence of, 267, 279, 333. See *Gregory VII., Kingdom*.
Papacy, curialist theory, 275; absolutism, 251; claim over empire, 305; infallibility, 252, 304, 309 sq. See *Empire*.
Papacy and constitutions, 273, 347; and popular government, 262, 266, 271, 272, 314 sq., 323. See *Plenitudo*.
Papal elections, 242 sq., 247, 250 n., 264, 270 n., 275. See *Popes, Rome*.
Papias, 125–128, 157, 174.
Parables, 87 sqq.
Pascal, 341.
Pastoral Epistles, 105 sq.
Paterini, 247, 248, 255.
Pattison, 356.
Paul, St., and Rome, 106.
Paul III., 329.
Paulinus of Nola, 193.
Pax terrena, 289 sq., 314.
Peckham, 300.
Pelagianism, 192.
Pelagians, 170.
Pelagius, 161 n., 188, 192, 196, 204, 205.
Pepuza, 129, 135, 138.
Perpetua, 140.
Persecution, 107, 131 sq., 137, 143 n., 215, 280, 320, 335.
Perseverance, 191. See *Elect*.
Persia, ancient kings of, 17.
Pessimism, 382, 384.
Petavius, 344.
Peter, St., successors of, 229; Petri Privilegium, 77 n.; letter to Pipin, 233 n., 238 n.
Peter of Aragon, 269.
Peter. See *Damiani*.
Peter of Florence, 249 n.
Peter Lombard, 260 n., 338.
Pharisees, 30.
Philaster, 228 n.
Philip, daughters of, 142 n.
Philip, Emperor, 266.
Philip II. (France), 253, 254.
Philip Augustus, 265 n.
Philo, 155.
Philosophy and theology, 153 sq. See *Theology*.
Philosophy of history, 12, 28, 32 sq., 105, 207 sqq., 225 sq.
Phocas, 230.
Phrygia, 135, 138, 139.
Pipin, 232, 233, 247 n.; donation of, 233.

INDEX

Pius II., 241.
Pius V. 247 n.
Pius IX., 227, 335, 337, 343, 344; syllabus of, 252 n.
Plato, 150; influence on theology, 152-156, 184.
Plenitudo Potestatis, 272, 310, 322, 337 sq. See *Societas Perfecta, Temporal Power, Deposing Power.*
Plymouth Brethren, 325.
Polanco, 339.
Polycarp, 125.
Pompey, 31, 40, 106.
Pontianus, 237.
Pope. See *Vicar, Papacy, Rome.*
Popes, martyred, 237 n.; medieval, ability of, 277; medieval, not canonised, 270 n.; vassals of emperors, 233, 235; emperor vassal of, 235; French ascendency over, 319. See *Avignon.*
Poverty, apostolic, 260 sq., 296, 299-305. See *Arnold, Franciscans.*
Praxeas, 139.
Praedestinatus, 228 n.
Predestination, 190 sqq., 196, 200; predestined, number of fixed, 191, 195; and probation, 204. See *Augustine, Grace, Elect.*
Premonstratensians, 260.
Priesthood in Kingdom, 12, 111.
Primasius, 161 n.
Prince, function of, 314-321.
Priscilla, 136.
Probabilism, 339-343.
"Pro Christo et Ecclesia," 362.
Proclus, 139.
Progress and authority, 282, 288.
Property, theory of, 316; Augustine's theory of, 212; Church, 212, 254.
Prophecy, Christian, 136, 139 n., 142. See *Joachim.*
Prosper, 193 n.
Prudentius of Troyes, 231 n.
Prussia, kingdom of, 330.
Psalm, hundred and tenth, 104, 112.
Puritanism, 57, 132, 137, 301 sq., 324; Montanist, 145, 146.
Puritans, 194, 360.
Purpose in life and in existence, 3-6, 84; in nature, 385.

Q

Quadratus, 142 n.
Quesnel, 221, 341.

R

Raban, 194 n., 231 n.
Rainalucci, 306, 313.
Ramsay, 106 n.
Rancé, de, 340.
Ranke, 337.
Rashdall, referred to, 229, 260, 279, 293, 299, 301, 327 sq.
Ratramn, 231 n.
Ravenna, exarchate, 230.
Raynaud, 344.
Realism, Christian instinct of, 121; causes of early Christian, 130 sqq.
Reason in nature, 5, 385.
Reformation, 333 sq., 347 sq., 354 sq.; eve of, 331.
Regalia, 258.
Regicide, 273.
Regnum, medieval, 270, 285. See *German Crown, Sacerdotium.*
Reign (earthly) of Christ, 53 n.; duration, 129; mediatorial, 51. See *Kingdom, Church.*
Remigius of Lyons, 231 n.
Renaissance, 331.
Renan, 312.
Rense, 306, 308.
Reordinations, 240.
Resurrection (twofold), 53 sq.; the first, 109, 113, 119, 122, 129, 170.
Reusch, 239 n., 339-343.
Reuter, referred to, 92, 147, 171, 174, 176, 178, 179, 181, 185, 188, 189, 192, 193, 195, 196, 197, 205, 218, 220, 227, 252, 268.
Revivalism, 143.
Resch, 39 n.
Richardson, 234 n.
Riehm, 22 n.
Riezler, referred to, 266, 268, 301, 303, 309, 311, 312 sq.
Ritschl, 13, 173, 358-362.
Robert of Naples, 303, 306.
Robertson Smith, 13 n.
Robinson, J. Armitage, 140 n.
Rome, sack of, 206; empire, Christian view of, 106; republic idealised, 273; empire idealised,

287; republican traditions, 260, 262, 325. See *Empire*.
Rome, position of pope in, 230, 242, 262, 265, 323; See of (Augustine), 218; and Constantinople, 229.
Romwald, 249.
Roncaglia, Diet of, 263, 264.
Roskovány, 238 n.
Rothad, 237.
Rothe, 363.
Rudolf of Hapsburg, 258, 270.
Rule of Faith, 148, 175.
Russian Church, 226 n.
Ryle and James, 41 nn., 43 nn., 45 n.

S

Sabatier, 297.
Sacerdos, 220.
Sacerdotium, 270, 285, 289. See *Imperium*.
Sallust, appealed to, 207.
Salmon, 136 n.
Salvian, 208.
Salzburg, 335.
Sanday, 51 n., 122, 123 n.
Sardica, Canons of, 161, 238.
Savonarola, 296, 304, 331.
Saxon Empire, 242.
Sayce, 17 n.
Schism, 175, 221; of East and West, 228, 239, 245, 259, 269, 299; of papacy, 274, 328; reformation, 348.
Schmiedel, 52 n.
Scholasticism, 279, 297, 354.
Schürer, 72 n., 346.
Scripture, sole authority of, 294, 309, 319; and tradition, 338.
Secularism, 362 sq., 375.
Seeberg, 194 n., 228 n.
Seleucid Kingdom, 40, 106.
"Semi-Pelagians," 189 sq., 192, 194, 203, 204, 336.
Serapeum, 163.
Sergius III., 240 sq.
Seven days of history, 129, 170, 298 n.; six days, 125, 126 n.
Sibyl, 45, 107.
Sicilies, kingdom of the, 269, 270 n., 294; Sicilian vespers, 269. See *Normans*.
Silvester I., 233 n., 236 n.
Silvester II., 240, 244.
Silvester III., 245.

Silvius, Aeneas. See *Pius II*.
Simony, 245, 246, 254, 261 nn., 267, 278, 302, 331.
Simplicianus, 190.
Siricius, 164 n., 236.
Sixtus IV., 305.
Sixtus. See *Xystus*.
Smedt, de, 274.
Socialism, Christian, 378 sqq.
Societas Perfecta, 101, 214, 251, 254 sq., 257, 274, 281, 293 n., 322, 344 n., 346, 371. See *Church, Kingdom, Plenitudo, Temporal Power, Sovereignty*.
Society, moral aim of, 288 sq., 325, 347; moral bond of, 210-213, 251; perfect, 164; Augustine on, 212; social influence of Christianity, 207. See *Christian Citizen, State, Dualism, Civitas*.
Sohm, 159 n., 342.
Solomon, 14, 43; psalms of, 40 sqq.
Sovereignty, 262, 272, 288, 314 sq.
Spirit, the Holy, 54, 99 sq., 136 sq., 143.
Spiritual (meaning), 316.
Spirituals. See *Franciscans*.
Stanton, 9, 26, 45, 53, 114, 121.
State, the, 210, 213; moral aim, 363; and Church, 251 (see *Church and State*); modern, 307, 315 sq., 321.
States, growth of modern, 258, 271.
Stephen II., 233.
Stephen III., 240 n.
Stephen of Hungary, 246 n.
Stephen, Sir J., 257 n.
Studium, 285.
Sulpitius Severus, 123.
Swete, 174 n.
Symeon, Junior, 163 n.
Symeon, Stylites, 163 n.
Syria, 40.

T

Taborites, 324.
Tarquini, 292 sq., 313, 335, 345, 347, 371.
Tatian, 130.
"Teaching of twelve Apostles," 122 n., 126, 142 n.
Teleology, 85.
Telesphorus, 237.
Templars, 260.

INDEX 401

Temporal power, 230, 233, 234, 241, 243, 250, 260, 262, 270 sq., 275, 277, 300, 316; defined, 292. See *Deposing, Plenitudo, Societas Perfecta*.
Tertullian, 100 n., 126, 136 n., 138, 139 n., 140, 141, 154 n.; Cyprian's Master, 141.
Thackeray, St. John, 52 n.
Theocratic ideal (Israel), 12, 13. See *Gregory VII*.
Theodora, 241 n.
Theodosius I., 226, n., 233 n.
Theology, task of, 84, 130, 153 sq.; councils, 174; twofold type, 130; source of divergence in, 148; and philosophy, 361; biblical, 358; in early Church, 148-158; early decay of, 228; scholastic, 260.
Theophylact, 124.
Thomas Aquinas, 153, 238 n., 279, 285, 296, 298; political doctrines, 271 sq.; and Augustine, 336 sq., 343; works of, 272; misled by forgery, 238 sq., 274; *de Regimine Principum*, 271-274; and Marsilius, 314 sq.
Tillemont, 344.
Tirol, 335.
Titius, 61 n.
Tolomeo da Lucca, 272.
Tout, 241, 263.
Transcendentalism, 154, 182, 196.
Trappe, la, 340.
Traversari, 331; family of, 249.
Trench, 324.
Trevelyan, 328.
Tübingen, school of, 83, 358.
Twelfth century, 259 sq.; and thirteenth, 275.
Tyconius, 161 n.
Tymion, 129, 135.

U

Ugolino. See *Gregory IX*.
Unam Sanctam, 274, 287, 319.
Unigenitus, 221 n.
Unity, Christian, 348.
Universal bishop, 229 sq.
Universalism of N.T., 96, 99; prophetic, 22 n., 23, 24, 26, 29; Augustine, 183, 198 sq.

Urban II., 259.
Urban IV., 238 n., 270, 271, 272.
"Usus" and "possessio," 299 sqq.

V

Valentinus, 150; Valentinian Aeon *Ecclesia*, 174 n.
"Vicar of Christ," 100, 267 n.
Victor, 139.
Victorines, 260. See *Hugh*.
Victorinus (Afer), 154.
Victorinus (of Petau), 157.
Vigilius, 230.
Villani, 290 sq.
Vincent (of Lerins), 203, 228 n.; Vincentian Canon, 148, 338.
"Vocatio non congrua," 191. See *Grace, Predestination*.
Volusianus, 207.

W

Waite, 120.
Walbert, 246, 249 n.
Waldenses, 264 n., 324 sq., 330.
Waldes, 324 sq.
Wearmouth, 231.
Weber, A., 293.
Wenrich, 257.
Westcott, 83 n., 122 nn., 379.
Wibert, 257.
William of Aquitaine, 249.
Willibrord, 231.
Witte, 287.
World, the, 361, 363; world to come, 44, 53.
Worms, Concordat of, 258.
Wycliffe, 326 sqq., 330, 334.

X

Xystus I., 237.

Z

Zachary (pope), 232, 247 n.
Zahn, 122, 123, 127, 139.
Zephyrinus, 136 n., 139.
Zosimus, 192.
Zwingli, 354 sqq.

www.ingramcontent.com/pod-product-compliance
Lightning Source LLC
Chambersburg PA
CBHW071436300426
44114CB00013B/1457